Penguin Handbooks
Equal Opportunities

Ruth Miller was born in Hamburg. She left school and Hitler's
Germany and came to this country 'au pair' shortly before the war.
In 1944 she became a journalist, obtaining a job on *Leader* (an
illustrated magazine, stable-mate of *Picture Post*). When *Leader*
folded, she joined *Housewife*, and then started freelancing.

She became interested in what people do for a living, and why and
how they do it, through interviewing famous personalities such as
Charles Chaplin, and strange people – a major and his wife who had
opted out on to a deserted crofters' island were among the oddest –
and people with extraordinary jobs like Pursuivant Bluemantle; but
she now finds more ordinary people and jobs fascinating, because
they are so varied. She has written on careers and related subjects
for *The Times*, *Good Housekeeping*, the *Daily Telegraph*, C.R.A.C.,
The Times Educational Supplement, *Where*, and *Living*. She is the
author of *Careers for Girls*, the forerunner of this book, which
appeared in four editions over ten years.

Ruth Miller is married to an engineer, and lives in a Victorian
house two minutes from Hampstead Heath.

Anna Alston took a degree in English at Oxford and qualified as a
careers officer. She was senior careers officer in Waltham Forest for
several years. She is married, has a daughter at primary school and is
now a freelance careers writer. She was co-author of *Working in
the Travel Business* and *Working in Photography*.

Ruth Miller

assisted by
Anna Alston

EQUAL OPPORTUNITIES

A CAREERS GUIDE
FOR WOMEN AND MEN

Sixth edition

PENGUIN BOOKS

Penguin Books Ltd, Harmondsworth,
Middlesex, England
Penguin Books, 625 Madison Avenue,
New York, New York 10022, U.S.A.
Penguin Books Australia Ltd, Ringwood,
Victoria, Australia
Penguin Books Canada Ltd, 2801 John Street,
Markham, Ontario, Canada L3R 1B4
Penguin Books (N.Z.) Ltd, 182–190 Wairau Road,
Auckland 10, New Zealand

First published as *The Peacock Book of Careers for Girls* 1966
Second edition published in Penguin Handbooks
as *Careers for Girls* 1970
Third edition 1973
Fourth edition 1975
Fifth edition published as *Equal Opportunities:
A Careers Guide for Women and Men* 1978
Reprinted 1978
Sixth edition 1981

Filmset, printed and bound in Great Britain by
Hazell Watson & Viney Ltd, Aylesbury, Bucks
Set in VIP Times

Contents

MAIN CAREERS IN ALPHABETICAL ORDER
(See index for all careers mentioned)

This book uses only the feminine pronoun though the information, unless otherwise stated, applies to both sexes.

viii   Contents

Introduction

This book serves two purposes; the first is to *provide unbiased accurate careers information*. Hard facts like entry and training requirements are checked with relevant organizations. Descriptions of the work involved – necessarily brief and only highlighting vital aspects – and descriptions of the sort of person likely to be good at/happy in the work, are based on practitioners' experiences and views and on my own observations in over twenty years of interviewing people at work.

I believe this is the most important difference between this Guide and organizations' own careers literature. To give just one example: before finally going to press each entry is sent to the relevant organization. Again and again organizations ignore my request to check only *the facts*, and they add 'integrity' to **Personal attributes**. Can you imagine anyone saying to her/himself 'I haven't got integrity, so career XYZ is not for me'?

The Guide is likely to be used mainly by young people between fourteen and twenty. However, it should be equally valuable to the increasing number of people in their twenties, thirties or forties who want to, or have to, change their occupation. Although *Late start* details are given under **Position of women** in each career section, they apply equally to men. Changing direction in mid-career is no longer odd, nor an admission of defeat or failure. Whether the contemplated change is the result of having made the wrong choice first time round, or whether it is due to people's change of interests, or to skills and occupations no longer being in demand – it is essential to realize that in many careers maturity is an asset; training facilities are available, and entry qualifications demanded of young entrants may be relaxed for older ones (see **Second Start in Education**, p. xxxvii).

Young people choosing their first career should prepare for the probability of having to learn new techniques, update skills and adapt to changed working environments in the future. We've all been told over and over again that technological developments, and resulting organizational ones, will have affected all our working lives by 2000 A.D. – but nobody knows how quickly, and to what extent changes will affect individual jobs. Informed guesswork suggests that, while many craft-level jobs will change out of all recognition, not *all* engineering works, for example, will install robots overnight. Copy-typing is likely to disappear altogether; in banks, and in insurance and solicitors' offices, new information-storing and retrieval technologies will drastically reduce tasks like filing and the looking-up of information. Doing away with dreary routine jobs will free staff to deal with customers'/clients' queries, say the optimists. No, say the pessimists (or should one say the realists?), it will lead to fewer jobs for people qualified only to do routine jobs.

To minimize the shock when change becomes necessary and to maximize the options open for changing to something that will be both in demand and congenial, people choosing careers now would be wise to go for as broad-based an initial training as possible, and be wary of jobs where initial pay is fine but no systematic training is given. What is absolutely vital to bear in mind throughout the choosing process is that it is mostly the unskilled jobs, needing little or no training, which are disappearing. The lower the qualifications, by and large, the greater the likelihood of unemployment. So it's important to stay in the education system, full- or part-time, as long as possible and to remember that, apart from C.S.E.s, G.C.E.s and further and higher education, there are alternatives such as T.E.C., B.E.C., City and Guilds Foundation and other courses (see pp. xv–xx).

Sixth-formers who cannot make up their minds what to do would be wise to remember that about one third of all graduate job vacancies are open to graduates from *any* discipline. Where disciplines are specified, the majority specify a science-based one.

Careers in this Guide are listed alphabetically. However, many if not most 'careers' are really 'areas of work'. Look in the Index and you see how many more jobs than career sections there are. Usually, one kind of training leads to jobs in a variety of settings, and you can usually mould training plus experience to the kind of job you will want to do when you know more about the whole spectrum and about your own likes, dislikes, strengths and weaknesses. For example, an engineering degree can lead to the top in the Civil Service or in industry, i.e. into prestigious, well-paid jobs where an understanding of new technologies helps with decision-making; it can lead to academic research; into exploring new export markets; to partnerships in professional consultancy or to setting up your own business, and so on. In each case the job's ingredients and the personal qualities required are different. The same goes for a first job in retailing: it can lead to a comfortable 9-to-5 office job or to hectic travelling across Europe checking transcontinental truck-drivers' schedules – quite apart from obvious retailing jobs like store-management and buying.

Use this Guide as a springboard, a first lap on the lengthy and possibly bumpy ride from vague first idea – Concorde pilot or TV reporter? – to final choice. Use the Guide in conjunction with the 'How to choose' aids (p. xlii), combined with discussion with careers advisers and parents, and if possible with people in the jobs you'd like to do.

As mentioned at the beginning, the book has two main purposes; the second of these is *to encourage girls to widen their career choice and speed their progress towards equality in the job market.*

Women now account for about 41% of the total workforce in this country, but only 2% are classed as 'managers'. Many more women manage, say, dry-cleaners', shops or typing-pools; many more men than women are bank managers or senior executives in industry. In the professions, women are beginning to make some progress (see list, p. xxxv), but having started from a very low baseline, they are still a tiny minority.

Because job segregation is still so strong, Equal Pay legislation (p. xxvi) isn't helping women much; average earnings per hour for women are less than three quarters of the earnings for men. The reason is not blatant flouting of the letter of the law, but the fact that women are still clustered in a narrow range of industries (especially catering, textiles, distribution) and in a narrow range of occupations, doing mainly unskilled or semi-skilled work which needs little training and therefore offers poor promotion prospects.

At a higher educational level tradition still puts women at a disadvantage: physiotherapists, for example, earn far less than electronics technicians; yet physiotherapists, nearly all women, need higher entry qualifications for a longer and more wide-ranging training than do electronics technicians – nearly all men.

When Sex Discrimination legislation (see p. xxvi) was passed more than five years ago few people realized how many intractable, persistent hurdles women had (and still have) to negotiate before 'equal opportunities' became more than a pious hope and a slogan. Legislation, we now know, merely set the stage – the action hasn't yet reached the end of the first act.

Very briefly, three main factors combine to keep women down, and out of most prestigious, well-paid and influential jobs. Firstly, *traditional career structures:* men's careers tend to have built-in training and promotion plans; women have to make it known to employers that they want a career, not just a job, even though they may be busy having children just at the time men are forging ahead. Secondly, *entrenched assumptions* which don't stand up to being tested: it is still widely assumed, for example, that women aren't worth training because they leave before they have repaid the time and money invested in that training. However, respectable academic research has proved that that is just not so. ('Young men don't stay in jobs longer than young women,' says the Chief Executive of one of Britain's most successful marketing companies, 'that's been proved beyond doubt. Besides, I'd much rather lose a member of expensively trained staff after five or seven years because *she*'s having a baby than because *he* is going to the competition.') Other disproved assumptions: women don't *want* responsibility; women aren't prepared to travel; women are absent more often than men. The last assumption is in fact a misleading sweeping statement: women *as a whole* are absent from work more often. But the level of absenteeism for men and for women depends on the level of responsibility involved in the job; the lower down the ladder, the higher the absenteeism rate – and far more women than men are on the lower rungs. In professional and management jobs, absenteeism does not differ significantly between the sexes.

The third factor lies in the *girls and women themselves* – their lack of confidence in their abilities; their apparent lack of 'venturesomeness'; their low job expectations. Social conventions and conditioning still make most girls into dear little stereotypes by the time they are thirteen – the vital stage when they choose their exam subjects. By choosing traditional girls' subjects girls limit their career choice *far* more than do boys who choose typical boys' subjects (see Sex Balance in Education, p. xxix).

This Guide is trying to re-condition careers advisers, parents, and career-choosers. This is why the female pronoun is used throughout, although the information applies to both sexes. That sounds like a gimmick – but why should it? Using the male pronoun when text applies to both sexes is normal practice: it is precisely this kind of social and semantic convention which is responsible for the snail's pace at which ideas are changing on what is and what is not a Good Job for a Girl.

How can girls be expected to see themselves as chartered engineers, TV service people, surgeons or bank managers while all the chartered engineers, TV service people, surgeons or bank managers they see on TV or in real life, and whom they read about, are male? Until girls have female 'role models' – women in traditionally male jobs with whom they can identify – the equal opportunity concept remains a vast oversimplification. There are indeed no medical school quotas now, and neither builders nor barristers may use the old 'we-have-no-ladies'-lavatories' excuse for keeping girls out of builders' yards or barristers' Chambers. But that sort of thing is only the tip of the iceberg of discriminatory traditions.

In terms of access, opportunities are theoretically pretty equal, but they are still totally unequal in the demands they make on boys' and girls' motivation, determination and self-confidence. To choose surveying, engineering or a management traineeship with one of the multinational companies, boys mainly need certain academic qualifications. Girls need those, plus the guts, the self-confidence, to stand out in a crowd, to differ from their peers, to put up with boring jokes about women's lib, and to be prepared to be asked personal questions about marriage plans at interviews. In other words, to make what would be a perfectly ordinary choice for an ordinary boy, a girl or young woman has still to be a bit extra-ordinary. That's why girls need positive encouragement from parents and careers advisers; but often the best they can hope for is amused acquiescence or raised eyebrows.

This Guide is trying to de-stereotype jobs and people, and to chivvy girls off the tramlines. (But a TV series about a perfectly ordinary couple where the husband is a primary school teacher and the wife a chartered engineer would be a lot more effective!)

Acknowledgements

I would like to thank the statisticians in the Universities Central Council on Admissions, the Department of Education and Science, and the Manpower Services Commission for letting me have up-to-date figures for the Sex Balance sections on pp. xxix–xxxvi, and for their patience in explaining statistical method, and jargon, to a layperson.

I would also like to thank the 120-odd organizations who answered my many questions, especially about the details I wanted for the **Position of women** paragraphs in each career section.

Most of the figures used in this book come from the above sources; some from publications by U.C.C.A., the Statistical Sub-Committee of the Association of Graduate Careers Advisory Services and similar bodies.

Finally, I would like to thank careers advisers, and careers information users, for suggesting improvements in presentation of the information. Wherever possible I have incorporated their suggestions.

Checklist

1. Initials, Qualifications and What They Mean

'O-level' in the General Certificate of Education normally refers to pass-grades, i.e. grades 1, 2 or 3 (or A, B, C). It covers O-level equivalents – such as C.S.E. Grade 1, or Ordinary Grades in the Scottish Certificate of Education.

NEW AWARDS: T.E.C. and B.E.C.

I. The *Technician Education Council* (T.E.C., S.C.O.T.E.C. in Scotland) awards have now replaced most of the former below-degree-level technician awards in all engineering, scientific, construction and other technical-practical and art and design careers. T.E.C. will have taken over the complete range by 1985 or 1986.

There are two 'levels of awards': *Certificates* and *Diplomas* are first-level awards, *Higher Certificates* and *Higher Diplomas* are second-level awards. Courses leading to awards are called 'programmes'. Programmes are made up of 'units', each dealing with one aspect of a course subject. A certain number of first-level units add up to a Certificate; with additional first-level units a Certificate can be converted into a Diploma; if second-level units are added a Certificate can be converted into a Higher Certificate and then, by adding more second-level units, into a Higher Diploma. (In the past, *technician certificates* were usually awarded after part-time study, *diplomas* after full-time study. Under T.E.C., a diploma indicates a wider spread of knowledge than a certificate; the student's 'mode of attendance' is immaterial.) All students take 'essential units' within a subject area – say sciences – and then add optional units according to interests/job – for example, hospital technicians would take different optional units within their sciences programme from those taken by science technicians in a university lab (see *Science Technician*, p. 413).

Awards lead to partial exemption from relevant bodies' examinations, such as the Institute of Medical Laboratory Sciences, Institute of Building, Institute of Electrical and Electronic Engineering Technicians, etc.

There are no rigid *entry requirements*: The scheme is flexible and programmes are tailored to fit entrants' educational level; the higher the entry-level, the quicker students will get their awards; but there is no time-limit within which programmes must be completed. There are no 'courses' which last a definite number of years.

For example, students with four relevant O-levels including maths, a science and English or 'a subject requiring English as a means of communication' (i.e. history, geography, social studies, etc.) can complete a Certificate programme by two years' part-time study. But students with fewer entry qualifications will take longer. The statutory minimum entry qualifications laid down by T.E.C. are three C.S.E. Grade III, in maths, a science and English 'or a subject requiring English as a means of communication'; but individual colleges and employers can, and do, set higher entry requirements in many cases. The scheme is still so new that no national pattern, covering all the various T.E.C. subjects, has yet emerged.

Although, theoretically, students can switch from full-time to part-time study and vice versa, in practice Certificate programmes are part-time; Diploma programmes are usually full-time. Most Diploma programmes last two years and entry requirements – set by colleges – tend to be three or four O-levels in relevant subjects. However, students with fewer entry qualifications should nevertheless apply; acceptance for individual courses depends so much on supply and demand, course directors' views, and programme content. It is also sometimes possible for students to catch up on missing G.C.E. subjects while following a Diploma programme.

Students with one relevant A-level and several relevant O-levels can start right away with a Higher Certificate – usually part-time – or a Higher Diploma – normally full-time, possibly sandwich.

T.E.C. Single Unit Scheme: Although, as stated above, T.E.C. programmes normally comprise 'essential' and 'optional' units if they are to lead to a Certificate or Diploma, it is also possible for students to take individual units in isolation. On completion of a unit, students are awarded a 'Record of Success'. This scheme is particularly useful for people who want to update a particular skill, or extend their knowledge in order to change to a new occupation. It is also very useful for women wanting to return to work after a gap.

Recognition of T.E.C. Awards: While the old National Certificates and Diplomas were usually acceptable in lieu of A-levels for entry to higher education, there is no 'blanket acceptance' of T.E.C. Certificates and Diplomas, simply because content, and therefore relevance, of individual programmes vary so much. Certificates and Diplomas are acceptable to higher education establishments in lieu of A-levels *if* students took appropriate units in relevant subjects and gained merits in all of them. Additional O-levels may also be required – there is no generally applicable ruling (as there is with B.E.C., see below). Students who want to use the T.E.C. route into higher education must ferret out the 'acceptability position' when planning their T.E.C. programme – and they should not rely on last year's, or similar programmes' acceptability! The extent to which T.E.C. awards qualify holders for exemption from professional bodies' own examinations also varies greatly. To find out which level of award leads to what extent of exemption, students must consult individual professional bodies. Generally speaking, Certificates and Diplomas in engineering subjects lead to Technician status; Higher Certificates and Diplomas to Technician Engineer status (see Engineering, p. 175).

II. The *Business Education Council* (B.E.C., S.C.O.T.B.E.C. in Scotland) is now responsible for awarding below-degree-level certificates and diplomas which used to be administered by a variety of bodies. Its awards have replaced a number of office/business studies certificates and diplomas. Organization is similar to, but (confusingly) not identical with that of T.E.C.

There are three levels of B.E.C. awards: *General* Certificates and Diplomas are first-level awards; *National* Certificates and Diplomas are second-level awards; *Higher National* Certificates and Diplomas are third-level awards.

Awards are given to students who have completed a 'course'; courses are made up of individual 'modules' – packages of skill and knowledge within a subject area. A certain minimum number of modules, at one of the three levels of attainment, adds up to a Certificate; if more modules are added a Certificate is converted into a Diploma. As with T.E.C. awards, diplomas indicate a wider spread of knowledge than certificates; the mode of attendance is immaterial; students may study part-time, full-time, or mix modes of attendance.

All students take certain 'core modules': all learn a bit about the inter-relationship between the various business functions and specializations (see Management, p. 264). But right from the start students choose programmes in one of four separate career areas:

General business studies – for students who intend to go into or are working in a medium-sized concern but do not, or at least not yet, want to specialize;

Financial studies – for students who intend to work in or are working in banking, accountancy, insurance, etc.;

Distribution studies – for students who intend to or work in retail or wholesale distribution;

Public administration studies – for students who intend to or work in local or central government, the police, the health services or other public body.

Within each of the four areas, students add modules relevant to their job or prospective job; B.E.C. awards are tailored to individual students' needs. Students may take different lengths of time to collect the modules necessary for completion of an award course. Minimum durations are:

For first-level award: 1 year part-time for General Certificate; 1 year full-time or 2 years part-time for General Diploma;

For second-level award: 2 years part-time for National Certificate; 2 years full-time or 3 years part-time or sandwich for National Diploma;

For third-level award: 2 years part-time for Higher National Certificate; 2 years full-time or 3 years part-time or sandwich for Higher National Diploma.

Entry requirements are flexible: with fewer than 4 O-levels, students first work for General (first-level) awards; with at least 4 O-levels (normally including English and maths) or a General B.E.C. award, students work for National (second-level) awards; with at least 1 A-level and 3 O-levels (including English and maths) or with a National award, students work for a Higher National award.

B.E.C./T.E.C. Computer Studies Awards

B.E.C. and T.E.C. have combined to provide a variety of National and Higher National awards in computer-related subjects; including programming, systems analysis, and various business-related aspects of computer work. Entry requirements again vary (see Computing, p. 134, for levels of computer work).

Recognition of B.E.C. Awards

Unlike T.E.C., B.E.C. does provide a structured way into higher education. Universities and C.N.A.A. agreed in 1980 to accept General Certificates and Diplomas with credit as an alternative to the O-level component of the general entry requirement, and National Certificates and Diplomas as an alternative to the A-level component. (For some degree courses, specific O- and A-levels are, of course, required.) For Business Studies degree students, transfer from and to Higher National awards may be possible.

Professional bodies in the commercial field either grant partial exemption from their own examinations to B.E.C. award-holders or require B.E.C. qualifications for entry to their own final examination. Extent of exemption depends on level of award and subject-relevance.

B.E.C. Post-Experience Certificate in Management Studies

This is a new award for people with considerable clerical/business experience who want to extend or update their knowledge and skills, and for women who want to return to work after a gap. The course normally takes one year part-time (it is planned for people in employment, but people temporarily *not* in employment – such as women who have the potential to return – can take the course); content and organization vary from one college or polytechnic to another. More post-experience awards are planned.

TRADITIONAL BELOW-DEGREE-LEVEL AWARDS
which are being phased out and replaced by T.E.C. and B.E.C. – but some will be running for a few years yet.

O.N.C. – Ordinary National Certificates and *H.N.C. – Higher National Certificates.* Awarded in a wide variety of subjects for students in relevant employment. O.N.C. entry requirements normally 4 relevant O-levels; H.N.C. entry requirement either appropriate O.N.C. or D. (see below) or 4 O-levels with at least 2 in relevant subjects and 2 A-levels. Courses normally take 2 years' day- or block-release plus one evening's study a week. Some courses can be taken by evening study alone. (This is not recommended: failure rate is much higher than by normal attendance.)

A good, relevant O.N.C. or O.N.D. is acceptable for degree and Diploma of Higher Education (see p. xx) course entry in lieu of G.C.E.s.

O.N.D. – Ordinary National Diploma and *H.N.D. – Higher National Diploma.* Equivalent 2-year full-time courses (H.N.D. may be 3 years' sandwich). O.N.D. entry requirements as for O.N.C.; H.N.D. entry requirements 4 O-levels and 1 A-level passed, for some courses another A-level studied (not passed).

O.N.C./D. courses are at Further Education Colleges; H.N.C./D. courses at Polytechnics, Further Education Colleges and Institutes of Higher Education (see p. xxi).

Higher National Diplomas are roughly at, H.N.C.s just below, pass-degree standard, and may qualify for post-graduate courses.

O.N.C./D.s and H.N.C./D.s qualify holders for partial exemption from relevant professional bodies' own examinations. Extent of exemption depends on level and content of award.

City and Guilds Certificates are normally awarded after part-time day- or block-release study to operatives and craftswomen/men in a vast

variety of practical and technical subjects. No entry requirements for
Certificate exams, but colleges, and employers, may require some
C.S.E.s (usually in maths and/or a science). (City and Guilds *technician*
certificates generally have been phased out and are replaced by T.E.C.
awards.)

City and Guilds *Foundation* Certificates are fairly new. They are
usually awarded after one year's full-time integrated education and
introduction to one of eight 'occupational areas': Agricultural Industries; Commercial Studies; Community Care (nursing; nursery nursing;
residential social work, etc.); Construction; Distribution (mainly retail);
Engineering (the largest area); Food Industries; Science Industries. No
entry requirements; Foundation courses are held in further education
colleges, in schools, or as 'link courses' between school and further
education college and practical experience at work. Courses are intended
for young people (mainly sixteen- to eighteen-year-olds) who are
interested in an area of work but do not know what specific jobs involve,
and who also need to improve their 'communication skills' (written and
spoken English and numeracy) before embarking on a career. A
Foundation Certificate is not a formal qualification, rather proof of
'vocational preparation'. So far only the General Nursing Council
accepts the relevant Certificate (Community Care) in lieu of one O-
level. However, all school-leavers without academic qualifications, or
only a few poor C.S.E.s and just a vague idea of what they want to do,
are likely to stand a far better chance of getting a job with a Foundation
Certificate than without one. The Certificate may also lead on to further
education courses or apprenticeships for which some C.S.E.s or even
G.C.E.s are expected or preferred (for example, T.E.C. courses for
which admission of students without G.C.E.s is at the discretion of the
college).

Dip.H.E. – Diploma of Higher Education: Courses started in the
seventies; they take two years full-time, some three years part-time,
and are held at Institutes/Colleges of Higher Education and Polytechnics. Entry requirements for school leavers: 2 A-levels (but A-level
grades accepted are probably lower than most degree students'). Mature
entrants – who account for a large proportion – are admitted according
to 'suitability'; this could mean having taken a re-entry course (see
Second Start in Education, p. xxxviii), or merely experience of life and
proof of appreciation/essential basic knowledge of subject to be studied.

Most Dip.H.E.s are 'modular'; students build up their own course
from a range of options within an area of study: for example in sciences,
social sciences, humanities. Courses vary enormously in content, organization and in vocational and academic value. Many courses guarantee
'Diplomates' entry into the third year of specific B.Ed. or other degree

(ordinary or honours) courses; some Dip.H.E.s are 'free-standing', which means Diplomates have to find degree courses which will accept their two years' study as equal to the first two years of that degree course. This is not always possible, and it may lead to problems getting grants; the subsequent degree course may not in such cases attract a 'mandatory' grant (see Grants, p. xxiv). Experimentally, some Dip.H.E.s are preparing students for local employment opportunities, but it is too early to say whether this will work.

The main advantage of the Dip.H.E. is that students can defer final career and course decisions – for example whether to take a B.Ed. or a science degree (assuming the Dip.H.E. modules were science ones), or leave the education system altogether after two years.

Although the Dip.H.E. was intended to be a qualification in its own right, its value in the job market is not very great so far. Few employers have heard of its existence or understand where it fits into the academic hierarchy; others think that students chose the Dip.H.E. because their A-levels were not up to degree course requirements, or because they wanted a soft option in higher education.

Diplomates are not normally accepted for graduate trainee schemes in industry nor for graduate jobs in the Civil Service. Most professional bodies grant exemption from their own exams in exactly the same way they grant exemption to (lower-entry-level) Higher T.E.C., B.E.C. and National awards holders.

COLLEGES AND INSTITUTES OF HIGHER EDUCATION

Colleges and Institutes of Higher Education developed in the seventies when teacher training was being reduced and changed. Most of the new establishments are amalgamations of former colleges of education; some are old colleges of education with a new title.

They still train teachers (B.Ed. and post-graduate certificate courses), but in order to use spare capacity and staff and also to enable teaching students to work together with other students, these new establishments have 'diversified' their courses. Students can now choose from a range of Dip.H.E.s and degrees and, in some establishments, they can also train for social work and some other professional qualifications.

Most of the establishments' titles and range of courses owe more to the whims of local education authorities and principals than to any concerted national education policy. The only feature all establishments have in common is that 'study programmes' are flexible. Courses often start with a 'common year' during which students can sample various subjects, and they can postpone both subject-choice and choice of qualification (Dip.H.E., B.A., B.Ed.) till the end of the first academic year.

These new establishments may be first choice for A-level leavers to whom universities and polytechnics seem frighteningly large and high-powered places, or who want to take a higher education course locally. Mature students make up a rather larger proportion of students than they do at university.

C.N.A.A. – Council for National Academic Awards; awards degrees at Polytechnics and other non-university educational institutions. C.N.A.A. degrees are comparable in academic standard (and usually status) to university degrees; their content and approach tend to be more directly geared to employment (i.e. vocational) in industry. Most of these degrees – for example in engineering, business studies – are sandwich courses, with periods in employment; C.N.A.A. students are often sponsored by employers.

C.N.A.A. arts degree courses tend to be easier to get into than university arts degrees; but competition for technological and business degrees is sometimes stiffer for C.N.A.A. sandwich courses than for university ones.

C.N.A.A. also awards Art and Design degrees (see p. 53).

2. Some Career Fields with at least Some Scope for Entrants without O-levels

Acting
Agriculture and Horticulture
Animals
Beautician
Building Crafts
Catering
Clerical Work (see also Banking, Civil Service, Purchasing, Shipbroking and Freightforwarding)
Dental Surgery Assistant
Design
Driving Instructor
Engineering Crafts
Fashion
Floristry
Hairdressing
Modelling

Nursery Nurse
Nurse (State Enrolled)
Photography
Police
Prison Service
Recreation Management
Retail Distribution
Science Laboratory Technician
Services
Shipbroking & Freightforwarding
Stockbroking

In many cases entrants can slot in according to their qualifications, at various levels.

3. Pay and Prospects

(a) PAY

The categories 'low', 'medium' and 'high' may be irritatingly vague. But a rough indication of relative earnings is the nearest one can get to being accurate and helpful. Precise figures would be misleading, not only because rates of pay change frequently, but because individuals with different priorities, abilities, and luck tend to earn different amounts in the same type of work, after the same amount of time. Even in jobs with fixed salaries, like the Civil Service, nursing, or air traffic control, speed of promotion depends on luck as well as ability (and mobility).

But above all, most jobs can be done in many different settings, each with different scope for earning and promotion – and different attractions for different people. For example psychologists in the prison service probably earn less than those in advertising; newly-qualified engineers in local government earn more than those with consultant engineers; with a few years' experience, engineers willing to move to where the demand is greatest – perhaps the Middle East – earn more than those who prefer to stay put; a hairdresser in London's West End earns more than one who prefers a cosy suburban salon; an electronics technician in a factory earns more than one who wants to meet people and services T V and hi-fi equipment for a neighbourhood shop.

Another point about earnings: jobs which are well paid to start with, but which require little or no pre-entry training, tend to be dead-end (and usually dull in the long run). Trainees – whatever their title – who are given day-release and/or other systematic training are naturally paid less than employees who are at their employers' disposal throughout the working week. Differentials between skilled and unskilled (or qualified and unqualified) people at the moment may be small, but the person who has had systematic training and understands the 'why' behind the 'how' is immeasurably better able to change the nature of her work, to switch jobs, and to adapt to the technological and organizational changes which will affect everyone during the rest of this century.

(b) PROSPECTS

Comments under this heading throughout the book may seem rather optimistic, but they assume that by the time today's career-choosers are qualified, the economy will have improved, or some way of sharing out the available work more fairly, may have been found. Perhaps shorter working hours all round, or a working life interspersed with educational leave, or with updating courses, or just longer holidays, will become normal procedure. Also prospects are always relative; for example, not every engineer will be able to get the ideal job anywhere she likes – but engineers generally have far better prospects than, say, town planners or clerks.

Two general points: firstly, in many jobs a foreign language is a great asset as it enables people to work abroad; and secondly, the broader-based the qualification, the better the chances of being able to adapt to changes in the employment market. Throughout the recession, unemployment among skilled people, whether craftsmen, technicians, or graduates, was far lower than among unskilled people.

4. Grants

Most students who have been offered a place on a 'designated' course are eligible for 'mandatory' grants, usually payable by the local education authority (where the student lives, *not* where the course is). 'Designated' courses are *full-time* first-degree, Dip.H.E., Higher T.E.C., B.E.C. and National Diploma and equivalent courses. However, mature students (see p. xxxviii) who have been accepted on a designated course are now eligible, whether they have A-levels or not. Courses in the Long-Term Adult Residential Colleges (see p. xl) also qualify for mandatory grants.

Mandatory grants are intended to cover fees and term-time maintenance. Additional allowances may be payable to mature students and for certain courses. Grants are means tested, the amount paid out depending on parents' or, in the case of married students, spouse's, income. Basic rates change every year.

All other students, i.e. all those not on designated courses, and people who have had mandatory grants in the past, may be paid 'discretionary' grants. The size, and indeed the award of any discretionary grant at all, depends on the economic situation, the policy of the local education authority, and on the student's suitability, in the council's view, for the course.

5. Careers Advice

Everybody up to the age of nineteen, and later if still in full-time education outside the universities, can go to *any* careers office for information and advice. So for any young person who is not happy with the careers service provided at school or college, there is an alternative source of help.

Some careers officers help adult career-changers and women returning to work, others say they must concentrate on helping young people. Information/counselling services specially for adults are available in many areas – ask at public library, citizen's advice bureau, Open University Regional Office (even if you do not intend to take an O.U. course).

Graduates, whatever their age, can use local university or polytechnic careers advisory services – contrary to what many graduates think, they do *not* have to go for information and advice to wherever they graduated, possibly many years ago.

6. Youth Opportunities Programme (Y.O.P.)

This provides a variety of temporary work-experience and training schemes for young unemployed people. Y.O.P. schemes do not guarantee subsequent employment, but they enhance young people's 'employability' by giving them the kind of experience which is specially useful for school leavers with either very poor leaving qualifications or none at all.

Details from careers offices, job centres, employment offices, youth clubs. (Girls are often offered only traditionally female work-experience in offices, hospitals, etc.; but they have every right to ask for Y.O.P. schemes in, say, a garage or an engineering workshop if such schemes are offered to boys locally.)

Sex Discrimination Legislation: Brief Summary of Main Provisions Relating to Education and Employment

The *Sex Discrimination Act* makes it unlawful to treat anyone on the grounds of sex (and, in the case of employment, on the grounds of marriage) less favourably than a person of the opposite sex.

1. Employment

The Act defines two kinds of discrimination:

DIRECT discrimination, for example sending boys but not girls on day-release courses when both are doing similar jobs; or *not* promoting the person next in line *because* she is a woman (or a man).

INDIRECT discrimination: applying the same conditions to both sexes which favour one sex rather than the other but are not justified. For example if an employer, when recruiting an *office* manager, demands that the candidate must have served a *technical* apprenticeship, he or she is discriminating against women because they are far less likely to have served an apprenticeship – which is irrelevant to the job to be done; or if an employer only recruits people aged 20–30, it indirectly discriminates against women who are likely to rear children during those years.

The Act's main exemptions apply:

to employment in private households;

to firms employing not more than five people;

where sex is a genuine occupational qualification (known as a G.O.C.), for example in acting or modelling (neither strength nor stamina are G.O.C.s);

where one sex is required for reasons of decency, for example on oil rigs where there is only one dormitory;

in certain jobs providing care and/or supervision such as prisons;

to jobs which genuinely involve work abroad in countries where women in such jobs are not acceptable. However, if, for example, an employer persistently employs men because he or she claims the job *might* take them to a country where women are unacceptable, but

in fact few male employees are sent to such countries, the employer
would be illegally discriminating;
to the Armed Forces, the Churches, competitive sports and charities,
work in mines, certain shift and night work.

The *Equal Pay Act* stipulates equal treatment as well as equal pay for
the same or broadly similar work. It covers conditions such as sick pay,
preferential mortgages, contracts of employment, etc. Job titles are
irrelevant: e.g. if a woman is called 'accounts clerk' and a man, doing a
similar work, is called 'factory clerk', she is still entitled to equal pay
and treatment. However, women's hourly average earnings are still less
then three quarters those of men. This is so because the Act, as it
stands, does not stipulate 'equal pay for work of equal value' and
employers are not required to undertake job evaluation schemes. In
traditionally female jobs, such as nurses' or dietitians' for example,
where direct comparison with men's pay is not possible, the Equal Pay
Act has proved useless.

The *Employment Protection Act* says that a woman may not be
dismissed because of pregnancy; she is entitled to 6 weeks maternity
pay and to reinstatement for up to 29 weeks after the birth of the baby.
These provisions apply only if the employee works till 11 weeks before
the baby is due and if she has worked for the same employer for at least
2 years full-time or 5 years part-time; if she wants to resume work, she
must have told her employer so *in writing* before leaving.

Positive Discrimination

The Sex Discrimination Act specifically permits 'positive action' to be
taken by employers, employers' organizations, education and training
establishments, in two kinds of situations:
1. Where in the past jobs (and training schemes) were available only or
mainly to one sex, special training may be provided for the other sex, to
redress the balance and improve job and promotion prospects for the
hitherto under-represented sex;
2. Special training may also be provided to help women who wish to
return to work after a gap.
Disappointingly little use has so far been made of the 'positive action'
provision. Few women probably know that they could press for
'catching-up' courses and training.

Complaints concerned with employment matters are dealt with by
Industrial Tribunals.
(Leaflets setting out rights and procedures in full available from Job
Centres.)

2. Education

Discrimination is unlawful in admission to and provision of educational facilities in both the public and private sectors. A few exceptions relate to establishments which are single-sex. All other classes and establishments must be open to all pupils/students regardless of sex. Girls who want to take technical drawing, and boys who want to do cooking must not be discouraged; medical schools may not operate a quota system, etc.

It is not only discriminatory to refuse entry, but also, for example, gently to persuade girls *not* to choose physics or craft, design and technology where laboratory and workshop facilities are restricted, and instead let them take biology which is less useful, later. It is also discriminatory to give boys more chance of work-experience schemes than girls, or to differentiate between the kind of schemes offered (for example to arrange that all girls work in hospitals once a week, all boys in engineering works).

To observe the spirit as well as the letter of the law, careers staff have a duty to widen the girls' careers horizons and to ensure that they are fully aware of all the opportunities, including the non-traditional ones, which are open to them.

As Sex Balance in Education figures (see p. xxix) show, changes in boys' and girls' exam subject choices are not encouraging. While the letter of the law *is* observed, in many schools the spirit of the Act is ignored.

Complaints about discrimination in education must first be made to the appropriate Secretary of State (for England and Wales or Scotland) for Education. If no satisfactory conclusion has been reached within two months, cases must be taken before county courts in England and Wales, sheriff courts in Scotland.

Advice and information about all sex discrimination matters is available from the Equal Opportunities Commission, Overseas House, Quay Street, Manchester M3 3HN. Advice on employment matters is also available from the Advisory, Conciliation and Arbitration Service (addresses from local employment offices). Also, local Citizens' Advice Bureaux, such women's organizations as Townwomen's Guilds, and the National Council for Civil Liberties (152 Camden High Street, London NW1) will advise and/or provide leaflets.

Women's Rights: A Practical Guide, by Anna Coote and Tess Gill (Penguin), contains full details on anti-discrimination legislation, including complaints procedure.

Sex Balance in Education
– Some Facts and Figures

Absolute equality in education is essential if women are to be equal at work. But traditional attitudes and assumptions still steer boys and girls into choosing different subjects at 13+. Girls' choices are far less useful in terms of further and higher education, job opportunities, and generally coping with technological developments.

Proportion of Total O-level Passes Gained by Boys and Girls

	1979		1975	
	Boys	Girls	Boys	Girls
Engineering Workshop	99·4	0·6	99·2	0·8
Mathematics	61·5	38·5	61·0	39·0
Physics	75·2	24·8	78·0	22·0
Biology	40·2	59·8	40·1	59·9
Chemistry	64·1	35·9	68·0	32·0
Technical Drawing	97·3	2·7	98·5	1·5
Craft Design and Technology	97·1	2·9	98·5	1·5
Sociology	24·6	75·4	28·0	72·0
Commercial Subjects	34·7	65·3	39·0	61·0
Cookery	1·8	98·2	1·0	99·0
Computer Science	72·9	27·1	—	—

The proportions are changing at an elderly snail's pace, despite rapid changes in women's life styles and later job aspirations. It is particularly disappointing that such a small proportion of girls is taking Computer Science, a new subject where there cannot be any traditional barriers to break down. (Computer facilities in schools are still limited; perhaps not all schools comply with sex discrimination legislation – see p. xxviii – about equal access to facilities.)

Marginally more girls than boys get 5 O-Levels, Grades A–C, or C.S.E. Grade 1 – 23·9% of girls and 23·4% of boys. But boys' choices include more 'useful' subjects, and so girls still limit their career options long before they can possibly know what they will want to do eventually. Most boys with several O-levels have at least one physical science and/or a technical subject apart from maths. If girls do choose a science, it is often biology which rarely fulfils later course or job entry requirements.

Only 5·7% of girls against 18·8% (1979) of boys left with O-level physics (which is essential for most technical traineeships). 22% of girls and 29% of boys had O-levels maths – here the gap *is* narrowing.

After O-levels, girls are still more likely to leave school than boys. In 1979 13·4% of boys and 11·4% of girls left with at least 2 A-levels, but 6% of boys and only 2·2% of girls left with two *science* A-levels (sufficient to get into many science and technology degree courses); 9·6% of boys and 7·3% of girls left with 3 A-levels – the crucial number for getting into the most prestigious and most sought-after degree courses; 4·7% of boys against 1·6% of girls got three Science A-levels – needed for medicine, the most competitive of all degree courses. (Considering that almost three times as many boys as girls have the necessary entry qualifications, it is interesting that now 40% of entrants to medical school are women.)

0·15% of boys and 4·9% of girls went on to full-time secretarial courses.

Higher Education

In 1979, 14% of boys and 11% of girls went on to full-time or sandwich higher education courses; 9% of boys and 6% of girls taking degree courses. 87% of boys and 75% of girls *qualified* to do so – i.e. leaving with at least 2 A-levels or 3 Scottish Higher levels – chose higher education as the next step.

The gap between numbers of men and women is steadily narrowing – but very slowly – by just under 1% a year. In 1969, out of every 100 candidates for admission to university, 70 were men and 30 were women. In 1979, out of every 100, 61 were men and 39 were women. Provisional figures for 1980 show an increase in applications from women of 5% over 1979.

Throughout the decade, women had a marginally better chance of acceptance than men. Of all male candidates in 1969, 51% were accepted; of all women candidates 53% were accepted. In 1979, 53% of all male and 55% of all female candidates were accepted. Women's marginally higher acceptance rate is interesting because, proportionately, far more women try for oversubscribed, difficult-to-get-into courses such as Law, Medicine, English; far fewer apply for often undersubscribed engineering and science courses. For example, 4,206 women applied for Medicine, where there were 2·99 applicants for each place; only 383 women applied for Physics where there were just 1·09 applicants for each place.

However, although numbers were still small, 1979 applications from women showed encouraging increases over 1978; e.g., Computer Science: up 42·6%; Electrical Engineering: up 40·9%; Production

Engineering: up 33·3%. Provisional figures for 1980 applicants and acceptances show that this trend is continuing: the proportion of women at university is increasing, and more women are choosing engineering/technology subjects.

Men are much more career-minded. Degree subject choices are of course limited by candidates' A-level passes, but these alone cannot explain all disparities. Women are far less likely than men to opt for degree courses which have a high value in the job market and for which *any* 2 A-levels are acceptable: 2,036 men (2·35% of male applicants) and 574 women (1·03% of female applicants) chose Accountancy; 2,335 men (2·7% of male applicants) and 721 women (1·3% of female applicants, or less than half the proportion of men) chose Economics; 831 men (0·96% of male applicants) and 1,706 women (3·07% of female applicants, or over three times the proportion of men) chose Sociology; and 2,338 men (2·7% of male applicants) and 4,625 (8·31% of female applicants) chose English.

Women as Percentage of all Entrants
by Subject Groups

| | *1979* | |
	Universities (degrees)	Polytechnics (all advanced courses)
Education	73·2	58·9
Medicine, Dentistry & Health (includes ophthalmic optics, pharmacy, etc.)	43·9	61·6 (excludes Medicine & Dentistry)
(Medicine only, included in above	(39·8)	—
Engineering & Technology	6·8	3·0
Agriculture, Forestry, Veterinary Science	36·0	—
x Science	35·6	24·6
y Social Administration & Business Studies	41·1	28·5
z Architecture & other professional/vocational studies	38·1	31·7
Languages, Literature, Area Studies	68·0	71·6
Arts other than Languages	53·6	52·3

x: Much smaller proportion of women in physical and computer sciences where prospects are good; far more in subjects like botany and biology where prospects are poor.

y: Far more women in non-vocational, poor-job-prospects subjects such as sociology and anthropology; more men in management-orientated, vocational subjects like accountancy and economics.

z: More women in catering, institutional management; far more men in architecture.

Differences in Subject Choices, Universities

	1979	
	Men %	Women %
Education	1·5	4·2
Medicine, Dentistry, Health	10·7	12·1
Engineering & Technology	21·3	1·8
Agriculture, Forestry, Veterinary Science	2·8	2·3
x Science	20·8	14·5
y Social, Administrative, Business Studies	27·2	28·8
z Architecture & other professional/vocational subjects	2·8	2·2
Languages, Literature, Area Studies	7·0	23·4
Arts other than Languages	5·9	10·7
	100·0	100·0

x: Much smaller proportion of women in physical and computer sciences where prospects are good; far more in subjects like botany and biology where prospects are poor.

y: Far more women in non-vocational, poor-job-prospects subjects such as sociology and anthropology; more men in management-orientated, vocational subjects like accountancy and economics.

z: More women in catering, institutional management; far more men in architecture.

Sex Balance in Employment and Training (see also Introduction, p. ix)

Women now account for about 41% of the total workforce. About 62% of women between 16 and 60 work, but about 40% of them part-time. Two thirds of women at work are married. One in ten of families with children under 16 has a woman as sole breadwinner. The proportion of women working, and the extent of part-time work, varies with age. Almost 70% of women aged 35 to 54 work; under 40% of those between 24 and 35 do so. The higher their educational qualification and/or specific job training, the shorter the 'domesticity gap', i.e. the sooner they want to return to work.

Despite the increase in numbers of women at work, there has been no corresponding increase in the spread of jobs they do or the industries they work in. Over half of all women in manual work are still concentrated in a narrow range of low-paid, low-skill industries and occupations – mainly in textiles, catering, hairdressing, laundries, cleaning, and light engineering assembly work. (No single industry employs more than 10% of working males.)

Sex Distribution in the Main Non-Manual Occupational Groups

	Men %	Women %
General and specialized management	7·4	1·5
Clerical Work	7·2	33·6
Professional & related in health, welfare, education	5·1	15·3
Literary, Artistic, Sport	0·7	0·4
Selling	3·3	8·1
Professional & related in technology, engineering, science, etc.	6·9	0·8
Professional & related supportive management	5·8	1·4

Clerical and Selling, the two groups in which women predominate spectacularly, are those in which jobs are most seriously threatened by chip-based technologies. The Professional/Technical and related work groups, which have the lowest proportion of women, offer the best employment scope.

About one third of boys and one girl in ten take up formal apprenticeships – and most of the girls go into hairdressing. Only 0·22% of engineering craft apprentices are girls (and engineering includes electronics – clean, light work and a growth industry – see Engineering, p. 163). 32% of engineering operatives (semi- and unskilled work) are women; they have little hope of promotion. Only 2·2% of engineering technician trainees are women. This is the area where job segregation is most disturbing; technicians in engineering and related fields (which include computer manufacture and servicing) are in demand whatever the unemployment figures elsewhere. But technicians need maths, and usually physics or at least a technical subject (see Sex Balance in Education; and **Position of women**, Engineering, p. 175, for the industry's efforts to attract more women.)

More boys than girls go straight from school into employment (i.e. without first taking a full-time further or higher education course), but far more boys than girls get systematic on-the-job training. In 1978, 366,294 boys and 84,010 girls were on non-advanced day-release courses; most of the girls took 'job-specific' courses such as shorthand or hairdressing; most boys were on courses which extended their skills range – and their job opportunities.

Proportion of Women on T.O.P.S. Courses, 1979 (for details of T.O.P.S., see p. xl)

Office skills (clerical)	90%
Craft courses in skill centres, e.g.: bricklaying, capstan setting	3%
Technical courses in Further Education Colleges, e.g.: motor vehicle servicing, electrical wiring, electronics	6%
Higher level science & technology courses including draughtsmanship, lab. science/technology	14%
Management/management services	22%

(6% and 14% bracketed: includes computer courses)

In the professions, the vast majority of women are still in traditionally female jobs. However, more women are now training for professions (i.e. are on relevant degree or similar courses) – and so they are beginning to catch up. The one profession in which the proportions should soon be equal is the one with the most difficult-to-get-into, and the longest, training: medicine.

University Graduates Entering Different Types of Employment, 1979
(% of total home Employment)

	Men	Women
Public Service	21·6	35·2
Education	3·6	9·4
*Industry	42·5	19·3
Chartered Accountancy	10·5	6·6
*Banking & Insurance	3·8	4·3
*Other commerce	8·6	12·1
Solicitors (private practice)	2·8	3·0
*Other employment	6·7	10·0

* Includes graduate secretaries

Proportion of Women in Some Top (and Other Good) Jobs, 1980

Bank Managers	about 1%	
Directors in 100 top U.K. Companies	well below 1%	
British Institute of Management members	1·36%	
Institute of Chartered Accountants full members	4%	(student members: 22%)
Institute of Cost & Management Accountants full members	1%	(student members: 10%)
Institution of Civil Engineers full members	0·25%	(student members: 2%)
Institution of Electrical Engineers full members	0·16%	(student members: 2%)
Institution of Mechanical Engineers	0·07%	(student members: 1%)
Institution of Electrical and Electronic Technician Engineers	about 1%	
Dentists – practising	17%	(dental students: about 60%)
General Practitioners – practising	17%	(entrants to medical school, 1980: over 40%)
Surgeons – practising	0·8%	(registrars: 35%)
Barristers – practising	10%	
Solicitors – with practice certificates	8%	(entering into articles, 1980: about 40%)

Royal Institution of Chartered Surveyors		(student members:
full members	0·9%	4·5%)
Society of Surveying Technicians	below 1%	
Engineering Technicians	2%	(trainees: 2·2%)
Architects – practising	5%	(students: about 16%)
Veterinary Surgeons	10%	(students: about 35%)
Advertising Account Executives	about 17%	
Air Traffic Control Officers	3%	
Driving Examiners	well below 1%	
Local Authority Chief Executives	well below 1%	
University Professors	about 2%	
Civil Service:		
Executive Officers (fairly junior grade)	35%	
Under Secretaries (senior grade)	2·7%	
Administration trainees (high-flyer graduate entrants)	47% of applicants 37% of appointments	

Second Start in Education

A Variety of Routes for 'Returners'

There are plenty of opportunities for catching up on missed educational opportunities. Adults who need G.C.E.s, or simply more knowledge, for courses or careers they want to start after a gap of some years, can join any further education college for part-time day or evening, or full-time courses. Most of these are intended for school-leavers, but adults are welcome, and at an increasing number of colleges 'AO' (alternative O-level) courses, which are designed specially for mature students, are available.

Students can take as many subjects as they like; just one, or several, building up their own full-time course. Most people take 1, in some cases 2, sessions a week, for 3 terms, to get an O-level (or AO-level), and about twice as long to get an A-level.

It is also possible to take G.C.E.s by correspondence course (but correspondence courses should be chosen with care!). If you cannot get advice from someone in education, go for a non-commercial organization, e.g. National Extension College, 18 Brooklands Ave., Cambridge.

Then there are a wide variety of *non-examination* courses. These include the traditional evening classes in all sorts of subjects, and various 're-entry' courses. These may be called *Wider Opportunities for Women*; *New Opportunities for Women* (men are rarely excluded, but most re-entry courses were started by women, for women wishing to return to work); *New Directions*; *Fresh Horizons*; *Return to Study*, etc. Courses vary in content, organization, level and quantity of work expected. Some are mainly confidence-restoring and 'diagnostic'; they help students to sort out their aims, motivation, level of confidence, circumstances, and then balance these with the available job opportunities, and the obstacles which may arise. Some courses teach only study technique: learning how to study is very important for people who left school years ago and/or never took studying very seriously. Other courses combine study technique with specific subjects.

Courses may be held on 1, 2, 3 or 4 days a week; day-time classes are morning only or between 10 and 3, to fit in with school-hours. Length varies from 8 weeks to one academic year (in a few cases two years).

There are also some fairly intensive 4 or 5 days a week (full or part-time) 'feeder' courses; these do not lead to A-levels, but successful completion is officially recognized as equivalent to degree course G.C.E. requirements. A few courses lead to science degrees – helpful for people who want to switch to or start a technological career.

A useful innovation for people who cannot commit themselves to attending classes regularly is the *FlexiStudy* scheme. Briefly, it is a combination of correspondence course with personal contact with a tutor by letter or telephone, and occasional face-to-face tuition. FlexiStudents have access to college laboratory, library and social facilities. So far some 50 colleges are taking part in the scheme. Write for free leaflet, 'National FlexiStudy', to National Extension College (address above).

There are some similar 'one-off', 'distance learning'-plus-college-attendance schemes, and the 'Open College of the North West' covers several F.E. colleges in Lancashire and Cumbria.

There is no national pattern or central information point. Whether there is a course locally depends entirely on whether there is someone in the education system with enthusiasm for helping potential returners. Many classes start in response to demand from potential students (please note!).

Mature Students and Higher Education

Universities and polytechnics can waive normal entry requirements for mature students (usually people over 21, sometimes over 23). The extent to which this is done varies enormously: again there is no national pattern. Most admission officers want 'evidence of ability to benefit from and cope with sustained post-A-level study'; but there are no generally agreed methods of assessing such evidence, nor of the standards required. Applicants may be accepted on interview only, but usually they have to write an essay as well; some universities accept only on results of special mature-entry examination. All higher education establishments welcome mature students, who tend to make up in enthusiasm and motivation what they lack in G.C.E.s.

There are no establishments which will *not* consider mature entrants; one college (Lucy Cavendish, Cambridge) is for mature women graduates and undergraduates only.

PART-TIME DEGREES

These were originally intended only for people in jobs, with all or most tuition in the evenings. Part-time *day* courses were pioneered by Hatfield Polytechnic and then Kent University. Several C.N.A.A. and university part-time day degree courses are now functioning, or in the planning stage. If there is no such course locally or within commuting distance, there is an alternative:

'ASSOCIATE' OR 'OCCASIONAL' STUDENTS

They take one or several units within existing degree (or sometimes diploma) courses. They may, but need not, take exams and accumulate credits which may ultimately count towards a degree. Only Hatfield Polytechnic has an official Associate Student programme, but this type of do-it-yourself part-time study arrangement is being made by enterprising individuals at several H.E. establishments. The scheme only works where the degree structure is 'modular', i.e. where the course consists of separate credit-earning units. There is no central information point; confusingly, reference books list some, but not all, H.E. establishments which accept part-time students. Contact registrars or admission officers at university etc. you would like to attend.

OPEN UNIVERSITY

No entry requirements; admittance is mainly on first-come first-served basis. To be able to cope with the course, most people find some preliminary G.C.E. or other re-entry study necessary. O.U. students 'build up' degrees by completing a number of 'course credits'. It is possible to accumulate the 6 credits required for a degree (8 for an honours degree) in 3 years; in practice most people take longer. There is no time limit; dropping out for a year or longer presents no problems.

There are now transfer agreements with C.N.A.A. and many university degree courses. These enable O.U. students with a certain number of credits to slot into the second year of a relevant full-time course. The other way round, students who had to drop out of full-time higher education (for other reasons than failing their exam!) may be able to finish in the O.U. These arrangements are specially useful for temporarily housebound people.

The O.U. also runs (shorter) non-examination courses (a) for people who want to update specific knowledge: for example scientists, social workers, maths and other teachers; and (b) in 'Community Education' which covers subjects like consumer affairs and child development. A *Return to Study* course is in the planning stage (autumn 1980). In the meantime, until it gets off the ground, existing short non-examination courses are yet another type of re-entry-to-education course.

For details of O.U. 'distance learning' methods and general information, write for free 'Guide for Applicants' to Open University, Walton Hall, Milton Keynes MK7 6AA.

LONDON UNIVERSITY EXTERNAL DEGREES

Students study by themselves, with a little tuition at some (not many) F.E. colleges, or with correspondence course. The National Extension College (Brooklands Avenue, Cambridge) has a tuition package which includes correspondence material, personal contact with a tutor and a student-to-student service intended to minimize the loneliness of the distance-learner.

O.U. and London External degrees do not overlap – they serve different types of students: O.U. degrees are broad-based and cover an 'area of study'; London External degrees cover specific subjects in depth; for example, modern languages (a great many), law, economics. One big drawback for mature entrants: of all universities, London is the most rigid in its entrance requirements and makes fewer concessions to mature students than other universities. Details from University of London, Senate House, Malet St, London WC1E 7HU: 'General Information leaflet for External Students'.

RESIDENTIAL COLLEGES

There are eight 'Long-Term Adult Residential Colleges' – and despite the title students do not necessarily have to live in. They are for people with few or no G.C.E.s who want to go on to higher education or professional training, or who merely want to stretch their minds. One college is for women only, one for men only; the others are mixed, and want more women students: only between a quarter and a third of applicants are women. Most students take 2-year courses, some take shorter ones; subjects so far covered are a mix either of liberal studies or of social studies; Hillcroft is hoping to start soon a mathematics/technology course, to enable women to get into the expanding computer-associated job area. Details from Hillcroft, Surbiton, Surrey (women only); Newbattle Abbey, Dalkeith, Midlothian; Coleg Harlech, Gwynedd, Wales; Co-operative College, Loughborough; Plater College, Oxford; Ruskin College, Oxford; Fircroft College, Selly Oak, Birmingham (men only); Northern College, Wentworth Castle, Barnsley, Yorkshire.

T.O.P.S.
– the Training Opportunities Scheme

T.O.P.S. is run by the Manpower Services Commission and helps people over 19 who have been out of full-time education for at least 2 years (it does not matter how much longer) and who want to learn new skills or update, or add to, old ones.

T.O.P.S. is flexible. Almost any full-time course which lasts at least a month and not more than a year and is likely to lead to employment may qualify for a T.O.P.S. grant (but for post-graduate university courses applicants must be at least 27). The final decision as to whether a person is given a T.O.P.S. grant is up to M.S.C. and possibly course administrators. It is up to individuals to make out a case for their sponsorship – so it pays to do careful research about likely employment opportunities resulting from the course for which a grant is wanted.

Craft courses, in anything from welding to catering, heavy goods vehicle driving to agriculture, TV servicing to carpentry, are at Government Skill Centres; most last 6 months and are followed by at least a year's 'learnership'. Technician courses in a vast variety of subjects, including T.E.C. (see p. xl) courses in things like microprocessor applications, are normally at Further Education Colleges, where T.O.P.S.-sponsored students work alongside 'normal' F.E. students. At management level, T.O.P.S. grants are available for courses – usually at Polytechnics – in, for example, Personnel, Transport, Marketing Management, and the Diploma in Management Studies which offers a large variety of options (details from C.N.A.A., and see Management, p. 263).

In theory, T.O.P.S. grants are also available for people who want to add to professional qualifications, for example for S.R.N.s who want to take the Occupational Health or the Health Visitor's Certificate; in practice this type of grant is now very difficult to get.

The vast majority of women still apply for clerical courses (see table, p. xxxiv) but these are now being drastically reduced (see Secretarial/Clerical Work for poor prospects for clerks, typists, etc.). T.O.P.S. organizers would greatly welcome more women on craft, technician and management courses (see **Prospects**, Engineering Technician, p. 177).

T.O.P.S. grants are higher than students' grants and are paid regardless of spouse's or own income and may include dependants' and other allowances.

There are only a few part-time courses at the moment (more requests might produce more such courses).

T.O.P.S. details from Job Centres and Employment Offices.

Useful Publications

(should be available in schools' and careers offices' libraries, at least for inspection)

1. 'How to choose' Aids:

Decide for Yourself
Your Choice Beyond School
Choosing a Job
Male and Female
Vocational Choice
Your Choice at 13+ (not what career to choose but which subjects *not* to drop in order to leave career options wide open)
Your Choice at 15+
Your Choice at 17+
all published by C.R.A.C., Bateman Street, Cambridge.
Which Career for You? by Catherine Avent, published by Robert Hale.
A CE Further Education Handbook for School Leavers (explains what F.E. is and provides) published by Advisory Centre for Education, 18 Victoria Park Square, London E2.
Higher Education – Finding Your Way, published by Department of Education and Science, Information Division, Elizabeth House, York Road, London SE1.

2. Reference Books:

A Compendium of Advanced Courses in Colleges of Further and Higher Education (full-time and sandwich), published annually by D.E.S. Regional Advisory Councils (Tavistock House South, Tavistock Square, London WC1). (Post-A-level courses, including 'one-off', T.E.C. Higher Diploma, and Professional Examination courses.) Similar information on part-time and 5th-form leavers' courses is published regionally (details from local careers offices/teachers).
Careers Encyclopedia published by Cassells/Daily Telegraph. Most detailed reference book available.
Polytechnic Courses Handbook, published annually for Committee of

Directors of Polytechnics (309 Regent Street, London W1). Details of individual polytechnics and their varied courses.

Directory of Further Education, all F.E. courses; including new 'distance-learning'/second-chance (see Second Start in Education, p. xxxvii) courses as well as T.E.C., B.E.C., City and Guilds, day-release, full- and part-time ones. Published annually by C.R.A.C.

Which Degree, covers all degrees and gives full course and institution details; now published annually by V.N.U. Business Publications (until 1980, Haymarket Press).

Degree Course Guides, booklets comparing individual courses within disciplines, published bi-annually by C.R.A.C.

Directory of First Degree and Diploma of Higher Education Courses, published annually by C.N.A.A. (344–54 Gray's Inn Road, London WC1). C.N.A.A. course details only.

Directory of Postgraduate courses (C.N.A.A. – as above).

Graduate Studies, published annually by C.R.A.C. – details of post-graduate courses. Since 1980 in 4 subject area volumes: Humanities and Social Sciences; Biological, Health and Agricultural Studies; Physical Sciences; Engineering and Applied Sciences.

The Handbook of Degree and Advanced Courses in Institutes/Colleges of Higher Education, published annually by National Association of Teachers in F. and H.E. Evolved out of previous Teacher Training summary of courses (see Colleges and Institutes of Higher Education, p. xxi); guide through maze of new B.Ed. and 'diversified' courses – essential mainly for prospective teachers.

The Compendium of University Entrance Requirements, published annually for Committee of Vice-Chancellors and Principals. Essential information on varying entry requirements. Useful section on mature students' entry.

Becoming a Teacher; Teaching Science and Mathematics; Teaching Handicapped Children; Teaching Craft, Design and Technology from D.E.S.

Grants to Students: a Brief Guide, published annually by D.E.S.

Second Chances for Adults, published annually by Macmillan – all types of courses for late starters; mid-career changers; women returning to work.

C.O.I.C. (Careers and Occupational Information Centre) publishes a wide variety of leaflets and booklets, including the 'Working In . . .' series specially for leavers without any qualifications. All these, and Information Sheets specially for graduates, should be available in schools' and careers offices' libraries.

ACCOUNTANCY

Professional accountant – Accounting technician

1. Professional Accountant

**Entry quali-
fications**

2 A-levels, 3 O-levels, including mathematics and English language.
(The Institute of Chartered Accountants of Scotland requires a degree.)
Over half the entrants are now *graduates* and the proportion is rising.

The work

Accountancy covers a wide range of functions, carried out in a variety
of settings. Its image as a deskbound profession, concerned almost
entirely with adding up figures, is out of date. Accountants' work falls
into 3 broad categories:
1. *Public* (illogically also called 'private') *practice accountancy*
2. *Industrial accountancy*
3. *Public service accountancy*

1. PUBLIC PRACTICE ACCOUNTANTS

They work in accountancy firms of self-employed partners or 'principals',
qualified salaried assistants, trainee accountants and accounting technicians (see p. 7). Firms vary enormously in size – from 2 to over 100.
Some work on their own, possibly from home. The bulk of practitioners'
work is auditing and taxation. Auditing means verifying and analysing
clients' books and ensuring that the annual balance sheet presents a
'true and fair' picture of the client's financial affairs. Auditing is done
on clients' premises. It may take anything from a few hours to several
months, depending on size and type of client's business. This means that
accountants spend a good deal of time away from their office, meeting
a variety of people. It may also involve travelling. Accountants also
advise their clients on personal and business financial matters, from
how to invest a small legacy to setting up a business or liquidating one.

Increasingly, large accountancy firms provide *management consultancy* services. Management consultants are called in, for example, to
investigate the reasons for a firm's decline and to advise on ways of
improving profitability. They may also undertake investigations into,
for example, the pros and cons of proposed mergers or takeover bids. In
the course of their work, management consultants collect information

on individuals' working patterns and established but perhaps outdated ways of working; unlike traditional accountancy, management consultancy involves interviewing people at all levels in an organization rather than mainly figure- and desk-work. It requires considerable expertise in business organization and practice.

2. INDUSTRIAL ACCOUNTANTS

They work for an employer on a salaried basis. They can be divided into *financial* accountants, concerned largely with internal audits, taxation, wage and salary structure, financial record-keeping; *cost* accountants, concerned with analysing costs by product and/or processes and procedures; *management* accountants, concerned with measuring the profitability of the whole enterprise, and forward planning. *Cost and Management* accountancy are now considered two aspects of the same thing, and this specialization is now usually called management accountancy. It is the fastest growing accountancy specialization (and it overlaps with management consultancy work). Management accountants assess the relative importance, value and cost of all aspects of a business (or public enterprise) – equipment, labour, raw materials, transport, sites, administration, marketing, etc. Every person's, machine's, department's, vehicle's, etc., contribution to the effectiveness of an organization, and their interdependence, can, with the help of computer systems and mathematical techniques, be assessed separately and as part of the whole operation. Management accountants might, for example, compare the relative cost of using a cheap new raw material which would necessitate more expensive machine maintenance and require mounting a marketing campaign to launch the changed product, against the cost of going on using the more expensive traditional raw material – taking into account, among other factors, what the competition abroad might do, and how staff would feel about the change. Or they might assess the cost of moving a factory to a cheaper site, considering increased transport cost, recruiting and training new staff. Like management consultants, their work requires interviewing all the people whose work affects the efficiency of the organization concerned. Having compared the financial results of alternative courses of action, management accountants present the information to the decision-makers at the top of the organization.

Management accountants need a broader understanding of business organization in general and of the type of business with which they are concerned than do financial accountants. They often move from salaried employment into public practice.

3. PUBLIC SECTOR ACCOUNTANTS

Accountants working for local government, the nationalized industries, the Health Service, etc., have much the same function and aims as industrial accountants: i.e. the most efficient use of resources. Only the emphasis is different: instead of improving profitability, public sector accountants are concerned with control and management of public authority finance. They advise on the financial implications of various courses of action and help sort out priorities when, with limited financial resources, new schemes or improvements or existing services have to be abandoned or curtailed.

Whereas accountants in industry present their information to business people who are themselves often knowledgeable about business matters, public sector accountants often advise and explain things to professional colleagues from other disciplines and elected councillors who may know very little about finance.

Prospects   Generally excellent. Demand exceeds supply even during the present recession. Because of the increasing complexity of financial management and planning, accountants are in great demand.

Accountants can remain specialists and move up the ladder to financial controller (titles vary) in industry or in the public sector; they can move sideways and up into general management (see Management, p. 259), into accountancy teaching, into systems analysis (p. 135) or into management consultancy. At middle-level there are a vast variety of jobs in all types and sizes of business and public enterprise. An accountancy qualification is also an excellent preparation for jobs in merchant and other banking, insurance, the Stock Exchange.

There are some opportunities for employment (but *not* in Public Practice) in the E.E.C., and in most other countries.

Pay: Very high (but low while under training contract) (see pp. 4–6).

Training   There are six main professional qualifications, each awarded by a different body:
1. Institute of Chartered Accountants of England and Wales;
2. Institute of Chartered Accountants of Scotland;
3. Institute of Chartered Accountants of Northern Ireland;
4. Association of Certified Accountants;
5. Institute of Cost and Management Accountants;
6. Chartered Institute of Public Finance and Accountancy.

The differences between the syllabuses are small – there is a basic body of accountancy knowledge which all accountants must master.

Non-graduate accountancy students must normally take a 9-month full-time Foundation course at a polytechnic. Most of these courses lead on to any of the professional examinations, but a few lead only to one or two. Students who are not sure which qualification they will ultimately take should ensure they start with a 'common' Foundation course. The Foundation examination syllabus covers accounting principles, law, economics, statistics, taxation.

The essential differences:

Only *Chartered* and *Certified*, but not *Cost and Management* and *C.I.P.F.A.* accountants, may, by law, audit limited companies' accounts, which is the public practice accountant's bread and butter.

Chartereds and *Certifieds* can work in industry *and* in the public sector, so studying for these two qualifications leaves all the options open.

The *Cost and Management Accountants*' syllabus covers industrial production and business organization in greater depth than do the others. For those intending to go into industry (far more professional accountants work in industry than in public practice) *Cost and Management* may be the first choice.

Those to whom prestige matters most would probably choose *Chartered Accountancy*. Those who want to go into the vast area of public service choose *C.I.P.F.A.*

The main attraction of *Certified Accountancy* is that, like Chartered Accountancy, it leaves all options open, and – very important for women – training is much more flexible (see below).

Another way of choosing one qualification rather than another is simply to choose the most easily available locally.

Training is always a combination of education and experience; all bodies now require non-graduate students to pass a Foundation examination before training for their own Professional examinations. Graduates may be granted partial or total exemption from the examination according to the relevance of their degree; Business Studies degrees may lead to the same exemption as Accountancy degrees. Each body has its own – important – list of exemptions.

1. Chartered Accountancy

Non-graduates enter into a 4-year 'training contract' in public practice. Before starting their training, they must complete the 9-month full-time Foundation course. While working under training contract students are normally granted a total of 22 weeks' study leave.

The syllabus covers accounting, auditing, structure and organization of business; principles of law, statistics and mathematics, economics; financial accounting; cost and management accountancy, taxation; computer systems.

Graduates enter into a 3-year training contract. An accountancy degree exempts totally from the Foundation examination; a related-subject degree qualifies for partial exemption. Graduates in 'non-relevant' degrees are encouraged to take a 'conversion' course (6 weeks to 6 months), part-time, during training: this exempts them from the Foundation examination.

Holders of B.E.C. higher-level awards (see p. xvii) may be exempt from the Foundation examination but train for 4 years; Diploma in Higher Education holders (see p. xl) qualify for similar exemption *only if their course content was relevant*. They all train for 4 years.

The training must be with the same firm of accountants throughout.

2. Association of Certified Accountants

Non-graduates: 4 years either in salaried employment in an approved accountancy department in industry, or the public service, or with a Certified Accountant in public practice. Those who intend to go into public practice must spend 3½ years in a practising accountant's office, of which at least 1 year must be post-qualifying. Students may, but need not, take the *full-time* Foundation course.

For *graduates* the training, whether in salaried employment or under articles, is 3 years. Graduates are granted partial exemption from examinations on a subject-for-subject basis. The syllabus covers much the same ground as the Chartered Accountancy examination, but it puts special emphasis on human relations in industry and on management skills.

Advantages of studying for the *Certified* Accountancy qualification:
1. Students are in salaried employment (they earn more than trainees under training contract). They may change employers and thus obtain varied experience.
2. They may interrupt training. However, employees have to do more studying in their own time than articled clerks. The failure rate is high.

3. Institute of Cost and Management Accountants

Students *may*, but need not, take a *full-time* Foundation course. Practical training usually takes 5 years without full-time Foundation course; or 3 years after completion of the full-time 9-month Foundation course. *Graduates* may be granted partial exemption from parts of the examinations, and complete training in 3 years.

The training can be interrupted; it need not be with one employer throughout. Training is the most industry-orientated. Day- or block-release may be granted.

4. Chartered Institute of Public Finance and Accountancy

Professional training takes 3 years while working as trainee in public sector accountancy/finance. A-level entrants' training must be preceded by a full-time 9-month Foundation course; for graduates with 'non-relevant' degrees it must be preceded by a 3-month Conversion course (check with C.I.P.F.A. for 'relevance' of individual degree courses). During professional training, trainees attend 39 weeks' educational courses, but this period is reduced for graduates with relevant degrees – length of reduction depends on degree course content.

Personal attributes

Academic ability; numeracy; ability to speak and write concisely; business sense; logical mind; ability to negotiate without self-consciousness with people at all levels within an organization; tact in dealing with employers and clients; a liking for desk-work.

Accountants in public practice: a confidence-inspiring manner; ability to put things clearly to laymen.

Cost and management accountancy and management consultancy: ability to communicate with and extract information from people at all levels of intelligence and responsibility.

Position of women

Proportions are still surprisingly low:

	Qualified Members	Students
Chartereds	4%	22%
Certifieds	5%	26%
I.C.M.A.	1%	10%
C.I.P.F.A.	approx. 5%	'significant increase'

There is little prejudice in accountancy generally except perhaps in some City firms and at the top in local government (see Local Government, p. 255). The reason for low proportions must be: (a) tradition, (b) the image of accountancy as totally desk-bound work without contact with people, and (c) the fact that fewer girls take O-level mathematics. Yet accountancy training helps women to get into senior management in industry (see p. 259). The accountancy bodies are genuinely trying to get more women into the profession and cannot understand why they recruit so few: a fair proportion have done extremely well in, for example, financial journalism, and some in management consultancy.

Career-break: Should be no problem with I.C.A. and A.C.A. There are lectures and journals which help to keep accountants up to date with developments. It is possible to work in most parts of the country and also to run a small practice from home. More difficult with other two bodies.

Late entry: No significant G.C.E. concessions, but cases judged on merit individually. It is difficult to find training vacancies, but the *Certified* Accountants help late entrants with finding training vacancies.

Part-time: Opportunities mainly in public practice.

Further in-formation
Institute of Chartered Accountants in England and Wales, P.O. Box 433, Chartered Accountants' Hall, Moorgate Place, London EC2R 6EQ

Institute of Chartered Accountants of Scotland, 27 Queen Street, Edinburgh

Institute of Chartered Accountants in Ireland, 7 Fitzwilliam Place, Dublin 2

The Association of Certified Accountants, 22 Bedford Square, London WC1B 3HS

The Institute of Cost and Management Accountants, 63 Portland Place, London W1N 4AB

The Chartered Institute of Public Finance and Accountancy, 1 Buckingham Place, London SW1E 6HS

Related careers
Actuary – Banking – Company Secretary – Computing – Insurance – Management in Industry – Purchasing and Supply – Statistics (Science) – Tax Inspector

---

2. Accounting Technician

Entry quali-fications
4 O-levels including an English and a numerate subject. Not more than one may be a craft (i.e. non-academic) subject.

The work
There is no legal requirement for 'accountants' to be professionally qualified (as for example solicitors and architects must be), except to audit public companies' accounts. In the past much of the work in accountants' offices was done (and still is done) by staff who either learnt by experience and never took an examination, or by clerks who had failed their examinations, or by over-qualified, and therefore bored, professional accountants. Only part of accountancy requires the professional accountants' academic ability and depth and breadth of knowledge.

A 'second-tier' or 'technician' qualification has now been introduced. Technicians' work may overlap with professional accountants', but broadly, the professional accountant is concerned with public companies' audits, and with financial management and advice; the technician with supplying financial and accounting information and services: the technician does the actual work on which professional accountants base their advice and management decisions.

Technicians may be employed in any type of accountancy department or firm; they are also employed in small companies as *sole accountant* to deal with day-to-day keeping of accounts. Work may involve contact with clients or customers, with other departments. While it is a mixture of desk-work and contact with people, the desk-work content of technicians' work is probably bigger than that of professional accountants – but it varies.

In small companies, which do not have professional accountants on the staff, technicians may even be called 'company accountant' (which is not a protected title).

Only professionally qualified accountants may 'set up in public practice' – a phrase which implies qualification to audit public companies' accounts; but any accountant, whether unqualified or with technician qualification, may, on a self-employed basis or in employment, prepare tax returns and generally 'do the accounts' for small traders, shop-keepers and individuals. Rather like auditing (see p. 1), this may involve visiting clients; and it often involves preparing accounts from rather chaotic private account-keeping, with bills stuffed into drawers, etc. This type of work brings accounting technicians into contact with a large variety of individuals.

Until early in 1981 there were two separate accountancy technician organizations – the Institute of Accounting Staff and the Association of Technicians in Finance and Accounting. I.A.S. students and members worked mainly in Certified Accountants' offices as the Institute was sponsored by the Association of Certified Accountants; A.T.F.A. students and members worked mainly in commercial and public sector offices as their body was sponsored by the Institute of Chartered Accountants, the Institute of Cost and Management Accountants and the Chartered Institute of Public Finance and Accountancy. Students had to decide for which institution's type of work to study before they knew much about what it involved. The two technician bodies talked about amalgamation for some years, but finally it was decided, at the end of 1980, to set up a new body to replace the two old ones. The Association of Accounting Technicians is sponsored by the four main professional accountancy bodies in England and Wales – the Institute of Chartered Accountants, the Association of Certified Accountants, the Institute of Cost and Management Accountants and the Chartered Institute of Public Finance and Accountancy. (The A.A.T.'s examinations and membership will be recognized, it is expected, by the I.C.A. in Scotland and Ireland.)

The A.A.T.'s aim is to encourage the 'professional development' of the large number of accountants who are doing highly skilled and responsible work but not at top professional 'consultant' level.

A.A.T. members can switch from one type of accountancy office to another, but it is expected that most will specialize – by experience if not in training – in one type of work, at least if they want to progress to relatively senior jobs. For example, they may work in public practice on auditing or tax matters – meeting clients; or on assembling financial information – doing mainly backroom work; and they may help small firms – shops, farmers, restaurants, etc. – with the preparation of their accounts (do their book-keeping, in fact).

A.A.T. members in large offices are likely to work with microcomputers and other new technologies. They may even be able to specialize in adapting existing accounting procedures to new technologies.

There is no 'bridge' to professional accountancy: qualified technicians would have to take the relevant training, but individual bodies may make concessions in terms of length of training, entry requirements, etc. to A.A.T. members.

Prospects Very good. There is considerable demand for technicians to work in accountancy departments and firms, and there is also scope to assist individuals and shop-keepers, etc., with account-keeping. However, technicians cannot be promoted to professional status (see **Training**).

Pay: Medium to high (see p. xxiii).

Training Education, and training in a suitable office, is to be closely integrated. Students who want to take the Association of Accounting Technicians' examination for membership must have worked in an approved accountancy practice or office for at least three years. They may work in any type of accountancy office – public sector, public practice, industry, commerce. The period in the office will provide the 'professional training'. 'Professional education' must be obtained by taking a B.E.C. or S.C.O.T.B.E.C. National Award (see p. xvii), either two years full-time, or three years part-time, while in relevant employment. The two elements – professional education and professional training – can, therefore, be concurrent, but full-time students will have to work in an office for three years before being fully qualified. The A.A.T. intends eventually to accept success in the B.E.C. or S.C.O.T.B.E.C. National Award examination to provide 'evidence of suitable professional education'; but until at least 1984 they will themselves examine students in areas where suitable B.E.C. courses are not available. They will also, until 1984, examine students who have already started the old Institute of Accounting Staff or Association of Technicians in Finance and Accounting courses.

The A.A.T. requires students to take *either* B.E.C. Business Studies (B1) courses, which cover non-specialized work in commercial, manufacturing and service organization (i.e. they are suitable for people who are not sure in what kind of organization they eventually want to work); *or* Finance (B2) courses, which are suitable for people who intend working in insurance, banking, building societies, etc. (However, *all* Business Studies National Awards are broad-based and holders can switch type of employment, possibly adding further 'modules' (see p. 265).)

Personal attributes

A methodical approach; liking for figure-work and desk-work. There is room in this work for those who prefer to work on their own but with limited responsibility as support staff to more highly qualified/experienced colleagues, and for those who, though unable to take the professional examination, wish to do responsible work and have contact with colleagues and clients.

Position of women

About 25% of accountancy technician students are women (the first few students qualified only in 1976), and the proportion may well rise. Accountancy technician training can be interrupted. There is scope for *part-time* work (mainly keeping accounts for small businesses which do not need full-time accounting staff).

Career-break: Should present no problem at all.

Late start: Very good scope indeed; full-time training is likely to be better than on-the-job training (where young school-leavers may be preferred).

Part-time: See above.

Further information

Association of Accounting Technicians, Berkshire House, 168–173 High Holborn, London WC1V 7AG

Related careers

Banking – Insurance – Purchasing and Supply – Shipbroking – Stock Exchange

ACTING

Entry quali- No rigid requirements. See **Training**.
fications

A career only to be contemplated by those who feel they could not possibly be happy doing anything else. Complimentary notices for school or college plays are rarely pointers to professional success, because being the best of a group of local performers is irrelevant when competing with the best from all over the country. In addition, luck plays a large part: being known to the right employer at the right time is as important as being good at the job.

Entry to this overcrowded profession is extremely difficult. There are 'casting agreements' between theatrical, TV, film and commercials producers which control the employment of actors and virtually restrict employment to Equity members. Equity (the actors' trade union) in turn strictly controls the entry of new members.

The work ## 1. THEATRE

Performers usually give 8 performances weekly. In repertory, there are often morning rehearsals as well, which leaves little free time. Reasonably priced digs near the theatre are rarely luxurious; theatre dressing-rooms tend to be cramped and uncomfortable.

Only a minute proportion of actors ever have a 'secure job' – contracts may be as short as 2 weeks; never longer than a year.

Apart from the conventional theatre, there has in recent years been a considerable growth in 'fringe theatre'. Companies are often set up by young players working as cooperatives (for a very small wage), taking plays into small halls, pubs, schools, etc. This type of acting – without proper stage – requires adaptability, devotion and special technique: it is not much easier to get into than conventional stage work.

2. TELEVISION

Provides over half the total of acting jobs, and is not easy to get into either: producers can pick and choose, and tend to choose players who have had repertory experience or have done exceptionally well at drama schools, TV work or in fringe theatre work. TV plays are video-taped (recorded), they are shot in 'takes' which are longer than film-takes, but not long enough to allow players to 'get into' the part as stage performances do. TV acting is more of a strain than filming or the theatre: rehearsal time is always cut to a minimum (3 weeks at the most), so it is impossible to have as many re-takes as in filming, yet there is no hope of doing better the next night, as in the live theatre. The TV studio atmosphere is hectic and tense. The majority of players prefer the stage, whatever their public utterances; but television provides their bread and butter and helps them to get known nationally..

3. COMMERCIALS

Work comes through theatrical casting agencies or some of the big advertising agencies. Work is never regular; TV commercials producers always look for fresh faces, and an actress who is currently advertising, for instance, a baby food, is unlikely to be used for some time, either for a competitor's food or for, say, a sophisticated drinks or fashion advertisement. Once established, actors and actresses sometimes appear in commercials which are written to suit their particular style, or they do 'voice overs' – the speaking but not the visual part of the commercial. Commercials are not a way into acting, but useful bread-and-butter jobs.

4. FILMS

The film industry has shrunk immensely in the last few years. There is very little work; nobody can hope to be a *film*-actress or actor today. Engagements tend to come at short notice. The decision whether to accept a tiny part in a TV soap-opera serial or wait for a hoped-for break in a film is always a difficult one. Once a performer has accepted a part, she must stick to it and not let a producer down if something better turns up – otherwise she loses her agent's or casting director's goodwill, which is fatal.

Acting is never easy, however good a player is. It gives great satisfaction, however, to people with stamina, real talent and lots of luck.

Prospects   Very poor indeed except for the outstandingly talented and lucky. A recent survey showed that at any one time over two-thirds of professional actors and actresses are out of work. An inquiry also showed that the chances of success are immeasurably better for students who have attended one of the established acting schools (see **Training**) than for those who have been to one of the 'academies' which are totally out of touch with the changing needs and techniques of the theatre and broadcasting, or those few who somehow slipped in without any systematic training at all.

'Graduates' from established drama schools do not normally have great difficulty in getting their first job. They are usually fixed up within a few months of leaving drama school. It is the second step into bigger and better repertory, or into TV, West End, etc., which is the problematical one – and which vast numbers never manage to make at all. It means coming to London, finding a good agent who will take a newcomer, and earning a living, yet being available if the hoped-for audition comes.

Pay: Depends too much on luck and talent to generalize about.

Entry requirements and training

No rigid G.C.E. requirements; acceptance at good drama schools depends on audition, but candidates considered suitable almost invariably have several O- and often A-levels, especially in English language and/or literature. The average ratio of acceptance at good schools is about 12 to 1; for women candidates it is about 45 to 1.

About 85% of players who earn their living at acting have been to schools which belong to the *Conference of Drama Schools* and one or two other well-known ones which for various reasons do not belong to the C.D.S. (careers officers have lists of these schools). The overwhelming majority of students from other schools and academies fall by the wayside, largely because they are not trained adequately in techniques of acting for TV cameras.

Performers' courses last 2 or 3 years. Students unlikely to succeed are asked to leave, or leave of their own accord, well before the end of the course. Courses prepare students for all types of work, but individual schools' curricula vary considerably. All cover the three main aspects: *movement, voice production* and *acting studies*. All students do all types of parts, from musical to mime, Shakespeare to Pinter. Courses include general stage-craft, play-construction, etc.

Drama can also be taken as part of a first degree course, but the primary purpose of these courses is the study of literary criticism, history and literature of the theatre; not vocational acting training. Graduates from these courses usually go into teaching or possibly into drama production (mainly TV); but there are far fewer such openings than there are drama degree students.

Post-graduate drama courses are also academic, not vocational.

Personal attributes

Good health; well-cut features, but not necessarily beauty; the ability to learn lines quickly; a good memory; great self-confidence; imagination and sensitivity to interpret any part; resilience, to ignore or benefit from the constant and public criticism from teachers, producers, directors, colleagues, and the critics; an iron constitution; a sense of rhythm, at least (preferably an aptitude for dancing and singing); outstanding acting talent and a 'stage personality'; grim determination.

**Position
of women**

Only about 1 woman applicant in 45 is accepted at drama school: the ratio of female to male students training is 3 to 1. Although there are *far* more parts for men than for women, more women graduate every year. In this profession it is of course not a question of discrimination at the employment stage, but entrenched tradition makes even women dramatists write more parts for men than for women. Actresses are therefore strongly advised to have a second string to their bow. Secretarial training is useful here, as 'temping' and part-time jobs enable an actress to be available for auditions while earning her living.

**Further in-
formation**

No central organization; consult list of recommended drama schools at Careers Office.

**Related
careers**

Barrister – Broadcasting – Speech and Drama Teaching, p. 492 – Speech Therapy. See also Arts Administration (Art and Design, p. 64)

ACTUARY

Entry quali-fications   *England and Wales*: 2 A-levels, one of which must be at least Grade B in a mathematics subject or Grade C in further mathematics, the other at least Grade C, and 3 O-levels including one English subject.
90% graduate entry.

The work   Actuaries use the theory of probability and other mathematical techniques to highlight and if possible solve financial problems, to suggest appropriate courses of action and to predict the financial implications of such actions; in other words, they 'work out the odds'. Their work is essentially concentrated academic desk-work, performed in a variety of settings. The majority of actuaries work on pension fund and social insurance schemes in life assurance offices, investigating such matters as relative life expectancies of various groups in the population, and assessing the effects of life-styles and characteristics on premiums and policies and investment. In other insurance branches – accident, fire, motor – actuaries assess risks and pin-point variables in the light of changing conditions and life-styles, and advise on reserves necessary to cover long-term liabilities. In government departments actuaries advise on public service pensions and insurance schemes. Though they are concerned with various aspects of people's lives and welfare (cushioning of the effects of old age, accident, sickness being the reasons for insurance schemes), actuaries do not have much contact with people outside their own office.

For actuaries who want to have more contact with people outside their own profession and perhaps apply mathematics to wider commercial matters, there are some opportunities in commerce and industry as financial analysts, advisers, planners. About 15% are in consulting practice, advising mainly on private pension funds. Consulting actuaries may negotiate with solicitors, tax inspectors and trade union officials concerned with pensions.

Prospects   A small profession, but steady demand for qualified people.
Pay: High (see p. xxiii).

Training   6–7 years' part-time study for school-leavers, 1 or 2 years less for graduates. No formal articles or apprenticeships. Training is on-the-job plus correspondence study (and discussion classes) for Institute of Actuaries' (England and Wales) or Faculty of Actuaries' (Scotland) examinations. Employers may give time off for day-time study, but considerable evening work is necessary too.

Students with good degrees in mathematics, statistics or economics qualify for exemption from parts of the Group A examinations, which include computer application; probability; statistics and compound interest; principles of actuarial treatment of statistical data; use of statistics in the study of population changes; finance and investment. The Final examination covers life offices, pension funds and friendly societies, finance and investment, general business insurance.

Personal attributes

Liking for concentrated desk-work; an analytical brain (actuaries tend to be good and devoted bridge-players); probing curiosity; pleasure in solving complicated problems; ability to interpret and express in clear English results of mathematical and statistical analysis; business sense for those who want to go into private practice.

Position of women

Of 3,448 fully qualified members of the Institute of Actuaries only 108 are women; but of 2,153 students, 235 are women, so the proportion is going up. No difficulties getting jobs and promotion.

Career-break: Possible for experienced actuaries who have kept up with developments, especially relevant legislation and data processing application (see p. 134). Temporarily retired members pay a reduced subscription which nevertheless entitles them to receive all journals and attend meetings.

Refresher Courses: Correspondence courses can be adapted.

Late entry: Only advisable for brilliant mathematicians because of the long training; also difficulty in finding training posts.

Part-time: In theory work could be done part-time, and by freelances; in practice no concentrated attempts to organize this seem to have been made by prospective part-timers.

Further information

Institute of Actuaries, Staple Inn Hall, High Holborn, London WC1V 7QJ
The Faculty of Actuaries, 23 St Andrew Square, Edinburgh (Scottish training and educational requirements differ in detail from the above)

Related careers

Accountancy – Banking – Civil Service – Insurance – Stock Exchange

ADVERTISING

Account Executive – Media Executive – Market Research – Creative Department

Entry quali- No rigid requirements; in practice usually A-level English or B.E.C.
fications award (see p. xvii). *Graduates* are increasingly recruited.
Graphic design, typography, etc., require art-school training (see Art and Design, p. 53), although some studios accept juniors with O-level art.

The work Advertising specialists work in:
1. agencies
2. company advertising departments
3. the media and for suppliers of advertising services (e.g. studios, film production, market research)

1. Agencies

Agencies plan, create and place advertisements on behalf of advertisers who appoint them to handle their 'account'. This may be a detergent, a package holiday, Government information, or a nationalized industry. Only 40% of advertising expenditure is concerned with persuading people to *buy*; advertisements are also used to get money for charities, votes for political parties, support for seat belts, to encourage energy saving or investment, to fill jobs.

Agencies vary in size and scope. Some employ up to 600 people, most under 50. Some specialize: for example, in technical or recruitment advertising. The largest agencies have a range of specialist services such as package design (see p. 56), film production (see Films, p. 79), market research and marketing (see pp. 18, 270) and public relations (see p. 379).

ACCOUNT EXECUTIVE

Agency staffs work in groups on individual accounts. Responsible for each account group of specialists is the *Account Executive*. She is usually in charge of several accounts, each dealing with a different product, and is the link between clients and agency. She must acquaint herself thoroughly with each client's product: this may involve asking

Research (see below) to identify the 'target group' (the people at whom the advertisement is to be aimed); to investigate the competition's product; to ensure the client's claims for the product can be substantiated. After the initial research, the group decide on a 'campaign theme', then the Account Executive discusses it with the client. When the brief and the budget are agreed, work on 'creating the advertisements' starts.

The Account Executive coordinates the work, watches the budget and presents progress reports to the client. Her work involves travelling if clients are scattered over the country or abroad.

The job requires self-confidence and diplomacy, as clients often have to be persuaded that the type and tone of a campaign suggested by the agency will be more effective than the client's own idea.

MEDIA EXECUTIVE

Media planners choose the channels of communication – newspapers, magazines, radio, television, posters and so on – which are most appropriate for any particular campaign and reach the target group most economically. Media planning decisions are based on information and statistics provided by *media research*. Computers are widely used to compare effectiveness and costs, but creative requirements – for colour, movement or sound – require subjective judgement.

Media buyers are responsible for the purchase of press or air time.

Planning, research and buying are the three media functions; they may be carried out by different people within the department, or the whole media operation may be the responsibility of a group of individuals assigned to a particular campaign.

MARKET RESEARCH

Before an advertising campaign is planned, facts are compiled about the product's uses, its advantages and limitations, competitors' products, distribution and so on. Facts and opinions are also gathered about its potential users – the target group: not just in terms of who they are, how much money they have and where they live, but in terms of their attitudes and behaviour. Some facts come from desk research, collecting information from a variety of published sources and the client's own records. Others may need specially commissioned research, ranging from statistics compiled by part-time interviewers questioning members of the public, to sophisticated behavioural studies involving trained psychologists.

CREATIVE DEPARTMENT

Once the account group has been briefed and a strategy agreed with the client, the *copywriter* and *art director* together develop the advertisement.

The advertising 'message' is translated into a 'communication' that makes an instant impact on the target group. Words and pictures must complement each other.

Copywriters must be literate and imaginative, but they must choose their words under considerable constraints – from the disciplines of the brief and the restrictions of the space or time available, to the obligations of the Code of Advertising Practice and legal requirements. An interest in commercial success and an understanding of people's ways of life and priorities are far more useful than literary leanings.

Television and cinema commercials may be created jointly by copywriters and producers, or written by specialist scriptwriters to the producer's brief. There is no hard and fast rule about who exactly does what, and whether the visual or verbal aspect is the more important.

The *Art Director* (see Art and Design, p. 53) is responsible for the physical appearance of print advertisements, deciding whether to use photography or illustration, commissioning and supervising its production and the type selection and typography. The typographer chooses type which is easily readable, fits the layout and reflects the character of the product.

The atmosphere in agencies is often relaxed and informal, but the pace and pressure are very demanding indeed. The decline in the number of people in agencies means fierce competition for any openings. Considerable talent, the right kind of personality and commitment are needed to survive and succeed.

2. Advertisers

Many advertisers incorporate advertising into marketing (see p. 270). *Brand managers* are responsible for the marketing policy for a product, including its advertising. Others have their own advertising departments, which vary in size. If a manufacturer creates and places all the advertising directly, the department may be much like a small agency. There is less scope for employees to work on different types of products simultaneously, but there may be a broader range of work.

Retailers' advertisement departments may deal with store and window displays, exhibitions, fashion shows, promotions and public relations, for example, using an advertising agency only for display advertisements.

Advertising departments are useful training grounds, giving experience in a range of work. There are more opportunities for junior copywriters in advertising departments than within agencies.

3. Media

Advertising departments are responsible for selling space or air time to advertisers, directly or through agencies. The *research section* provides information about readers or viewers; it helps advertisers pin-point target groups. The *promotions section* may have its own creative department, which works in three areas: projecting the medium to advertisers, to distributors, and to retailers on behalf of advertisers. *Sales representatives* are responsible for selling advertisement space or air time; this may include telephone canvassing, trying to get classified advertisements (which may involve having to put up with being rebuffed, and trying again). *Media Managers* are responsible for ensuring that advertisements comply with the Code of Advertising Practice, which may involve checking copy claims and possibly asking for changes to be made before accepting copy.

Prospects   Now more limited than they used to be; the advertising industry has contracted considerably in the last few years. Considerable persistence – apart from talent – is needed to get a job. Virtually all jobs are in London.

Pay: High (see p. xxiii).

Training   A combination of practice and theory. Examinations are set by C.A.M. (Communication Advertising and Marketing Education Foundation). At least 1 year's experience in the communications industry (e.g. advertising, public relations, broadcasting, marketing) is required before students may register for evening, correspondence or day-release (rarely granted) courses.

1. The C.A.M. Certificate

Covers Marketing, Advertising, Public Relations, Media, Research and Behavioural Studies, Communications. Each may be taken independently, over a number of years, but 2 years' evening classes are usual.

2. The C.A.M. Diploma

For C.A.M. Certificate holders, available in Advertising, Marketing, Public Relations, or Media.

Partial exemptions from the Certificate stage may be granted to holders of relevant B.E.C. awards (see p. xvii), or degrees in Business Studies or Communication Studies, Diploma in Marketing or Management Studies, post-graduate degree in Business Administration.

C.A.M. qualifications are not obligatory, but their importance is increasing.

There are few in-service training schemes, but some agencies take several graduates (any discipline) each year; many advertisers have management training schemes which can lead to advertising jobs.

Secretaries occasionally progress to executive or copywriting positions; their chances are greater with a small specialist agency (for example, a recruitment agency) or in an advertising department, but they are never *very* great.

Personal attributes

Business acumen; interest in social and economic trends; flair for salesmanship; communication skills; ability to work in a team; ability to stand criticism whether justified or not; ability to work under pressure; resilience; persistence.

For creative people: discipline; originality; strong feeling for uncomplicated images and 'messages'; willingness to produce the kind of words/artwork that are best for the campaign, whether artistically first-rate or not.

For research: objectivity; a logical, analytical brain.

Position of women

Although the majority of advertisements are aimed at women, only about 1 in 6 account executives are women, and about 1 in 5 copywriters; women do best in research, and an increasing number of brand managers (see Marketing, p. 270) are women. Though the Women's Advertising Club keeps an eye on women's promotion, they have not been able to do much about unequal promotion at senior level. It is an area where discrimination is difficult to prove, as there is no career-structure; promotion does not depend on qualification and experience but on 'suitability' for any particular job.

Career-break: Prospects only reasonable for experienced researchers or for successful executives who have 'kept their hand in' with freelance work.

Late start: Little opportunity unless there has been previous relevant commercial experience.

| **Further in-formation** | C.A.M. Foundation, Abford House, 15 Wilton Road, London SW1V 1NJ |
| | Institute of Practitioners in Advertising, 44 Belgrave Square, London SW1X 8QS |

| **Related careers** | *Management in Industry – Marketing – Public Relations – Retail Distribution* |

AGRICULTURE AND HORTICULTURE

PRACTICAL WORK: *Agriculture*: Livestock – Farm Mechanic – General Farming Work; *Horticulture*: Crop Production – Amenity Horticulture
ADVISORY WORK, TEACHING, MANAGEMENT, RESEARCH, FRINGE SPECIALIZATIONS

Entry quali-fications   Entry at all levels from no qualifications to degree.

The work   Agriculture and Horticulture cover a wide range of jobs. There is scope at all educational levels. Jobs range from work for the loner who chose agriculture for the peace of working on the land, or horticulture for its scope for beautifying the urban environment, to work for people primarily interested in using the latest technologies to improve the world's food crops, or who want to work with animals. To be commercially viable, units are increasing in size, and use of management techniques and specialization within both agriculture and horticulture are now usual.

Practical Work

(Usual qualifications: Apprenticeship, National Certificate or Ordinary National Diploma.)

AGRICULTURE

1. Work with Livestock

(a) *Beef Cattle*: Work varies according to size and type of farm. Some farms rear calves and feed some mature animals; others fatten cattle through to slaughter.

(b) *Dairy Herd*: A 50-cow herd can be worth £50,000, so this is highly responsible work. Work involves rearing, feeding, milking and following strict hygiene maintenance routines.

(c) *Pigs*: Some farms breed pigs for sale; others buy young pigs and fatten them for sale as bacon or pork; yet others both breed and fatten. Extent of automation varies: on some pig farms feeding and cleaning of pens is mechanized, on others it is not.

(d) *Poultry*: Highly specialized: holdings concentrate either entirely on egg production, or on hatching – often in fully automatic giant incubators where thousands of chicks are hatched at the same time; or on rearing broilers, which are chicks fed scientifically specified diets to reach exact weights within a defined period. Some poultry units resemble a cross between a laboratory and a modern factory, with indoor, clean work. There are few farms where looking after poultry means feeding birds in the farmyard.

(e) *Shepherd*: Hill farms usually concentrate on large numbers of sheep: on lowland farms sheep may form part of a unit and shepherds spend a lot of their time helping with other farmwork. Shepherds work with (and may train) dogs.

On the whole the larger and/or more mechanized the farm, the greater the degree of specialization. Individuals need not stick to one specialization throughout their career, though some prefer to do so. Livestock workers are expected to drive tractors.

2. Farm Mechanic

All farmworkers must be able to cope with running repairs; many units employ farm mechanics who are in charge of machinery maintenance, repairs and adaptation of all types of mechanical gadgets. On large units there may be several mechanics; usually there is only one.

3. General Farm Work

Working conditions vary according to size of farm (anything from 30 to several thousand acres). Some workers live in the farmhouse, others in digs in the village. Some are near towns or Young Farmers' Clubs; others may be isolated. On large farms there will be colleagues; on small farms there may be only one young worker. Hours are generally long and irregular, especially on small farms where there are not sufficient staff to work a rota system, and where there are no holidays during the summer months. Although all farmworkers are on their own for some of the time, only hill farm shepherds are alone all day.

People who do not want to specialize and take responsibility for animals or machinery can work on holdings which are not divided up into specialized, self-contained units. These are usually not highly mechanized and tend to be smaller than average.

HORTICULTURE

This can be divided into *Crop Production* – market gardens, commercial units, glasshouses, fruit farms and nurseries (many commercial enterprises concentrate on 'high cash value' crops such as cut flowers, ornamental plants, lettuces, cucumbers) – and *Amenity Horticulture*.

Crop Production

(a) *Market gardens*: Vegetables, salad crops, tomatoes and flowers are grown. Market gardens are 'cultivated intensively', which means the land is used to grow more than one crop a year. This makes the work varied. Market gardens are increasingly mechanized, but planting and thinning out of delicate plants is normally done by hand. Grading, washing and packing may all be done by hand, or may be mechanized.

(b) *Nurseries*: Some grow a variety of herbaceous and other plants, ornamental trees, shrubs, bushes, fruit trees, etc.; others specialize in one or two. Nursery workers learn propagation (producing plants from seed, by grafting, or from cuttings); they dig up plants and pack them for dispatch, and they collect and identify seeds. They may also sell produce and advise customers on how to look after it.

(c) *Glasshouses*: These form part of most nurseries and market gardens, for the production of out-of-season and delicate plants; some concerns consist almost entirely of glasshouses. The work is usually the least hard physically. Those in charge of a glasshouse must understand ventilation, temperature control, etc.

(d) *Fruit Farms*: Work consists of pruning, grafting, cultivation and spraying of trees. In orchards, the autumn and most of the winter is spent grading and packing. (Poultry-keeping may be done as a sideline.)

Experienced horticultural workers can become plantation assistants on fruit research stations; quality inspectors and crop estimators for canning and quick-freezing stations run by large commercial firms.

Jobbing Gardening in Residential Areas

Jobbing gardeners' work is seasonal, and it is advisable to have another string to one's bow – say, secretarial work for the winter and gardening jobs by the hour or day in other seasons. Some firms maintain private gardens on contract and employ jobbing gardeners.

Garden Centres

This is a combination of selling, advising, growing. Staff answer customers' queries and they grow the produce they sell. Garden centres are busiest at weekends. They are in towns and on the outskirts.

Amenity Horticulture

This is a relatively new specialization. Its purpose is to provide and maintain pleasant open-air environments for townspeople to relax in: parks in towns; country parks; picnic areas off motorways; National Trust properties; nature trails. Work involves maintenance of ornamental gardens and, often, nursery work. It may also include maintenance of bowling greens, golf courses, tennis courts, etc. Amenity gardeners are usually employed by public authorities rather than by commercial enterprises. The work involves contact with the public and often helping with recreational activities, such as sitting at cash-desks for open-air concerts, usher and patrol duty (see also Diploma in Management Studies, Recreation Management, **Training**, p. 391). There is more of a career-structure (and day-release) in this type of horticulture than in commercial concerns.

Horticulturalists may work in tiny nurseries or large commercial establishments; as the only employee or as one of a large staff; on the outskirts of a town, or in the depths of the country. Hours are sometimes irregular, and it is usually impossible to take a holiday in the summer.

Prospects   In horticulture prospects are better than in agriculture; poultry work, especially the broiler industry, offers the best opportunities. Setting up on one's own, whether in market gardening or poultry farming, demands considerable capital and experience.

Pay: Low to medium (see p. xxiii).

Advisory Work, Teaching and Management

Entry quali-   Higher National Diploma or degree (see below).
fications

The work   ## 1. ADVISORY WORK

The Agricultural Development and Advisory Service (includes horticulture) and commercial firms employ specialist advisers who visit individual growers and farmers to help them with production problems. Advisers also lecture to allotment societies, farmers' clubs, women's organizations and schools. The work combines meeting people with work in the country – an unusual combination.

Horticultural specialists advise, for example, new and inexperienced growers on where to plant what. They may diagnose plant disease and type of soil and advise on marketing questions.

Poultry specialists discuss the best type of breed for farmers' individual purposes, advise on feeding and housing problems, and help farmers keep abreast of developments in poultry technology.

Livestock and Dairy specialists advise on such matters as grass production, silage, making the proper use and choice of feeding stuffs and balancing rations, and on new milking equipment. Dairy specialists can also become *milk officers*, taking samples of milk at farms for laboratory testing. Milk Marketing Boards employ staff to inspect producers' herds, milk and milking parlours.

2. TEACHING

Work is in secondary schools (mainly in rural areas), in technical and agricultural colleges, and as Rural Economy Instructors travelling round a county lecturing to women's organizations, allotment societies, etc. The work in schools may be combined with running school gardens, or with teaching other subjects. Teachers sometimes teach part-time in several schools. Subjects include processing farm produce; farmhouse budgeting; dairying and poultry-keeping; cheese-making; horticultural practice; environmental studies. Not all subjects would be taught to the same form or even in the same school; the rural studies teacher's work is much wider in scope than it used to be.

3. MANAGEMENT

Practical work shades into management. The first step on the management ladder may be supervising several dairy-herd workers or being in charge of quality control of the cut-flowers section in a nursery.

As farms – and horticultural units – are growing in size, the range *but not the number* of management jobs is increasing. At the top of the ladder are *farm managers*, who are responsible for the day-to-day running of the farm, control of staff, marketing of produce, record keeping, farm accounts, dealing with suppliers. Work, and level of responsibility, vary according to type (privately owned or belonging to food manufacturers) and size of farm.

On small and medium-sized farms, managers may also be practical farmers and help out in whatever section help is needed; in other jobs, the work is entirely administrative, though the 'office' may be makeshift. On larger farms, *farm secretaries* (see p. 424) may be employed.

Prospects   1. *Advisers*: good only for those with good qualifications who are willing to move round the country.

2. *Teachers*: Some form of 'rural studies' is now taught in about half the country's schools. The work is ideal for those who like teaching (see p. 485) and who want to do work which is connected with the country, if not entirely a country job.

This is virtually the only job in agriculture and horticulture in which there is any opportunity for part-time work.

3. *Management*: Jobs are very difficult to get – there is very stiff competition.

Abroad: Some opportunities in developing countries; amenity horticulturalists may be able to work in E.E.C. countries; agricultural engineers in developing countries.

Pay: Low to medium (see p. xxiii).

Personal attributes

Advisers: Very much the same as for practical work because practical work has to be done during training: ability to get on well with all kinds of people and to convey practical and factual information clearly; diplomacy when attempting to persuade growers to try new methods.

Teachers: Much as for advisers, with, of course, an interest in children. See also personal attributes for teachers, p. 491.

Managers: Ability to recruit and cope with permanent and seasonal labour; ability to take decisions, knowing that these are subject to the vagaries of nature; enjoyment of responsibility.

Research

Entry qualifications   Degree.

The work

Research is usually concerned with a particular aspect of crop production or of animal husbandry. Work may be largely or entirely theoretical, involving study of scientific journals and papers as well as collaboration with scientists from other disciplines; it usually involves experimental work in the laboratory and may involve practical work observing animal behaviour, plant growth, effects of climatic conditions, etc. (see also Scientific Research).

In Horticulture most of the work is connected with pest control, plant diseases, soil chemistry, cultivation methods, crop suitability for canning and freezing.

In the Poultry and Dairy industries the main fields of research are genetics, biochemistry, nutrition, stock management, and breeding principles and methods.

In the poultry industry and in horticulture there is research into taste preservation after freezing and into producing the right kind of product for processing. Researchers work closely with technologists in food processing – see Food Technology, p. 417.

Researchers work for research establishments, botanical gardens, in industry, in the Civil Service Science Group.

Training   Training patterns can be adjusted to fit individual requirements. It is
possible (though it takes a long time) to start without any G.C.E.s and
eventually get a degree. The main types of course for those with fewer
than 4 O-levels or C.S.E.s are:

1. The Agricultural Training Board's or similar *Local Government
Training Board (Amenity Horticulture) Apprenticeship Schemes.*

Three years supervised practical training in one branch (either horticulture or agriculture). These schemes normally include day- or block-
release and may also include a 1-year full-time certificate course (see
below). This type of training leads to a Craftsman's Certificate and
possibly to City and Guilds Certificates or, if the 1-year full-time course
is included, to the National Certificate in Agriculture or Horticulture.
There is no need to decide on any specialization within either agriculture
or horticulture before starting initial training.

2. Full-time or sandwich courses at Colleges of Agriculture

(a) *National Certificate courses*: Normally 1 year full-time.

Entry requirements: At least 1 year's practical work on farm or holding
(which may have been part of the apprenticeship scheme); and evidence
of having studied English, mathematics and a science (i.e. O-level or
C.S.E. passes are not essential; but college places are often scarce:
G.C.E.s or C.S.E.s help to get a place).

Most courses are in general agriculture or in general horticulture, but
a few are specialized, for example in poultry husbandry, in amenity
horticulture and in commercial horticulture. On the whole, specialization starts *after* the general course: in 'supplementary' courses, for
example, in dairy husbandry, grassland farming, glasshouse production,
etc.

(b) *Ordinary National Diploma (O.N.D.) Courses*: 2 years full-time or
3 years sandwich.

Entry requirements: 4 O-levels, including 1 science, and 1 year's
practical work (or National Certificate credit standard). O.N.D. courses
are available in several specializations and in general horticulture and
general agriculture.

O.N.D.s lead to 'technician' level and eventually to supervisory and,
with further training and/or experience, possibly to management level.

(c) *College awards*: A variety of specialized (varied length) courses,
usually for students with O.N.D.s or Certificates with credit. These
courses are useful for students who during training decide on a
specialization they had not previously thought of.

(d) *Amenity horticulturalists* may take further training in *recreation
management* (and manage sports centres, etc., see p. 390).

(e) *Higher National Diploma (H.N.D.)* at Agricultural Colleges: 3 years
sandwich.

Entry requirements: At least one science A-level with at least 3 O-levels normally including mathematics and an English subject and preferably a science, or a good O.N.D. Agriculture or O.N.D./C. Sciences. Candidates must normally have had a year's practical experience.

H.N.D. courses are concerned with the managerial, scientific and technological aspects of agriculture and horticulture; they are intended for people who will go into management or advisory work (in industry: A.D.A.S. now takes only graduates). Courses are available in amenity horticulture, commercial horticulture, general agriculture, agricultural marketing/business administration, poultry husbandry, dairy technology. Further specializations may be introduced.

Post-H.N.D. courses are also available, mainly in new technologies in management and farm organization. These courses may be taken after some time at work.

3. Degrees: 3 or 4 years.

Entry qualifications: 2, or more often 3, A-levels, including at least 1, usually 2, sciences, and 3, O-levels, or good O.N.D. Agriculture or T.E.C. Sciences, and 1 year's practical work.

Degree subjects, apart from general agricultural and horticultural sciences, include *forest science*; *agricultural engineering*; *agricultural economics*. Little actual farm work is included in degree courses, which are intended for future advisers, researchers, teachers or managers.

Fringe Specializations

1. CONSERVATION

Concerned with the preservation of the country's plant and animal life.

Conservationists research into and try to balance the long-term effects of modern aids to farming such as pesticides, and of changes in the use of land. The removal of a hedge – for more efficient ploughing, for example – may destroy shelter for certain animals which then disappear from the area but had previously been useful in keeping down other harmful animals. Conservation takes in *ecology*, which is the study of how plants as well as animals exist together and act and react upon one another in their natural surroundings, and what happens when the natural balance is disturbed through intervention by man in order to use land and resources for more immediately efficient purposes.

The greatest demand is for graduates with degrees in horticulture, botany, zoology or geography. Conservationists work mainly for research organizations, specially the Natural Environment Research Council. (See Scientist, p. 400.)

2. FORESTRY

This is a small specialization. The Forestry Commission and, increasingly, private owners' cooperatives, employ *forestry officers* who plan afforestation programmes and are responsible for the management of groups of forests. Though an administrative job, it also involves driving and walking through forests. It includes responsibility for fire protection; wildlife protection; disease identification and control; recreation-area planning and control; possibly marketing management (the production of home-grown timber is increasing). *Foresters* are responsible for the day-to-day management of individual forests. They have more direct contact with the general public – they are often asked by children and their teachers about plant- and wildlife.

Forestry Officers must be graduates in forestry. Foresters normally now take the Ordinary National Diploma in Forestry. There is also a 2-year basic training for forest workers.

Forest work usually involves living in the forest all the year round; being on one's own for days on end and yet being good at dealing with the general public.

3. AGRICULTURAL ENGINEERING

Agricultural engineers apply engineering principles to food production. As the world's non-renewable and slowly-renewable resources are being rapidly used up, it is essential to make the most efficient use of natural resources. This involves recycling processes; exploring and using new sources of energy and, above all, incorporating new technologies in the design, manufacture and maintenance of agricultural equipment. Agricultural engineers may be involved in 'environmental control' – providing the right housing for livestock; in product planning; mechanizing procedures; crop storage and processing. The work is related to food technology (see p. 417) and professional engineering (p. 163). There is ample scope for work abroad, especially in developing countries.

Training   Either a first degree in agricultural engineering (it is possible to start without A-level mathematics as long as students had good O-level grades and take a special mathematics course during their first degree course year); or H.N.D. or degree in related subjects (geography; sciences; agriculture), followed by 1- and 2-year post-graduate courses at the National College of Agricultural Engineering which is now part of the Cranfield Institute of Technology.

4. FISH FARMING

Breeding and rearing fish for food or sport. Most fish farms (there are approximately 400) are one- or two-person businesses, but there are some large-scale fish farms. Like all animal husbandry, this is usually a 7-day-a-week job and involves unsocial working hours. There is no prescribed training and entry; the usual ways into this new and growing industry are:

1. For day-to-day management: 1-year full-time gamekeeping and fishery management course. People with practical farming experience are given preference for course places.

2. For unit-managers, forewomen, own-business fish farmers: 2-year full-time Diploma in Fishery Management. Minimum age 17; 4 O-levels, preferably including chemistry and 3 months' practical fishery experience required.

3. For research and management: degree in biological science or agriculture, usually followed by post-graduate course.

Details from Institute of Fisheries Management, 36 Springfield Road, Wallington, Surrey; and Ministry of Agriculture, Fisheries and Food, Whitehall, London SW1.

Position of women

A large proportion of unskilled farm workers, but very few apprentices and not many more on full-time courses, are women. Farm management is an almost totally male preserve: farmers tend to be traditional in outlook, and while there are more male applicants than jobs women are unlikely to get farm management posts. Farmers genuinely believe that women would not be able to help with the tough work, and managers, at least on small and medium-sized farms, do occasionally help with whatever needs doing. Up to now, very few women have taken the long training required for management, which is necessary to convince farmers that they are able to cope with all the work. Women are unlikely to be considered for forestry work, mainly because of the need to live in often isolated areas and to be able to do physically hard work. In amenity and commercial horticulture, and especially in agricultural engineering, they have equal opportunities of getting top jobs.

Career-break: There should be no problem for those who progressed into management level jobs before the break.

Late start: On the whole this is not advisable, as trainee vacancies tend to go to young applicants. However, 1-year courses for horticultural Certificates are available under T.O.P.S. (see p. xl).

Further information	Agricultural Training Board (includes horticulture), Bourne House, 32–34 Beckenham Road, Beckenham, Kent, BR3 4PB
	Women's Farm and Garden Association, c/o Lilac Cottage, Birch Green, Colchester, Essex, CO2 0NH

Related careers	*Animal Nursing Auxiliary – Landscape Architecture – Science Technician – Scientist – Veterinary Surgeon*

ANIMALS

Animal nursing auxiliary – dogs – horses – veterinary surgeon

1. Animal Nursing Auxiliary

Entry quali-
fications
4 O-levels, including English language and a physical or biological science or mathematics.

The work
Animal nursing auxiliaries assist veterinary surgeons in their surgery and occasionally on visits. They hold and pacify animals during examination and treatment; in the surgery they sterilize and look after instruments. They collect and analyse specimens, prepare medicines, and take out stings and stitches. Auxiliaries also clear up after unhousetrained animals and after operations; they may assist in the reception of patients. They work in 'small-animal' practices, i.e. those dealing with domestic animals, and for the R.S.P.C.A. and other animal welfare and research organizations.

The hours are usually long and irregular. Animals have to be cared for at weekends which may mean going to work on Saturday and Sunday, perhaps just to feed them.

Some veterinary surgeons' practices employ only one auxiliary, so she may be rather isolated from her contemporaries and have little companionship. Most of the working day will be spent with her employer.

Prospects
Poor on the whole, but once trained, auxiliaries have a much better chance of congenial work than untrained girls. There is no career ladder though – no promotion prospects.

Pay: Low (see p. xxiii).

Training
Minimum age for enrolment as trainee is 17; practical work may start earlier.

Training is on-the-job, plus private study. There are some day- or block-release courses.

A potential trainee must first find a job with a veterinary practice or hospital approved by the R.C.V.S. as a training centre and must then enrol with the R.C.V.S. as a trainee. The syllabus covers anatomy and physiology, hygiene and feeding, first-aid, side-room techniques (analysing specimens and preparing slides), and the theory and practice of breeding and nursing. Finals may be taken after at least 2 years' traineeship.

Trainee vacancies are sometimes advertised in the *Veterinary Record*, and prospective trainees may themselves advertise for jobs. Letters to local veterinary surgeons and animal research and welfare societies may also bring results; and the R.C.V.S. will provide a list of those veterinary practices and centres which are approved as training centres.

Personal attributes A love of animals and a scientific interest in their development, behaviour, and welfare; lack of squeamishness; a willingness to take orders, and yet to act independently when necessary; readiness to work well both alone and with others; a sure, firm, but gentle grip; patience.

Position of women This is still a female preserve: out of 1,250 A.N.A.s, 1 is male; out of 714 students, 4 are male.

Career-break: This is a young woman's job.

Late start: Difficult to find training vacancies as surplus of young applicants who are satisfied with very low wages.

Part-time: No part-time training, a few part-time jobs.

Further information *Animal Nursing Auxiliaries Guide*, price 75p plus letter postage from Royal College of Veterinary Surgeons, 32 Belgrave Square, London SW1X 8QP

Related careers *Animal Technician, p. 415 – Dogs – Horses – Veterinary Surgeon*

---

2. Dogs

Entry qualifications None required.

There are two kinds of work with dogs: (1) breeding, boarding, greyhound training, and quarantine kennels (licensed by the Ministry of Agriculture, Fisheries, and Food); (2) dog beauty parlours.

1. KENNELS

The work   Work is always hard and usually dirty. The kennel maid's day starts at 8 a.m. and usually ends at 5 p.m. but she must be prepared to stay up all night, for example when puppies are about to be born. Regular time off is difficult to arrange except in large establishments; someone is always needed to feed the animals. Quarantine and greyhound kennels are usually run on more professional lines than small private boarding and breeding kennels, with more regular working hours.

A kennel maid cleans kennels, grooms the dogs, and deals with minor ailments. Dogs who are really ill are looked after by full-time attendants (see Animal Nursing Auxiliary, p. 34). In breeding kennels, she trains puppies and learns all about preparing for dog shows. In greyhound kennels, exercising the dogs is an important part of the work.

Prospects   There are far more applicants than jobs. Poor ratio of managers to kennel maids.

Considerable capital and experience are needed to set up boarding kennels. A good deal of land is required for exercise yards. Breeding pedigree dogs must be done on a big scale to be really profitable.

Pay: Very low (see p. xxiii).

Training   Two methods:

(a) 6–12 months as working pupil in a kennel. Pupils learn grooming, handling, training, stripping, clipping, diagnosis of sickness symptoms; first-aid; nutrition; breeding principles. Courses are usually residential and cost around £10 to £60 per week. Teaching kennels must be chosen with great care – some teach little, and use pupils as cheap labour.

There are no set courses or examinations.

(b) On-the-job. Starting as a junior in good kennels can lead to just as good jobs in the future, if the junior does some private reading, and asks questions of senior staff.

Personal attributes   An unsentimental affection for dogs; a placid but firm manner; patience.

2. DOG BEAUTY PARLOUR

The work   Pet shops and dog beauty parlours (sometimes attached to department stores) employ girls to clip, groom, and strip poodles and other breeds. Usual shop working hours, with occasional weekend duties.

Prospects   Fair only for the really good trimmer and clipper. Setting up on one's own requires great business sense and knowledge, and capital.
Pay: Very low to high (see p. xxiii).

Training   Two methods:
(a) 6–12 months as working pupil in breeding kennels specializing in show animals (poodles usually). Pupils learn general dog care as well as shampooing, handling scissors and electric clippers, and learning how and when to give various types of trim (details as in **Training** (a) under Kennels).
(b) On-the-job, 2–3 years as junior. Leads to just as good a job eventually.

Personal   Patience and firmness; dexterity; imagination to show off the animal's
attributes   best points and hide its weaker ones; a good appearance and a pleasing manner; ability to deal with dogs' owners; for the better paid jobs, organizing ability.

Position   This is almost all female work; kennels are also usually run and owned
of women   by women; but dog beauty parlours (more profitable) are sometimes run and/or managed by men.
   Like all jobs with animals (except veterinary surgeon) this is largely a young woman's job: only those with management experience are likely to be able to return after Career-break.

Late start: No.

Part-time: No.

Further in-   Jobs and courses advertised in Dog World and Our Dogs.
formation

3. Horses
(Riding instructor; groom; stable manager)

Entry quali- 4 O-levels including an English subject or B.H.S. Assistant Instructor's
fications   Certificate.

The work   Physically hard, outdoors in all weathers, and varied depending on the type of stables, i.e. looking after hunters in the winter and children's ponies in the summer. Thus hours are often long, including weekends, especially during the summer (sometimes up to 14 hours a day).

Accommodation varies. 2 or 3 working pupils or grooms may have to share a room. Grooms usually live in (unless their home is near the stables) because their working day may start at 6 a.m. Instructors are not usually obliged to do so.

1. RIDING INSTRUCTOR

The work She teaches children and adults, both in private lessons and in classes, and accompanies riders who hire horses by the hour. She starts early and may finish late, because many pupils come before or after their work. She may also train horses and ponies, and she usually has to spend some time looking after the horses, and cleaning tack and stables. Senior instructors are also responsible for general stable management.

Prospects Only fair. Though opportunities are increasing, there are still more candidates than good jobs. Setting up on one's own requires considerable capital, experience, and business knowledge. Good instructors are wanted frequently for work in equestrian training centres, and quite a few work on travel organizations' pony-trekking holidays (summer only).

Pay: Low to medium (see p. xxiii).

Training Two methods of training for the British Horse Society's Assistant Instructor's, Intermediate Instructor's and Instructor's Certificates:
(a) *At a Fee-charging School*
Courses last about 3 to 15 months; fees vary enormously.
(b) *As Working Pupil*
Courses last normally 1 year and usually consist of 9 months' stable routine and management: i.e. mucking-out, feeding, and watering, riding exercise, and some instruction; and a 3-month concentrated course of instruction while still doing light stable duties. Working pupils may receive pocket money but usually pay for their board and lodging (around £5–£40 a week). After at least a further year's work and at a minimum age of 22, they can take the B.H.S. Instructor's Certificate.
NOTE: Some establishments call themselves schools but are stables which hire out horses. They tend to use working 'pupils' as cheap labour. Pupils should choose a school which is 'Approved' by the British Horse Society, and is a member of the Association of British Riding Schools.

Personal attributes Authority; physical agility; the ability to express oneself clearly; patience; a liking for children; not too much ambition.

2. GROOM/STABLE MANAGER

The work   A groom works in and may eventually manage hunt, racing and show jumping stables, private stables, livery stables (which look after horses for private owners), riding schools, or stables with horses for hire, or at a stud.

She cleans stables; looks after the well-being of the horses – feeds them, and watches out for and reports any symptoms which make her suspect that a horse is sick; and keeps the saddle and the rest of the tack in perfect condition.

At a horse or pony stud, the groom also looks after the brood mares and cares for their foals. She may also break in ponies.

Prospects   Though opportunities are increasing, there still are usually more candidates than good jobs. Plum jobs, such as travelling with show horses, are very rare indeed. This is usually a job, rarely a career.

Pay: Low (see p. xxiii).

Training   Training is usually as a working pupil, and lasts from around 6 months to over 1 year. Students usually first take the B.H.S. Assistant Instructor's Examination, or the Certificate of Horsemastership Examination. At age 22 they would then go on to take the B.H.S. Stable Management Certificate.

Personal attributes   Physical stamina; liking for being out of doors in all weathers; indifference to getting dirty; willingness to work irregular hours, often by oneself.

Position of women   About 10 times as many women as men are instructors, but the majority of grooms and the vast majority of stable managers are men. This is largely a young woman's field, as far as jobs are concerned, but quite a few women own their own riding schools or stables.

Part-time: There may be some part-time work for riding instructors at local riding establishments; payment by the hour is anything from £1 to £6.

Further information   British Horse Society, The National Equestrian Centre, Kenilworth, Warwickshire CV8 2LR

Related careers   *Agriculture and Horticulture – Animal Nursing Auxiliary – Animal Technician, p. 415 – Dogs – Veterinary Surgeon*

---

4. Veterinary Surgeon

(General practice; official appointments; commercial organizations; teaching)

Entry quali- 3 science A-levels and 3 O-levels, and some experience of work with
fications animals.

The work ## 1. GENERAL PRACTICE (including work for animal welfare organizations)

Work includes carrying out operations in the surgery as well as visiting patients in their owners' homes. In urban practices vets are concerned with small animals; in country practices with small as well as with farm animals.

Veterinary surgeons are expected to provide a 24-hour service, but most practices are organized so as to provide reasonable time off, and holidays.

It is usual to start as an assistant in an established practice and later either become a partner or set up on one's own (which makes time off more difficult to arrange).

2. OFFICIAL APPOINTMENTS

Officers in the Animal Health Division of the Ministry of Agriculture, Fisheries and Food, and in the Agricultural Research Council cover a wide range of duties:

(a) *Field Service*: Practical experience elsewhere is essential for accept-ance as Veterinary Officer.

The Ministry's Field Service Officers are stationed throughout the country, usually in county towns, and deal with the prevention and control of notifiable diseases of animals and poultry, the tuberculin testing of cattle, the inspection of animals on farms and in markets, and other duties in connection with government regulations and schemes for the maintenance and improvement of farm-animal health standards. The work involves a considerable amount of visiting farmers, markets, etc., and therefore dealing with people as well as with animals.

(b) *Research Officers* and *Scientific Officers* are employed by the Ministry's Central Veterinary Laboratory as well as by the Agricultural Research Council. Officers are concerned with causes, treatment, and prevention of animal diseases; with the development, production, and uses of biological products for the diagnosis of such diseases, and for immunization against them; and with the effects of modern agricultural practice on animal health and production. Immediate practical farming problems as well as long-term applied and fundamental research projects are dealt with.

(c) *Officers in the Veterinary Investigation Service* of the Ministry carry out laboratory tests for the diagnosis of disease on carcasses and organs from cattle, sheep, pigs, and poultry submitted to Veterinary Investigation Centres by veterinary surgeons in practice all over the country. The Veterinary Investigation Service also takes part in field investigations into outbreaks of disease among farm animals in consultation with local veterinary surgeons in general practice, and advises on the most suitable treatment.

3. COMMERCIAL ORGANIZATIONS

Work with manufacturers of agricultural products, feeding stuffs, fertilizers, pharmaceutical products, etc., is similar to that of research officers in the Scientific Civil Service.

4. TEACHING

At universities; usually combined with research work.

Prospects

General practice: Good.
Official appointments: Limited.
Commercial organizations: Fair.
Universities: Poor.
Abroad: With post-graduate experience some openings on short-term contracts on schemes of technical assistance in developing countries.
   Pay: High (see p. xxiii).

Training

Degree courses usually last 5 years and are divided into pre-clinical (anatomy, physiology, biochemistry, pharmacology) and clinical (animal husbandry, medicine and surgery, veterinary public health).

During training, usually in their vacations, students must spend at least 6 months with a veterinary surgeon, to gain practical experience.

Personal attributes

Scientific interest in animals and their behaviour and development, rather than sentimental fondness for pets; powers of observation; a firm hand; the ability to inspire confidence in animals (i.e. total absence of nervousness) and in their owners; self-reliance and adaptability; indifference to occasional physically disagreeable conditions of work.

For some posts: organizing ability and powers of leadership; for others, ability to work as one of a team.

Position of women

14% of registered (practising) veterinary surgeons are women, and 35%

of students. In the past it was believed that veterinary departments, like medical schools, operated (unofficial) quota systems, but now the proportion of women students *admitted* is slightly higher than that of applicants, compared with men. Women who get as far as filling in U.C.C.A. forms are known to be more highly motivated than men: they know the hard physical work they will have to undertake. Even if they eventually set up an urban practice, dealing mainly with pets, they have to deal with all kinds of animals and diseases during training.

Career-break: May present problems. Veterinary practice changes rapidly: young graduates are preferred to 'returners'.

Late start: As there is such stiff competition for degree course places, it is unlikely that anyone over 30 would be accepted, though there is no official upper age limit.

Part-time: Some opportunities as assistant in general practice; very occasionally in research; by running small practice from home; or as Temporary Veterinary Inspector with Ministry of Agriculture, Fisheries and Food.

Further in-formation
Royal College of Veterinary Surgeons, 32 Belgrave Square, London SW1X 8QP
British Veterinary Association, 7 Mansfield Street, London W1
Civil Service Commission, Alencon Link, Basingstoke, Hampshire
Agricultural Research Council, Cunard Building, 160 Great Portland Street, London W1

Related careers
Agriculture and Horticulture – Animal Nursing Auxiliary – Animal Technician (p. 415) – Dogs – Environmental Health Officer – Horses – Medicine – Scientist (Biology, p. 406)

ARCHAEOLOGY

Entry quali- 2, often 3, A-levels and 3 O-levels. Mathematics or science and modern
fications language at O-level normally required.
For classical archaeology, Latin or Greek at O- or A-level.
For conservation, chemistry at A-level.

The work Excavation work is only one aspect of this science of gaining knowledge
of the past from the study of ancient objects. Though archaeologists
need a broad knowledge of the whole field they may specialize in one
geographical area. For example there is Norse, Anglo-Saxon, and
classical archaeology. Most archaeologists also specialize in particular
objects of study, for example coins, weapons, sculpture, or deciphering
inscriptions. Excavation technique is another, highly technical specialization.

Many archaeologists work in museums (see Museum Work). Others
work for the Ancient Monuments division of the Department of the
Environment, the Royal Commission on Historical Monuments, the
archaeological section of the Ordnance Survey, a few for county and
regional units and local authorities.

Prospects Very limited. There are many more archaeology graduates than jobs.
Pay: Medium (see p. xxiii).

Training 1. B.A. in archaeology, ancient history, anthropology, or classics with
archaeology, or any honours degree followed by a 2-year archaeology
diploma, or, with A-level chemistry, B.Sc. in Conservation of Archaeological Materials.
2. Diploma in Archaeological Practice of the Council for British
Archaeology (Ordinary or Higher Level).
Part-time or full-time course. Exemptions may be granted to those with
archaeology degree or professional training.

Personal Deep curiosity about the past; intellectual ability well above average;
attributes artistic sensibility; patience; manual dexterity (for handling delicate and
valuable objects). For excavation, physical stamina.

Position About 20% of archaeologists are women, most of them working in mus-
of women eums. Women have reasonable chances of directing excavation work.

Career-break: Prospects for returners depend on previous experience.

Late start: Advisable only for women who already have a relevant degree and/or hobby experience.

Part-time: Probably more on a short-term project basis than regular part-time work.

Further information   The Council for British Archaeology, 112 Kennington Road, London SE11 6RE

Related careers   *Archivist – Museum Work*

ARCHITECTURE

Architect – architectural technician

Architect

Entry quali- 2 or 3 A-levels and 3 O-levels. Individual Schools of Architecture have
fications widely differing requirements, ranging from *any* 2 A-levels, and mathematics merely as one of the 3 O-levels, to 3 specified mixed science/arts
A-levels.

The work Architecture bridges the arts–technology gap. Its challenge is to
produce a practical yet artistically pleasing design within a given budget.
Tasks range from converting old houses into flats to designing a hospital
or a housing estate. New methods and materials are constantly being
developed, and the architect must understand their potentialities and
limitations. She must be interested in the social and psychological needs
of the community and in changing life-styles.

In whatever field an architect works, the method of working is
basically the same. She receives instructions from her client or employer
on the type, function, capacity, and rough cost of the building required.
Then she does research: she may question the 'social' decisions on which
the client based the brief and may herself collect information on the
needs of the building's – or estate's – future users. This 'sociological'
aspect of the work is now much more important than it was even a few
years ago. It involves discussing with householders, hospital staffs,
teachers, office workers, their expectations from the new accommodation as well as their criticisms of the old. When the architect has a clear
picture of exactly what purpose the new building is to serve, the design
work begins. This starts with producing, perhaps jointly with colleagues,
a sketch scheme of the floor plans, the elevations, and perspective
drawings. Several such schemes may have to be produced before one is
finally approved.

The next stage is to prepare contract documents, which will include
detailed drawings and specifications, and estimates of cost. At this stage,
if the scheme is a big one, consulting engineers (see p. 168) and quantity
surveyors (see p. 479) may be appointed. Necessary planning consents
must have been obtained from the local authority.

When the contract for the work has been awarded to a building
contractor, the architect is in overall charge. She is responsible for

certifying payment to contractors, and for inspecting the work in progress. She regularly visits the building site, issues instructions to the contractor's agent or foreman and discusses any difficulties with him. Site visits involve walking through mud and climbing scaffolding. The architect is normally also responsible for the choice or design of fittings and the interior design of the buildings she undertakes. (See Art and Design, p. 56.)

An architect can work in different *settings*: in private practice; in the architects' and planning departments of a local authority; with a public body such as a new-town corporation; with a ministry; or in the architect's department of a commercial firm large enough to have a continuous programme of building or maintenance work.

In private practice her client may be an individual, a commercial firm, a local authority or other public body. It is usual for private practices to specialize, but not exclusively, in either houses or schools, or offices, etc. In private practice architects normally work only on design and not, as in other categories, on design and maintenance.

In local authorities the architect works on a wide variety of buildings, such as one-family houses, blocks of flats, schools, swimming-baths and clinics. Usually she also collaborates with private architects employed by the authority for specific schemes.

For other public bodies such as nationalized boards or ministries, the architect's work is less varied and is largely confined to the organization's particular building concern: for example hospitals for the Department of Health and Social Security.

The same applies to an architect working for a commercial concern. Her work is confined to that organization's particular type of building: for example, hotels and restaurants for a large catering organization; shops for a merchandising group.

The majority of architects are salaried employees, but they may become junior partners and later principals in a firm, or set up on their own. But to start a firm requires a good deal of experience, capital and contacts.

Prospects   They fluctuate according to economic climate. Apart from joining architects' firms or departments, there is also some scope in interior design studios, designing interiors of shops, hotels, aircraft, etc.

Abroad: Limited opportunities to set up in practice in the Commonwealth or to work (not set up in practice, though) in E.E.C. countries.

Pay: Medium to very high (see p. xxiii).

Training   The normal pattern of training is a 5-year full-time course, with 1 year of practical experience after the 3rd year and a second year of practical experience at the end of the course, making a minimum of 7 years.

There are a few part-time (day-release) courses, but this method of training is not recommended: it takes even longer than the normal training and the failure rate among part-time students is higher than among full-time students. Subjects studied include history of architecture, design and construction, town planning, environmental science, some sociology, economics, traffic studies.

For interior designers, architectural training need only be up to R.I.B.A. Part I standard. It must be followed by a specialized art-school course (part- or full-time) and practical experience.

NOTES: (1) Architecture, Planning and Landscape Architecture are closely related disciplines. There are some courses which start with a combined studies year so that students can delay specialization until they know more about the whole field. But courses must be chosen with care: practising architects whether in private practice or public employment must be on the Register of the Architects Registration Council of the United Kingdom. Only 'recognized' courses (38 in 1980) lead to Registration. Up-to-date lists of 'recognized' courses are available from the R.I.B.A. (which 'recognizes' courses on behalf of the A.R.C.U.K.) and from the A.R.C.U.K. Course titles can be misleading, for example 'Architectural Studies' may or may not be a 'recognized' course.

(2) For candidates who are not quite certain whether to commit themselves to a 7-year training it is useful to know that the first 3-year stage of training, on most courses, leads to an Honours degree in its own right, and therefore to all the 'graduate jobs' for which no particular discipline is specified.

Personal attributes
A practical as well as creative mind; an interest in changing life-styles and social priorities; self-confidence to put over and justify new ideas; mathematical ability; some dexterity in drawing; the ability to deal with legal and financial questions; a reasonably authoritative personality; an aptitude for giving clear instructions and explanations; good health; good eyesight.

Position of women
Only about 16% of students and 5% of working architects are women. There has been little change in recent years. Yet there have been genuine attempts on the part of architects to recruit more women. It is true that women architects are still often expected by partners, or employers and clients, to be good only at designing kitchens and colour schemes; nevertheless women who want to be considered 'architects' rather than 'women architects' have had fair opportunities for some time now which they have not sufficiently exploited. Lack of candidates rather than prejudice is the main reason for the small number of women.

There is as yet (1980) no woman Director of Architecture in Local Government (see p. 255), and it is unlikely that many have applied for such jobs, but many women are senior partners in private firms and senior architects in public sector employment. Altogether *opportunities* are probably 'more equal' in this than in most other professional areas, yet they are sadly under-used.

Refresher training: No courses, but *ad hoc* arrangements for returners to work in architectural offices. Some returners take post-graduate courses and specialize in something like traffic planning, urban design, planning, etc.

Late start: Suitable applicants considered for training without 2 A-levels, but they *must* have basic mathematics and show academic ability; possibly difficulty in getting practical training in times of unemployment, and in finding jobs. About 11% of final-year students are over 30.

Career-break: Opportunities for those who have kept up by way of reading journals, attending occasional lectures and seminars. Architects are strongly advised to 'keep their hand in' and do *some* work throughout the break, however sporadic.

Part-time: 28% of women architects work part-time, virtually all of them in private practice. There is little opportunity in the public sector, but heads of departments agree that at least up to middle level jobs it should be possible to organize.

Further in-formation	The Director (Education and Practice), Royal Institute of British Architects, 66 Portland Place, London W1N 4AD Royal Incorporation of Architects in Scotland, 15 Rutland Square, Edinburgh Architects Registration Council, 73 Hallam Street, London W1N 6EE
Related careers	*Architectural Technician – Design – Engineering – Landscape Architecture – Planning – Surveying*

Architectural Technician

Entry quali-fications   Preferably 3 O-levels, including mathematics, a science subject and a subject involving the use of written English, but see **Training** and T.E.C. awards (p. xv).

The work   Architectural technicians work in architects' and planners' offices both in private practice and in public employment. Duties vary considerably according to the size and the structure of the office. They may include any or all of the following: collecting, analysing and preparing technical information required for a design; preparing technical drawings for the builder and 'presentation' drawings for the client; administration of contracts; liaison with clients and with specialists such as, for example, quantity surveyors; taking notes at site meetings; site supervision; collecting information on performance of finished buildings (which means contact with satisfied and possibly dissatisfied clients); office management. Technicians often do responsible work but not normally any creative designing.

Prospects   Vary according to economic climate. There are no prospects of becoming an architect without taking the full professional training (see p. 46). This is not substantially shortened for technicians, but with a good T.E.C. Certificate or Diploma (see p. xv) students *may* be able to transfer to architectural training (i.e. it is a way in without the usual A-levels).

Pay: Medium (see p. xxiii).

Training   On-the-job with day-release for T.E.C. Certificate or by full-time T.E.C. Diploma (see p. xv), and then to Higher T.E.C. awards and membership of S.A.A.T.

Personal attributes   Accuracy; ability to draw; technical ability; interest in architecture and environment; liking for teamwork.

Position of women   Very few women indeed, only because very few have tried.

Career-break: Theoretically no reason why qualified technicians should not return. T.E.C. training system can be adapted to help with up-dating skills.

Late start: Not advisable, as young entrants, of whom there are sufficient, are preferred.

Part-time: Not much opportunity at the moment.

| **Further in-formation** | The Secretary, Society of Architectural and Associated Technicians, Palladium House, 1–4 Argyll Street, London W1V 1AD |

| **Related careers** | *Surveying Technician* |

ARCHIVIST

Entry quali- Usually A-level Latin and a reading knowledge of French, and an arts
fications degree (preferably in history).

The work The archivist's work combines scholarly research with the selection, preservation, arrangement and description of documents, such as official records of central and local government and courts of law, or private documents such as title deeds, business records, family papers. The archivist assesses the value for posterity of papers being currently produced and she preserves and puts in order, for reference purposes, all types of records which were produced in the past. She helps members of the public with their research, whether they are professors of history, solicitors in search of evidence, or students working on projects. She must understand methods of preservation and repair, and of microfilming.

Archivists work in county record offices, for research institutions, occasionally for firms or families who want their history researched and written up, and for the Public Record Office, which is the depository for the records of central government from the Domesday Book to today.

Prospects The supply and demand for archivists are about even. It is usually necessary to go wherever there is a vacancy, both for the first job and later for promotion.

Pay: Medium (see p. xxiii).

Training 1-year post-graduate full-time course for the Study of Records and Administration of Archives Diploma. Subjects include palaeography, record office management, research methods, editing, some history and law.

Personal A strong sense of history; liking for quiet, painstaking research;
attributes curiosity.

Position Just over half of Britain's archivists are women; they have a fair share
of women of top jobs.

Career-break: Return difficult, as there are always sufficient young (and cheaper) job applicants.

Late start: Probably difficult, for above reasons.

Part-time: Training: possible. Work: not many opportunities at present, but theoretically it should be possible to work part-time.

Further in-formation The Honorary Secretary, The Society of Archivists, South Yorkshire County Record Office, Ellin Street, Sheffield S1 4PL

Related careers *Archaeology – Librarian – Museum Work*

ART AND DESIGN

FINE ART – DESIGN: graphic design or visual communication; 3-dimensional design; textiles/fashion – ART THERAPY – ARTS ADMINISTRATION

The work
Covers two separate but overlapping fields: ART, which is largely painting and sculpture and is not a career in the usual sense; and DESIGN, which could be called 'applied art', as it covers design for commercial application. The terminology is vague, constantly changing, and confusing. For example *industrial design* (engineering) is also called *product design*, and comes under the broader heading *3-dimensional design*. Similarly, *graphic design*, with all its sub-categories – illustration, typography, photography, etc. – is now often called *visual communication* or *communication design*.

In the Art and Design C.N.A.A. degree (see below), the areas of specialization are: (1) fine art; (2) graphic design; (3) 3-dimensional design; (4) textiles/fashion. Within these broad categories there are many specializations.

1. Fine Art

An extremely small number of artists are talented enough to make a living by painting and sculpting alone. Anyone determined to paint or sculpt for a living must either have a private income or a second string to her bow.

Commissions for murals and sculptures for public buildings are extremely rare, and private commissions even more so.

The majority of painters and sculptors also teach, and for that they need art plus teacher training (and part-time teaching is very difficult to get). Others combine fine art with design in overlapping areas, for example studio-based craft, or such graphic design specialization as book illustration or advertising. But in these areas opportunities are also rare and mainly for successful artists. A few artists do picture restoring and copying, but again there are few openings.

2. Design

The function of the designer, who is, broadly, a specialist combining artistic talent and training with sufficient technical and business knowledge to appreciate the requirements of an industry, is still evolving. There is no career structure; no particular qualification leads to any particular level of responsibility or type of job. But most designers start as assistants and work first in the area of specialization in which they trained. Later, with experience and evolving interests, they can switch specializations, or at least sub-specialization. For example, a 3-dimensional designer might switch from light engineering to furniture or interior design; a graphic designer from typography to photography; a fashion/textile designer from fashion (see p. 190) to floor-covering or wallpaper, etc. Sometimes 3-dimensional-trained designers switch to visual communication – but the switch the other way round is less likely. A few later combine several design categories.

Titles in industry are arbitrary and mean little; an assistant designer may have more scope for creativity and decision-making than a designer or even design director. Many industrial employers are not yet used to working with designers; the contribution the designer is expected or indeed allowed to make varies from one job to another. For example, sometimes the bias is towards technical expertise: the designer is expected to state, through design, exactly how a product is to be manufactured or printed; sometimes the bias is towards creativity, and the designer is expected to put forward ideas for totally new products. Most frequently she is responsible for the visual appearance of the product.

She usually works with a team of experts from different disciplines – both technical: engineers, printing technologists, etc., and business: buyers, marketing people, etc. This teamwork is one of the important differences between artists and designers: designers cannot just please themselves: their ideas on what is 'good design' and what is not have to be adapted to fit in with commercial and technical requirements.

Though the designer's work varies from one field of design to another, the end-product always has to fulfil at least two demands: it must look right and perform its function adequately. For example, a poster must attract attention and be easily readable; a tin-opener or a fridge must work well, look good and last; a biscuit pack must attract attention, fit into shelf-displays, keep its contents fresh, and open easily; a machine tool must serve the engineer's stated purpose, be easy and safe to handle and clean, and all these products must be manufacturable within given cost-limits. Designers must fully understand the purpose of the product they are designing and its marketing and manufacturing problems. They must know the limitations of and potentialities of materials and machines available for production.

At first as design assistant, the trained designer gains useful experience when carrying out rather simple 'design-technician' rather than design tasks. For example she may translate a designer's idea for a product into detailed working drawings: this requires technical know-how rather than creativity. In furniture design, for example, she would specify how to fix A satisfactorily to B in manufacturing terms without spoiling the appearance.

One designer usually has several design assistants (now sometimes called design technicians) working for her; the size of design teams varies greatly. Designers and design assistants work in various settings: in advertising agencies; manufacturing concerns' design departments; architects' offices; interior design studios; design consultancies, and many others. Organizing freelance work either on one's own or with colleagues on a design consultancy basis is complex and requires experience: newly-trained designers should try and gain experience as staff designers first. They need to know a lot not only about production problems and organization, but also how to deal with clients and finance.

Main Specializations in Art and Design

1. FINE ART

(see p. 53).

2. GRAPHICS OR GRAPHIC DESIGN OR VISUAL COMMUNICATION

This is concerned with lettering, illustration, including photography; the design of symbols. It ranges from the design of books, book jackets, all kinds of advertisements (posters, packaging, etc.), to the visual 'corporate identity' symbol of organizations, i.e. presenting the image of that organization in visual, instant-impact-making terms; for example a symbol might be required for use on all of an airline's, hotel chain's, local authority's or company's equipment and property; from planes to cutlery; letter-heads to delivery vans and perhaps even items of clothing.

Visual communication includes 'visual aids' for industrial and educational application. This is an expanding area: instructions and/or information are put over in non-verbal language, with symbols taking the place of words. Symbols are used as teaching aids in industrial training; as user-instructions in drug and textile labelling; as warning or information signs on machinery, on road signs. Symbols may be in wallchart or film-strip form, or on tiny labels as on medicine and detergent packages, or on textile labels, or on huge posters.

Symbol design, whether single or in series, requires great imagination, social awareness, logical thinking.

Visual communication also includes TV graphics: captions, programme titles, all non-verbal TV presentation of information, election results, trade-figure trends, etc.; packaging, publicity and advertising; stamp and letter-head design. Graphic designers work in advertising agencies, in design units, or in manufacturing firms' and other organizations' design departments. Television absorbs only a tiny proportion.

There are few openings in general book and magazine illustration and design, but there is considerable scope in technical and medical graphics, which require meticulous accuracy rather than creative imagination. There is also some scope in the greeting-card trade and in catalogue illustration. Much of this is considered hackwork by creative artists.

3. 3-DIMENSIONAL DESIGN

This can be divided conveniently into *Product Design* and *Interior Design*. The former embraces the design of such things as furniture, jewellery, pottery, silver, etc., as well as the design of certain aspects of products made by the engineering industries. The latter is usually referred to as Industrial Design (Eng.). Interior design embraces the design of office, domestic, hotel, ship and airport interiors; exhibition and window display and sets design.

(a) Product Design

This covers the design of all kinds of consumer-goods (for example domestic appliances, or suitcases), and of machine-tools, mechanical equipment, cars.

It is fairly generally agreed now that manufacturing industry must pay more attention to design than it has in the past. But there is no general agreement on how this is to be brought about. Many engineers and manufacturers still believe that with a bit more design training, engineers can cope with the aesthetics and ergonomics (ease of handling and cleaning, convenience in use, legibility of instructions). But most progressive manufacturers now agree that engineers must work *with* design specialists who, for their part, must have a thorough understanding of engineering principles and production constraints.

The proportion of 'design input' and 'engineering input' varies from product to product. Designers talk about a 'spectrum' – for example, in the manufacture of a plastic egg cup the 'engineering input' is very small, the 'design input' large; at the other end of the spectrum is a gas turbine, where the design input may be confined to the lettering of the instructions and the colour (which is, however, important, as it affects the 'work environment', which affects industrial efficiency). In between the two extremes are appliances such as food mixers, record players; the engineer designs the components and says how they must be arranged to do the job; the industrial designer is primarily concerned with the appearance and ergonomics of the product.

Between the first sketch and the final product there may be many joint discussions, drawings, modifications, working models and proto-types. The designer negotiates with the engineer; design technicians develop the product through the various stages. Designers and engineers work in teams – whether the team leader is an engineer or a designer varies according to (a) type of product, (b) firm's policy, and last but by no means least to engineer's and designer's personalities.

Product designers need such extensive knowledge of relevant engi-neering and manufacturing processes that they tend to stay within a particular manufacturing area. The greatest scope is in plastics, which covers a wide range of products, from toys to complex appliances and equipment.

(b) Interior Design

Interior designers work in specialized or general design consultants' studios; large stores; for a group of hotels or shipping companies; in private practice or local authority architects' offices. A considerable knowledge of architecture is required in order to know how to divert drains, move walls safely, or enlarge a shop window satisfactorily. The job of the interior designer, besides being responsible for such things as the management of contracts, is to specify the nature of an interior – how it is made, built and finished – as well as selecting the finishes and fixtures and fittings.

Planning interiors for a hotel, shop, liner, etc., needs research before designing starts. Beginners often spend all their time on fact-finding: the different items of goods to be displayed; the number of assistants required in a new shop; the kind of materials suitable for furnishing a ship cruising in hot climates. They also search for suitable light fittings, heating equipment, furnishing materials, and they may design fixtures and fittings.

The term 'interior design' is often interpreted rather loosely, and some jobs require less training and creativity. This applies particularly to work done by assistants in the design studios of stores or architects' offices, in showrooms of manufacturers of paint, furniture, furnishings, light fittings, wallpaper, etc., and in the furnishing departments of retail stores, and in specialist shops. In these settings, interior designers may advise customers or clients on the choice and assembly of the items needed. This may mean suggesting colour schemes, matching wallpaper and curtains, sketching plans for room decoration, or advising on the most suitable synthetic fabric for a particular furnishing purpose. As stores estimators and home advisers, they may go to customers' houses to give advice or even only to measure up for loose covers and curtains. Some stores employ interior designers as buyers in furniture and furnishing departments, and paint, wallpaper and furnishing fabric manufacturers may employ sales representatives.

(c) Set Design

The work requires a knowledge of period styles, structures and of lighting techniques, and a wide range of interests, to help visualize the right kind of set for any particular play or TV programme. Limited scope.

(d) Design for Exhibition and Display

Combines some of the work of interior and set designer with model-making and graphic design. Exhibition design is usually done by specialist firms. Exhibitions are often rush jobs, and designers may help put up stands and work through the night before opening. Exhibition designers also work in museums (see p. 290).

(e) Window Display

Closely allied to exhibition design, but can be specialization on its own. The essence of window and 'point of sale' design is communication: the display designer must present the store's or shop's image, attract attention and persuade the passer-by to buy. Window display can consist of merely putting a few goods in the window or a show case, or it can be a highly sophisticated exercise in marketing, using specially designed models (see Model-Making below) and specially chosen merchandise to produce a 'theme' and marketing policy. In stores there may be a *display manager*, a *display designer* and several display assistants or technicians who make/arrange the props and merchandise. Reasonable scope.

(f) Studio-Based Design (glass, jewellery, silverware, stained glass, etc.)

Design and production by designer-craftsmen who run their own small-scale studios or workshops where each article is made individually. This is almost as precarious a way of making a living as painting or sculpting. However, some studios survive, selling to local shops and individual customers.

(g) Model-Making

This includes the design and/or making up of models for window and exhibition display, and the making of scale models for architects, planners, and interior-design and product-design studios. Many designers, architects, etc., find that their clients are better able to judge a design if they see it in 3-dimensional model form rather than as drawings.

Model-makers use the traditional materials – wood, plaster, fabric, etc. – and also the new synthetics. They usually work in specialist studios and firms, but some work in other types of design studio. There is more scope here for manual work requiring some creative ability than for pure artistic design. This is an expanding field.

4. TEXTILES/FASHION
(see also Fashion, p. 190)

Textile design includes printed and woven textiles, carpets, lino, wallpapers, and plastic surface coverings and decoration. There are few openings in manufacturing firms. One of the difficulties is that thorough knowledge of manufacturing methods is essential, but it is difficult to get a job with suitable firms.

Textile designers work on their own more frequently than do other designers. They usually work through agents who show their designs to manufacturers. Fashion collections are held three times a year, furnishing collections usually twice.

General prospects

As in all creative work, success depends on ability, luck, personality and such imponderables as current taste and economic conditions. Few designers ever make a name for themselves.

The ratio of opportunities to qualified applicants is more favourable in the less glamorous and more technical field of product design than in interior, set, or textiles and fashion design.

There will never be as many creative top-level jobs as there are aspiring designers, but there is scope for 'design assistants' or 'technicians' whose work varies in level of creativity and responsibility; such work as making working drawings from designers' scribbled outlines; model-making; or, in communication design, trying to get as near the designer's intended effect with restricted number of colours and within printing constraints; and there is a vast range of jobs in product design which require technical competence, an appreciation of what constitutes good design and *some* creativity rather than creative genius.

Prospects are reasonable for people who *want* to design for industry and appreciate that it is teamwork, but *not* for failed artists.

Training

The difference in status between a degree and some other full-time courses bears little relation to their relative usefulness in career terms. A thorough training is as essential as is training for any other career, but there is no particular type of course which *necessarily* leads to a definite grade or kind of job (except in the case of teaching). Also there is controversy among design teachers and among employers about the content of courses and about the value and relevance, for individual jobs, of the various qualifications.

Apart from degrees in Art and Design, there is a large variety of so-called 'Vocational' courses. Most of these courses are now validated by D.A.T.E.C., an offshoot of the Technician Education Council (see p. xv). Some Business and Technician Education Councils Awards lead to design or design-related options; for example for people interested in design and business management, or in textile technology and design. Some courses lead to the examinations of the British Institute of Interior Design or to the British Display Society's examination.

3-Year Full-Time or 4-Year Sandwich Degrees in Art and/or Design

Educational requirements: 5 O-levels; or 3 O-levels and 1 A-level; or 2 O-levels and 2 A-levels, including 3 academic subjects and 1 subject showing the candidate's ability to use English; plus 1-year foundation course (or, exceptionally, certain 6th-form art courses).

Degrees are normally awarded in 4 separate areas of specialization: fine art, graphic design, 3-dimensional design, and textiles/fashion. Within their specialization, students normally study one principal and one or two subsidiary subjects. In graphic design, for example, typography may be the principal subject with photography and lettering as subsidiaries. In 3-dimensional design, product design may be the principal, with ceramics and/or silversmithing as subsidiary.

Students sometimes work for some weeks in a studio or design department in industry. Contact with whatever branch of design they hope to take up should play a vital part throughout the course. All students spend 15% of time on complementary studies which include History of Art.

Within these broad outlines, individual courses vary greatly.

Courses are normally preceded by a full-time foundation course which should be 'diagnostic' to help students decide on the specialization in which to qualify. There are many aspects of design which school-leavers cannot know about, and this course is expected to lead many students to one of the less well-known design fields. However not all foundation courses give such broad training and candidates should find out something about the courses. Acceptance for the foundation course is no guarantee of acceptance for the degree course itself.

There are some new art/technology, art/management, creative arts and similar 'mixed' degree courses (2 A-level entry).

Post-graduate training is almost always required for designers who aim at top jobs. There are post-graduate full-time courses (1 to 3 years) in most design specializations, for example, in film, in TV graphics or (course started 1976) in Graphic Information for Technical, Scientific and Educational Application. The highest qualification is the Royal College of Art Master's Degree (M.Des.R.C.A.).

University Courses

Very few universities offer degree courses in design, but there are plenty of university courses in fine art, history of art and, for students with arts degrees, post-graduate courses in history of art. Fine arts and history of art qualifications lead to work in museums and art galleries, in art publishing, in research and teaching. Prospects are severely limited.

See also Arts Administration, p. 64.

Vocational Courses

These vary considerably in length, entrance requirements, quality and extent of specialization. Some are almost indistinguishable from degree courses, but they do not usually contain any complementary studies, and can therefore devote all their time to professional design studies. Many Vocational courses are approved by the Chartered Society of Industrial Artists and Designers (which is the professional association for designers), and they may be as useful in career terms as degree courses (possibly even more so). The Society approves only courses which have up-to-date equipment at their disposal and which include professional practice. This covers client contact; administration; designing to cost; manufacturing processes. Entry requirements for these courses may be the same as for the degree course, but often they are slightly lower.

Other Vocational courses must be chosen for their relevance to the student's objectives. Some are suitable for the student who wishes to concentrate on, for example, lettering or typography, costume jewellery, glass decoration, photography, model-making, interior decoration, window display, book-binding, picture restoring, etc., but who does not aim to be a designer responsible for the creative conception of projects and products. Other courses, for example ceramics in Stoke-on-Trent, millinery in Luton, corsetry and lingerie in Leicester, are geared to local industries. They cover a particular design field in depth and may lead to top jobs in those fields. In some specializations, for example, model-making, window display, picture restoring, it is also possible to learn on-the-job as trainee, sometimes but rarely with day-release. It is essential, when taking such a post, to make sure that it includes some kind of training and is not a dead-end unskilled job.

Subjects in which courses can be taken (not usually at all levels) full-time or part-time day-release or evening classes

Antique restoration

Book design and production and
  bookbinding

Book illustration

Ceramics

Conservation

Decorating and sign-writing

Display and exhibition design

Dress design and manufacture

Embroidery – hand and machine

Enamelling

Etching

Fashion

Film

Fine art

Furniture design

Glass design and decoration

Interior decoration

Interior design

Jewellery

Lettering and illumination

Lithography

Metalwork

Millinery

Modelling and sculpture

Model-making

Mosaic

Package design

Painting

Paper conservation

Photography

Picture restoring

Product design or industrial
  design (engineering)

Sculpture

Set design

Shoe design

Silversmithing

Stained glass

Technical graphics

Technical illustration

Textile conservation

Textile design (including carpets
  and lino, synthetic surface
  coverings)

Toys

TV design

TV graphics

Typography

Art Therapy

Work and training

This is a growing field. Its purpose is twofold: painting and other art forms help withdrawn patients to express themselves and relieve tension, and seeing patients' work helps psychiatrists pinpoint patients' thoughts and problems. The majority of art therapists work – usually on a sessional basis – in psychiatric and mental handicap hospitals with children and with adults, individually and in groups; some work with maladjusted and some with physically handicapped children. Art therapy is not so much a career in itself as a field in which practising artists with the necessary human qualities can do useful work. Postgraduate 1-year special training is essential.

Personal attributes

All careers in art and design require resilience, self-confidence and exceptional talent.

Especially for design: ability to work as one of a team; creative sensibility and imagination coupled with a logical analytical mind; an interest in science and technology; curiosity and a desire to solve technical problems; perseverance; an interest in the social environment and in the community's needs, tastes and customs; the ability to take responsibility, and criticism; willingness at times to lower one's artistic standards in the interests of economic necessity or technical efficiency.

For freelances and senior staff jobs: business sense; the ability to communicate with employers and clients who commission the work but are possibly not themselves interested in art.

For 'technician' jobs: considerable manual dexterity, technical ability and some creativity.

Position of women

Only a small proportion of designers are women. In the most promising specialization, Product Design, the proportion of women is minute; very few women take up this specialization – largely, probably, because of the considerable engineering content during training (and mathematics O-level requirement). A woman in a manufacturing industry design-engineering team needs special drive and self-confidence to overcome traditional resistance to (a) designers in industry; (b) women in manufacturing industry.

In set and exhibition design women still have to persuade employers that they are able to cope when in an occasional rush designers have to put up sets and display stands.

There is no logical reason whatever why there are so few women in good jobs in graphics; more women than men take the appropriate training.

In fashion/textiles again more men than women succeed. Design is one of the areas where discrimination is difficult to prove but it seems to exist.

Career-break: If experienced and established, designers can take up freelance work; some return to work, but competition from recent art school leavers is likely to be stiff.

Late start: If to earn a living, advisable, if at all, only in strictly limited areas – perhaps in typography.

Part-time: As freelance.

Further in- Design Council, 28 Haymarket, London SW1
formation Chartered Society of Industrial Artists and Designers, 12 Carlton House
Terrace, London SW1Y 5AH
British Institute of Interior Design, 22–24 South Street, Ilkeston,
Derbyshire DE7 59E
Art and Design degrees: Art and Design Admissions Registry, Imperial
Chambers, 24 Widemarsh Street, Hereford HR4 9ET
British Association of Art Therapists, 13c Northwood Road, London
N6 5TL
British Display Society, 24 Ormond Road, Richmond, Surrey

Related *Advertising – Architecture – Broadcasting – Cartography –*
careers *Engineering – Fashion – Landscape Architecture – Museum*
Work – Photography – Teaching (Art, p. 493)

Arts Administration

The City University, London, runs courses in Arts Administration both
part-time, for people in relevant employment, and full-time, with a one-
year Diploma course. At Leicester Polytechnic the Performing Arts
C.N.A.A. degree course includes Arts Administration. Courses combine box office management; planning exhibitions; orchestral management. The great majority of students are graduates, and most have had
some administrative or secretarial experience in something connected
with the visual or the performing arts. Students must have extensive
knowledge of whichever type of artistic activity they wish to administer;
music graduates go into symphony orchestra administration; fine arts
graduates into art gallery or similar administration. But for regional arts
centre work any form of experience/training in the arts may be
acceptable. Scope, however, is very limited indeed, for training and for
work, but women are doing well.

See also p. 296, Music Administration.

BANKING

Entry quali- 4 O-levels, including an English and a numerate subject, or B.E.C.
fications General Award (see p. xvii); A-level holders and graduates slot in
higher up the training ladder.

The work Many jobs involve dealing with people as much as dealing with figures.
Trainees start in the general office, where they learn how to deal with
payment and collection of cheques and other basic banking procedures.
Routine figure work is now largely done by machines: trainees spend
some time in the Machine Room (see Computing and Data Processing,
p. 134). First important promotion is usually to cashier (at least in
clearing banks, in which the majority work). Cashiers are often called
a bank's ambassadors – like sales-staff in stores, the impression they
make determines the bank's image.

After a spell at the counter, trainees are moved around the various
departments and then decide whether they would like to specialize (or
stay cashiers). The main specialist departments are: *Securities*, which
deal with investments (stocks and shares, mortgages, etc.) – work
involves advising customers, keeping up with economic trends, discussion with businessmen, City experts; *Foreign Exchange*, dealing with
travellers' cheques and foreign transactions generally; *Trusts*, dealing
with trusts and wills in which customers have appointed the bank to
look after their own or their dependants' interests; advising people who
have been left money how best to invest it; explaining intricate money
matters to bewildered heirs.

Advisory services (various titles): banks are increasingly involved in
commercial planning, advising, for example, when mergers, takeovers
or liquidations are negotiated. Small and medium-sized businesses often
rely on banks for financial advice. Branch managers, acting within the
policy laid down by Head Office, have powers to decide what overdrafts
to grant to individuals and firms. This requires considerable commercial
expertise and judgement, and may involve research into, for example,
the viability of a particular type of venture which a customer wants to
start, or into the housing situation to determine whether a customer's
proposal to convert an old house into flats makes commercial sense.

Prospects Banking is one of the employment areas where chip-based technology
is likely to reduce the demand for all but management staff.

The first few years in banking are largely routine, with little scope for
initiative. Trainees who do not lose heart, and who pass their exams,

stand a fair chance of promotion to middle-management (head of section or small department) and to sub- or assistant manager of a small branch. Promotion to senior management – branch or assistant manager – depends on candidate's willingness to move to wherever there happens to be a vacancy, ability and luck. The clearing banks all prefer to promote from within: there is hardly any movement from one of the Big 4 to another. The Merchant Banks – which do not have any (or a few very rich) individual customers but deal with commercial concerns, and the Bank of England recruit mainly graduate trainees.

Note: Girls and women who enter as clerks or secretaries are not 'banking trainees' and are unlikely to be granted day- or block-release for the exams which are necessary for promotion in professional banking. (See Secretarial and Clerical Work, p. 422.)

Pay: Medium to occasionally high (see p. xxiii).

Training

On-the-job training with day/block-release.

New structure of Institute of Bankers' examination:

Stage 1: B.E.C. National Award in Business Studies (O-level entrants) or a one-year 'Conversion Course' for those with one or more A-levels. Those with two or more relevant A-levels (Law, Economics, Accountancy) and graduates go directly into

Stage 2: Eight papers set by the Institute leading, after banking experience, to Associateship (A.I.B.).

Stage 3: Financial Studies Diploma: a degree-level qualification for those expected to achieve senior management.

Entry qualifications: Associateship or Degree plus two direct entry papers. This Diploma is useful only in Banking. B.E.C. Higher National Award (see pp. xvii, 265) or a degree or Accountancy qualification may lead to wider choice of management jobs.

Personal attributes

Meticulous accuracy; a clear, logical mind; tact; courtesy; a feeling for figures and interest in work with data-processing equipment (see p. 134). For senior jobs: ability to deal with many different types of customers, sometimes in difficult situations.

Position of women

Banks need large staffs for routine work which, traditionally, women have done. Far fewer girls than boys are granted day-release right from the start; possibly because fewer *ask* for it. It is up to girls to take only jobs as trainees (and not as clerks or secretaries), and to make sure they are granted day/block-release on the same basis as boys. Only 1·5% of Institute of Banking members are women but the proportion of women working for the professional examinations is now about 15%. Under 1% of bank or senior departmental managers are women. This may partly be due to the fact that women are not as willing as men to move to wherever there is a vacancy one step higher up the ladder; but banking is certainly one of the careers in which opportunities are not equal. Women have to be considerably more determined, and more intelligent, than men, to be given equal chances of promotion to senior management.

Career-break: Probably no problem at lower and middle levels; but so far no woman who has interrupted her career seems to have got anywhere near the top.

Late start: It is unlikely that over-25s would be taken on as trainees.

Part-time: Not in professional banking – only as clerk or secretary.

Further in-formation	Banking Information Service, 10 Lombard Street, London EC3V 9AS
	Institute of Bankers, 10 Lombard Street, London EC3V 9AS
	Stock Exchange, 61 Threadneedle Street, London, EC2

| **Related careers** | *Accountancy – Actuary – Insurance* |

BEAUTICIAN (women only)

Beauty specialist – sales consultant

**Entry quali-
fications**
None laid down, but some schools ask for chemistry; see **Training**.
Minimum age for employment as beauty specialist: usually about 25.

The work
There are two types of job: beauty specialist (or therapist) and sales
consultant (or 'beauty consultant' or 'sales representative'). The two
jobs occasionally overlap.

1. BEAUTY SPECIALIST OR BEAUTICIAN OR BEAUTY THERAPIST

Gives treatments ranging from simple make-up and 'facial', to massage,
electric depilation (removal of superfluous hair), and treatment for skin
conditions, such as open pores. The fully qualified specialist uses various
types of electrical apparatus. She knows when to deal with a skin
complaint herself and when to advise her client to see a doctor.

Treatment salons are run either by cosmetics firms or as part of a
hairdressing establishment; some are run by an owner-manager. The
majority of clients are middle-aged. A beauty specialist treats about 8
clients a day. She is on her feet all day and must always look fresh and
well-groomed. She works in an exclusively feminine world.

2. SALES CONSULTANT

Usually works in the perfumery department of large stores, occasionally
in luxury hotels (at home or abroad), on liners, or at airports. She is
usually under contract to a cosmetics firm and travels round the country,
working for a week or two each in a succession of stores or shops.

She sells and promotes her firm's products and tries to win regular
customers. She answers questions on skin-care and make-up problems,
and may give talks and demonstrations.

Prospects
Poor to fair for gaining experience. More girls take the expensive
training than can find jobs. For *experienced* women there *are* good jobs:
cosmetics buyers for stores, at the head offices of cosmetics firms,
training consultants, and travelling for cosmetics firms. For those also

trained in hairdressing there are some opportunities in television (see p. 82) and as hair-dresser/beauty specialists in psychiatric hospitals which recognize the importance of beauty care in rehabilitating patients.

Pay: Medium to relatively high (see p. xxiii).

Working for Yourself

Some beauty specialists set up on their own. The initial financial outlay on equipment is between £250 and £1500. The town hall will advise on necessary licences.

Income: Low to very high (see p. xxiii).

Training

It is essential to work as an assistant in a store perfumery department or chemist's shop, before starting training. To succeed a beautician must be able to express herself quite easily. A foreign language is a great help, and the best jobs require several languages.

Professional Training

1. 2-year (1-year for over-21s) full-time course for City and Guilds Beauty Therapy Certificate. 3 O-levels preferably, including a science.

2. Private beauty courses. Minimum age usually 18. Most good courses last from 5 to 6 months (some are longer) and cost usually between £250 and £800. Courses are divided between theory – anatomy, physiology, diets, salesmanship, salon organization, and sometimes electrical treatments – and the practical work: giving facials, different types of massage, make-up, etc.

3. Higher Diploma in Beauty Therapy (first course started 1976). Courses last 2 years full-time; special emphasis on TV make-up requirements, and remedial aspects. 4 O-levels and 1 A-level in approved subjects which must include at least 1 science subject.

Courses Given by Cosmetics Houses for Sales Consultants Only

Minimum age usually 25. Schools attached to some cosmetics houses give free training (though some demand a premium).

Women must have several years' selling experience and must be good saleswomen. The courses usually last a few weeks, and subjects dealt with are facials, simple massage, eyebrow shaping and make-up, both for day and evening. These courses qualify as sales consultant, but *not* as beauty specialist.

It is wise to take either a hairdressing (see p. 203) or secretarial (see p. 422) training as well as beauty training. It widens the choice of jobs later, either by starting as a secretary in a beauty salon and working up into the beauty side, or by getting into a hairdressing salon which has a beauty department.

6-month full-time courses are now being held at a few Colleges of Further Education. Candidates should have O-level English and science, and must be at least 21.

Personal attributes

A liking for women of all ages; a friendly, confident manner; tact; courtesy; an attractive, well-groomed appearance; *naturally* good skin; cool dry hands; good health; business sense.

Career-break: No special problem, but see **Prospects**.

Late start: Beauty specialists' work is very suitable for late entrants. Many salons prefer women who are nearer in age to the majority of clients than young school-leavers are.

Part-time: Fairly easy to find for the over-30s.

Further information

City and Guilds of London Institute, 76 Portland Place, London W1N 4AA

Confederation of Beauty Therapists, 69 London Road, Sevenoaks, Kent

---

Related careers

Broadcasting (Make-up, p. 82) – Hairdressing

BOOKSELLING

Entry quali- None laid down, but good general education essential.
fications

The work
The accent is on selling and keeping stock moving, rather than on literary pursuits, yet staff must be well read and keep on reading books and reviews in order to be able to advise customers and answer queries. Reading should cover a wide field rather than only one's own interests, but in good bookshops staff usually specialize in one or two subjects. Customers are often left to browse undisturbed amongst the stock but must be offered help and advice when they want it.

Assistants' duties include daily dusting and filling and tidying shelves and display-tables. This also helps to learn the stock and remember where titles are shelved. Assistants also write out orders, keep records and may do some bookkeeping. They may pack and unpack parcels and perhaps carry them to the post.

One of the most interesting and most skilled parts of the job is helping customers who have only a vague idea of what they want or cannot explain what they have in mind. It may involve tracing titles in bibliographies and catalogues.

Book-buying – selecting a small proportion of the vast number of new titles published each month – is a highly skilled and often tricky task. Several members of staff may be responsible for buying within one or more subject areas. They have to be able to judge what will interest their particular customers, whether to buy a new title at all and how many copies to order. New titles are ordered before reviews have appeared so staff must trust their own judgement. They must also judge how much reliance to place on the recommendation of publishers' representatives.

Managers may take part in buying – it depends on how experienced their staff and how large the shop. Above all, the manager tries to give her shop an 'image' to attract a nucleus of regular customers. This is done partly by the choice of books in stock and partly by the method and type of display and arrangement of the shop as a whole. The manager is also responsible for the stock control system (as she would be in any other kind of shop).

Prospects
Not very good. Far more people want to work in bookshops than there are vacancies. Bookshops thrive only at Christmas, but some owner-managers of small bookshops do reasonably well and there are some openings with department and multiple stores' book departments.

Pay: Low (see p. xxiii).

Training   The majority of staff in individual bookshops learn on-the-job, but an increasing number of booksellers encourage their staff to work for the Booksellers' Association Diploma. Study may be by correspondence course, by attendance at residential courses organized by the Booksellers' Association or – rarely – by day-release courses. Employers belonging to the Booksellers' Association's Charter Scheme are obliged to provide some training for staff.

Staff in the book departments of stores and similar organizations who want to qualify for managerial posts may take part-time day-release courses in retail distribution (see Retail Distribution, p. 396) which are designed for all engaged in non-food retail distribution. Courses concentrate on the business of selling rather than on selling a particular commodity, but students may undertake 'project' work dealing with bookselling.

Personal attributes   An excellent memory; wide interests and extensive general knowledge; pleasure in reading and handling books; a liking for meeting people with various interests; a helpful friendly manner and the knack of making diffident customers who are not well-read feel they are welcome; the ability to work well in a large team or in a very small shop or department; a calm temperament; good health and strong feet.

Position of women   About 55% of booksellers are women; many are *part-timers*. Neither *career-break* nor *late start* should present any problems, but see **Prospects**.

Further information   Booksellers' Association of Great Britain and Ireland, 154 Buckingham Palace Road, London SW1

Related careers   *Librarian – Publishing – Retail Distribution*

BROADCASTING

(Radio and Television – including Film Work)

Studio manager – producer's assistant – assistant floor manager – floor manager – researcher – production assistant – producer/director – vision mixer – news – local radio.

PROGRAMME SERVICES: camera work and recording – make-up – costume – designer

Entry qualifications

For most jobs, a degree or specialist qualification/experience is necessary. Selection boards do not *demand* degrees, but the sort of lively minds broadcasting needs usually have taken a degree. Candidates with a poor degree and a good record of extra-curricular activities – university journalism, dramatics, or politics, etc., are more likely to be accepted than studious single-minded people.

No particular subject is the most useful. An economics or history degree may provide a background for current affairs programmes; an English or music degree for drama and music programmes. Science and technology graduates are needed for science and special features and for educational broadcasting – from schools programmes to the Open University – *and* for current affairs.

Selection boards look for well-informed all-rounders as well as for specialists. Journalistic experience is very useful indeed.

(See also Opportunities in Programme Services, p. 77.)

The work

There are a large number of different jobs in television and radio, but there is very little a school-leaver can do right away, or even train for specifically. Most jobs are done by people with training and/or experience which in itself has nothing to do with broadcasting but is valuable – particularly drama or journalism. Presenters and newscasters have usually been journalists. Secretarial jobs usually lead only to better secretarial jobs, but occasionally to producer's assistant (see below). Radio is a good basis for learning about broadcasting. Many enter it as a springboard for television, and then prefer to stay in it. Working hours in broadcasting are very irregular. All who work on programme production are liable to work until transmission stops for the night. Staff often have to work under great pressure.

STUDIO MANAGER (Radio)

The only training scheme of any size in radio is that for S.M. She is responsible for the technical presentation of programmes, and for achieving the artistic effect the producer wants. The job demands sufficient knowledge of radio to operate the equipment, but not necessarily to understand how it works.

To be able to interpret a producer's wishes, an S.M. must have wide cultural and current affairs interests. She must be good at dealing with other studio staff, with actors, and with people who come to give talks or be interviewed and who may have no previous broadcasting experience.

S.M.s may eventually become radio producers, or they may go over to television, usually at assistant floor manager level, or into sound recording (see below).

PRODUCER'S ASSISTANT formerly PRODUCTION SECRETARY (B.B.C. TV)/ PRODUCTION ASSISTANT (I.T.V.)

Entrants who go straight into television (either service) still often start as secretaries. If they are lucky and very good, they may become a producer's assistant (i.e. glorified secretary). In I.T.V. this job is called production assistant. In B.B.C. language 'production assistant' is the term for a more advanced position (see below).

The producer's assistant is the producer's right hand and memory. She sees to it that the right instructions about make-up, costumes, sets, rehearsal times, and studio bookings, etc. go to the right people. She usually attends rehearsals and may later have to re-type the shooting script, incorporating all the day's changes, ready for the next day's rehearsal or performance. During transmission, she sits next to the producer in the control-gallery, mainly timing the programme. This may be a step up towards:

FLOOR ASSISTANT AND ASSISTANT FLOOR MANAGER (Television)

The work varies according to the size and type of production. Duties usually include practical tasks such as marking out in chalk the actor's movements on the floor, making sure that all props are available, and taking charge of the prompt-book. Assistant floor managers usually start their on-the-job training with the easier talks and discussion programmes, and later go on to drama series, etc.

The next step up is to:

FLOOR MANAGER

In I.T.V. the floor manager in dramatic production is usually known as a stage manager, and the same term applies in the B.B.C. on Outside Broadcasts.

A floor manager is roughly the equivalent of stage manager in the theatre (see p. 462). Her duties may include relaying the producer's instructions to the actors. For this she is in touch with the producer by a tiny transistor radio. She is responsible for cueing the actors, and this itself may be complicated. Actors working on different sets in one production often cannot see each other and the floor manager may have to dash from set to set, keeping out of camera sight as she does so.

RESEARCHER

Researchers are usually graduates and/or ex-journalists; many have been floor managers; a few were originally secretaries and graduated to research via producer's assistant. Researchers are usually engaged on a contract basis (rather than as staff) and, unless they are promoted to production assistant (see below), they may be out of a job after 3 or 4 years. Research may be anything from looking through newspaper cuttings and finding a suitable person to be interviewed – not by researcher but by interviewer/presenter – on a news programme, to spending several months researching the background for a documentary or drama series. Researchers must be good all-rounders, able to pick out relevant facts from a mass of material. They usually write 'briefs', which may range from a few questions which an interviewer is to ask on a programme, to exhaustive background material for a documentary scriptwriter. Researchers in current affairs must also be able to think up programme ideas, and they work under tremendous pressure. Specialist researchers, for example for scientific or medical programmes, are often freelances.

PRODUCTION ASSISTANT (in I.T.V. this level of job may be called trainee or junior director, or senior floor manager)

She may also do some research; and she may direct outside film sequences and, occasionally, studio camerawork. Production assistant is the first of the 'production-shaping jobs'; it is an important one in the hierarchy: the pyramid narrows considerably at this level; production assistants may spend some time in the control gallery, and occasionally they may do senior floor management, especially in drama productions. The next step up is to:

PRODUCER/DIRECTOR

The producer and/or director's exact functions vary. They include responsibility for initiating, budgeting, casting, and the shape or 'treatment' of programmes. These top jobs are very responsible and are done by specialists in a particular field, such as current affairs, drama, or science or technological topics, with long, often technical, experience in the medium.

VISION-MIXER

Up to six cameras may be in operation during a production. The producer in the control room decides which camera's picture to send out to the audience, and tells the vision-mixer, who switches to the selected camera as the order is given. This needs concentration and quick reflexes.

Training for above jobs Mostly on-the-job. There is no specific pre-entry training which is certain to lead to the above jobs, but there are some film and TV courses (see below, and Art and Design, p. 53).

NEWS STAFF

Newsroom staff compile and write scripts for the presenters; reporters and correspondents 'get the stories' and present some themselves. The essence of broadcast news is brevity. TV and radio journalists must be instant fact-selectors and decision-makers. They may be sent anywhere at any time.

Entry and training The B.B.C. runs a regular, I.T.N. an occasional, news and current affairs training scheme (about 2 years' duration) for entrants between 21 and 25 – about 700 applicants for 12 to 16 vacancies. Entrants are almost invariably graduates (any subject) with keen interest in current affairs, but 'general education' plus proven journalistic ability (i.e. good job on a good paper) are also acceptable.

LOCAL RADIO

Local radio stations are run on a shoestring. A manager (titles vary between companies) is in charge. She may have a deputy or programme organizer for day-to-day organization of output. Stations have between

2 and 10 producers, and about the same number of station assistants (or programme assistants or junior producers).

Broadly, a *producer* is responsible for initiating and developing programme ideas and for involving the local community. She must therefore know people and issues in the locality in which she applies for a job. She may produce anything from local current affairs to request and phone-in programmes (though there may be some specialist producers). She may also interview, and present programmes.

Station assistants research and prepare programmes and also interview (on and off the air); they are also usually responsible for operation of studio and control-room equipment.

No rigid entry qualifications, but all candidates must have a good microphone voice, be well informed on and interested in a wide range of contemporary topics and trends, both national and local, and have sufficient knowledge to handle recording and transmission equipment. Producers and station assistants are usually given a few weeks' basic training.

Programme Services

SOUND AND VISION

Film and *television* camera and sound work are two quite separate fields.

1. Film

A considerable amount of television material is shown on film; whole programmes are filmed, for example for schools broadcasts, documentaries; and film is used as an important ingredient of all types of programme: light entertainment, current affairs, children's programmes, plays and series, etc. The same camera crews work in the film studio and on location. They travel a lot, and at short notice.

There are three basic jobs in films: *editing*; *camera*; *sound*.

Entry requirements and training Interest and 'hobby experience' are crucial. There are a number of film/TV courses at art schools, either as part of an Art and Design degree course, or 2/3-year Diploma courses, or at post-graduate level. Course emphasis (and entry requirements) vary enormously: for example on closed circuit educational television films; on feature or instructional films; with technical or creative bias, etc.

Equally useful in later job-opportunity terms, but more difficult to get into (several hundred applicants for every training vacancy) is the B.B.C. film training scheme (1 year approximately; age 18 to 25). No specific G.C.E. requirements, but several O-levels are in practice essential; above all, candidates must show 'evidence of lively interest in film-making techniques' and know enough about cinematography principles to absorb advanced film training; they also need 'special knowledge of some of the following: photography, the cinema, music, magnetic sound recording, sport, news, current affairs'. Film training includes separate schemes for:

Film Editors

A considerable amount of film is shown on TV, either as all-film programmes or as part of video-taped plays, documentaries, news, features, etc. Film forms about 25% of the total output. Editors work entirely in the cutting-room, 'editing down' material shot in the studio or on location. A great deal of their work is done on their own initiative, as directors do not have time to be with editors all day. The job is highly creative as it is the editor who shapes and fashions the final programme which audiences see. Editing can lead to directing.

Assistant film editors look after the practical side of running the cutting-room. They do the 'joins', log film on its way out of and back into the studio and laboratories. They learn by watching, and often cut sequences under the editor's supervision. Cutting-room work is almost invariably done under great pressure.

Film Camera Crews

Crews usually consist of 2 to 4. The head of the camera crew is in charge of *lighting*. She works in close cooperation with the director; knows the script thoroughly and arranges the all-important lighting and camera angles for each individual shot, so as to achieve the atmosphere the director wants. Lighting is an important step to directing.

Assistant camera crews load and change magazines, make sure the right equipment is available at the right time and place and in working order, and they learn how to operate cameras and lighting equipment. Promotion is pretty slow – it takes about 10 years to reach lighting cameraman/woman status.

Film Sound Recordist

She is concerned with dubbing, sound-transfer and above all with mixing sound from various sources. This may include location recordings on tape, and sounds produced by effects machines. Achieving the correct balance, controlling the 'input' from various sources is a highly skilled job, requiring great technical skill and musical creativity.

Assistants manipulate microphones and other recording equipment and learn by watching. (Far fewer apply for sound than for vision jobs; chances of acceptance and of promotion are, therefore, rather better.)

Projectionists (Film Assistants Class II)
They operate projection equipment and may also work on dubbing.

Virtually all promotion to camera work, recordist, editor, is from inside the broadcasting organization – i.e. via recruitment into an Assistant grade; but editors, camera crews and recordists also often work as freelances, or they may be recruited with full film/TV school training. The greatest hurdle for those who do not start as assistants is getting a union card without which they cannot get jobs.

Note on the Film Industry: There is no basic difference between filming for TV and making films for the cinema, or making instructional, educational and advertising films. There are no regular on-the-job training schemes outside TV, and jobs in films are even scarcer. Virtually all film makers outside television are freelances and lead a very precarious existence.

2. Television

Most television programmes are pre-recorded. When recording a programme, as well as during 'live' transmission, previously recorded and/or filmed material may be slotted in. The operational/technical side of creating programmes and then getting them on TV screens all over the country (or the world) is highly complex. It requires creativity, technical expertise and a calm, unflappable temperament.

Confusingly, operating and controlling vision and sound equipment is done by the *engineering* division staff in the B.B.C. (which is the only broadcasting organization with a comprehensive training and career structure). There are two separate but overlapping entries and ladders for two overlapping but separate categories of staff:

1. *operational* vision and sound staff responsible for interpreting the producer's (non-technical) instructions and for producing the required sound and vision effects which are finally heard and seen;
2. electronic and communications *engineering* staff.

1. The first category start as *trainee assistants* in Technical Operations.

Entry re-   Minimum age 18 (in practice, maximum about 25). O-levels in English
quirements   language, mathematics and physics; *or* English language and a T.E.C.
Certificate in Electrical Engineering, Electronics or Applied Physics. Applicants must also have a keen interest in, and some 'hobby experience' of, hi-fidelity reproduction, tape-recording music, or colour

photography or lighting for amateur dramatics. Ability to read a musical score and/or knowledgeable interest in current affairs are also expected. Acceptance depends very much on interview.

The work　There are four *Technical Operations* TV specializations:

i. *Trainee Camera Assistants* help in setting up and operating electronic cameras and associated equipment in studios and on outside broadcasts. Promotion is to Assistant and later Camera man/woman, Vision Supervisor, Vision Controller and ultimately possibly to Technical Manager responsible for Lighting.

ii. *Trainee Sound Assistants* help in setting up and operating sound recording and reproduction equipment; they 'collect sound effects', and may eventually become Sound Supervisors responsible for control and balance of the various sound sources which are combined for final transmission. They are London based.

iii. *Trainee Audio Assistants* do similar work to Sound Assistants but they work in the regional (smaller) centres, and are also involved in the operation of radio sound equipment.

iv. *Technical Operators (Radio).* Apart from operating and later controlling sound equipment they are concerned with collecting and 'routing' material. They do not work in television, but once inside Technical Operations, it is often possible to switch to television (and many people who do radio work as a way into television stay in radio because it is more interesting and varied than they thought).

Training　Normally starts with a 3-months course, B.B.C.-run, and continues on the job with further full-time courses for two to three years. Promotion is not *guaranteed* even when the training has been successfully completed but B.B.C. engineering training is highly valued by all sound and vision recording studios outside the B.B.C.

NOTE: Candidates with qualifications from Art School TV departments or specialist TV schools, or candidates with music technology qualifications (see p. 295), usually have to start as trainee assistants in Technical Operations. However, there are some opportunities in independent (much smaller) companies or as freelances. B.B.C. training is generally considered the best for all vision and/or sound operational jobs.

2. The second category start as *Technical Assistants*. Outside the B.B.C. this kind of job is called 'technician' (see *Technician Engineer*, p. 175). Technical assistants are the professional engineers' support force.

Entry requirements　Minimum age 18 (in practice, maximum around 25). O-levels in English language, mathematics and physics *and* having studied (i.e. not necessarily passed) A-level physics and mathematics. T.E.C. Certificate in Electrical Engineering, Electronics or Applied Physics plus O-level English language *may* be acceptable. Acceptance depends very much on interview. Technical assistants must show that they understand the basic principles of electricity and magnetism and have a good grasp of their practical application. 'Hobby experience' as for Technical Operations Trainee Assistants.

The work (T.A.s and professional engineers)

There are two specializations: *Technical Assistant/Television* and *Technical Assistant/Radio and External Broadcasting* (as with Trainee Assistants/Technical Operations, radio work may lead to TV work).

Technical Assistants/Television assist in any of the B.B.C. Engineering Departments. On the 'operational' side, they work in Studio/Engineering/Outside Broadcasts and Television News. They cope with emergency repairs and sudden equipment failure and generally act as technical 'back-up'. Television Network Engineering staff are responsible for operation and maintenance of the equipment used to route, control and distribute signals from various sound and vision programme sources. All this work can be hectic and needs quick decision-making and a cool head.

Other B.B.C. departments are concerned with research, development (see Engineering, p. 163, for engineering functions), planning, installation, commissioning and maintenance of all the complex equipment and plant used for producing, recording, transmitting and routing programmes. Some of the most technologically advanced work in telecommunications is done in or with the B.B.C.

Training

Starts with a 3-months, B.B.C.-run course and continues on the job with further courses for about 2½ years. After satisfactorily completing training, technical assistants are eligible for promotion to B.B.C. Engineer posts. However, the majority of B.B.C. Engineers enter as graduates with degrees in Electrical or Electronic Engineering, Applied Physics or other relevant science subjects, or with T.E.C. Higher awards in Electronics or Telecommunications (or with relevant H.N.D./C.s). For posts in Research and Designs (the same as 'Design' in Engineering, p. 164) minimum entry qualification is now a 1st or 2nd Class Honours Degree. There is also scope for engineers with higher degrees.

Engineers are also required by the independent companies, most of their engineers and assistants (titles and organization vary) being on 'operational' (i.e. technical back-up rather than research etc.) work; and there are no comprehensive, permanent training schemes. Staff are normally recruited with T.E.C. and Higher T.E.C. awards or degrees or with B.B.C. training.

All engineering staff, at every level, have to be prepared to work unsocial hours. The higher up the ladder, the more 'normal' the hours worked.

Although there is no official or organized route for this it is possible for engineers to switch to camerawork, lighting, floor manager, and later producer or director. It is easier to get into broadcasting with engineering qualifications than any other way.

MAKE-UP

Entry requirements and training
Nothing rigid. City and Guilds beautician and hairdressing or vocational art course may be a help in this competitive field. But unqualified persons who pass a practical test are taken on for about 2 years' make-up and hairdressing training. The first 3 months is a basic training and trial period. After that, training consists of carrying out practical duties, starting with simple make-up and hairdressing and gradually learning the intricacies of make-up for colour, and of period-style and other complicated procedures.

The work
Television make-up is highly skilled. It requires the ability to understand and defeat the camera's often unkind effects on faces. It also requires a thorough knowledge of period hairstyles. An experienced senior assistant is usually in charge of each dramatic production and makes up the star actors. Juniors see to the rest of the cast and also look after the simpler make-up required for non-dramatic productions.

COSTUME

(a) Designers

Entry qualifications
Costume design diploma plus, preferably, relevant experience.

The work
Costume designers are in charge of the hiring, design and adapting of up-to-date and period costumes. They are called in on new productions in the early stages, to discuss the costumes and to advise whether to hire, make specially, or adapt. Later they liaise with designers and make-up staff. They need a thorough knowledge of period styles, but further research is often needed to make certain of representing the exact year or season. First job usually as *trainee costume assistant*.

(b) Dressmakers

Entry qualifications
City and Guilds or equivalent standard.

The work   Dressmakers make up costumes designed by the supervisor, and do alterations to costumes which are hired or from stock.

(c) Dresser

Entry quali- Ability to sew; a calm temperament and a practical approach.
fications

The work   Last-minute ironing and maintenance of costumes. They also help actors to dress, especially in quick changes which make TV a terrifying medium for many performers.

DESIGNER

Entry quali- For set designers: art and design or architectural training with relevant
fications   specialization plus experience. Graphic designers have usually had experience in commercial studios or advertising (see p. 55). Scenic designers normally need Art and Design degree.

The work   The designer is responsible for set-dressing and for designing the sets. She is called in by the producer when an idea is beginning to take shape. A designer's interpretation of the atmosphere the producer has in mind, and her own suggestions, are vitally important to the success of the production.

   The designer has assistants whose work is often more technically skilled than 'creative'. They draw ground-plans and make working drawings, draw up specifications, make models of sets, and make and search for props.

   Graphic designers and graphic artists (assistants) create credit titles, 'linking material', captions, maps and general illustrations.

Prospects: Competition for all jobs is very keen indeed and only the best stand a
Broad-   chance. It is impossible to lay down what the best is in any particular
casting   case, as requirements are so complex and varied.
generally   *Pay*: Varies enormously.

Personal   *For all broadcasting*: creative imagination; wide interests generally, a
attributes   special interest in a particular subject; a clear, quick, logical mind; appreciation of what audiences want; a strong constitution; the ability to work as one of a team and to take responsibility; a sociable nature; a fairly thick skin; tact; calmness in crises; speed of action; self-confidence.

Position of women

On the programme production side, women do reasonably well up to about middle level jobs (about one third are women); but it is only recently that, thanks to considerable pressure, women have started being seen on the screen as reporters and interviewers; and there are still very few women indeed in policy-decision-making jobs. Companies are now trying to find women presenters and reporters, so 'suitable' women should have fair chances, but nobody has ever been able to find out exactly what qualities a woman must have to be considered 'suitable'.

On the vast technical side there is only a minute proportion of women (about 10 out of 10,000). All entrants are expected to have had 'hobby experience' with electronic equipment – and that rules out the vast majority of young females. Any woman who really wants to get into broadcasting should consider getting in via an engineering degree or technical qualification. She would stand out and be noticed, and might be able to transfer to programme production.

Career-break: Depends on how well established before the break, but many women have returned.

Late start: Fair scope for women with relevant experience and qualifications, especially for experienced journalists.

Part-time: Possibly as freelance on a contract basis.

Further in-formation

B.B.C., Appointments Officer, Broadcasting House, London W1
Independent Broadcasting Authority, 70 Brompton Road, London SW3
for individual companies

Related careers

*Acting – Advertising – Art and Design – Journalism – Music –
Photography – Stage Management*

December 1980: A *National Broadcasting School* starts operating in 1981. Initially it will train for radio only. Courses (both full-time 4 to 12 weeks, and evening-only) in (a) ENGINEERING (entry with O-level English, science to A-level or T.E.C. or City and Guilds Telecommunications or Electronics or relevant experience); (b) PROGRAMMING (entry with 3 O-levels or relevant experience); (c) JOURNALISM (entry with 2 years' experience in professional journalism). But apart from stated entry requirements, the School intends to apply rigorous 'suitability' tests. It is expected there will be ten applicants for every place. Grants are not likely to be paid, so the evening-only courses are particularly likely to be oversubscribed by would-be broadcasters still in some other employment.

BUILDING

Building crafts – Building management

Entry quali- Craft training: average ability in mathematics, a science (other than
fications biology or domestic).
Technician training: see T.E.C. p. xv.
Degree: 2 A-levels, 3 O-levels, including mathematics.

The work The building industry is made up of companies ('contractors') of all
sizes, from international giants employing thousands of staff, including
architects, chartered surveyors and chartered engineers, to small 'jobbing builders' employing one or two craftsmen/women and taking on
additional people as required. (Many craftsmen work part of the time
on their own and part of the time for contractors.) Large companies
have their own design departments and execute large-scale projects
such as housing estates, large office blocks, hospitals etc. Smaller firms
– and often large ones too – work to plans drawn up by the client's
architect. Firms may subcontract work to specialist firms of plumbers,
tilers, smaller general builders etc. On large projects the client, or the
client's architect, appoints a *clerk of works* (see below).

Levels and organization of work are very much less well-defined than,
for example, in the engineering industry. Many contractors started at
craft level and built up their own business, but this is becoming less
frequent; the need to understand the new technologies and materials,
the need to organize work efficiently and to work to given standards are
'professionalizing' the building industry. There is, therefore, increasing
scope for people with specialist qualifications, but there will always be
scope for craftsmen and craftswomen who are good at their job and also
have organizing ability to build up their own business. Knowledge of
basic crafts like bricklaying is essential even for managers.

BUILDING CRAFTS

The main trades or crafts are:
1. *Bricklaying*: measuring and marking out a job; checking verticals and
horizontals with guide and plumb lines and spirit level; laying the bricks
using mortar and trowel. Bricklayers must be able to read drawings.
2. *Carpenter and joiner*: laying floorboards; hanging doors and fitting
window frames; erecting roof timbers and staircases; making built-in

furniture; knowing about the qualities and uses of different types of timber. Carpenters must be able to read drawings.

3. *Plastering*: preparing surfaces of inside walls and ceilings; making up the plaster; applying and spreading it evenly; using moulds for decorative work.

4. *Roof slating and tiling*: preparing rafters with roofing felt and battens; hanging tiles and slates on battens; fixing lead or zinc flashings; covering roofs and walls in materials such as asbestos and weatherboarding.

5. *Painting and Decorating*: knowing about different types of paints and finishes; preparing surfaces; painting; hanging wallpaper.

6. *Plumbing*: installing, maintaining and repairing water supply and waste systems; understanding complicated plumbing systems in houses where the system has been changed or added to after conversion.

7. *Heating and ventilating fitter*: installing heating and ventilating (including air conditioning) systems; understanding basic heating, etc., systems.

In most of these trades craftsmen and women may work, on their own at times, in people's homes as well as on new constructions.

BUILDING MANAGEMENT

The term is used to cover a wide variety of jobs and skills. It includes responsibility for seeing that the work is carried out in the right sequence with the right materials at the right cost, for organizing the labour force and for the supply of materials. It may include organizing the financial side (paying wages, paying for materials, etc.) but that depends on the size of the firm. Some building management jobs are site-based (there may be a site-office), some are office-based; nearly all jobs involve some site-visits; and many jobs – at least for large firms – involve working away from home at times. Building management jobs normally involve dealing with labour; to succeed in this kind of job – to be respected by the labour force – building managers, whatever their specific job, must understand the rudiments of building crafts. Job titles and specializations (which vary very much between firms) are:

1. *Buyer (Purchasing Officer)*: selects from the design drawings the materials and services needed; contacts suppliers and subcontractors to obtain the most competitive prices; ensures materials are available at the right time.

2. *Estimator*: calculates the likely cost of materials (from door handles to concrete), labour and plant, and the time needed for the project when the firm is tendering for a contract. Also analyses costs of existing projects to provide guide to future estimates.

3. *Planning engineer*: at pre-tender stage is involved in the decision about how the tender can be adjusted. When tender is accepted, she

produces charts showing sequence of operations. Works closely with contracts manager. In large companies will use computer for this (see p. 134). She will have had experience of estimating, buying or contracts management.

4. *Site engineer*: in charge of technical side of an individual project. Sets out the positions and levels of the building to ensure it is placed in the correct position in accordance with the designs. Oversees all the work on site, including quality control (see Structural and Civil Engineering, p. 168).

5. *Site manager (site agent)*: in charge of the contract. Ensures the designs and specifications are understood by the foremen; plans and coordinates materials and labour. Sees that building keeps to the plan and time schedule (see Building Surveying Technician, p. 478). May have young engineers under her control. Used to be called 'general foreman'.

6. *Production controller (Productivity)*: works on incentive schemes; measures work done by operatives as part of productivity control; takes part in construction planning at site level. Some specialize in work study, and/or industrial relations.

7. *Contracts Manager*: oversees several projects. Moves from site to site ensuring that work is progressing according to plan. Plans movement of machines and labour to minimize delays and time wasting. Has overall responsibility for completion of projects to correct standard at the right time.

Clerk of Works: Other building management specialists work for the contractor; the clerk of works is employed by the client (or client's architect). She may be employed full-time by a local authority or, in the private sector, on a contract basis. She works from an office on site and is responsible for seeing that the work is carried out according to the architect's specifications. As the only person on site not working for the contractor she can be rather isolated, so needs to be confident and self-sufficient. On large schemes she may supervise several other clerks of works specializing in, for example, heating and ventilating or electrical installation.

Training

Crafts: School leavers are strongly advised to train with a firm operating the National Joint Training Scheme for skilled building operations. Trainees normally serve a 3-year apprenticeship combining full-time, off-the-job training in the first year with, later, day-release and practical experience, leading to City and Guilds Craft Certificates. (This scheme covers crafts 1–5. Plumbers serve a 4-year apprenticeship for Basic and Advanced Craft Certificates. Heating and Ventilating fitters follow an engineering craft course, see p. 181.)

Management: 1. T.E.C. certificate/diploma in Building Studies with appropriate units (see T.E.C. p. xv), usually on-the-job with day-release. Successful completion leads to technician membership of the Chartered Institute of Building.

2. For jobs with big building organizations, 3-year full-time or 4-year sandwich degree in building/building technology/building construction and management. Most give exemption from Institute of Building's Final examinations parts 1 and 2.

3. Clerk of works: as above, followed by evening or correspondence course for Institute of Clerks of Works' Intermediate and Final examinations. (T.E.C. certificate or diploma in Building Studies gives some exemptions.) Membership of the Institute of Clerks of Works is compulsory before sitting the examinations. Some local authorities give day-release.

Personal attributes

Building crafts: see engineering crafts p. 183.

Building management: technical and practical aptitudes; good at organization; willing to work outdoors in all weathers; ability to manage the work force.

Prospects

There is a shortage of skilled craftsmen and women in most areas. Trained and experienced managers are also in demand, but large-project building fluctuates with the economic situation.

NOTE: Building management overlaps very much with surveying and civil/structural engineering technician jobs.

   Pay: Low for crafts when training; medium to occasionally high for crafts and management when qualified (see p. xxiii).

Position of women

There are as yet few craftswomen; more women have entered building management and are proving very successful. There is no reason why there should not be many more at all levels.

Further information

Building Industry Careers Service, 82 New Cavendish Street, London W1M 8AD

Institute of Clerks of Works of Great Britain, 41 The Mall, London W5 3TJ

Construction Industry Training Board, Radnor House, London Road, Norbury, London S W16 4E L

Related careers

Agriculture and Horticulture – Architecture – Engineering Crafts and Technician – Surveying Technician

---

BUILDING SOCIETY MANAGEMENT

Entry quali- 2 A-levels, 4 O-levels, including an English and a subject proving
fications numeracy, or B.E.C. National award in Business Studies or Financial
Studies. Also *graduate* entry.

The work There are nearly 200 members of the Building Societies Association,
but there is no uniform building society organization. In the 'Big 5',
each of which has its own distinctive structure and policy, management
trainees tend to go up the promotion ladder within that society. Then
come about 30 societies in which branch management is sufficiently
similar for management staff to move between these societies for
promotion. The remaining societies are small and mostly local ones.
They do not usually have an organized management and training
structure. It is almost impossible to move 'up' from management in a
small, local society into one of the bigger ones. So people who want to
make a career in building society management should try for a job in
one of the Big 5 or in one of the medium-sized societies.

In practice, in the large and the medium-sized societies there is now
a two-level entry. Clerical staff may do some counter-work and deal
with clients, but few manage the leap into management. Trainee
managers who must have the required entry qualifications (see above)
do some counter-work to begin with to learn how to deal with clients,
but most of their time is spent on such building society work as mortgage
principles and processing; assessing applicants' suitability for mortgages;
and liaising with surveyors, estate agents, solicitors and investment
specialists. Increasingly, they learn how to adapt traditional office
procedures to new technologies. After 2 to 3 years, trainee managers
are expected to be fully-fledged managers of small branches, or they
may become assistant managers in a bigger branch. The branch
managers' main job is 'getting business': 'selling' *their* branch and
society in competition with other societies. This means managers must
make contact with solicitors, estate agents, large local companies, etc.

In a large branch an assistant manager would be responsible for the
administration of the office and for interviewing all but the most
important clients. The manager himself is responsible for finding out
why, for example, a client might be taking his/her business elsewhere:
she may arrange to visit such a client and find out in what way her
branch or society has displeased a client. But much of the manager's
time is spent on routine mortgage processing.

Prospects   After the rapid expansion of the 1970s, building societies are 'consoli-
dating'; new branches are not opening in such great numbers as they
did a few years ago. Also, as fewer clerical staff will be employed as
office technologies change, there is a reduction in junior
management/supervisory staffs. However, prospects are fair, and promotion prospects to bigger-branch management and regional management are also reasonable, but only for people willing to move to
wherever the next step-up vacancy happens to be.

Training   Trainee managers work for the examinations set by the Chartered
Building Societies Institute. The big societies run their own in-house
training courses and there are some C.B.S.I. residential courses. The
bulk of exam-preparation has, however, to be done by private study;
day-release is granted by some societies.

Personal   Ability to inspire confidence in clients; organizing ability; numeracy,
attributes   communication skills; liking for routine desk-work.

Position   So far there are very few women branch managers, but about 10% of
of women   students for the C.B.S.I. exam are now believed to be women. Building
societies tend to be conservative bodies and, while discrimination is
difficult to prove, male trainee managers progress more quickly.
Societies say women are not willing to move to another town to gain
experience, but no specific cases of refusal to move were produced. As
the various societies' policies on everything vary greatly, prospective
trainee managers could 'shop around' and find out which society has a
significant proportion of women trainees.

Career-break: No evidence yet of any woman manager having tried to
come back; it is likely that young trainees are preferred as technologies
and policies change rapidly.

Late start: At present, societies take on trainee managers up to about
30; but it seems that no older women with relevant previous experience
have tried for trainee management jobs.

Part-time: Not at the moment. No reason at all why it should not be tried.

Further in-   Chartered Building Societies Institute, Fanhams Hall, Ware, Herts.
formation   Building Societies Association (for member societies), 34 Park Street,
London W1Y 3PF
Individual Societies.

Related   *Insurance – Banking*
careers

CAREERS OFFICER

Entry quali- Degree, teaching or comparable professional qualifications, or industrial
fications experience.

The work Careers officers' main job is helping school children make wise career-
decisions, but they also deal with adults: anyone who is in full- or part-
time education, or any adult who wants or has to change careers, is
entitled to go to the local education authority careers office for
information and advice. (See Careers Advice, p. xxv.)

Careers work in schools is a long-term process. Ideally it should start
early enough to discuss the career implications of dropping and taking
up particular subjects for O-levels or C.S.E. and to stress the importance
of leaving as many options open as long as possible. Careers officers also
help young people, possibly using interest and aptitude questionnaires
and tests, to clarify their thoughts about their own personality, abilities,
career expectations and desired life-style. They normally give individual
vocational guidance interviews to fifth formers, whether they are leaving
school or staying on, and follow-up interviews where necessary.

Careers programmes are planned to suit the various age and ability
groups and may include a variety of media and methods. A careers
officer may give talks or hold discussion groups in school. She may
organize or help to organize careers libraries; arrange talks by specialists
in schools or at careers conventions; arrange for individuals and groups
to visit places of work. She may also arrange work experience periods
to give children who are interested in a career but vague about the
actual work and/or environment a chance to get first-hand information,
and to widen others' career horizons. Films, TV, tape-recordings, are
also used in careers programmes.

Careers officers work closely with careers teachers. Some specialize
in work with pupils who leave with few or no qualifications; others in
work with those who go on to higher education, or with the physically
handicapped, or they work entirely with further education and polytechnic students. An important aspect of the work is finding suitable
jobs for school leavers. Employers notify the careers services of
vacancies which are circulated to careers officers. Careers officers
also 'canvass' employers and other careers officers for young people
where necessary; for example, if the individual wants a job which is
only available in certain areas, such as apprentice jockey.

In order to inform pupils adequately, careers officers must themselves
be well informed about developments, trends and impending changes in

education, training, the job market. They divide their time between giving out information and collecting it: they visit employers, they talk to personnel officers and to the people who are actually doing the work; they attend meetings where they are told about the industrial and the further/higher education scene; and they visit colleges and other educational institutions. Careers officers are involved in organizing government schemes to help unemployed young people (Youth Opportunities Programme).

Like teaching, careers work must not be judged by one's own personal experience of it. It would be wrong for a pupil who had no or poor advice at school to dismiss careers work as nothing but giving routine talks and handing out careers literature. The quality of careers work varies enormously from one area to another; there are still not enough careers officers to make the service work as well as it is intended to.

Prospects   Reasonable; though there is a shortage, employment prospects depend on level of public expenditure. Promotion prospects are good for those who are able and willing to move around the country to get varied experience.

Pay: Medium (see p. xxiii).

Training   1-year courses at universities and polytechnics for vocational guidance diploma (course titles vary). Careers officers may be seconded for training after a traineeship. The syllabus includes organization of education services; occupational and social psychology; public and social administration; organization of industry; counselling aims and methods; practical work with pupils; visits to a variety of places of work and talks with/by employers.

Personal attributes   Ability to get on with and understanding of people of all levels of intelligence and temperaments; interest in industrial and other employment trends and problems; sympathy with rather than critical attitude towards other people's points of view; organizing ability; willingness to work in a team; ability to put facts across clearly and helpfully; ability to gain young people's confidence and to put them at ease however shy and worried; insight and imagination to see how young people might develop.

Position of women   About half of all careers officers are women, but a very much smaller proportion are in senior jobs, let alone at the top. Women careers officers feel that there certainly has been discrimination in the past: women have had to be better qualified and have wider relevant experience than men for the same type of promotion.

Late start: Women who, before the break, had any kind of job which involved dealing with a variety of people, preferably in various work situations, stand a good chance of acceptance for training. Maturity and variety of experience can be an asset. Vocational guidance diploma courses are available under T.O.P.S. (see p. xl).

Career break: Should not present any problems (but see **Prospects**).

Part-time: Not at the moment, but no reason why this work could not be done on a part-time basis.

Further in-
formation
Institute of Careers Officers, 37a High Street, Stourbridge, West Midlands
Careers Service Training Committee, Local Government Training Board, 8 The Arndale Centre, Luton LU1 2TS

Related
careers
Management in Industry – Personnel Management – Teaching – Youth Work (Social Work, p. 452).

CARTOGRAPHY (Map Making)

Cartographer – cartographic draughtsman

Entry quali- Depends on type of work – from 2 O-levels to degree. See **Work** and
fications   **Training**.

The work   Cartography is concerned with the evaluation, compilation, design,
reproduction, draughting and editing of maps. A map in this context
covers any type of chart, plan or three-dimensional model representing
the whole or sections of the earth or of other parts of the universe.

Both cartographic data collection and reproduction methods have
changed drastically in the last few years. Apart from 'old-fashioned'
aerial photography such advanced technologies as seismic sensing and
electrostatic mapping are being used. But cartography does *not* involve
exploring uncharted territory, taking photographs from helicopters or
setting up satellite photography! It is an indoor desk job though very
occasionally cartographers may accompany the information gatherers.
While the cartographer determines what data are needed for any
particular map and may discuss which type of data collection is best in
any particular case, the actual collection is done by specialists such as
surveyors (see p. 468), specialist photographers (see p. 347), electronic
data processing people (see p. 134) or by historical or archaeological
researchers. *Cartographers* interpret the information collected by other
specialists, *cartographic draughtsmen/technicians* represent the information in three-dimensional or graphic form. Apart from tracing and
drawing, draughtsmen use highly sophisticated reproduction methods
and materials.

The largest single employer is the Ordnance Survey. Other employers
include various Ministries (Defence and Environment particularly),
nationalized industries, local authorities, commercial map publishing
houses, motoring organizations and exploration departments of oil
companies.

The kinds of maps which are produced include: cartographic por-
trayals of airfield approaches with landing charts for pilots; maps
showing traffic flow or the distribution of population, housing, employment, and industry for planning purposes; maps for the Forestry
Commission showing the progress of land acquisition, planting, thinning,
and felling; maps of the surface of the moon and maps of ancient Rome.

Prospects   Limited. Jobs are mainly in London and Southampton (Ordnance Survey).

Training   *Cartographer*: Geography or Topographic Science degree or post-graduate Diploma in Cartography or 2-year full-time Cartography Diploma. Entry requirements: A-levels in geography and one other science, O-levels in mathematics, English and a science subject (which must be a different subject from that offered at A-level).

For work with the Ordnance Survey, Southampton:

Cartographic Assistant: Maximum age 19; 2 O-levels including either English language or mathematics, geography, art or technical drawing or comparable subject, a science or a language.

Cartographic Draughtsman: Maximum age 25, 3 O-levels (chosen from the same as above), 4 months in the Ordnance Survey Department's Drawing School.

For work with other employers, draughtsmen now work for a T.E.C. award in Cartography, Planning and Land Use. Entry is flexible (see T.E.C., p. xv) but in practice cartography employers demand 4 O-levels including mathematics and a 'subject demonstrating facility in the use of English'. Trainees complete the Certificate course in 2 years' day-release. Entrants with lower qualifications take at least 3 years.

Personal attributes   Patience; great accuracy; good colour vision; keen interest in physical surroundings; powers of observation.

Position of women   *Cartographers*: Comparatively few women have qualified, but those who have had no special problems.

Cartographic draughtsmen: About one in six are women.

Career-break: Should be no problem for qualified cartographers who keep up with technological changes; but see *Prospects*.

Late start: Very few opportunities.

Part-time: Not normally; but graduate cartographers might be able to get sporadic rather than part-time project work.

Further information   British Cartographic Society, R. W. Anson, Department of Construction, Oxford Polytechnic, Headington, Oxford OX3 0BP

Related careers   *Architectural Technician – Art and Design*

CATERING

Hotels – restaurants – industrial catering – contract catering – school catering – hospital catering – institutional management

**Entry quali-
fications**
3 O-levels (including English, one science and a mathematics subject) are required for admission to all courses likely to lead to supervisory and management work. But in this essentially practical area, it is still possible, though rare, eventually to get a good job without paper qualifications.

A-level and graduate entry: see **Training**.

The work
Catering is the umbrella term for providing accommodation and/or food and drink services. A growth industry, it now employs over a million people. It covers several overlapping branches and a vast array of totally different types of concern. The main branches are: *hotels* – vast number of small ones, small number of large and/or luxury ones, motels, pubs; *restaurants* – all types, sizes and standards; *industrial catering* – staff canteens, restaurants and overlapping with *contract catering*; *school catering*; *college* and *university catering*; *hospital catering*. Catering in the last four is also called '*institutional management*' (see below, p. 106), but there is not necessarily any greater difference between jobs in commercial and in institutional (i.e. non-profit-making) catering than there is between individual jobs *within* commercial and *within* 'institutional' catering. The continued use of 'institutional management' owes more to tradition than to logic. The difference is in emphasis on various aspects rather than in operation and management methods.

There is no need to specialize in one branch of catering at the outset; people switch from one to the other. But for senior hotel management, training and experience in food and drink service *as well as* in accommodation services is necessary; for non-residential catering, experience of accommodation services is *not* necessary. Job titles often mean very little: two jobs with the same title may involve totally different tasks and levels of responsibility. Though catering does not have a clear-cut career structure, there are basically several rather vague and overlapping levels of skilled work: *craft level*: cooking, housekeeping, junior reception, etc.; *supervising* a small number of people doing cooking, housework, etc.; *junior to middle management*:

in charge of a section or department in hotel, restaurant, etc.; and *senior management*.

In senior management, work often overlaps with other managerial jobs and does not necessarily involve any contact with the public (the reason which brings most entrants into this industry). Senior managers in a hotel or restaurant chain may, for example, work entirely at head office; in industrial catering they may be responsible for a group of catering units, visit individual managers and liaise with head office; or they may investigate latest 'catering systems' (see p. 100). Job content varies not only according to catering branch but also according to type and size of hotel, restaurant, canteen, etc. Concerns range from the small and/or old-fashioned hotel run by an individual with total disregard for current catering practice, to units and chains run on sophisticated management principles with the latest technological aids.

The majority of catering jobs (except industrial and schools) involve work at 'unsocial hours', i.e. while customers are enjoying themselves. Success in all jobs (except at craft level) depends largely on other people's work: motivating others to do their jobs well, and efficient utilization of equipment and deployment of staff are essential catering management functions.

INDUSTRIAL CATERING

This covers the provision of meals – snacks to dinners – at places of work. Meal service is provided either by catering staff employed by the organization itself, or, increasingly, by *catering contractors*. These supply a number of clients with a complete meal service, running 'catering units' on the premises in factories, offices, universities, boarding schools, holiday camps, motorway restaurants, at airports, and, with mobile units, on racecourses, agricultural shows, film locations, etc. Catering contractors' staff can change the setting in which they work without having to change employers. Senior managers are in charge of a number of units; most staff work on the same premises regularly for a period.

The unit manager's job is administrative. She only cooks herself if fewer than about 20 meals are being served. Her main task normally is organizing the staff's work and timetable so as to achieve as even a flow of work as possible – though in the nature of meal services, peaks and valleys of activity and therefore occasional frayed tempers are unavoidable. Other main management tasks include: *menu-planning* – the complexity of this varies enormously according to the range of meals to be provided, from a narrow range of unexciting standard dishes to a wide selection including directors' dining-room 'specials', and according to the importance attached to nutritional values and tight budget control. Caterers must be able to provide at least 2 weeks' changing menus within several given price ranges and at different grades of sophistication. *Costing* – ingredients, labour costs, etc. *Purchasing*, which includes negotiating with suppliers and setting out 'specifications' detailing, for example, the uniform size and weight of the lamb chops in an order of several hundreds.

Managers normally attend meetings with directors and/or personnel manager and also discuss improvements or complaints with staff representatives. They are expected to keep up with technological developments and may be responsible for, or advise on, purchasing new equipment; but that work may also be done by specialists on a consultancy basis. Managers are usually responsible for, or for advising on, table arrangements, type of service, equipment and other maintenance.

In industrial catering, unlike most types, working hours are the usual ones. There is normally no evening and weekend work (although some industrial caterers work mainly at weekends).

There is a wide choice of jobs: from preparing sophisticated snacks for a West End showroom, or a dozen *haute cuisine* lunches for partners in a stockbroker's office with the help of one or two assistants, to running a large self-service canteen or a factory's several staff dining-rooms and feeding up to 2,000 a day with the help of a staff of 50 – including 2 or 3 assistant managers.

SCHOOL CATERING SERVICE

Much the same as in industrial catering, with special emphasis on catering for children's tastes, and nutritional values.

After training, caterers supervise the preparation of dinners, either at individual school kitchens or at centres from which up to 1,000 meals are distributed in insulated container vans to a number of schools – altogether about 6,000,000 meals a day. (But this is not the same as 'Systems Catering', see p. 100.)

Promotion is to school meals organizer, advising on buying, planning, staffing, kitchen management, nutrition, etc. Organizers cover part of or the whole of a local education authority area and do a good deal of travelling. Some kitchens are antiquated; some up-to-date.

School meals staff are employed by local education authorities, not by individual heads of schools, with whom, however, they work in close cooperation. They do not, as a rule, have anything to do with supervising children during meal-times. During school holidays such work as stock-taking is carried out; in depressed areas a skeletal meal service is often provided during holidays.

RESTAURANT MANAGEMENT

Basically the same tasks. The range of eating places (and hence the variety of types of job) is even greater, ranging from coffee bar and speciality house where only a few dishes are served (and perhaps cooked in full view of customers or supplied from central sources) to large 'popular' and to exclusive *haute cuisine* restaurants. Restaurant managers must know how to attract and keep customers. Budgeting is often not as tight as in industrial and institutional catering. Menu-planning complexity depends on type of restaurants, with special scope for culinary creativity, for example, in vegetarian and in luxury restaurants, for management skills in narrow-range large or chain restaurants.

Catering for fluctuating numbers of customers with the minimum of waste is a highly skilled job. Rush hours tend to be more hectic than in industrial catering because it is impossible to have enough staff for busy days without being overstaffed on slack ones, except by the employment of casual or part-time staff, which creates additional problems.

Managers' responsibilities vary greatly according to type and size of restaurant. For example, if the restaurant is one of a chain, overall planning and ordering may be done at head office; in other places the manager may be given a very free hand to 'give the restaurant that personal touch', as long as she keeps menus within a given price-range and reaches the minimum profit target.

According to type of restaurant, managers spend varying amounts of time on 'customer contact'. Except in lunch-only restaurants, working hours, though not necessarily longer, are more spread out, with some evening and weekend work.

Pub ('Licensed House') *Management* is almost invariably done by married couples. It is a way of life rather than a job, as it means being tied to the bar during licensing hours, 7 days a week. Most managers work for breweries which own pubs; some own or manage 'free' houses. Work involves purchasing, stock- and record-keeping as well as bar service. Thorough knowledge of licensing laws is essential. Interest in entertainment trends and more than just a 'liking for people' of all kinds are essential. Specialist training and experience in bar and cellar work required.

In some leisure centres (holiday camps, race courses, etc.), bar staff are the licensees and have their own 'franchise' – they run their own bars, i.e. instead of working for a salary they 'rent' the bar on the premises.

HOSPITAL CATERING OFFICER

Basically again same tasks; hospital catering officers organize provision of meals for patients and staff, which means meals for between 200 and 3,000 people, many of whom are on the premises (and need meals) round the clock. They usually prepare diets under the overall direction but not day-to-day supervision of dietitians. Unlike other catering managers who may have learnt largely on-the-job, hospital catering staffs (management level) invariably have had systematic specialist training. This is the only catering specialization with a career structure (apart from school meals). At the top *catering advisers* work as National Health Service Regional Officers (see Health Service Administration, p. 206), i.e. not actually in hospitals. They advise on planning kitchens, catering technologies (see Systems Catering, below), staff training and staffing requirements, etc. *Catering managers* are responsible for the catering arrangements in a group of hospitals. *Catering officers* are responsible for provision of meals in individual hospitals. (See Dietetics, p. 155, for dietitian catering officers.)

Assistant and *Deputy Catering Officers* are steps on the ladder to Catering Officer. In small hospitals, *catering supervisors* may be in charge of the whole catering operation; in larger hospitals they are responsible for a section.

Experience in hospital catering is very useful training for other specializations.

SYSTEMS CATERING

This is a new development, and a type of operation rather than a branch. Market research (see p. 270) identifies the most popular dishes within given price-ranges for given consumer-groups. Dishes are part- or fully prepared, and often even 'trayed up' in vast production kitchens. Then they are transported, usually frozen or chilled, in special transport to the 'point of consumption', which may be many miles away. Finally, at the point of consumption food is 'reconstituted', for example in an aircraft galley. That may mean instant cooking in convector or similar oven, or merely taking out of the container into which the dish was put in the production kitchen and serving.

Managers must understand the technologies involved and their effects on ingredients, and they must be good organizers, but 'reconstituting' the food means merely setting dials and turning knobs rather than cooking.

Production kitchens leave little scope for creative cooking; every dish is prepared to recipes specifying such details as the size, weight, colour and often even the position of meat or cucumber slices, of sprouts or strawberries. But in experimental kitchens where new dishes and technologies are tried out, the work combines advanced cooking skills, an understanding of the effects on the ingredients of being prepared in these unorthodox ways, and managerial skills.

At present, catering systems are used mainly by airlines, in some industrial and contract catering, and in chains of speciality houses. Their use is likely to spread.

There is also scope for *food technologists* (see p. 417) and specialists in management skills. Organizing transport of food and equipment; forward planning; equipment maintenance and sales are all fringe catering management occupations. Managers do not usually have much 'customer contact' in systems catering; some cover wide areas supervising various 'systems', others liaise with equipment manufacturers.

TRANSPORT CATERING

This is often done by catering contractors; increasingly 'catering systems' are used. In airline catering for example, all meals are prepared, and many 'trayed up' in production kitchens on or near airports, for consumption hundreds of miles away. Menu planning involves taking into account climatic conditions at point of consumption; commercial facts such as air commuters' 'menu-fatigue' (business people travel the same routes regularly; frequent menu changes must be made or customers are lost to the competition); research into which dishes and wines 'travel well'. *Airline catering* is very tightly cost-controlled; but in *marine catering* priorities are different: for passengers and crews at sea, meals are the highlight of the day. Proportionately more money is spent on food at sea than in the air, so sea-cooks and chefs have greater opportunities for creative cooking, and therefore for getting good shore-based jobs later.

Victualling ships – ordering supplies for trips sometimes several months long – is another catering specialization. Work is done in shipping companies' offices. Previous large-scale catering experience is essential.

MIDDLE MANAGEMENT AND SUPERVISORY POSTS

In all large-scale catering, assistants – various titles and various levels of responsibility – may be in charge of one catering function – purchasing, budgeting, food preparation for example – or of several functions. They are either trainees, or people who prefer not to or cannot train for top jobs, or fully-trained people waiting for better jobs.

PROFESSIONAL COOKS

A variety of openings at various levels of skill and responsibility. For example, in large-scale *haute cuisine*, a chef heads a hierarchy of assistant chefs, each responsible for one type of cooking – meat, vegetables, pastry, etc. The chef may be responsible for budgeting, buying, planning – or this may all be done by a food and beverage manager, or at head office; responsibilities depend on type and size of organization worked for. In small *haute cuisine* restaurants, 2 or 3 cooks may do all the work. In simpler restaurants, convenience foods are used extensively and cooks' ability to produce palatable, inexpensive yet reasonably varied menus is the most important aspect of the work. It is no easier than, but very different from, *haute cuisine*.

FREELANCE COOKS

For *directors' dining-room service*, one cook prepares up to about 12 lunches a day, single-handed. This may be part of the company's industrial catering unit with planning, shopping, etc., done centrally, or it is done by *freelance cooks*, who do their own planning, budgeting, shopping. They may have several lunch-time clients each requiring service on 1 or 2 days a week. Freelance cooks also cook for private dinner parties and, on a regular or occasional basis, they cook evening meals for families (one or several), usually to relieve working mothers of shopping and cooking chores. They need their own car to transport equipment and shopping. They must be able to budget and cook within various price-ranges. Sometimes they get jobs cooking for families on self-catering holidays abroad, and with travel agents' chalet-party package tours, working in ski resorts all winter, at the seaside all summer. This type of work usually includes general house-keeping.

Cooking still usually involves some physically hard work – the larger the kitchens, the tougher the job often is; but some large kitchens are highly mechanized. Even with modern design and equipment kitchens still tend to be hot, noisy, and damp, and at times very hectic. A lot of standing and some heavy lifting are inevitable.

In large kitchens there are many cooking jobs without managerial responsibilities, but anyone who wants to progress beyond the kitchen-hand stage must take systematic training; home-cooking experience is not enough. It is important to distinguish between courses for professional cooks and for *haute cuisine* for home cooking. Cookery classes and schools do not always make this difference quite clear.

Personal attributes   *For all catering (in varying degrees)*: organizing and administrative ability; ability to discuss matters with all types of people – unskilled kitchen staff and managing directors, salesmen and shop stewards, committee chairmen and colleagues; interest in people as well as in preparing food and in management; some manual dexterity and visual imagination; ability to remain unruffled in inevitable crises; physical stamina. For *Freelance Cooks*: as above, plus business acumen.

Hotel Management

MANAGER

The work The manager's work varies enormously according to size and type of hotel. In large hotels, the general manager is coordinator and administrator. Departmental managers are in charge of specialist services: reception, sales, food and bar service, housekeeping, etc. The manager deals with correspondence, has daily conferences with departmental managers and may be in touch daily or weekly with head office. Although she tries to be around to talk to guests (not only when they have complaints), most of her time is spent dealing with running the business side, making decisions based on information given her by accountants, personnel manager, sales manager, accommodation manager, etc.

She does not normally have to live in, though she may have a bedroom or flat on the premises. Her working hours are long, and often busiest at weekends and during holidays. Managers are expected to speak at least one foreign language. They must be able to switch from one task to another instantly, and change their daily routine when necessary – which it often is.

Among the manager's most important tasks: creating and maintaining good staff relations, as success depends entirely on the work done by others under her overall direction; giving the hotel the personality and the character which either the manager herself, or more often her employers, intend it to have; and being able to make a constantly changing clientele feel as though each of them mattered individually, though the extent of emphasis on personal service varies according to the type of hotel.

In small hotels the manager may have a staff of about 15 to 30, and instead of several departmental managers, possibly 1 general assistant. She often has to live in, and she usually has less off-duty time than managers in large hotels. There are *far* more small (and unglamorous) hotels than large or small luxury ones. Many small and medium-sized country hotels are owned by companies and run by married couples (who have little time off together). In the past the husband was invariably the manager, the wife assistant or housekeeper or receptionist. Under equal opportunity legislation, women must be given equal opportunities on companies' training schemes.

GENERAL ASSISTANT – ASSISTANT-MANAGER

The work In small hotels she helps wherever help is needed most – in the kitchen, in the bar, in housekeeping. Although the work is extremely hard, it is the best possible experience, some hotel managers say the only valuable experience – better than theoretical training (though the ideal is a sound basis of technical training complemented by experience). In large hotels she assists the manager and may be entirely responsible for certain departments: housekeeping, reception, food and drink service, etc. Some remain assistants, either by choice or because managers' jobs are not available.

An assistant departmental manager may be as responsible and as well paid as a general manager: it depends on size and type of hotel.

Personal attributes *For top jobs*: exceptional organizing ability and business acumen; outgoing personality; the wish to please people, however unreasonable customers' demands may seem; an interest in all the practical skills – cooking, bar-management, housekeeping, etc.; willingness to work while others play; ability to shoulder responsibility and handle staff; tact.

For assistants/managers of small hotels: partly as for Managers, but exceptional organizing ability is not necessary; instead, a liking for practical work is essential, and willingness to work hard and get things done without taking the credit.

RECEPTIONIST

The work Head receptionists are assisted in large and medium-sized hotels by junior receptionists. They keep the chart or 'bedroom-book', which shows at a glance provisional and definite bookings. To steer a course between unnecessary refusal of bookings and over-booking is skilled work. Receptionists deal with correspondence; they must be able to do straightforward book-keeping, type and compose their own letters: they notify other hotel departments of arrivals and departures, and keep the Tabular, or 'tab. sheet' (a ledger into which all charges are entered to the relevant room numbers), which involves collating chits handed to reception by the kitchen, hall porter, bar, etc., and transferring charges to guests' accounts and on to the Tabular. Many hotels have computerized reservations and accounts systems, which give instant information on a whole hotel group's vacancies; on guests' accounts; and possibly supply position regarding clean linen, beverages, etc.

Receptionists also act as general information office, answering guests' queries, such as train times, or the address of a good hairdresser. In motels, guests 'buy keys' as they arrive to rent a suite with garage for one night at a time. Receptionists explain the procedure and hand over the keys.

They work in or near (and sometimes do the flowers for) the entrance hall, and are always at the centre of activities. They work shifts. Especially in country hotels, they may live in; meals on duty are supplied free, sometimes in the restaurant, more often in the staff dining-room with other senior staff.

Head receptionists are usually responsible directly to the manager; theirs is considered one of the most important posts in the hotel business and can be a stepping stone to general management.

Personal attributes

A friendly, helpful personality; an uncritical liking for people of all types; a good memory for faces – visitors appreciate recognition; ability to take responsibility and to work well with others; considerable self-confidence; a methodical approach; a liking for figures; meticulous accuracy. *For top jobs*: business acumen; good judgement of people; leadership.

HOUSEKEEPER

The work

Except in small hotels, housekeepers do not do housework, but supervise domestic staff. Other duties include: checking rooms – for cleanliness, general comfort, bedside lamps, etc.; laundry – giving out clean linen, seeing to its repair and replacement; pass-key control; room service organization and supervision; discussions with heads of other departments; training and engaging staff and arranging work schedules. In a large hotel a head housekeeper may have a staff of 200 under her.

In small and medium-sized hotels the housekeeper may be responsible for choosing and maintaining the furnishings, decoration and general appearance of bedrooms and lounges. In large hotels there may be one assistant or floor housekeeper to every floor, or every two floors; the head housekeeper's job is therefore more onerous. She is immediately responsible to the manager.

Housekeepers generally only have direct contact with guests when there are complaints, or when special attention is needed – if guests fall ill, for example. Success depends largely on ensuring that the domestic staff do their work well.

There are similar housekeeping jobs in halls of residence and especially in the *Hospital Service*. Career structure is better in the latter than in hotels.

Personal attributes　　Organizing ability; practical approach; an eye for detail; practicality; ability to handle and train staff.

HOTEL SALES MANAGEMENT

A new fringe hotel management career. Hotel sales managers work for large hotels and hotel groups. They sell 'hotel facilities' – efficiency, service, atmosphere, as well as conference and banqueting facilities. A hotel sales manager for example may approach large business concerns and try to fix contracts for business executives to stay regularly at her hotels and, jointly with tour operators (see Travel, p. 499) and airlines etc., she 'builds' package tours.

No career structure or definite way in yet. Hotel sales managers come either via hotel management, or marketing (p. 270) or any other type of business experience. (H.N.D.s with Tourism specialization are useful preparation.)

Personal attributes　　Business acumen; numeracy; extrovert, friendly personality.

INSTITUTIONAL MANAGEMENT

The work　　This is management in non-profit-making, mainly residential establishments: college and university halls of residence, welfare homes and hostels; the domestic side of hospitals and of boarding-schools; as well as, increasingly, in commercial conference and training centres; also non-residential work: school catering service; meals on wheels; social service departments' day centres.

Managers may be called bursar, warden, domestic superintendent, organizer, institutional manager. Titles are arbitrary and do not indicate any particular level of responsibility, status or duties.

There are almost as many different types of 'institutions' as there are of hotels, and there is considerable overlap between catering and institutional management. The difference is one of emphasis and setting in which the work is done. Some jobs in institutional management have more in common with running a hotel – for example running a large conference or management training centre – than with other institutional management jobs, in which residents' general well-being and emotional needs as well as their creature comforts have to be considered (such as old people's homes, where the job is part catering, part social work). In hospital, institutional managers are level-pegging with senior nursing officers.

An institutional manager may be responsible for all or some of the following aspects of a community's creature comforts: general management; staff management; ordering, costing, menu-planning, and preparation and serving of meals; purchase and maintenance of kitchen and equipment; planning or having a say in the planning of additional building; choosing furnishings and decoration; overall budgeting for the running of the establishment; making arrangements, in establishments with long vacations, for residential conferences, vacation courses, etc.; dealing with residents' and staff's suggestions and complaints and taking action accordingly; helping to establish a friendly atmosphere both among staff and among residents; in small establishments, first-aid and home-nursing (but *not* responsibility for sick residents); taking minutes at meetings, drawing up agendas, etc.; acting as hostess and as general information bureau.

Most jobs are entirely administrative, but in small hostels and welfare institutions, and hospitals, the manager occasionally has to help out with housework or cooking. Many (by no means all) jobs are residential; accommodation varies from bedsitter to self-contained flat for couples (with spouse not necessarily working in the organization concerned).

Institutional managers are occasionally expected to spend a good deal of their time in the common or public rooms with the residents – the degree of privacy varies.

Assistant institutional managers – which may mean housekeepers – are usually beginners seeking experience or those unwilling or unable to take the more responsible jobs, but in large organizations, especially hospitals, it is a step on the ladder.

Personal attributes   A sociable temperament; a liking for and ability to get on with all kinds of people as well as a liking for things domestic; a practical approach; ability to handle staff and willingness to lend a hand wherever necessary; calmness in crises; disregard of criticism – institutional managers are often blamed for domestic hitches beyond their control.

Prospects   Good in all branches and occupations. The higher the level of management, the stiffer the competition, however. There is no rigid career structure, except in hospitals and school catering. Promotion depends on a combination of qualifications, experience, individual organizations' management development policy, personality and mobility: experience in variety of type of establishment is essential for work with some large companies.

Pay: Varies. The luxury hotels do not necessarily offer better-paid or more varied jobs than large limited-menu restaurant chains.

Training   This is rather haphazard with a variety of courses and qualifications. Large catering organizations now often expect specific qualifications for the various levels and types of jobs, but there is still no universally applicable career structure. Below degree level entry, on-the-job training, with day- or block-release, is probably as useful a preparation for advancement as full-time training. But day-release is not easily granted in catering and employment *without* day-/block-release is not recommended.

1 Pre-entry courses

1. For entrants with at least O-levels in English, mathematics and a science: 2 year full-time courses for T.E.C. Diploma (see p. xl) in *Hotel, Catering, Institutional Management and Food Technology*. Students take 'core units', which give them a broad-based catering training, and special option units to prepare them for a specific aspect of catering. T.E.C. Diploma leads to 'technician' level, i.e. practical/supervisory-jobs, but a first job depends on the individual, type of organization and supply and demand.

NOTE: T.E.C. minimum entry requirements (see p. xl) are lower than 3 O-levels, but colleges set their own entry requirements and as T.E.C. Diplomas are replacing former O.N.D.s (which required 4 O-levels) colleges do not feel they can lower entry requirements further (see Craft courses below).

2. For entrants with *either* 1 A-level (and possibly another subject *studied* to A-level) and 3 O-levels (including English, mathematics and a science) *or* with a T.E.C. Diploma (with relevant option units): 2-year full-time or 3-year sandwich T.E.C. Higher Diploma courses. T.E.C. Higher awards probably lead to junior/middle management jobs.

3. For entrants with at least 2 A-levels and 3 O-levels (including English, mathematics and a science and, for some courses, a modern language (whether a T.E.C. Diploma is acceptable in lieu of A-levels depends on relevance of units studied – there is no blanket acceptance as with old O.N.D.)): 3-year full-time or 4-year sandwich degree courses. These vary in emphasis on various catering aspects but include supervision of food and beverage preparation (and some practical work); catering management principles and practices; catering technologies (for example, equipment and processes used in 'fast food' restaurants, 'systems catering'); specialist work such as airline catering; sales management and marketing; accounting; computer application; the various aspects of tourism; the implications of the growing recreation and leisure industries.

4. For graduates with *either* a relevant degree or comparable qualification, *or* any degree plus proof of interest in/experience of catering: 1-

year full-time courses for post-graduate diplomas (old H.N.D./C.s are acceptable too, T.E.C. Higher awards *may* be).

Both catering degrees and post-graduate diplomas lead to exemption from Professional Examinations of Hotel Catering and Institutional Management Association (H.C.I.M.A.), the professional hotel and catering organization.

II Courses for people in relevant employment

1. For entrants with *either* 4 O-levels (including subjects demonstrating command of English and numeracy and a science) *or* with 3 years' relevant work with experience and at least 2 years' part-time study: 2 year part-time day- or block-release course for H.C.I.M.A. Part A examination, leading to H.C.I.M.A. membership.

2. For students with at least 12 months' responsible work in the industry and, usually, Part A H.C.I.M.A. Part B (former Final) examination: 1-year full-time, 2-year sandwich or 3-year day- or block-release course. (Whether T.E.C. awards will qualify for entry to Part B courses will not be known until T.E.C. courses have run for some years.)

NOTE: It is usually possible to study for T.E.C. awards by full- or part-time study but very few colleges run part-time T.E.C. catering courses.

3. Mainly for people in relevant employment with few or no O-levels: 2-year part-time City and Guilds Craft Certificates in *General Catering*, *Basic Cookery* and various other hotel/catering subjects such as *Housekeeping/Cleaning Science*, *Food Service* and *Reception*. In some colleges City and Guilds courses are also available full-time. These courses may also qualify, with experience, for T.E.C. and H.C.I.M.A. courses.

In some Further Education Colleges and 6th forms, City and Guilds foundation courses combine general educational subjects with an insight into, or preparation for, jobs in the broad hotel and catering area. No entry qualifications.

Personal attributes

For all catering management (in varying degrees): organizing and administrative ability; ability to discuss matters with all types of people – unskilled kitchen staff and managing directors, salesmen and shop stewards, committee chairmen and colleagues; interest in people as well as in preparing food, and in management; a certain amount of manual dexterity and visual imagination; the sort of temperament which remains unruffled in inevitable crises; physical stamina.

Position of women

Traditionally, and illogically, catering and hotel-keeping (not institutional management) have been a man's world. In hotels until very recently there were hardly any women above departmental or assistant or small-hotel management. As yet no woman is manager of any of the well-known large luxury hotels; very few are near the top. Women traditionally only run hotels in which there is no management hierarchy. To break the tradition, women have to be exceptionally well qualified and they must be mobile: companies say that the reason for not promoting more women is that women are not willing to gain varied experience by moving around the country.

This is a career area where discrimination is difficult to prove; qualifications do not always prove suitability for individual jobs.

In up-market restaurants, men are traditionally managers; women chefs are still very rare indeed, and most managers have *been* chefs at least for a time. In large commercial kitchens, most of the staff are men, but in school and hospital kitchens, where the work is just as arduous, there are mainly women cooks.

In industrial catering, women are beginning to have equal chances at all management levels. In hospitals, institutional-management-trained women have top jobs in domestic management, but top catering officers – concerned with food and drink, not housekeeping – are more frequently men. Schools and institutional catering managers are usually women. The fact that women do hold large-scale catering management jobs in some areas shows that it is only tradition which has kept them out of other catering management areas.

Career-break: No problem in institutional management for women who can live in and/or work irregular hours; nor in industrial and schools catering.

Refresher training: Most catering courses can be adapted.

Late start: No problem. Admission to courses depends on experience and motivation rather than age and G.C.E.s. 6-month and 1-year catering courses are available under T.O.P.S. (see p. xl).

Part-time: Very limited opportunities at management level, good opportunities at craft level (i.e. cooking, housekeeping, junior reception). Freelance catering offers possibilities.

Further information   The Hotel, Catering and Institutional Management Association, 191 Trinity Road, Tooting, London SW17
Hotel and Catering Industry Training Board, P.O. Box 18, Ramsey House, Central Square, Wembley, Middlesex HA9 7AP

Related careers   *Dietitian – Food Technology – Home Economics – Services (Catering Corps) – Teaching (Housecraft) – Travel Agent and Tour Operator*

CHIROPODY

Private practice – hospitals and health authorities – industry

Entry quali-
fications
Minimum age 18. 2 A-levels and 3 O-levels.

The work
Chiropodists diagnose and treat foot diseases and functional and constitutional foot disorders; they inspect children's and adults' feet to prevent minor ailments from growing into major ones. When patients need their shoes adapted, chiropodists give the necessary instructions to surgical shoemakers or shoe-repairers; they also construct special appliances themselves. Chiropodists can choose the environment in which to work:

1. *Private practice*: This is the most remunerative work. The chiropodist treats patients in her own home and, occasionally, may visit patients in their homes. Private practice can be lonely work (even though patients are seen all day) but group practices are now being set up in some areas, partners renting premises jointly or using rooms in one of the partner's homes as a surgery.

2. *Hospitals and area health authority clinics*: Chiropodists are employed on a sessional (3-hourly) basis or full-time.

3. *Industry*: Concerns where staff are on their feet all day often employ full- or part-time chiropodists.

   In both (2) and (3) chiropodists enjoy the companionship and social facilities of a large organization. Some combine part-time work with private practice, to have a small regular income which supplements private practice income.

Prospects
Good, but private practice may diminish. In employment, only fair chances of promotion to senior appointments.

Pay: Medium (see p. xxiii).

Training
For State Registration, which is essential, 3 years, full-time, at chiropody schools which prepare students for the Society of Chiropodists' examinations. Two-thirds of the training is practical and includes treatment of patients under the supervision of experienced chiropodists, the preparation of appliances and shoe-fitting. The theoretical training includes the life sciences, anatomy, physiology. Candidates must make

sure that a chosen course is recognized by the Society of Chiropodists (the Society is the qualifying body); other courses are useless.

Personal attributes
A high degree of manual dexterity; ability to get on with people greatly affects chances of promotion and of having a flourishing private practice. However, unlike many other careers with patients, a shy, retiring woman may get on well, providing she is even-tempered.

Position of women
At the moment, 53% of practising chiropodists, and 63% of students, are women. Proportionately there are more men than women in senior jobs and in private practice.

Career-break: No problem if kept up with developments. Reduced 'non-practising membership' subscriptions are available.

Refresher courses: *Ad hoc* arrangements with 1 month 'up-dating' can be made.

Late start: Good opportunities, with relaxations in G.C.E. requirements. Upper age 45. 15% of entrants are over 25.

Part-time: Ample scope for work, no part-time training.

Further information
The Society of Chiropodists, 8 Wimpole Street, London W1M 8BX
The Institute of Chiropodists, 59 Gloucester Place, London W1

Related careers
Physiotherapy

CIVIL AVIATION

Air traffic control officer – cabin crew – ground staff – pilot

1. Air Traffic Control Officer

Entry quali-
fications
5 G.C.E.s including English language and maths; 2 must be at A-level, of which one must be maths, geography or a science subject. Many entrants are *graduates*.

The work
Teams of A.T.C.O.s control the movement of aircraft when taking off, *en route*, and when coming in to land. They regulate the flow of traffic on routes through a particular portion of airspace. When an aircraft is planned to leave a particular Air Traffic Control Centre's airspace, an A.T.C.O. coordinates the flight details (position, speed, etc.) with colleagues in the adjacent A.T.C.C., which may be another U.K. airport or a European Centre. Captains of aircraft are in fact in two-way radio communication with a series of air traffic control officers from the moment they request permission to start engines till the moment they stop engines at their destination.

On any particular day or night shift an A.T.C.O. deals with either aerodrome, approach or airways control. The work is enormously responsible and very highly skilled. It involves, for example, the safe 'stacking' of aircraft in the airport's 'holding area' until there is approach and ground space for each to start the landing sequence; and it involves ensuring that aircraft flying along the same routes at different speeds and in different directions preserve safe distances, horizontally and vertically, at all times. In making the necessary mathematical calculations the A.T.C.O. is assisted by computers, and must know what data the computer should be fed with (see Computing, p. 134).

An A.T.C.O. spends most of her time sitting – wearing earphones – in front of a radar tube or display board which gives details of aircrafts' position and flight path. The international air-traffic language is English, so the A.T.C.O. talks, and is talked to, in her own language, but foreign pilots, especially when they are under pressure, do not always speak English very clearly. The A.T.C.O. must make up her mind quickly and ask the pilot to repeat anything she does not understand.

All A.T.C.O.s must be willing to do shift work. In emergencies duties can be changed at the last moment.

Prospects Fair.

      Pay: Good.

Training 2¾-year course, including a period at the College of Air Traffic Control (Bournemouth) and at A.T.C. units. Training includes flying up to private pilot licence standard, all aspects of air-traffic control, meteorology, navigation, telecommunication, principles of radar and associated techniques.

Personal attributes A cool and calm temperament and the ability to feel or at least show no excitement whatever in emergencies; ability to concentrate; a good and quick brain; indifference to being the only woman in a large group of men; ability to work as one of a team.

Position of women About 3% of A.T.C.O.s and about 10% of A.T.C.O.s in training are women. The proportion is small only because so few women apply for training: a slightly *higher* proportion of women than men applicants is in fact accepted for training.

Career-break: In theory, retraining is given to women who want to come back; it is too early to say how this will work in practice.

Late start: Acceptance for training up to 34 for people with relevant experience only.

Further information Air Traffic Control Service, Room T 1223, Space House, 43/59 Kingsway, London WC2B 6TE

Related careers *Pilot – Scientist*

---

2. Cabin Crew
(Stewardess and Steward)

Entry qualifications Minimum age usually 18.

No qualifications laid down; usually O-level standard (not passes) in English and one European language, some catering or nursing experience, or 1 year in a responsible job which involved dealing with people.

The work   The cabin crew welcome passengers, supervise seating and safety-belt arrangements, and look after air-sick travellers, babies, and children travelling alone. Stewards and stewardesses serve meals (but do not cook them), and sell drinks and cigarettes in a variety of currencies.

They 'dress the plane' to see that blankets, head-rests, magazines, cosmetics, etc. are available and in good order, and make necessary announcements over the public-address system. They deal with any emergencies and write reports after each flight, with comments, for instance, on the behaviour of unaccompanied children.

Most of the time cabin crews are airborne waiters and waitresses. From the moment seat-belts are unfastened they are continuously busy, working at great speed in a confined space.

Duty hours vary from one airline to another and are likely to be changed at the last minute because of weather and other 'exigencies of the service'. Normally on European routes cabin crews are 'on' for 4–6 days with a good deal of night duty; they are then off-duty for 2–4 days. On long-distance trips they may be away from home for 3 weeks, but that would include several days' rest at a foreign airport.

The farther the destination, the more chance of sightseeing. On short routes cabin crews may fly backwards and forwards for a month without seeing more than the airport at their destination. On long-distance trips crews often change planes at 'slip-points' and stay for a few days' rest, living in luxury hotels at their airline's expense.

To transfer from European to transatlantic routes entails finding a job with another airline. Transfer to an independent or foreign airline is easier after working with British Airways than vice versa.

Prospects   Vary according to economic climate. British-trained crews are in demand by American and other foreign airlines if they speak the appropriate language.

Pay: Medium (see p. xxiii).

Training   About 6 weeks with Europe-only airlines to about 8 with transatlantic ones. Subjects include meal-service, first-aid, airborne procedure, emergency drill with swimming-bath lesson in the use of the inflatable dinghy and life-jacket.

Personal attributes   An attractive appearance; a likeable personality; calmness in crises; common sense; efficiency.

Position of women   See p. 117.

Further information   Individual air travel companies.

3. Ground Staff (some examples)

(a) PASSENGER SERVICE ASSISTANT (titles vary)

Entry qualifications Usually O-level standard English and mathematics and geography. Minimum age usually 18.

The work Passenger service assistants see that passengers and luggage get on to the right plane, with the minimum of fuss. They check-in luggage, which involves checking travel documents; check-out passengers at boarding gate. They answer passengers' questions on travel connections and similar matters.

Other duties carried out by experienced P.S.A.s include: load-control – preparing information for aircraft loaders on luggage weight; cargo documentation for Customs clearance; checking that planes leave with the right meals, cargo, baggage.

P.S.A.s work in uniform, and do shift work. They move about the airport all day, rarely sit down.

(b) SALES STAFF (again titles vary)

Entry qualifications Usually O-level standard English, mathematics, geography, a foreign language.

The work Sales staff sit in airport offices and answer questions on international flight connections; make fare calculations (in various currencies), sell tickets over the counter and over the phone. Bookings are made to and from all over the world; each reservation must be related to reservations made elsewhere and reservation vacancies available for any particular flight at any given moment. This is called 'space control'. Reservations staff use computerized information systems: at the push of a button they can see, on their computer terminal, exactly what the present reservation situation is on any flight.

Senior sales staff may call on travel agents, business houses and other important customers to explain special travel schemes, and 'sell' their own particular airline, both passenger and cargo services.

Sales staff may do shift work, though less so in senior positions.

Training (a) and (b) Short on-the-job training with some lectures.

Personal attributes An orderly mind; a liking for meeting people very briefly; a calm, helpful manner; good speech and appearance.

(c) COMMERCIAL MANAGEMENT; FLIGHT OPERATIONS AND FLIGHT PLANNING

Entry quali-fications
Vary with different airlines and according to supply and demand. Considerable A-level and graduate entry for traineeships. Some promotion from sales staff.

The work
The administration of flight programmes, which cover many thousands of flight-miles, millions of tons of freight and ever-growing 'passenger throughput' is a highly complex undertaking. Staff organize the airline's fleet of planes over its network, making the most efficient use of each aircraft, e.g., ensuring that as far as possible outgoing freight is replaced with return-flight freight, and that the 'turn-round' time on airports is as short as possible, while allowing time for maintenance, loading, etc. 'Aircrew management' involves arranging individual crew members' schedules, taking into consideration maximum flying hours allowed; rest-days ('stop overs') abroad, etc.

Apart from this planning work, staff are also responsible for ensuring that at all times aircrew have all the information they need before each take-off, throughout the planned itinerary. This involves discussions with a variety of departments and individuals; keeping detailed records, being prepared for emergencies.

Prospects
Vary according to economic climate.

Pay: Low to medium (see p. xxiii).

Training (c)
Through airlines' own training schemes, lasting 2 to 3 years, *or* B.E.C. Higher Awards or degree, followed by shorter airline training. Schemes vary between companies and according to expansion or contraction rate of airline industry.

Personal attributes
Drive, organizing ability, indifference to breaking new ground in what used to be an all-male job. Liking for working under pressure.

Position of women
Air stewardesses and stewards are all 'cabin crew'; now a woman can be senior stewardess in charge of an aircraft's cabin crew. *Groundstaff* examples: traditionally mainly women. *Commercial Management*: So far very few women have tried. For equal chances of promotion beyond middle level they have to be better all round than the men with whom they compete.

**Further in-   There is no central organization; main British airline: British Airways,
formation**   P.O. Box 10, Heathrow Airport, Hounslow, Middlesex. Addresses of
                  other airlines through usual travel agencies and newspapers.

**Related   *Linguist – Management, Hotels and Catering – Travel Agent*
careers**

4. Pilot

**Entry quali-   2 A-levels and 3 O-levels; subjects must include mathematics and
fications**   English language, and either physics or chemistry or physical science;
                  in practice 1 scientific subject at A-level.
                  Graduates, preferably in science or engineering, stand the best chance
                  of acceptance. Upper age limit: 26 (25 for Helicopter Training Scheme).

The work   The pilot's most taxing task is assimilating a mass of separate bits of
                  information presented to her by an array of indicators on the instrument
                  panel, and by colleagues, to 'process' it in her mind, and to take whatever
                  action may be necessary. Procedures during the flight and specially
                  during take-off and landing are complex enough, but what makes the
                  pilot's job the arduous one it is is the fact that she must at all times be
                  prepared for the unexpected. Instrument failure may require her,
                  instantly, to override whatever the computerized equipment's instruc-
                  tions are, or evasive action may have to be taken to avoid a mid-air
                  collision. Throughout her working life a pilot probably never has to
                  cope with such 'incidents', but she must be *able* to do so.
                  Her first job for at least 2½ years is as co-pilot. Then, as pilot, she has
                  total responsibility for the aircraft, crew, passengers. Navigators are now
                  rarely employed, and flight engineers not on all aircraft: the pilot must
                  in any case be able to perform navigating and engineering tasks.
                  Her work starts at least an hour before take-off, when she either
                  prepares her own or is presented with a detailed flight plan. This gives
                  such information as exact height at various stages on her precisely
                  defined route; meteorological information; take-off and landing weights
                  which are vital data in case of emergency action.
                  On 'short hauls' (in Europe) pilot and crew are busy all the time. On
                  long hauls there can be long hours with only routine checks to go
                  through. This can be difficult in an unexpected way: pilots get bored,
                  because there is no real work to do, yet the need for alertness is as great
                  as ever.

Prospects   In the 1980s, when the last of the war-time pilots – who make up a large proportion of present pilots – retire, demand was expected to increase. However, because of the world-wide recession this increase has not materialized. There is some small demand for other types of pilots (plane or helicopter): on air taxis; crop spraying; aerial photography; oil rig supplying; weather and traffic observation; flying privately or company-owned planes and helicopters, and especially for instructors in flying clubs. In recent years a few pilots have managed to pay for their own initial training and then 'built up' the number of flying hours needed to be eligible for a Commercial Pilot's Licence (see **Training**) while working as instructor.

   Pay: High (see p. xxiii).

Training   The overwhelming majority of students at the recognized air training schools are sponsored, but the only regular sponsor of any number of pilots, British Airways, has discontinued its sponsorship schemes for the time being. Basic training lasts at least 20 months for non-graduate entrants, about 1 year for graduates. The syllabus includes aerodynamics, meteorology, electrical engineering and electronics, aircraft design and systems, flight procedures and aviation law. Flight training starts on the ground, in simulators.

   The first qualification is the Commercial Pilot's Licence (C.P.L.), but to fly in an airliner as co-pilot the basic requirement is the C.P.L. plus Instrument Rating. Ratings are qualifications in particular aspects of flying and in flying particular types of aircraft; the types of aircraft a C.P.L. holder may co-pilot depend on her Ratings. Before a pilot is qualified as Captain of an airliner she must have the Airline Transport Pilot's Licence (A.T.P.L.) and many thousands of flying hours.

   Full-time, non-sponsored training to C.P.L. costs over £20,000 but quite a lot of people now get only a Private Pilot's Licence (P.P.L.). They then gain sufficent hours to take an Instructor's Course; as Instructors they are paid and they can accumulate the 700 hours' flying-time necessary to qualify for exemption from the full-length, full-time C.P.L. training. This roundabout way of qualifying is *very* much cheaper and can be done while, most of the time, earning a living in part-time employment.

Personal attributes   Above-average intelligence; ability to fight boredom and be alert at all times; mental agility; self-confidence; leadership qualities; ability to take instant decisions; total unflappability; very well balanced personality; desire to break down traditional sex-barriers.

Position of women

There were 12 women commercial pilots in 1980 (including 6 captains); a few more worked on air taxis, crop spraying, etc., and especially as instructors in flying clubs. Once trained, women have no more problems getting jobs (*outside airlines*) than men. But despite the Sex Discrimination Act it is unlikely that women will have equal opportunities as airline pilots for a long time to come, as many men learn flying in the Services, and companies say that all pilots must be able to work on all routes and in some destination countries there is no accommodation or provision for, and/or reluctance to deal with, women pilots.

The British Women Pilots Association has about 200 members and helps with advice and (small) scholarships (Hon. Sec.: Mrs M. E. Tucker, B.A. Terminus, P.O. Box 13, London, S.W.1.).

British Airways opened its training sponsorship scheme to girls in 1977, but none has been sponsored yet.

Further information

Civil Aviation Authority, FCL 3, Aviation House, 129 Kingsway, London WC2B 6NN

British Women Pilots Association (address above)

Related careers

Air Traffic Control Officer – Engineering – Surveying

CIVIL SERVICE

The Civil Service is Britain's largest employer. It offers opportunities at all educational levels, in virtually all career fields. There is a tradition of training and encouragement to use day-release facilities which enables ambitious entrants to proceed in easy stages up the Civil Service hierarchy.

For *graduates* the Civil Service has one of the most sophisticated training programmes anywhere.

There are two main categories of entrants:

(a) Specialists with professional or other qualifications or skills, who follow the career for which they trained *before* joining the Civil Service. They include architects, economists, psychologists, scientists, engineers, librarians; and also secretaries, typists, caterers (details under individual career headings).

(b) A large group of school-leavers and graduates. According to their education qualifications they enter one of the general Civil Service groups or grades.

This section deals mainly with the second category – the non-specialists.

The work The type of work done is immensely varied: virtually every facet of contemporary life has some connection with a government department; only a few examples of the vast number of subjects dealt with by Civil Servants can be given. In the Home Office, for example, staff, at any level, might be concerned with the administration of prison and borstal management and reform; or with the award of orders and other decorations. The Central Office of Information is concerned with projecting Britain's image abroad through films and feature articles on life in Britain and British institutions, and it also produces reference and publicity material for use in this country on anything from home safety to new methods of bee-keeping. In the Department of the Environment staff liaise with local authorities on, for example, housing policies and environmental health matters and traffic policies. The Department of Education and Science is concerned with the overseeing of the work of local education authorities, and is responsible for long-term policy on the expansion of museums, art galleries, sports facilities, and with various research councils. The Department of Industry organizes research into science and technology and its application to industry. It runs laboratories and over 100 research establishments. Other Ministries deal with transport, defence, agriculture, etc. In the

Training Services and Employment Service Divisions – parts of the Manpower Services Commission – Civil Servants are concerned with the efficient use of manpower and productivity. They deal with training and re-training needs and activities, with industrial tribunals, with giving job information and guidance to school-leavers, mid-career changers and to women who want to return to work. At executive level, Department of Employment Civil Servants are in contact with the general public at job centres and employment offices; at administrative level, the work is mainly policy-making, at regional and central offices.

Most vacancies up to and including O-level standard candidates are filled by departments recruiting locally. Others are filled by admission (see below) into a 'grade'. Candidates can express a preference for any particular Department, and the Civil Service does its best to fit them in. It is possible to transfer from one Department to another later on.

The atmosphere in individual offices depends as much on the person in charge as it does in any department in any large organization. As a rule, public servants do not work under as much pressure as many people in industry, but the work is no less stimulating. At administration trainee (see below) level and above it is likely to be intellectually more challenging: complex policy matters are discussed and the consequences of alternative decisions and policies assessed. An important difference between Civil Service and private-sector management careers: Civil Servants are always primarily advisers – someone higher up and finally a Minister takes the final decision; in industry, executives at comparable level are more likely to be responsible for the consequences of their own decisions.

Social and welfare facilities vary in extent and quality, but they always exist. Sports grounds and social clubs are available in larger centres. Civil Servants working away from home are helped with accommodation problems. Canteen facilities or luncheon vouchers are usually provided.

Holidays are often better than in industry. 4 weeks is usual, even for most of the junior staff; 6 weeks for those in the highest posts. Most Civil Servants work a 5-day week.

1. ADMINISTRATION TRAINEE (leading to Principal, and then up senior administrative hierarchy)

Entry quali-fications   *Maximum* age: 28.

Honours or post-graduate degree. Degree subject is immaterial. In the past senior Civil Servants usually had arts degrees; now the need for relevant, expert knowledge in top-level administration is generally accepted, science and technological qualifications are greatly welcomed.

Method of entry and training: Written examination and series of tests and interviews, lasting 3½ days in all, at Civil Service Selection Board. Successful candidates are told the initial estimate of their potential at the time of selection; this assessment is progressively revised. Trainees spend 2 to 4 years (the first 2 are probationary) in this grade and during that time they have several 'postings' to different types of work and 4 to 5 months of formal training at the Civil Service College. Throughout the trainee period they are supervised, and encouraged to put forward ideas and take decisions.

The work   Senior Civil Servants are responsible, under Ministers, for policy-making and laying down broad lines of organization and development. In an industrial or commercial organization this would be the function of senior executives. They advise Ministers on policy, and are often involved in legislation which gives effect to that policy. They assemble material for Ministers' speeches in the House and draft replies to Parliamentary questions. They reply to letters from M.P.s about the work of the Department, and may represent the Department in negotiations with other governments, other Departments, outside organizations, and occasionally members of the public.

Prospects   Good for promotion up the Civil Service hierarchy. Administrative Civil Servants become responsible for controlling progressively larger and/or more important sections of the work of their Department. The proportion of desk and paper work, of dealing with committees and attending meetings with other Civil Servants and/or people outside varies greatly between and within Departments. Administrative Civil Servants may switch Departments, but more often they move on to different sections within their Department. Individuals' preferences and abilities are taken into consideration.

Pay: High (see p. xxiii).

Personal attributes   High intelligence; capacity to grasp all issues involved in a problem and to weigh up facts, conflicting opinions and advice, to make decisions; ability to extract the main points from a mass of detail and to write balanced and concise reports; ability to hold and delegate authority; the art of inspiring loyalty, stimulating and guiding enthusiasm; tact for dealing with Ministers, staff and outside parties; enjoyment of responsibility.

2. EXECUTIVE OFFICER

Entry quali-
fications

Maximum age: 44.

Two A-levels and 3 O-levels in approved subjects which must include English or English language, or promotion from Clerical Officer grade. A large proportion of entrants are *graduates*.
Method of entry: Competitive interview and tests.

The work

Executive officers are either 'general executives' or 'departmental executives'. Departmental executives are only employed in certain Departments and have special titles, for example Immigration Officer (see p. 216).

General executives work in most Departments. Their work varies widely. An executive officer may be in charge of a group of clerical officers assisting more senior officers, or she may be responsible for work of her own. This ranges from the granting of import and export licences (according to laid-down criteria) to acting as secretary (which is *not* the same as doing 'secretarial work') to a committee, which may deal with anything from transport to ancient monuments or housing policy. An executive officer might also work on individual 'cases', seeing a case through from beginning to end; such work might bring her into contact with the general public. H.M. Customs and Excise offers a wide range of casework in connection with the detection of contraband at ports, and visiting manufacturers of dutiable goods.

In the Department of Health and Social Security she might be visiting hospitals to discuss, for example, proposals for using new technologies in kitchens or intensive care units. She would be a link between specialists at the hospital, and administrators, as well as specialists in her Department. In this type of work, the executive officer's and administrative Civil Servant's (who started as administration trainee) duties overlap.

In level of responsibility, executive officers' work is broadly comparable to that of junior to middle management in industry.

Prospects

Very good for promotion to Higher Executive officer. After 2 years Executive Officers may be considered for selection as Administration Trainees along with graduate entrants.

Pay: Medium to high (see p. xxiii).

Personal
attributes

Organizing ability; a liking for paper work; enjoyment of a measure of responsibility.

3. CLERICAL OFFICER

Clerical officers are employed in most government departments. In addition, there are departmental clerical officers who work mainly in branch offices, such as Job Centres, Tax Offices, and Offices of Customs and Excise.

Entry quali-fications 5 approved O-levels, including English language. Many candidates have A-levels.

The work A clerical officer does much the same wide range of jobs as a clerk in industry and commerce. She deals with incoming correspondence, sees that it is distributed to those concerned, writes letters or drafts them for a senior officer, handles correspondence with the public, assembles statistics and keeps records.

There is often more variety of work than in comparable jobs in a private firm. For example, in the Immigration Department of the Home Office, a clerical officer may deal with students visiting this country, with permits for employment, or with aliens whose residence permits have expired. Clerical officers may do some interviewing of the general public in the office as well as paper work.

Prospects There are opportunities for promotion to executive officer. Clerical officers are given day-release to study for examinations. But see Clerical Work (p. 422) for effect of 'chip' on office work.

Pay: medium (see p. xxiii).

Personal attributes Accuracy and a liking for desk-work. There is room both for good mixers and for those who prefer to work on their own.

4. CLERICAL ASSISTANT

Entry quali-fications *Either* O-level English language and 1 other subject; *or* short test.

The work A clerical assistant or junior clerk does routine work for clerical officers: filing, sorting, keeping records. She may also deal with inquiries from the public.

Prospects Clerical assistants are encouraged to take day-release classes and prepare for examinations. Promotion prospects are excellent, but see Clerical Work (p. 422) for coming changes due to the 'chip'.

Pay: medium (see p. xxiii).

5. PERSONAL SECRETARIES

Entry quali- Minimum age: 18. 3 O-levels, including English or English language,
fications   and shorthand and typing speeds of 100 and 35 words per minute
                 respectively, or equivalent audio-typing skills. However, many posts are
                 filled by promotion from the typing and clerical grades.

The work   Personal secretaries work for senior Civil Servants; their duties cover
                 the usual secretarial functions (see Secretarial Work, p. 422). Occa-
                 sionally there are opportunities for travel, especially in the Diplomatic
                 Service (see below).

Prospects   There are posts of great responsibility as secretary to heads of
                 Departments, and for promotion to supervisory duties.
                 Pay: Medium (see p. xxiii).

6. TYPING AND SHORTHAND-TYPING GRADES

Entry quali- For typists, a typing speed of 30 words per minute; for *shorthand-typists*,
fications   shorthand speed of 100 words per minute, or equivalent audio-typing
                 skill.

The work   As in any office – see Secretarial and Clerical Work, p. 422.

Prospects   With improved shorthand and typing, prospects of promotion are
                 excellent. Study by day-release is strongly encouraged. But see Clerical
                 Work (p. 422) for coming changes due to the 'chip'.
                 Pay: Medium (see p. xxiii).

7. THE DIPLOMATIC SERVICE

Entry is to Grade 7 or 8 (Administrative), to Grade 9 (Executive) and
to Grade 10 (Clerical) as follows:
   Grade 7 and 8: As for administration trainee, plus proof of ability to
learn languages.
   Grade 9: As for executive officer, but preference is given to candidates
with A-level in a foreign language.
   Grade 10: As for clerical officer. Preference given to candidates with
O- or A-level in a foreign language.

The work   Staff work in foreign and Commonwealth countries as well as in London.
                 During a working life-time usually about 8 to 10 tours are served

abroad, each lasting 2 to 5 years, i.e. roughly two-thirds of an officer's career is spent abroad. Work is very varied. Staff may work on trade, political, cultural relations, general administration, aid administration, or the dissemination of information. They meet many inhabitants of the country they work in and are expected to know or learn the relevant language. However, knowing one particular language well does not mean that all the career will be spent in the country where that language is spoken. Members of the Diplomatic Service must be prepared to serve anywhere in the world. Those who cannot or do not want to do so are usually asked to resign.

Prospects   The functions of the different grades overlap. Promotion prospects from one to another are good. Promotion from Grade 10 to Grade 9 is usually by examination; promotion to higher grades, and for those with some experience, is on merit without further examination.

Pay: High (see p. xxiii).

Training   The Diplomatic Service attaches great importance to proper training. New entrants at any level usually have a short course of lectures and visits designed to acquaint them with the organization and working of the Service and its place in the machinery of government. Specialized courses are also arranged in most types of work with which members of the Service will be concerned. Great importance is also attached to language study; even when no full-time language training is given, officers are expected to learn something of the language of the country in which they are serving and are given encouragement and assistance to enable them to do so. (Language allowances are paid to officers who reach certain levels of proficiency.)

Personal attributes   An officer must be part saleswoman, part political analyst, part public relations woman; she must have a calm and reliable personality; a persuasive, confidence-inspiring manner, have the ability to make friends easily and to put down roots instantly, yet not mind being uprooted at short notice: the diplomatic service is not so much a job, more a way of life; it needs balance, staying power, great curiosity about the way other nations live, without having any preference for any particular nation.

8. DEPARTMENTAL AND SPECIALIST POSTS

Apart from the posts for professional specialists mentioned earlier and careers described under separate headings, there are some other posts of interest to *graduates*, though only limited numbers are recruited each year; for example:

Inspector of Ancient Monuments in the Department of the Environment. Such inspectors are concerned with the preservation of ancient monuments and historic buildings. This includes inspecting and reporting on the conservation and restoration work done by the Department, and general inspection of monuments which are, or should be, scheduled under the Ancient Monuments Act. Such monuments may be of any date from the neolithic period to the last century. Inspectors must therefore have a thorough knowledge of history; preferably also experience of archaeological field work and some knowledge of architecture. Inspectors may have to research and write guide books and reports. They may also have to appear in courts of inquiry.

Recruitment is to the grade of Assistant Inspector. Candidates should have a relevant first- or second-class honours degree – or a postgraduate qualification (for example a diploma in the history of art).

Pay: Medium to high (see p. xxiii).

9. RESEARCH POSTS

Research officers are recruited for various Departments, usually for specific projects. Virtually any type of subject may have to be researched. Research officers collect, analyse, and assess information, and prepare reports and surveys on the basis of which reports are drawn up and policy decisions made by high Civil Servants.

Research projects vary vastly. They might include collecting information about foreign countries' economic structure or agricultural resources, for the Diplomatic Service; perhaps cooperating with university sociology departments on inquiries into the causes of delinquency and the treatment of offenders, for the Home Office – just about every Department needs researchers occasionally.

Entry requirements   Honours degree. For some posts degrees must be in economics, geography, or other relevant subjects; though for others degree subjects are not specified. For posts in the Diplomatic Service reading knowledge of a particular non-European foreign language may be required. Technological/science degrees are now often specially useful, even if the degree subject is only used as background knowledge.

10. SCIENCE GROUP: covers both science and engineering work

Most scientists in the Civil Service are concerned mainly with research and development (see Scientist, p. 400, for definition of types of work). They work in about 120 government or government-sponsored research establishments. Research covers a wide spectrum – from projects concerned with defence to projects concerned with 'improving the quality of life': here scientists may be engaged on research into improving building methods; nutrition (to increase food supply in developing countries as well as food production yields in this country); transportation; long-range weather forecasting; conservation and recycling resources. Physicists, mathematicians, engineers, computer scientists, statisticians, seem to be in steadiest demand. But demand levels for the various disciplines change frequently.

Entry qualifications

Either:

(1) With 4 O-levels, often now 1 A-level and/or more O-levels, including an English, a science and/or mathematical subject, as *assistant scientific officer*. Like other Civil Servants they may take day-release to continue their studies for T.E.C. awards (see p. xv) or equivalent. Recruitment at this level is straight into particular jobs, as vacancies arise.

(2) With T.E.C. Higher Award or degree as *scientific officer*. This is the main recruitment grade, and entrants are recruited either centrally, much as administration trainees, or by individual research establishments.

There are also opportunities for entry for those with post-graduate qualifications and/or research experience in industry.

Position of women

The Civil Service was the first large-scale employer to accept that there is a case for adapting employment patterns to women's lives. A report, *Women in the Civil Service*, said that 'conditions of service ought to reflect the different social patterns under which most men and women live their lives'. The report's recommendations were accepted in principle in 1971 but little progress has been made in implementing them effectively. Women are, as a result of the report, *eligible* for reinstatement in their former grade after a gap for domesticity; they are *eligible* for part-time work and they are *eligible* for unpaid leave during school holidays. But none of these provisions is a *right* and little is done to publicize them.

It is up to individual heads of departments and to Establishment (personnel people) to decide whether such arrangements are practicable in each particular case. Women find it very difficult indeed to get unpaid leave; of over 4,000 Principals (male and female) 12 women work part-time and of 3,606 women Higher Executive Officers 5 work part-time. (A look at Civil Service statistics, incidentally, again proves the practical advantages of having technical/scientific qualifications: about 5% of women in the Data Processing and the Science Categories are part-timers!) In the general administration grades, where there are no staff shortages, many women believe that even *asking* for part-time work or unpaid leave could affect promotion chances.

Present admission proportions reflect the relative educational attainments of men and women:

Administration Trainees: More than twice as many men as women are accepted, which is not surprising as A.T.s are honours graduates and more than twice as many men take honours degrees.

Executive Officers: The proportion of women being *accepted* is consistently higher than the proportion *applying*. Again this is not surprising: fewer female 2-A-level leavers go to university so more bright ones are available for 2-A-level jobs.

In senior grades men still far outnumber women and little has changed in the last ten years. This may be largely due to past policies and to higher 'wastage' rates among women, although nobody knows at the moment. However, in 1980 the Civil Service set up a committee to review developments in the position of women. (See also p. xxxvi.)

Career-break: See above.

Part-time: See above.

Late start: The age limit for Executive Officers was raised to 45 in 1980. The previous age limit, 28, had been challenged as 'indirect discrimination' under the Sex Discrimination Act: as women may be occupied with bringing up children while men try out and change careers, it was argued that women were less likely to have made final career decisions at age 28. There is no upper age limit for clerical staff.

Further information	Civil Service Commission, Civil Service Department, Alencon Link, Basingstoke, Hampshire
Related careers	*See those mentioned in the text – Local Government*

COMPANY AND INSTITUTIONAL SECRETARY
(Chartered Secretary and Administrator)

Entry quali- 2 A-levels and 3 O-levels or 1 A-level and 4 O-levels; or B.E.C. National
fications   Certificate/Diploma in Business Studies or Public Administration.
         G.C.E.s must include an English and a mathematics subject. See
         Training for *graduate* entry.

The work   This is very different from that of a secretary to an executive. A
         chartered secretary is responsible for the engagement, payment and
         control of staff; for calling meetings of the board of directors and
         arranging shareholders' meetings; for preparing agendas, statistics and
         minutes; for assembling information on financial, technical, and legal
         questions; and for preparing reports on these subjects in clear, concise
         language. She attends meetings, contributes to discussions, and supple-
         ments orally the information already prepared in the reports and
         memoranda.

         As Company Secretary she is responsible also for keeping a register
         of shareholders and other statutory books, and for the payment of
         dividends. Although qualified accountants are employed by most
         companies the Company Secretary must have a good knowledge of
         accountancy and some legal knowledge.

         As secretary to an institution, trade association, learned society, etc.
         she carries out similar work, but she may be described as a manager,
         administrative assistant, bursar, or registrar, and she may have fewer
         financial duties. She acts as a link between the governing council and its
         members, just as the Company Secretary is the link between the board
         of directors and the shareholders. She arranges annual general meetings,
         etc., and she may edit a journal. She deals with inquiries from the public
         and from prospective members.

         Membership of the Institute of Chartered Secretaries and Adminis-
         trators is now also considered a useful qualification for management
         jobs generally (see Management in Industry, p. 259), not necessarily
         just for Company Secretary. The broad-based training enables members
         to co-ordinate other specialists' work or to specialize in one particular
         aspect of commerce such as financial or export management or
         accountancy.

Prospects   Good, as it is an adaptable qualification.
                  Pay: Medium to high (see p. xxiii).

Training   The Institute's examination is in four parts, each part divided into two
                  modules and each module consisting of two subjects. Students who fail
                  one subject retake the module, not the whole examination part as in the
                  former structure. The Part I examination gives a general grounding in
                  administrative techniques and covers communication, principles of law,
                  economics and statistics. Parts II, III and IV are geared to the type of
                  setting in which the student intends to work. The three options are (i)
                  the *company secretarial* stream, (ii) the *general and financial adminis-
                  tration* stream, and (iii) the *public service* stream.
                     Such subjects as personnel management, economic policies and
                  problems are studied in all streams. Company secretarial students take
                  for example a taxation module; general and financial administration
                  students take a management administration module.
                     The differences in the syllabus are not very great and it is likely that
                  whatever stream a student chooses to study, she could later switch to
                  work in one of the other settings.
                  There are various ways to study:
                  1. Best for school-leavers, as it does not require a final career decision
                  at the outset, is to take a Higher B.E.C. award in Business Studies or
                  Public Administration followed either by employment plus part-time
                  study (day-release is generally granted by public employers and large
                  companies) or by a 1-year full-time course for Parts II, III and IV.
                  Subject-for-subject exemptions are normally granted to B.E.C. Higher
                  award holders.
                  2. By taking a degree (in any subject) followed either by a full-time 1-
                  year course for Parts II, III and IV or by employment plus part-time
                  study. (Graduates are granted subject-for-subject exemption.)
                  3. Entirely by part-time study while in appropriate jobs. This takes at
                  least 4 years: it is advisable to choose a job with day-release.
                  4. Entirely by correspondence study perhaps supplemented by evening
                  classes.

Personal   A flair for administration; common sense and good judgement; numer-
attributes   acy; interest in current affairs; tact, discretion.

Position   About 5% of Institute members are women – this represents a
of women   considerable increase in the last few years. Though there are no doubt
                  pockets of resistance to women in many companies, women who have
                  qualified have had no problem getting jobs – more often in public
                  service and general administration than as company secretary.

Career-break: Should be no problem. There are 'Revision Courses' which can be used as *refresher* courses. Also, there is no time limit for completing the 4-part examination; so it is possible either to resume studies after returning to work, or to study by correspondence course, preferably with evening classes, while housebound.

Late start: Good opportunities. Mature students with previous experience in administrative, accounting or secretarial work do not need to have the normal entry qualification. Full-time 1-year courses qualify for T.O.P.S. grants (see p. xl).

Part-time: Fair possibilities. Many professional associations and institutions want only part-time secretaries. It may also be possible to attend the part-time day-release courses while *not* in employment – depends on individual colleges' policy.

Further information   The Institute of Chartered Secretaries and Administrators, 16 Park Crescent, London W1N 4AH

Related careers   *Accountancy – Health Service Administration – Secretarial and Clerical Work*

COMPUTING or ELECTRONIC DATA PROCESSING (E.D.P.) or INFORMATICS

Systems Analyst/Designer – Applications Programmer – Software/Systems Programmer – Operator – Data Preparation Staff

Entry quali-
fications
Nothing rigid: opportunities at all education levels, but see **Training**. Programmers and Operators are normally given aptitude tests by employers; ability to think logically and pay attention to detail is more important than mathematical ability, and, for many jobs, paper quali-fications.

The work
Computing is not one career with defined training and career structure. It is a *function* performed in virtually any job area. Computers are a tool with which computing people help others do their job more effectively. Computing people work in virtually any job area, but the vast majority of computing jobs are in commerce and industry.

The terms 'compute' and 'computing', say the experts, are really out of date. They have a mathematical connotation and were correct when, in the early days, computers' strength lay entirely in the speed and accuracy with which they could perform complex arithmetical opera-tions. But now a computer is an 'information handler' and deals with texts as well as numbers. Experts prefer titles like 'electronic data processing' [E.D.P.], or data processing, or, in the Civil Service, Automatic Data Processing [A.D.P.]. Some people prefer 'informatics' or 'information technology' – terms which cover the whole microchip-based information-handling industry, including telecommunication and word processing. However, 'computer' and 'computing' have become part of the language – the terms have stuck.

A computer can classify, store, re-arrange, sort and reproduce information, or 'data'. It can present data as required – instantly, at given but not necessarily regular intervals, or on demand. It can answer questions fed into it and it can analyse its own and the computer-users' replies. It can do all these things only because a computer specialist has given it a set of instructions – (its 'brain') which are called a 'program' (see below).

The actual machine is known as 'hardware'. Designing, developing, manufacturing, servicing and installing (and, usually, selling) are done by engineers (see p. 163) – mainly but not only electronic engineers, and by physicists, mathematicians, and various other specialists. To perform its information-processing tasks, the hardware relies entirely on 'software' – the programs (never program*mes*). Hardware without software, computer people explain, is as useless as a mousetrap without cheese. This section deals with 'software' jobs.

The computer's capacity or 'intelligence', and the complexity of the tasks it can perform, depend on the complexity and quality of the software. For example, a microcomputer in a small factory may be programmed to carry out one particular function – such as working out the payroll. A mainframe – large computer installations with distant 'terminals' (see below) – can be programmed to deal with a variety of tasks; it *appears* to perform them all simultaneously, but in fact it deals with one after another in the minutest of minute fractions of a second. For example, all the country's car records are stored in a mainframe computer. Individual police officers all over the country have access to the mainframe via police stations' individual 'terminals'. These are v.d.u. (visual display unit) screens attached to keyboards which look and are operated much like typewriters. Police officers 'key in' (type) the car number and within seconds the car owner's name and address appear on the v.d.u. Similarly, supermarkets' checkout terminals are connected to a central mainframe computer store/warehouse, and at any time the level of stock of any of the thousands of items on sale in hundreds of supermarkets is known, and can be automatically acted upon. One computer system can instruct another computer system to set the re-stocking procedure in motion.

There are a vast number of types and levels of computer jobs. Because of the explosive growth of the technology, job titles, career paths, training structures and job hierarchies are vague, vary from one organization to another and are still evolving (and will go on evolving).

However, computer jobs can be divided into four main groups, each with many variations and sub-groups.

1. *Systems Analyst/Designer*
2. *Applications Programmer*
3. *Software or Systems Programmer* (also, confusingly, called *Software Designer*)
4. *Operator* and *Data Preparation Staff*

1. SYSTEMS ANALYST AND/OR DESIGNER

There are three stages to her job. First, she investigates and analyses the existing system – or lack of it – in the organization which is intending to buy a computer. In many organizations methods of working have evolved haphazardly and in the process have become inefficient. For example, in a department store which has increased its volume considerably over the years, the method of recording sales, ticketing goods, making out bills, stock control and dealing with suppliers may be totally unsuited to the size of the organization today. The systems analyst spends several months getting to know the intricacies of the business, observing and talking to staff in all departments and at all levels – from junior clerk or packer to buyer or marketing and managing directors – to assess routines, bottlenecks, objectives. The work requires business acumen, knowledge of commercial practice and an ability to get people to talk freely about their work and to accept changes in old-established routines. When the systems analyst has reduced the old system into a logical sequence of procedures, she writes a Report on how computerization would affect the organization's staff, and how it would improve efficiency and profitability. If the Report is accepted by the Management, the systems analyst 'tidies it up' (fills in the details), hands over to the programmer (see below) and probably supervises the implementation of the computer installation.

Systems Analysts and Designers in the past worked invariably *for* manufacturers but *with* the users who were intending to buy the particular manufacturer's computer. Now many also work for 'software houses' or 'systems houses' – consultancies which provide professional services rather as chartered accountants do. Systems analysts/designers may therefore have to advise potential users which particular manufacturer's systems to buy, so they must be knowledgeable about and critical of the various systems available. They must be good at explaining complicated matters to laymen – the potential computer users.

The attraction and challenge of this computing job is the mixture of tasks and of talents required: applying highly specialized technical knowledge; improving an organization's efficiency; assessing competing computer manufacturers' claims for new products. On top of applying technical know-how, systems analysts/designers must be very good at dealing with people. They must make the computer acceptable to staff. Traditional working methods and hierarchies may have to change; retraining has to be arranged and accepted, and staff reductions may have to be faced.

2. APPLICATIONS PROGRAMMER

The relationship between Systems Analyst/Designer and Applications Programmer has been likened to that of architect and builder. Applications Programmers work to 'program specifications' – a description of what the program is to achieve – provided by the Systems Analyst/Designer. There is a spectrum of applications programmers – senior ones, especially if they work with a 'business-expert' type Systems Analyst, do almost their own 'systems design' – some work to a 'loose specification', using great expertise and ingenuity; others work to a 'tight specification', need less expertise and have less scope for ingenuity.

Applications programming covers various stages. The Applications Programmer roughly assesses the time needed to complete the program, breaks down the program into separate components, and then breaks down each component into individual step-by-step sequences of instructions upon which the computer can act. All this needs logical, analytical reasoning, but *not* mathematical skills. Then comes 'coding', which is the conversion of each instruction-step into the appropriate programming language (most of which are now easily learnt). So the job which laymen often think of as programming, i.e. writing in symbols in a given computer language onto coding sheets, or keyboarding (like typing) instructions straight into a computer terminal, is only part of the vast and varied programming skills area.

Applications Programmers' programs usually instruct a particular machine to perform a particular task; for example to enable a chain of hotels to keep a constantly updated record of vacancies, or a hospital group to keep track of the many waiting lists within the various specialties, and the various hospitals within a hospital group.

But there is also another type of applications programming. Because so many computer users have the same or similar needs, they can now buy 'applications packages'. These are programs produced 'for stock', and bought by users 'off the shelf'; they deal with applications like stock control, payrolls and personnel records. 'Applications packages' are produced by consultancies or by manufacturers. Applications programmers can therefore choose the kind of environment they want to work in – from bank to hospital, from manufacturer to consultancy (and that may mean a large one, or a one/two person concern).

Senior programmers have almost as much contact with non-computer people as have systems analysts; others, especially those who concentrate on coding, have little contact with the outside world.

Applications programmers can move into 'data base management' (which means, basically, being in charge of all the computerized information within an organization), or they can go into the better paid, more prestigious, and more varied systems analysis – but most stay in programming.

3. SOFTWARE OR SYSTEMS PROGRAMMERS OR SOFTWARE DESIGNERS

(Titles are used arbitrarily by different organizations.) Their work is the most theoretical/scientific. They design and develop the software or 'controlling program' which is incorporated into the hardware during

production, and which forms the essential part of the computer system. Without these experts' ingenuity and high technology expertise computers cannot function. Thanks to their work the information stored in the computer is 'on tap' as required. The work is a combination of applying computer science principles, creativity, high technology expertise and analytical reasoning. Software Programmers work jointly with engineers, mathematicians, operational researchers, physicists and other highly-trained specialists. They are the only computer people who
(a) *must* have a technological/scientific background and who
(b) work almost entirely with other highly-qualified experts and have little contact, at work, with non-computer people. Their work is basically Research and Design [see Design and Research and Development, p. 163 under Engineering].

4. COMPUTER OPERATOR AND DATA PREPARATION STAFF

Operators' jobs vary so enormously that there can be no accurate description of their work. For example working on a 'mainframe' computer (large computers with distant terminals), the operator might sit at a console in an air-conditioned room feeding instructions into the computer to 'run' a particular program, and then she would 'obey' the computer's command (which appears on a T.V.-type screen) to 'load' a particular disc or tape next.

Computer operating usually consists of carrying out a sequence of operations with meticulous attention to detail. Computer time is expensive and an operator's mistake can be costly. Mainframe operators work in all types of large organization; they usually have to do shiftwork, as the computer, to pay its way, must be in use 24 hours a day.

With the advent of minicomputers (which can be programmed to perform *a few* tasks at a time) and microcomputers (*one* task at a time) computer operating has changed drastically. Operating the small computers is done either by people whose work has been computerized – former ledger clerks, store or book keepers or hospital records officers, for example – or by clerks taken on for this type of work. It is easily learnt and requires keyboarding (typing) skills; these can be learnt on the job. An important difference between the work of mainframe computer operators and that of mini- and microcomputer operators is that the latter do not work in air-conditioned computer rooms away from the rest of the office staff; mini- and microcomputers can be part of any office (professional as well as commercial, or any other), the work is therefore a new version of traditional office work, carried out in the usual office environment (see also Secretarial and Clerical Work, p. 422).

Data Preparation or 'Input Equipment' staff operate ancillary equipment; their work is in process of change too. 'Old' computers require information to be translated into a form which they can 'read', and which has first to be entered onto punched cards or tapes. Increasingly, operators now key in instructions to the computer direct, or via terminal or micro/minicomputer.

Operators and Data Preparation staff must have a feeling for machinery and some manual dexterity. They must be prepared to be on their feet a great deal and to carry loads that are often quite heavy.

Data Preparation staff can become operators. There is a hierarchy of operator jobs leading, via senior operator and supervisor of a team, to shift leader and operations manager. Titles, and levels of responsibility attached to titles, vary from one organization to another.

Operators with analytical reasoning ability (assessed by in-house tests) can go on to applications programming; those with organizing ability have considerable scope for promotion on the administrative side.

Training This is still evolving. Experience is, on the whole, more important than paper qualifications but experience is often difficult to get without qualifications. It is still possible to start with a few O-levels as Operator and, with in-house training and preferably day-release, become an Applications Programmer and then a Systems Analyst – if the conditions and the personality and ability are right. Because of the quick expansion and rapid developments in the whole computer area, training is disorganized and haphazard, with several overlapping types of qualifications. Many people at the top of the profession now are unqualified, because when they started their careers there were no relevant qualifications. Others have got on without qualifications because of the shortage of computer staff, but new entrants should aim at a qualification (though the only work for which a degree is *essential* is Software/Systems Programming).

One of the biggest and most prestigious employers of computer staff suggests that prospective applications programmers and systems analysts should accept *any* job in computing, even as unskilled data preparation staff; they can then work their way up.

There are now various bodies which award computing qualifications. The main ones are:
B.E.C./T.E.C. (see p. xviii): Certificates and Diplomas and Higher Certificates and Diplomas in Computer Studies; in Business Studies with Computer options; in Applications Programming and in Systems Analysis (titles vary and may change from one year to the next).
Royal Society of Arts: mainly in operating.
City and Guilds: in operating and in applications programming.

National Computing Centre: all levels and aspects of computer jobs.
British Computer Society: The main professional body; awards its own qualifications, from applications programming upwards.

These are now the most common and the recommended training routes:

Systems Analyst/Designer

1. 4-year sandwich Computer Science or Computer Studies degree which includes a year's practical computing experience. Specific titles of degrees are misleading; it is essential to find out whether a computing degree, whatever its title, includes commercial computer applications experience. *Or*
2. Degree in Business Studies with computing specialization, *or*
3. Post-graduate computer course at polytechnics, *or*
4. *Any* degree; many employers consider a degree as proof of ability to learn, and they train staff themselves (after having given them an aptitude test), *or*
5. Business management experience, *or*
6. Accountancy qualification.

Applications Programmer

Either any degree, *or*, with at least one A-level and usually other studies to A-level, T.E.C./B.E.C. Higher award [see pp. xv, xvii] in Programming – these can be taken either on a full-time basis (usually two years for a Higher National Diploma) or by day-release while in relevant employment; *or* British Computer Society's qualification.

Some employers take entrants with 2 A-levels for in-house training. A-levels are not usually specified, but a language is considered the most useful subject by some employers; mathematics at O-level is required by most.

Software or Systems Programmer/Software Designer

Degree in computer science (titles vary – check that degree is concerned with the technical software work and *not* with commercial computer application/systems analysis), *or* in mathematics, *or* in electronics, *or* in physics.

Operators/Data Preparation Staff

Employers' requirements depend partly on type of operating/data preparation to be done and partly on supply and demand. Full-time pre-entry training is not as useful as on-the-job training with day-release. Many employers require 5 O-levels including a language and mathematics; others even require an A-level; yet others accept people with manual dexterity and practicality with lower entry qualifications – candidates are given aptitude tests.

B.E.C./T.E.C. National Certificates/Diplomas (see p. xiii) in Computer subjects normally require entrants to have 4 O-levels, including mathematics, but entrants with fewer O-levels (and no maths) may be taken on on basis of aptitude tests.

NOTE: Private schools diplomas (full-time courses) vary enormously in value. Check with National Computing Centre or British Computer Society before enrolling.

For unemployed young people and school-leavers who pass an aptitude test (no specific entry requirements):

The Data Processing Threshold Scheme. This consists of 42 weeks of integrated practice (work with computer-users) and theory at technical colleges. Students work for the B.E.C./T.E.C. National Certificate in Computer Studies. Although the scheme was originally intended to lead to junior computer jobs only, many Threshold students have gone on to programming and some to systems analysis.

Prospects

Computing defies all career-prospect criteria. Present enormous shortages in systems analysis, systems/software design and in programming are likely to persist throughout the eighties, but the shortage of operators/data preparation staff may dwindle as computers increasingly do their own operating and programming.

Pay: Very high (see p. xxiii).

Personal attributes

Systems Analyst/Designer: well above average intelligence and powers of logical reasoning; imagination to put themselves into the shoes of the people whose jobs they may be 'analysing away' or at least changing; tact and diplomacy; ability to get on well with people at all levels in an organization's hierarchy; a confidence-inspiring manner; curiosity; creativity to visualize how old-established methods might be changed; ability to explain complicated procedures in simple language; ability to take an overall view of a situation and yet see it in detail; business acumen; numeracy.

Applications Programmers: Powers of logical thinking; numeracy; powers of sustained concentration; great patience and willingness to pursue an elusive problem till solved; liking for concentrated deskwork; ability to communicate easily with people in computing *and* with lay people. Programmers who hope to progress to systems analysis should note the different personal qualities required.

Software Programmers/Designers: Very high intellectual ability; originality; research-inclined mind; imagination; interest in high technology and its implications and rapid developments.

Operators: Practicality; liking for routine work; organizing/administrative ability for those wanting to get promotion.

Position of women

This is such a new career that no barriers have had to be broken down, and women do very well indeed in all areas except in *Systems/Software Programming* (for which a science-based degree is needed). Even here, the few women who have taken a relevant degree also do very well. In *Systems Analysis* women's special ability to gain people's confidence has been extremely useful at the investigation stage, and women are particularly successful both in employment and as freelance consultants. One of the biggest and most prestigious software houses is run, and almost entirely staffed, by women. So many women do freelance *applications programming* when they have a family that this has been called the new cottage industry. The majority of *operators* and *data preparation* staff are women, but this is a dwindling employment area.

When it becomes generally known that high mathematical ability is not essential for Systems Analysis or for Applications Programming, even more women are likely to enter, and succeed in, this expanding career area.

Career-break: Analysts, designers, programmers: As computer technology is changing so fast, *all* computer people have to up-date their knowledge constantly. Women who have kept in touch during the break by at least reading relevant journals, and have preferably also attended lectures etc., are welcomed back and can attend short up-dating courses. But the *complete* break should not be more than about 2 years. (It is possible to do *part-time* freelance applications programming.) Operators and data preparation staff may find it difficult to return in future; school leavers tend to be preferred for the dwindling number of jobs.

Late start: Good opportunities for graduates and people with business or related experience in applications programming and in systems analysis. For *Systems/Software Programming* up-to-date science background is essential. *Operator*: see *Career break* for likely problems.

Part-time: Good opportunities, especially for applications programmers and systems analysts (irregular project-based work for the latter rather than regular-hour part-time work).

Further information

National Computing Centre, Oxford Road, Manchester M1 7ED
British Computer Society, 13 Mansfield Street, London W1M 0BP
Institute of Data Processing Management, 51–54 Goschen Buildings, 12–13 Henrietta Street, London WC2E 8NU
Institute of Administrative Accounting and Data Processing, Walter House, 418–422 Strand, London WC2R 0PW

DANCING

PERFORMING: ballet dancer – modern stage dancer. TEACHING: teaching children – teaching adults. CHOREOGRAPHY

Teaching and performing are two separate careers. There are two kinds of performer: (1) Ballet dancers, and (2) Modern Stage dancers.

Performing

Entry quali-fications

No specific educational requirements, but a good general education is essential for ballet dancers.

1. BALLET DANCER

The work

The ballet dancer leads a dedicated life. Her days are spent practising, rehearsing and performing. She has little spare time and may not indulge in such activities as cycling, riding, etc. lest they develop the wrong muscles. She will meet few people who are not in some way involved with ballet.

She is usually attached to one particular company and may be on tour for much of the year.

Prospects

Not good. Ballet companies have only a few vacancies each year. Once she is a member of the *corps de ballet*, a talented dancer has a chance of rising to solo parts and understudying bigger roles, but it is rare indeed to rise to principal dancer status. Even a successful dancer's professional life is short; only the very exceptional still get engagements in their middle thirties. There are increasing prospects with contemporary dance companies for dancers not suited to classical ballet.

Pay: Medium to high for the few who do succeed (see p. xxiii).

Training

Serious training must have started by the age of 10 with a professional teacher who prepares pupils systematically for one of the officially recognized major dancing examinations: e.g. those of the Royal Academy of Dancing, the Imperial Society of Teachers of Dancing, or the British Ballet Organization (R.A.D., I.S.T.D., B.B.O.).

The best training is given at professional schools which give general education for G.C.E.s and a thorough drama and dance training.

Promising pupils usually take scholarship auditions held by the Royal Academy of Dancing. Under the Academy's scheme promising pupils are given free classes twice a week for up to 5 years (provided they keep up to standard, and don't grow awkward or too tall).

Full-time professional training must start not later than at 16. It lasts for about 3 years.

There are ballet schools all over the country but pupils from the London ballet companies' schools have a far better chance of eventually finding a place in these companies, which recruit most of their *corps de ballet* from their own schools.

Ballet training includes national and character dancing, mime, history, art and literature, and usually French (most technical terms are in that language).

Before accepting a pupil, good schools insist on a thorough orthopaedic examination, which is repeated at regular intervals throughout training.

Personal attributes Strong back, perfect feet; intelligence; intuition; emotional depth; musical talent; the ability to take criticism without resentment; a strong constitution; complete dedication.

2. MODERN STAGE DANCER

The work The modern stage dancer performs in musicals, pantomime, cabaret, on TV, and in light entertainment generally. She is not usually attached to a company, but appears in individual shows, usually with spells of unemployment in between. She does not work quite as hard as a ballet dancer – practising is not so all-important.

Prospects For the fully trained first-rate dancer (about 1 in 10) prospects are fair. But like other entertainers, a dancer must be prepared for months of 'resting', meanwhile earning a living in some other way yet being available to attend auditions. If she is lucky, she may get a long run in the West End, a tour, or a television series.

Unless she has made her name in her early twenties she will find it difficult to go on getting engagements, however competent she is.

Pay: Medium to high for those who do succeed (see p. xxiii).

Training 3 years full-time, preferably but not necessarily at one of the professional schools (see Ballet Training). At auditions, she must be able to demonstrate her ability to dance up to intermediate ballet exam level. The modern-stage dancer should also have some training in voice production and drama. The latest starting age for serious, but not necessarily professional, training is about 14.

Personal attributes Attractive appearance, especially shapely legs; resilience; versatility; enterprise in tracking down jobs; sense of rhythm.

Teaching

Entry qualifications For qualified teacher status, training which is required for teaching in ordinary (i.e. not *dance*) schools: 2 A-levels and 3 O-levels (see Teaching, p. 485). Very exceptionally, 1 A-level may be acceptable.

The work A dancing teacher may teach both children and adults, or she may specialize in teaching one or the other.

1. TEACHING CHILDREN

The teacher who specializes in teaching children works in 3 main fields: ordinary schools; dancing classes; specialized professional schools.

(a) *Ordinary Schools*
Full-time or visiting part-time teachers teach dancing to O-level, mainly to improve children's poise and deportment.

(b) *Dancing Classes and Schools*
These are intended for children who don't have dancing lessons at school. They may be run by a teacher who hires a hall for the purpose, or they may be in a dancing school which caters for both children and adults.

Children are usually prepared for 'Ballet in Education' exams or other officially recognized dancing examinations (see Ballet Dancing Training). This ensures that children are being properly taught even though they do not intend to become professionals.

(c) *Professional Schools*
Dancing is an essential part of the curriculum; the teacher deals with specially talented children who hope to become professional dancers.

Prospects Excellent. More and more parents want their children to learn dancing.

There are also good opportunities for teachers in Europe where non-professional dancing for children is now very popular. Royal Academy of Dancing and Imperial Society of Teachers of Dancing examiners often go abroad to organize, teach and examine.

Pay: Medium (see p. xxiii).

Training　*Leading to qualified teacher status*
This is changing at the moment; a new Council for Dance Education and Training has been set up. It issues up-to-date lists of 'accredited' courses which would normally lead to teaching in *dancing* schools; these courses do not lead to 'qualified teacher status' (nor do they usually qualify for admission to post-graduate teacher-training). To teach dancing in ordinary schools, training is *either* a 4-year course at one of the few dancing schools *which have a link with a College of Education*; *or* a 3- or 4-year College of Education course which has a dance component – it is important to check prospectuses carefully before choosing such a course, as the 'dance component' varies from a few hours to a substantial proportion; *or* a degree in Dance or in Performing Arts (titles and course content vary) followed by a 1-year post-graduate teacher-training course.

Personal attributes　The ability to explain and demonstrate steps and movements; a fine sense of rhythm and some proficiency at the piano; a liking for people of all ages; imagination; endless tact and patience; good appearance; graceful movements. (See also Teaching, p. 491.)

2. TEACHING ADULTS

The work　Most adults and teenagers are interested in learning mainly ballroom dancing, including Latin-American and whatever may be the current craze.

A ballroom-dancing teacher may work either in a general dancing school, of which ballroom dancing is one department, or at a school which specializes in ballroom dancing. She may also teach in youth clubs and hold ballroom classes for children as a sideline.

Prospects　At the moment first-rate both for those who want to work as assistants in dancing schools, and for those who want to open their own schools, but the dancing boom may not last indefinitely. There are occasional, but very few, opportunities for dancing-teachers-cum-hostesses in hotels.

Pay: Medium (see p. xxiii).

Training　For ballroom specialists, training takes 1 year to 18 months, and can be taken on an apprenticeship basis. Students pay fees at first; later they receive a salary.

Personal attributes　Much the same as for teachers of children; even more tact, patience, and self-confidence are needed.

Choreography

The work   The dancer who has exceptional imaginative powers and the ability to interpret music in terms of dancing may ultimately do choreography. This is dance composition: the grouping of dancers and sequence of dances which make up the entire ballet. In modern stage dancing, a choreographer may direct within a wide range – from the production numbers on TV which involve scores of dancers, to the unexacting dances of a seaside concert party.

Choreography is not a career for which a novice can be trained. Years of experience of ballet and a thorough musical training are needed (see Music, p. 293).

Position   *Performing*: far more men are coming into the profession; there is now
of women   a far greater shortage of *first-rate* male than of first-rate female dancers.
Teaching: this is still a predominantly female occupation (especially teaching children) but there is no reason why more men should not train for teaching.

Part-time: Good opportunities.

Further in-   Council for Dance Education and Training, Room 301, 5 Tavistock
formation   Place, London WC1H 9SS (for addresses of accredited ballet schools)
Imperial Society of Teachers of Dancing, Euston Hall, Birkenhead Street, London WC1H 8BE
Central Register and Clearing House (qualified teacher status B.Ed. and post-graduate courses), 3 Crawford Place, London W1H 2BN

Related   *Acting – Music – Remedial Gymnast – Teaching (Speech and*
careers   *Drama, p. 492; Physical Education, p. 492)*

DENTISTRY

General practice – community health dentist – hospital dental surgeon – ancillary work

Dental Surgeon

Entry quali-
fications
2 or 3 A-levels, at least 2 sciences at A-level (usually 3); if only 2, 1 additional science among the 3 O-levels. Individual schools' requirements vary slightly.

The work
A dentist (or dental surgeon) preserves teeth by filling, crowning, and scaling. She extracts teeth and designs and fits artificial dentures. She also does surgical operations on the jaw, and orthodontics, which is the improvement of irregular teeth, mainly in children. The preventive aspects of dentistry are very important, involving regular teeth inspection for children.

1. GENERAL PRACTICE

The majority of dentists are in general practice. Most of them treat National Health patients almost exclusively, though some treat both private and N.H.S. patients. A very small minority treat only private patients.

A dentist in general practice has the best financial prospects and the greatest independence, but she is also likely to work the hardest. She may be in a partnership, or in practice on her own, working in her own premises with her own equipment, and employing her own dental surgery assistant (see p. 152).

It is usual to begin as an assistant or associate in a practice, with a view to becoming a partner later, but primarily to learn how a practice is run. This involves a good deal of organization, filling-in of forms, ordering stocks, and contact with technicians.

It is also possible to buy the 'goodwill' of a dentist who is retiring or moving away, or simply to put up a plate and wait for patients.

2. COMMUNITY HEALTH DENTIST

The school dental service's aim is to give every school child a dental inspection once a year and to offer whatever treatment may be necessary. A school dentist may also provide dental inspection and treatment at child and maternity clinics for expectant and nursing mothers and for children under five. In country areas the dentist sometimes holds clinics in surgery-caravans.

3. HOSPITAL DENTAL SURGEON

In hospitals, a dentist looks after sick patients whose teeth need urgent attention, and does jaw operations and complicated extractions. Out-patients may need only ordinary dental treatment.

Dental work in hospitals has the usual hospital advantages of life in a community, colleagues to discuss difficult cases with, and social and sports clubs.

Prospects   Good in all fields. Qualifications are now accepted in E.E.C. countries. Some scope in Commonwealth countries.

Pay: Medium to high (see p. xxiii).

Training   5–6 year courses at dental schools attached to universities. The first year is a preliminary science course (as for medical training). Students with A-level physics, chemistry, biology or zoology or mathematics are exempt from it.

Some dental schools have discontinued this course. Even when dental schools do accept students for a preliminary year, local authorities do not normally pay grants for what is in effect an A-level course.

Dental training lasts for 4 or 5 years. The syllabus covers anatomy and physiology, the uses of dental materials, design and fitting of dental appliances, pathology, some medicine, general as well as dental surgery, anaesthesia, orthodontics, children's and general preventive dentistry, radiology, dental ethics, and relevant law.

Practical work on 'phantom heads' begins in the second year, and work on actual patients during the second or third year of the dental course.

Personal attributes   Manual dexterity; a methodical and scientific approach; and good health (especially good feet, for standing all day).

Left-handedness is not a disadvantage.

Dentist in general practice especially: The ability to establish easy relationships quickly with people, and give confidence to the nervous. (The growth of the practice depends almost entirely on the patients' personal recommendations.) Organizing ability.

Community health dentist especially: The ability to get on with children.

Hospital dentist especially: The ability to work well as a member of a team.

Further information General Dental Council, 37 Wimpole Street, London W1M 8DQ

Related careers *Dentistry: Ancillary Work – Medicine*

Ancillary work

(Dental therapist – dental hygienist – dental surgery assistant – dental technician)

If you are interested in dentistry but do not have the necessary qualifications for dental training, there are 4 careers available in dental surgeries: dental therapist, dental hygienist, dental surgery assistant and dental technician.

1. DENTAL THERAPIST

Entry qualifications
Minimum age for training 17.
4 O-levels, including English language, and a science subject, preferably biology.

The work
Dental therapists do operative work; they work in the hospital, school, mother and child welfare dental services, helping dentists to give treatment to children and to teach them how to care for their teeth. They work under the direction of a dentist who prescribes the treatment to be given; this includes simple fillings, extraction of deciduous teeth, and cleaning, scaling and polishing teeth. Dental therapists always work under supervision, mostly in double-surgery clinics. Their responsibility is therefore limited. Most of the patients are very young – in welfare clinics under 5, in school clinics mostly under 11. Dental therapists do not work for dentists in general practice.

Prospects
Very good for getting jobs, but with no promotion prospects.
Pay: Medium (see p. xxiii).

Training
2 years full-time, only in London. Practical training (on which more time is spent than on theory) is on dummy heads, so that students learn how to scale, polish, fill and extract teeth without worrying about

hurting the patient; they also work on patients, under supervision. Theoretical training includes anatomy, physiology of the teeth and jaw, some radiography, some dietetics – enough to understand why some foods are good and some bad for the development of children's teeth.

Personal attributes Considerable manual dexterity; conscientiousness; some interest in science; good health, especially healthy feet; a way with children.

Further information Management Committee, School for Dental Therapists, 37 Wimpole Street, London W1M 8DQ

2. DENTAL HYGIENIST

Entry qualifications Minimum age for training 17.
4 O-levels, preferably English language and a science subject. Candidates are given a manual dexterity test.

The work A dental hygienist also does 'operative work'. She does scaling and polishing under the supervision of dentists, but she does not do any fillings, etc. An important aspect of her work is preventive dentistry. She gives talks, sometimes with colour slides to illustrate her points on the need for oral hygiene; for instance, to children she explains the bad effect on teeth of too much sweet-eating; to mothers at ante-natal clinics she talks about the need for correct diet during pregnancy.

Unlike a dental therapist, she works with adults as well as with children, and for dentists in general practice as well as in community health clinics.

Prospects Good: more dentists in general practice, especially in partnerships, are now also employing hygienists, but there are no promotion prospects.
Pay: Medium (see p. xxiii).

Training 9 months to 1 year full-time at dental hospitals. Training is similar to that of therapists, but the extracting and filling of teeth are not included. Some time is spent in learning how to talk about oral hygiene to audiences of children and adults.

Personal attributes As for therapists, plus the ability to express oneself lucidly and to address an audience.

Further information   General Dental Council, 37 Wimpole Street, London W1M 8DQ

3. DENTAL SURGERY ASSISTANT

Entry qualifications   None laid down, but school *up to* G.C.E.-level is essential, preferably with 1 or 2 passes. Some schools demand G.C.E. passes.
Minimum age for training usually 17.

The work   A surgery assistant does no 'operative work'. She is the dentist's 'third hand', handing her the right instruments at the right time; she also looks after her instruments, does sterilizing, gets out patients' treatment cards, helps with filling in forms and filing, and often does general secretarial work. She may act as receptionist.

Surgery assistants work wherever dentists work, i.e. in general practice, in community health clinics and in hospitals.

Prospects   Good.
Pay: Medium (see p. xxiii).

Training   Most dentists train their own assistants, but some prefer those who were trained at a dental hospital, for a period varying from 6 to 18 months. The type of training differs slightly from one hospital to another, but it is always almost entirely practical, with some lectures and demonstrations. The reason for variation in the length of training is that in some hospitals courses concentrate on training only. In others, assistants earn a little during training for help with routine work, looking after instruments, etc.

In London, there is one course for dental surgery assistants which lasts 1 year full-time, and during a second year, when students are working as assistants to dentists, they complete the course in evening classes. (2 G.C.E. passes are expected.)

The majority of dental surgery assistants, however, learn on-the-job. They go straight from school or from secretarial college into a dentist's surgery and are trained mainly by him. They are advised to attend evening classes.

After the training, plus at least 2 years' work, they can pass the examination for the National Certificate awarded by the Examining Board for Dental Surgery Assistants.

Personal attributes   A polite, friendly manner; some manual dexterity; a well-groomed, neat appearance; good health.

Further information   Association of Dental Surgery Assistants, Bank Chambers, 3 Market Place, Poulton-le-Fylde, nr Blackpool, Lancashire

4. DENTAL TECHNICIAN

Entry quali- None specified. Some knowledge of chemistry and physics desirable.
fications

The work Dental technicians construct and repair dentures, crowns and other orthodontic appliances. They work either in commercial dental laboratories where work for individual dentists is carried out, or in hospital dental laboratories. It is highly skilled work.

Prospects Excellent. There is a great shortage of dental technicians.
      Pay: Low to medium (see p. xxiii).

Training At present, 5 years' apprenticeship with day-release, for City and Guilds Dental Technicians' Certificates. Apprenticeships may be shortened to 3 years soon. 3-year full-time courses are available in some hospitals.

Personal Willingness to work as the only woman in an all-male laboratory; great
attributes manual dexterity; patience; accuracy.

Further in- National Joint Council for the Craft of Dental Technicians, 64 Wimpole
formation Street, London W1M 8AL

Position *1. Dentists*
of women 17% of practising dentists are women, but about ⅔ of students are now female. Of all the top professions, dentistry is the most promising for women. They have truly equal chances of promotion in the health services; they are welcomed in private practice by partners and by patients; and it is a profession which can be carried on anywhere in the country.

Career-break: No problem: there are refresher courses. The Dental Retainer Scheme encourages women dentists to work at least 12 sessions and attend 7 education sessions a year, while paying reduced membership fees.

Late start: Dental schools vary in their attitude to mature students and judge each case on her merits – acceptance depends largely on the number of years students would have after qualifying: over-35s tend to have more difficulty getting a place than under-35s. There is, usually, no relaxation in G.C.E. requirements – but prospective dentists can take missing A-levels at evening classes. No employment problem once qualified.

Part-time: Excellent opportunities for employment, none for training.

2. Dental Therapists, Hygienists and Surgery Assistants
Virtually 100% female profession.

Career-break: Should be no problem.

Late start: Young students are given preference for training usually, but mature entrants are also considered. Mature entrants could try for training under T.O.P.S. (see p. xl) for Dental Hygienists' and Dental Surgery Assistants' 1-year full-time courses.

Part-time: Excellent opportunities for employment – none for training.

3. Dental Technicians
Although most technicians are men, more women are now training and their position is much as for other dental staff now.

Career-break: No problem.

Late start: Unlikely.

Part-time: No problem.

Related careers	*Dentistry – Medicine, and Related Careers – Nursing – The Services – Science Technician*

DIETETICS

Preventive dietetics – Therapeutic dietetics

Entry quali-
fications

2 science A-levels, one of which must be chemistry; 3 O-levels which must normally include English and mathematics. See **Training**.

The work

Dietitians apply scientific principles of nutrition to normal and to therapeutic diets. Their functions have broadened in the last few years as healthy eating habits became recognized as a vital part of preventive medicine.

Dietitians' work divides broadly into *preventive* and *therapeutic* dietetics.

Preventive work, mainly in the community: As food becomes ever more expensive and as more 'convenience' and other processed foods come on the market it is becoming more and more important that shoppers should be able to assess the nutritional values of various foods, and the possible ill effects on health. Preventive dietetics is part of health education. In preventive work the dietitian tries to get her message across to as many people as possible *before* they need therapeutic diets. To do this she works 'through' other professionals – those who reach wider sections of the community than the dietitian could hope to reach. She endeavours to keep nurses, social workers, health visitors, midwives, teachers and G.P.s up to date on nutritional matters; she gives talks in schools, to youth clubs, P.T.A.s, Rotary Clubs etc. There is an element of public relations work in preventive dietetics: the dietitian has to make herself and her work known and get herself *asked* to speak to groups.

She also works out diets for special groups; for example cheap and simple-to-prepare meals for the elderly; for parents with large families, little time and little money; for people living alone; and for ethnic groups who have to observe certain dietary rules but cannot afford to buy their own food-stuffs here because they are too expensive.

Preventive dietetics overlaps with *therapeutic work* which involves advising individuals, mainly hospital in- and out-patients, on specific diets. For therapeutic work, the dietitian uses her expertise together with skill and imagination to make diets 'stickable-to' even when, for example, patients may have little understanding of the need to avoid certain ingredients in their diets and include others.

Dietitians to not normally do any cooking themselves; even direct supervision of diet-kitchens is now the exception rather than the rule. They act as consultants to catering managers in hospitals (or a group of hospitals) and other institutions. Most dietitians are employed by the National Health Service and are hospital-based. At the top of the N.H.S. dietetics tree is the District Dietitian. She decides how to use her staff to best advantage – whether to designate one dietitian to do the health education work in the community and let the rest work with patients in hospitals, or whether to let everybody do a bit of everything. Preventive work in the community is still rather new and district dietitians are still experimenting how best to use their staff.

Some local authority social services employ dietitians entirely for community work; some local education authorities employ them for work in the school meals services.

Dietitians occasionally become catering managers in hospitals or other large organizations either because they cannot get suitable jobs *in* dietetics, or because they prefer the possibly greater managerial content of large-scale catering management (see Catering, p. 96) to dietetics. Experienced dietitians may become lecturers, and/or do research.

Prospects   Fair on the whole. Experienced dietitians are usually in demand, but first jobs are not necessarily available where they are wanted. Industry now employs far fewer dietitians than in the past, but there are some openings in the developing countries and in the E.E.C. (for dietitians who speak the relevant languages). British qualifications are not yet recognized in the U.S.A. and Canada but it is likely that they will be when all dietitians are graduates.

Pay: Low to medium: possibly improving as profession now becoming all-graduate.

Training   This is changing. Diplomas are phasing out, and since 1980 new entrants take a 4-year degree course (titles vary; some courses including the term 'nutrition' are recognized by the Dietitians Board as entitling holders to State Registration, and some are not – Registration is essential for dietitians wishing to work in the National Health Service). Degree courses include at least six months' practical work. The syllabus includes physiology; biochemistry; microbiology; nutrition and food science; diet therapy; health education; large-scale catering systems and principles; economics of nutrition.

Graduates with relevant degrees (i.e. which include human physiology and human biochemistry) may take a new 2-year postgraduate Diploma course (first course started in 1980).

Personal attributes For all dietitians: interest in science as well as in food; curiosity about and sympathy with other people's ways of life and standards of food preparation; ability to get on well with people of all ages, temperaments, backgrounds in one-to-one consultations. For dietitians who hope for promotion: sufficient self-confidence, intellectual ability and communication skills to fulfil the dietitians' new role as health educator, and consultant, to other professionals.

Position of women Still 99 per cent female profession, but amongst students there are now about 10 per cent men. Proportionately more men than women in lecturing posts.
Career-break: Presents no problem; although there are no formal refresher courses, *ad hoc* arrangements are made by hospitals.
Late start: No age-bar in jobs, mature students welcome on degree courses.
Part-time: Fair opportunities for work, none for training.

Further information British Dietetic Association, 305 Daimler House, Paradise Street, Birmingham B1 2DL

Related careers *Catering – Food Technology – Home Economics – Medicine – Science (Biochemist, p. 406; Chemist, p. 405)*

DRIVING INSTRUCTOR AND DRIVING EXAMINER

DRIVING INSTRUCTOR

Entry quali-fications
4 years' clean driving licence: minimum age theoretically 21; in practice licences rarely granted to anyone under 25.

The work
The majority of instructors work on their own. This is more lucrative, but also more precarious, than working for one of the big driving schools. Hours are irregular and long: far more pupils want lessons after work or at weekends than during normal working hours. It is essential to have someone at home who will deal with telephone bookings, inquiries, cancellations. Most instructors teach between 6 and 12 pupils a day.

Being a good driver is not the most important aspect of instructing: instructors must like teaching and have the natural ability to do so; they must be able to put themselves into the position of a nervous, possibly not very talented, learner. They usually drive all day and every day through the same streets, which can be dull. The attractions of the work are, largely, being one's own boss; developing learners' road sense and driving technique; talking, during lessons, to a variety of people.

Prospects
Depends on area: it is essential, before investing in a dual-control car, to find out whether the area is not already saturated with instructors.

Pay: Varies from low to medium (expenses are very high) (see p. xxiii).

Personal attributes
Organizing ability, business acumen, ability to get on with all types of people and to put them at their ease; complete unflappability and fearlessness; mechanical aptitude; teaching talent; endless patience; ability to criticize tactfully and explain lucidly.

Training
Instructors must now pass the Department of the Environment's stringent written and practical examination. There are instructors' schools, but potential instructors may learn as they wish. Syllabus covers driving techniques; teaching skills and practice; knowledge of design and mechanism of cars; road procedure as in Highway Code but in very much greater depth.

DRIVING EXAMINER AND TRAFFIC EXAMINER

Entry quali-fications
Minimum age 26; experience of having worked with the public, in a position of some authority; 6 years' clean driving licence and wide experience of driving in last 3 years; active interest in and knowledge of all motoring/road/traffic trends and problems; some mechanical knowledge of cars and other vehicles; elementary knowledge of road transport law as it affects commercial, passenger and goods vehicles; preferably some experience of driving heavy goods or public transport vehicles and/or motor-cycles.

Acceptance is by competitive examination held, at irregular intervals, by the Department of the Environment, plus interview, driving test and 4-week course followed by special test.

The work
Driving Examiners are Civil Servants. They test learner-drivers of cars and other vehicles. They work as members of a team under a senior examiner, attached to one of over 300 test centres throughout the country. They conduct normally 8 or 9 tests a day. During the test, when examinees tend to be nervous, examiners may not converse (to ensure that examinees are not, and cannot claim to have been, distracted); they make detailed notes on driving technique and road sense, throughout each test-drive. Their decision is final; they must keep records of each test in case an examinee complains. The work is highly concentrated and, for work as responsible as this, can be rather repetitive.

Traffic Examiners, also Civil Servants, investigate, by observation on the road, by inquiry of operators and by examination of drivers' records, whether laws concerning operation of vehicles (such as hours a driver may be in charge of a vehicle without rest period) are being observed. Examiners do not have to examine vehicles' mechanical conditions.

Prospects
Fair. Recruitment is however only sporadic. For promotion examiners usually have to move to another area.

Pay: Medium (see p. xxiii).

Personal attributes
Air of authority; patience; tact; ability to concentrate constantly; unflappability.

Position of women
Driving Instructors
About 15–20% now are women (a great increase in the last few years). Women instructors have no special problem getting pupils.

Career-break: There is a danger that, during the break, another instructor may set up in the area. Continued driving during the break would be essential.

Late start: Most instructors and examiners have had some other job before; maturity is an asset.

Part-time: It is possible to have a small number of pupils, but it is never possible to work during school-hours only. Summer months are the busiest time. So far no part-time examiners.

Driving Examiners

The first few women applied in 1977; by 1980 only about 20 had been appointed. The Department genuinely wants to attract more women, but the 'preferred' experience (see above) makes it difficult for women to be eligible. But those who have had experience of driving heavy goods vehicles or buses would stand a good chance. (*Note*: Heavy Goods Vehicle Driving instruction is available under T.O.P.S. (see p. xl).)

Further information	Department of the Environment (Register of Driving Instructors, or Driving and Traffic Examiners), Lambeth Bridge House, London SE1 7SB
Related careers	*Mechanical Engineering – Teaching*

ECONOMICS

Entry quali-
fications   Degree in economics; A-level mathematics is usually essential.

The work   Economics is concerned with the organization, utilization and distribution of productive and financial resources, nationally and internationally. This includes the study of political, industrial and social
relationships and institutions, and of conflicting economic theories.
Economists work in a wide variety of settings – in urban and regional
planning, in industry, commerce, the Civil Service, in financial and
industrial journalism, as organizers or researchers in trade unions and
in management consultancies. They also try (but do not often succeed)
to identify the causes of problems like inflation and unemployment, and
suggest courses of action which might solve or ease the problem. Some
economists specialize in, for example, the economics of energy
resources, the car industry, agriculture, transport.

An economics degree can be a 'general' qualification for administration; and it can be a 'specialist' qualification – for work in systems
analysis, statistics, market research, investment analysis, cybernetics,
operational research.

Prospects   Fair, as such wide application.

Pay: Depends largely on type of employer; medium to very high (see
p. xxiii).

Training   Most degree courses include as 'core' studies: economic and political
theory and economic history. Specializations to choose from include
agricultural economics, economic geography, urban development,
industrial or financial economics, transport studies, operational
research. Economics can be combined with accountancy, geography,
law, sociology, planning, mathematics or a physical science. The content
of individual courses and the emphasis given to the many aspects of
economics vary greatly from one course to another.

Personal
attributes   Numeracy; interest in political and social affairs; analytical powers.
Resilience, to be able to persevere when events prove research and
theories wrong, and when suggestions are being ignored.

**Position
of women**
About one quarter of economics students are women; they do not seem to have any special difficulties getting jobs. A comparatively large proportion do well in financial journalism and in investment analysis. The subject is adaptable enough to enable women to work in *some* area at all stages of their career. Instead of part-time work they do sporadic freelance work, *if* established and experienced.

**Further in-
formation**
No central organization.

**Related
careers**
*Accountancy – Computers – Cybernetics – Information Work –
Journalism – Management in Industry – Operational Research –
Planning*

ENGINEERING

Professional engineers – technician engineer and technician – engineering crafts

1. Professional Engineers

Entry quali- 2 or 3 A-levels, including maths and physics, and 3 O-levels. Precise
fications requirements vary from one degree course to another. Increasingly,
English language and/or a foreign language at O-level are specified. For
chemical and agricultural engineering A-level chemistry is essential.
Chemistry at O-level is essential for entry to most courses.

T.E.C. Certificates and Diplomas may be accepted in lieu of A-levels:
acceptability is not automatic and depends on units taken and the
degree course directors' views on T.E.C.

The work Engineering offers scope for working with people, for communicating
ideas, for using creative imagination, for helping to shape the future of
society and the physical environment at home and all over the world.
Engineers are essential for the improvement of the quality of life
generally. Opportunities for professional engineers exist in a very wide
variety of settings indeed – in hospitals and atomic power stations; in
research establishments; in manufacturing industry; in the Civil Service
and local authorities; as teachers or as consultants in professional
practice; in fact, in virtually any area of employment. Engineers have,
probably, more choice of environment in which to work than most other
professionals.

Engineers and technologists apply scientific principles, theories and
methods to practical ends. The majority work most of the time at desk
and/or drawing-board, at meetings with clients and colleagues. They
work in teams with other specialists such as architects, scientists,
systems analysts, product designers, as well as with other engineers.
Though during training all engineers spend some time supervising work
on the construction site or factory floor, qualified engineers can choose
jobs in which they have to do none of this kind of work. Nor is there any
physically hard or dirty work in professional engineering. As the object
of engineering is the design or improvement of the 'hardware' of living
– engineers have influenced if not designed every bit of equipment and
machinery in use anywhere – it is closely involved with the life of the
community.

An engineering qualification is also much under-rated as a way into more glamorous-sounding (better paid) and more difficult-to-get-into careers – e.g. Marketing (see p. 270), Industrial Management (see p. 259), Public Relations (see p. 379), Broadcasting (see p. 73) and other graduate employment. Employers who want 'graduates' often now prefer science and engineering to arts graduates. Their specific knowledge can be useful in an age when technology has a bearing on virtually any type of business; their analytical approach to problem-solving is invariably useful, even when the problem is not a technical one. So even young people who are not planning to spend their lives as engineers, but want to go into anything from merchant banking to journalism, might well consider taking an engineering degree as a stepping-stone. Engineering need no more be a vocational course than an arts degree (engineering courses are *much* easier to get into than arts degree courses); the chances are that, during their course, students may find that engineering itself has more to offer than they thought.

There are degrees which combine engineering with economics, languages and other subjects, and there are post-graduate courses in Business Management, Systems Analysis, Transport, etc., which can be taken either immediately after qualifying or a few years later (after the *career-break*, p. 175).

Engineers specialize in two dimensions: in one *branch* or discipline, and then, after training, in one *function*, or type of activity. This applies to a greater or lesser degree to all branches of engineering (function can be changed more easily than discipline). The main *functions* are:

1. DESIGN

This is the most creative of the engineering functions and is the core of the engineering process. The design engineer creates or improves a product which can be manufactured and maintained economically, performs satisfactorily and looks good, or she may design a new, or improve an established, engineering process. Most designers work to a brief. For example, a car manufacturer's marketing department may request that next year's model within a given price range should incorporate fuel-saving and/or safety devices (which may have been perfected in Research or which Research may be asked to work on); and that the model should incorporate certain visual features which seemed to 'sell' a competitor's model; the design engineer may add her own, totally new, ideas.

Her job is to find efficient and economic solutions to a set of problems. She must investigate materials and processes to be used in the manufacture of the product, which means she has to consult experts from other disciplines; but *she* specifies what goes into the manufacture of the product and what processes are to be used.

Because the work of design engineers varies so enormously, the job is impossible to define precisely. Designing an aircraft which is a team effort has little in common with adding a feature or two to an established type of transistor. Most work is done in 'design offices', where several graduates assisted by technicians work under a *chief design engineer*; some designing, in electronics for example, is done in the laboratory. A design engineer can choose whether to be part of a team that designs, say, a whole new airport, or whether to work on simple, straightforward design on her own.

Personal attributes   An urge to put new technologies to practical use; creativity; imagination; academic ability; ability to coordinate the work of others.

2. RESEARCH AND DEVELOPMENT

In some organizations research and development are two separate departments; in some the two, plus *Design*, go together. But most typically research and development form one department, with design a separate, but very closely linked one.

Research and development engineers investigate, improve, adapt established processes, products and components of products, and they may create new ones. The work is essentially experimental, laboratory-based, but the 'laboratory' could be a skid-pan on which new tyre-surfaces are tried out, or a wind-tunnel in which to experiment with aircraft models. Whenever the product is not too unwieldy, research and development build (or let the technicians build) prototypes, which are then discussed with marketing and production colleagues.

While there is some extending-the-frontiers-of-knowledge kind of research, most of engineering research is 'applied', i.e. aimed at maximizing sales and profits; or at saving precious resources.

Work comes from several sources: *design engineers* may want to use a new material or process which they have heard of but they need to know more about its 'behaviour' before using it; *production engineers* may ask research and development to investigate why there is a recurrent fault in a particular production process or product; the *marketing* department may complain that a particular aspect of a competitor's fridge, aircraft, or traffic signal component makes the competitor's product sell better: research and development would investigate the better-selling product, and then try and come up with something even better. Research and development is very much team work; there is scope for specializing in the more academic research or the more practical development side of the work.

Personal | Academic ability; imagination; perseverance in the face of disappointing
attributes | research results; interest in following up ideas which have profitable
application; ability to work well with colleagues from other departments.

3. PRODUCTION

This is rather confusing. It is both a separate engineering branch with
its own degree and Chartered Institution, and it is an engineering
function. To confuse matters even more, terminology is vague. Some
so-called production engineers in industry are not engineers but became
specialists in production by working their way up via foreman. Sometimes arts graduates go into production because they are practical and
good at organizing, and they pick up technical knowledge as they go
along. Production engineers are also called production planners or
production managers – terms which may, or may not, denote different
levels of responsibility and qualification.

Broadly, production engineers organize and control the manufacture
(or construction) of any kind of product – a car; a component used in
car manufacture; a can of peas; the can into which peas are put; a mass-
produced dress; a sewage works. It is the production engineer's job to
achieve an even flow on the production line or construction site. She
must see that labour, equipment and materials are used efficiently and
that the product is completed at the correct quality and cost, in the right
quantity, at the right time. The variety of settings in which production
engineers work is enormous: it can be a huge (and noisy) heavy
engineering plant; it can be a large, but very quiet, highly automated
workshop; increasingly also small manufacturers in light engineering, in
clothing and food processing employ production specialists.

Production engineering invariably contains a large 'man-management' element: as foreman or production supervisor, a junior (or
trainee) production engineer might be in charge of a production line,
responsible for the work done by perhaps 100 operatives; later, as
production planner (or whatever her title) she might be responsible for
ensuring that the right materials used in the production process are
available on the shop-floor at the right time in the right quantities and
that 'dispatch' is ready to receive the finished product: she might later
be responsible for long-term production planning and development –
that would be part of Management (see p. 259).

In the past, production engineering was usually done by practical
people with some knowledge of engineering processes. As manufacturing processes become ever more sophisticated, and as industry recognizes the need for greater efficiency and streamlining, production
engineering has grown in importance (and status). It is now an important
equal of other engineering branches *and* functions.

Production managers often do work which has much in common with personnel management. An important part of their job is smoothing out problems on the shop-floor before they flare up into disputes; they deal with union officials, as well as with staff problems which might affect the department's productivity.

Personal attributes

Organizing ability; practicality; ability to get on well with people of all types at all levels in the hierarchy – from operatives to heads of research and managing director; ability to keep calm under pressure and in inevitable crises; liking for being very much at the centre of action.

4. TECHNICAL SALES

Sales engineers spend most of their time away from the office, meeting people. Selling engineering products ('specialist selling'), which may be selling anything from machine tools to oil rigs, domestic freezers to road maintenance equipment and service, combines salesmanship with technical knowledge. Customers may be laymen to whom the virtues of a product have to be explained, or highly professionally qualified (more so than the sales engineer possibly) people who ask searching questions about its performance and properties. Sales engineers also act as link between prospective customer and manufacturers, passing on criticism of and requests for products and changes (see also Marketing/Selling, p. 270).

Searching out new customers is an important part of selling. Some sales may take months of meetings and negotiating. Sales engineers may travel abroad a good deal, or they may have their own 'territory' near home – it largely depends on the type of product.

Personal attributes

Outgoing personality; adaptability to use the right approach with different types of customers; perseverance, and indifference to the occasional rebuff; commercial acumen; interest in economic affairs.

The main *branches* of engineering are:

1. MECHANICAL ENGINEERING

Mechanical engineers work in all branches and all functions; they are concerned with the application of the principles of mechanics, hydraulics, thermodynamics to engineering processes. They have a vast choice of end-product to work with and environment to work in: literally no industry is closed to them; they also work in hospitals and research establishments. The engineer who wants to help humanity as directly as possible, who wants to see the application of her efforts to the alleviation of suffering and discomfort, can work in *Medical Engineering* (see below); the engineer who wants eventually to go into technical sales or into marketing, can take her mechanical engineering training into anything from car manufacture to computers or North Sea oil extraction.

2. ENVIRONMENTAL ENGINEERING
(Heating and Ventilating Engineering, Building Services Engineering)

This used to be part of mechanical engineering; but is now a specialization on its own. Environmental engineers are concerned with heating, lighting, ventilation, air conditioning, noise and air pollution and its control. They are called in as consultants by civil engineers and architects on building projects from hospital to airport, office block to housing estate, chain store to underground station.

3. CIVIL ENGINEERS

They are concerned with the design, planning and construction of motorways, bridges, dams, large buildings (in conjunction with architects usually), waterways, sewage plant, oil rigs, and, increasingly, with traffic and transportation planning and management. More than any other branch of engineering, civil engineers tend to be consultants, called in by local authorities or architects for whom they plan and design projects. Consultant engineers design for and negotiate with clients and professionals from other disciplines – i.e. this is office and conference-table work rather than supervision on site. Civil engineers working for contractors supervise construction projects and deal with contractors' agents and foremen; they may also do design work.

4. STRUCTURAL ENGINEERING

This overlaps with Civil Engineering. Structural engineers may be called in as consultants by architects and by civil engineers – they are specialists on choosing materials and processes used in, and designing, large-scale constructions.

5. ELECTRICAL AND ELECTRONIC ENGINEERING

It is almost impossible to draw a dividing line between the two. Broadly, *electrical engineering* is concerned with the use and generation of electricity to produce heat, light and mechanical power: electrical engineers work in generating stations, distribution systems and on the manufacture of all kinds of electrical machinery from tiny motors for powered invalid chairs to heavy motors for industrial plant. They are also concerned with research into the use of electrical power, for example for use in transport and heating systems.

Electronics is mainly concerned with:

(a) *Communications*: This includes telephones (the *Post Office* employs large numbers of electronic engineers to improve and extend its telephone and telegraph services), radio and television (see Broadcasting, p. 73), where engineers research into, maintain and operate transmitting and receiving equipment.

(b) *Instrumentation and Control*: This is concerned with automatic control devices, from the operation of equipment on the moon, by ground control, to nearer-home gadgets such as automatic oven- and central-heating time-clocks.

Then there is the vast area of computer-controlled equipment. Anything from a factory mass-producing fish fingers or plastic cups to railway-signalling or supermarket re-ordering installations can be computer-controlled. (See Computing, p. 134).

(c) *Microelectronics*: This is the most dramatically developing and expanding sub-section. Briefly, it is electronics writ small in terms of cost and size, and writ very large indeed in terms of present and potential uses and employment opportunities (at technician, technician engineer and professional levels). Microelectronics is concerned with the design, development and production of scaled-down, minuscule electronic devices – notably the 'chip' – and with their application. The chip affects virtually every industrial, commercial, scientific and professional activity but it can do nothing by itself: electronics specialists develop its potential and 'program' (instruct) it to perform the precisely defined task for which it is intended. (Programming in this context differs from data processing programming: electronics and other engineers use their programming skill as an additional tool – they are not 'programmers'.)

Mass-produced, general-purpose as well as specialized chip-based equipment is now used (or soon will be) in such varied spheres as hotel, aircraft and theatre seat reservations; supermarkets (those bleeping checkouts keep the warehouse management informed of the precise level of stock of every item in every store at any time); document storage and retrieval systems (see Information Scientist, p. 247); in hospitals, libraries, banks, television production companies, commercial and professional offices. In manufacturing, 'robotics' – assembly-line work done by programmed robots – is developing fast. Scientific applications include weather-forecasting; computer-aided design in civil and structural engineering; dating archaeological discoveries. In hospital, a doctor's request to the laboratory for a blood sample analysis can soon be transmitted verbally instead of by writing out chits: voice recognition by machine is now possible but not yet in practical use.

6. MEDICAL OR BIO-MEDICAL ENGINEERING

This is not yet a discipline on its own but a combination of electronic, electrical and mechanical engineering. Medical engineers at the moment usually take a degree in either mechanical, electronic or electrical engineering and then either take a post-graduate course or join a team working on medical engineering projects. These are often carried out jointly with consultants in hospitals, who specify what they want any particular equipment to do. Kidney transplants, heart surgery, and many less spectacular procedures are only possible thanks to the imaginative cooperation of doctors and engineers.

Medical engineers also design aids for severely handicapped people – for example, artificial, remarkably usable, limbs for thalidomide children, or custom-built 'transport' for severely handicapped patients.

Medical engineering is often overlooked as an alternative to medicine for people who want to be closely involved with alleviating disabilities.

7. MUNICIPAL ENGINEERS

Municipal engineers work for public authorities. They do civil engineering (see above), and are often also responsible for refuse collection and disposal, the maintenance of public parks and gardens, street lighting, and – a very important aspect of their work – highway planning, car parking, and traffic management schemes. Traffic/transport engineering is becoming an important specialization in itself with special post-graduate or first degree course training. While the majority of municipal engineers take civil engineering degrees, other engineering and some other degrees may be acceptable.

8. CHEMICAL ENGINEERING

Chemical engineers are concerned with the design and development of laboratory processes, and with their translation into large-scale plant, for the production of chemicals, dyes, medicines, fertilizers, plastics, etc. Their expertise in designing and managing plant in which chemical processes take place is also used in food processing, brewing, paper, textile and other industries. They are also concerned with converting noxious waste into useful by-products, or at least into harmless substances. Though chemical engineering is possibly the most highly specialized branch (and the only one for which A-level chemistry is *essential*), it has far wider application than is often believed: many chemical engineers do work in oil refineries and other heavy industry, but there is wide scope elsewhere.

9. PRODUCTION ENGINEERING

See *Production*, above, p. 166.

10. NAVAL ARCHITECTURE

Despite the title, the work is engineering rather than architecture. Though it is concerned with the design and construction of craft which float on or under or hovers just above the water, its main concern is with the efficient and economic operation of craft, of any size from sailing dinghy to supertanker, hydrofoil, oil rig, nuclear-propelled submarine and naval vessel. Naval architects work for the Services as well as for ship- and boat-building firms. A small branch.

11. AERONAUTICAL ENGINEERING

Concerned with aircraft design and construction and space research, as well as with planning, operation and maintenance of airlines' fleets of aircraft and aircraft components. They work for aircraft manufacturers, airlines and the Ministry of Defence. They are also involved with hovercraft and other high-speed transport systems, many of which are still on the drawing board. This is a small branch of engineering, and a greater proportion work in research and development, fewer on production.

12. AGRICULTURAL ENGINEERING

See Agriculture, p. 31.

Prospects (all professional engineering) Good for engineers as a whole, *very* good for electrical, electronics, mechanical and production (function *and* branch) engineers. The broader the application of a specialization, the better the prospects (e.g. naval architects are less adaptable than mechanical engineers). However, as all engineers have a common base, many switch branches during their careers. Many now go into industrial management, or into commerce where an understanding of new technologies and their implications is very useful.

There is also considerable scope *abroad*, especially for chartered engineers (i.e. those who have had experience in a responsible job).

Opportunities are in the Middle East, the developing countries and Europe (where speaking the relevant language is essential).

Pay: Medium to high (see p. xxiii).

Training Engineering degree which leads to 'professional engineer' status and usually to a first job as 'graduate trainee'. The degree can either be in one engineering branch right from the start, or it may be a course which starts with a general engineering first year, allowing students to postpone specialization until they know a bit more about engineering generally. There are also an increasing number of courses which combine engineering with another subject, for example economics, marketing, a modern language or management. Courses, even within individual disciplines, vary in content, some being more industry orientated, others more academic in approach. Before choosing a course prospective students should first study C.R.A.C. *Course Guides* and *Which Degree* and then individual prospectuses.

Sandwich courses are particularly suitable for students who want to go into industry, as it gives them a chance to sample the industrial scene, and it is reassuring for the prospective employer if a job-applicant has had experience of the working world. Many of the large companies now sponsor students (i.e. pay them while they are studying). Sponsored students are 'industry-based', they spend all their work-experience periods with their sponsor's organization; 'college-based' sandwich students have their work-experience periods organized by polytechnic or university and may get experience of a range of employers during their course. There are 'thin sandwich' courses which last 4 or 5 years, with students spending alternately 6 months with employer and 6 months studying; 'thick sandwiches' are 5-year courses with a year each at the beginning and at the end with an industrial employer, and 3 years' studying in the middle.

To be registered as a *Chartered Engineer*, graduates must have spent a few years (at least 3 usually) in 'a responsible position', and must normally have passed a 'professional interview' and been admitted to corporate membership of one of the member Institutions of the Council of Engineering Institutions (each branch of engineering has its own Institution; there are 16). Some Institutions now stipulate a first- or second-class honours degree for membership.

It is possible to switch to engineering with a 'related' degree, which may be, for example, in planning, physics, mathematics or, for certain branches, chemistry. Such graduates would have to satisfy the Institution they wish to join that they have acquired the necessary engineering knowledge (i.e. provide evidence of work done).

It is also possible to become a Chartered Engineer without joining one of the Institutions. The Council of Engineering Institutions sets its own two-part examinations which lead to Registration as Chartered Engineer. Graduates in an engineering discipline normally qualify for exemption from the C.E.I. examinations but the C.E.I. has kept open a non-graduate part-time route to qualifying. It is possible to qualify via T.E.C. and Higher T.E.C. awards (or possibly by taking a special polytechnic course) and then to take the C.E.I.'s own examinations. This route is not recommended: it is lengthy and the drop-out rate is very high. People who cannot take a full-time degree course, for whatever reason, are advised to qualify as Technician Engineers (see below).

In 1980 a Committee of Inquiry into the Engineering Profession published *Engineering Our Future*, a report which became known as 'Finniston', after its Chairman, Sir Monty Finniston. The report's recommendations as a whole were not accepted by the government. But the proposed changes in engineering *education*, or similar changes, may well be implemented in the next few years. In any case prospective engineers and, especially, 'the undecided', who have the right A-levels for, but little interest in, traditional engineering, should be aware of Finniston. They should read *Engineering Our Future* (in its abridged form) because Finniston shows the diversity of functions carried out by professional engineers. These include, apart from the obvious design, development, etc. (i.e. technical ones), such activities as market appraisal, export, marketing, commercial and financial management, etc. Finniston should also help to give technician engineers the status they have long deserved.

Very briefly, proposed changes are these: training should be more manufacturing-industry orientated (for that reason, proposals affect mechanical, electronic/electrical and production engineers more than they affect civil, structural and agricultural engineers); courses should have a greater practical content and include, for example, application of new engineering technologies, manufacturing problem-solving techniques, case studies and project work; courses should be followed by structured training on the job. It is proposed that there be 3 levels of training and qualifications:

1. *Registered Associated Engineers (R.Eng.(Assoc.))*. They would be the 'support force' (technician engineers). Qualification to be at Higher T.E.C. level. Training could be a mixture of part-time and full-time education or entirely full-time, taking 3 to 4 years. Entry with T.E.C. Certificate or 1 relevant A-level. Structured post-qualification training and experience essential before designated R.Eng.(Assoc.).

2. *Registered Engineer (R.Eng.)*. For mainstream professional work. Qualification to be based on a 3-year Bachelor of Engineering (B.Eng.) degree. There would be a 'bridge' for T.E.C. entrants. Again, structured post-qualification training and experience before designated R.Eng.

3. *Registered Engineer Diplomate (R.Eng.(Dip.))*. Qualification would be based on a new 4-year Master of Engineering (M.Eng.) degree course intended for students who, *during their first year on the B.Eng. course*, show leadership potential on the technological *or* on the management side. The first year of the B.Eng. course would be 'diagnostic', so there is no need (indeed no possibility) for school-leavers to choose an elite or mainstream degree course. After the diagnostic year, the B.Eng. and M.Eng. students follow different courses. Structured post-graduate training and experience before designated R.Eng.(Dip.).

Individual degree courses would, as at present, vary in precise content, and A-level requirements, in emphasis and in organization; they would be run at universities and polytechnics.

Position of women

About 2% of Chartered Engineers are women, which is a lower proportion than in any other European country (except Ireland) or the U.S.A. The proportion varies slightly among branches, with a greater (but still tiny) proportion in electronic and electrical engineering.

The reason for the appallingly low proportion is probably partly that far fewer girls than boys take mathematics and physical sciences at O- and A-level. But that is not the whole explanation: there has, in recent years, been an increase in girls taking sciences at school, but there has not been a corresponding increase of women on engineering degree courses. Even in 1979, of all home university students starting technology/engineering degrees only 6·8% were women. Engineering departments have gone to considerable lengths to attract girls, but it is the mistaken image of job opportunities which seems to keep women away.

Women graduates have no special problems getting jobs. Though there are still many firms who discriminate (in practice if not in theory), there are more employers who genuinely want women engineers than there are women applicants. Naturally, only women who do not mind being the only, or one of a few females in a male environment will be happy and successful in engineering. But then (and this cannot be emphasized too strongly) an engineering degree can lead to so many non-engineering jobs. Women engineers are, sometimes, at an advantage when competing with men, because employers realize that women who took up engineering have initiative, whereas for men engineering may be just a career for which they happen to have the right A-levels.

In *Production* women are even more of a rarity than in the other functions (14 women out of 20,000 Members of the Institution of Production Engineers). However, production depends far more than is generally realized on dealing with people; for that reason women can be particularly good at it – once it is accepted that women can also manage men (and in light engineering (electrical and electronic) many assembly lines are all female).

Both the Engineering Industry Training Board and industry are genuinely trying to attract more women into engineering. In conjunction with universities, the E.I.T.B. is now running annual residential 'Insight' weeks for 6th form girls who are thinking of an engineering career but do not know exactly what the jobs involve. In 1980, several conferences were organized to inform careers advisers, parents and girls about the opportunities open to women engineers. In addition, the E.I.T.B. offered bursaries worth £500 to women engineering graduates and generally tried its best, along with the Women's Engineering Society and the Equal Opportunities Commission, to persuade industry to adapt traditional employment structures to women's life patterns (career-break, need for part-time work, etc.).

Career-break: Because of the pace of technological change, a complete gap of several years may be difficult to bridge. Women should at least try to keep up with reading professional journals. However, several schemes for organizing refresher-training were being discussed in 1980: one proposal was that women who want to return to work should, for 6 months, have an 'industrial tutor' – someone in the organization who takes the returners under her/his wing and helps them get up to date. Because of the enormous shortage of engineers, employers are willing to help returners, so in future the career-break is unlikely to be the problem it is at the moment. There are also possibilities of transferring to Technical Writing (p. 403) or (especially) to Teaching (p. 485).

Late start: Not advisable except for exceptionally highly motivated women because first jobs might be difficult. In any case, A-levels have to be recent and up to date.

Part-time: Rare, except perhaps in research or as consultants.

Further information　　Council of Engineering Institutions, 2 Little Smith Street, London SW1 (also as for Technician Engineers, p. 180).

2. Technician Engineer and Technician

Entry qualifications　　Preferably 4 O-levels, including mathematics and a physical science (see **Training** below).

The work　　Technicians are the link between skilled craftsmen and professional engineers. At the top end the technician's job overlaps very much with the professional engineer's: many graduate engineers (see above) are in fact technicians.

Technicians work in all engineering branches and functions (see p. 163), usually under the supervision of professional engineers – at least to begin with. In production, technical sales, marketing, maintenance and after-sales service, experienced technicians often work on their own.

The technician scene is very confusing to anyone outside engineering. There are two grades of technicians: *Technician Engineer* and *Technician*. Their respective duties often overlap. However, *technician engineers* are officially described as 'that group of people who operate immediately in support of chartered engineers ... and sometimes independently', and *technicians* as 'that group of people who apply proven techniques and procedures and carry a measure of technical responsibility under guidance of chartered or technician engineers'. The two technician groups comprise a multitude of levels of skill, expertise, responsibility, training, ambition. Some do work which is equal to that done by chartered engineers in the firm next door; others do work which overlaps with craftsmen's.

Work is as varied as that of chartered engineers and the settings in which technician engineers and technicians work are equally varied and range from hospital to aerospace laboratory, from professional consultant's drawing office to large factory or local authority engineer's department.

Tasks include, for example:

In all branches: draughtsmanship, which may be routine work, but may involve using initiative and special knowledge, and producing working drawings from designers' rough notes and/or instructions; or assisting professional engineers in Research, Design, Development (see pp. 163–7); taking charge of *production processes* and procedures (see Production, p. 166); being responsible, for example, for one or several production lines or for continuity of supplies, or dispatch. Production functions are often subdivided and carried out by technician engineers under a production manager.

Mechanical engineering: as estimating engineer, responsibility for costing projects or parts of projects; supervision of installation of equipment on customer's premises or in firm's own factory; vast variety of *repair and maintenance* work and supervision and coordination of it in anything from garage to hotel, hospital to factory; *after-sales service* to investigate, for example, complaints when central heating has gone wrong (the work is done by technicians or craftsmen, technician engineers diagnose the trouble).

Electrical and electronic engineering: probably the widest scope. Wherever there is electronic equipment, technician engineers and technicians are needed for installation, maintenance, fault tracing, repairs, sales, servicing. This means they are needed in hospitals (see

Medical Engineering above, p. 170); at airports, in places like the Stock Exchange, the Post Office – any organization which uses electrical or electronic equipment (see Computing, p. 134). While large organizations, for example, hospitals, supermarkets or factories, employ their own technicians and technician engineers, the majority are employed by equipment manufacturers and are sent out to service, sell, investigate and repair, which means they visit a variety of customers.

The Post Office employs a large number for work at exchanges and for calling on subscribers (and to work in the road). Technicians work in broadcasting (see p. 77); in hi-fi and similar equipment shops where they repair and service customers' equipment (this again may involve visiting customers' houses); and in commercial recording studios – for example, *balancing engineers* (who must be able to read music and have a good ear) are responsible for producing the required levels of sounds from various sources.

Radio and television servicing is often a simple job; technicians (not technician engineers) employed by TV rental and similar firms are trained to service one or two types of models and call on customers to repair TV sets on the spot, or replace faulty parts. (It is important to find out, when taking this type of job, whether technician training (see below) is available or whether it is a dead-end job without prospects of progressing.)

Civil and Structural Engineering. Technician engineers in traffic management may be in charge of compiling a 'street inventory' prior to the installation of traffic signals (finding out where gas and electricity mains are; what shops/schools and other 'traffic generators' there are); they organize traffic counts and collate accident data. Others cost projects, supervise construction work; work out what equipment is required on bridge or road works; liaise with clients and, in municipal work, with local residents. They also become *building inspectors* for local authorities, or they specialize as design draughtsmen; they investigate new materials and processes; or assist with making land and site surveys (see Surveying, p. 480).

Prospects Very good indeed, especially for electronics and electrical technician engineers. Even during the worst of the recession the demand for technicians and technician engineers exceeded the supply. Experienced technicians and technician engineers are also often able to get work *abroad*. Technician training is broadly based and, once trained, technicians, and even more technician engineers, can switch type of work.

Pay: Medium to high (see p. xxiii).

Personal attributes

Interest in technology and a methodical approach are needed in all technician jobs. There is room for backroom types who like to get on with their work on their own, for those who like to work in a team, those who like to work in a drawing office or laboratory, and for those who enjoy visiting clients and customers. For some jobs, but by no means all, manual dexterity. For others, ability to explain technical points in plain language and liking for meeting people.

Training

There are a variety of training schemes. It is important when getting a job as trainee or learner or junior (or whatever the title) to find out whether systematic training is given. Jobs which do not include systematic training are not 'technician engineer' or 'technician' jobs in the correct sense of the term.

The most up-to-date training pattern is that recommended by the Engineering Industry Training Board; it is widely adopted by employers.

Training starts with 12 months at a training centre which covers basic engineering processes including machining, fitting, welding, electrical wiring, electronic assembly, soldering and sheet metal work. About a third of the time is spent in college on learning the theory to complement the practical training. After the first year, specialized training starts. It is planned to enable the technician to master the six skills which are required in all technician jobs to a greater or lesser degree: choosing materials and components and understanding processing of materials; handling and using measuring tools or instruments; collecting and communicating information; understanding the manufacturing and commercial activities of the employer; planning and organizing one's own work as well as the work of others; diagnosing and solving problems and analysing faults.

Carefully worked out manuals explain, for example, how to consider when writing reports what the recipient's level of technical knowledge is, and what information should be transmitted in any particular situation to client and colleagues and how to transmit it; how to design specifications; how to plan projects: all tasks which are concerned with the organizing of work as much as with doing it.

The length of training varies, largely according to entrants' school qualifications, from 2 to 4 years. Examination structure has just changed (although the old method may still operate in some colleges).

The normal pattern of training is now based on Technician Education Council (T.E.C.) courses (see p. xv). Length of training depends on entry qualifications and aim.

1. Entrants with C.S.E. Grade 2 or 3 in maths, physics and English, and preferably, but not necessarily, in technical drawing or engineering, take a 3-year, part-time, day-release course leading to a T.E.C. Certificate which, with practical experience, leads to registration as

Technician (Tech. C.E.I.). Technicians can then go on to take a Higher
T.E.C. Certificate by two years' further part-time, day-release training
and become registered as *Technician Engineers (T.Eng.(C.E.I.))*. However, minimum entry qualifications are in practice set by colleges, and
many require 4 O-levels.

2. Entrants with O-levels or C.S.E. Grade 1 in maths, physics, English
and one other academic subject normally take a 2-year full-time or a 3-
year sandwich T.E.C. Diploma, or a 2-year, part-time day-release
Certificate, leading to Technician status. Then they do a further 2-year
full-time or 3-year sandwich course for a T.E.C. Higher Diploma (or
they can take a Higher Certificate – see above under 1). Entrants with
at least 1 relevant A-level (usually maths or physics) and at least 4
relevant O-levels or C.S.E. Grade 1s (maths or physics must be included
at O-level or A-level) can go straight into a T.E.C. Higher award course
(either part-time, full-time or sandwich). Some colleges require a second
A-level subject to have been studied, but not necessarily passed.

T.E.C. courses, called 'programmes', are much more flexible than
were the old National Certificates and Diplomas which they are
replacing. T.E.C. programmes are made up of individual 'units', a
certain number of which add up to a Certificate; if more units are added,
a Certificate becomes a Diploma. In practice, most part-time day-
release programmes lead first to a Certificate; sandwich and full-time
programmes lead right away to a Diploma. The procedure is the same
at Higher Certificate and Higher Diploma level. A Diploma, at each
level, denotes greater breadth of knowledge and skills than a Certificate.

Each programme within an engineering discipline contains 'essential
units' taken by all students within the subject area – for example,
electronic or mechanical engineering – and a number of additional
optional units which fit in with the students' individual interests and job
requirements.

Technicians   (Tech.   C.E.I.)   and   Technician   Engineers
(T.Eng(C.E.I.)) are registered with the Engineers Registration Board.
In certain engineering areas the City and Guilds Full Technological
Certificate also entitles holders to be registered as T.Eng.(C.E.I.).

**Position
of women**

There are even fewer women in technician engineering than in professional engineering. The biggest technicians' institution, the Institution
of Electrical and Electronic Technician Engineers, has well below 1%
of women among its 18,000 members; there are even fewer women
technicians and technician engineers in other specializations. Yet
women are genuinely welcomed by employers, quite simply because
there is an enormous shortage of technicians.

The E.I.T.B., in conjunction with employers, organizes several
schemes to recruit and train women technicians. Those who have

finished their training do extremely well. There is no logical reason whatever why so few women take up this type of work – it is only tradition and misconceptions about what technicians do, where they work and what their reception would be, which keeps women away.

Women trainees may occasionally have to overcome some resistance from men who fear all the easy jobs will go to women (for example Post Office technicians have said they fear that women will get all the cushy in-the-exchange jobs, while the men do the outside jobs), but there are ample opportunities in organizations where there is no opposition to women. In electronic engineering, there have long been unskilled female operatives (recruited without the necessary qualifications for technician training – and without any intention of 'training them up' usually), so women technicians do not *have* to enter all-male set-ups.

Career-break: Returners will probably be very welcome – it is too early to be sure. They have to keep up with developments by reading journals or attending occasional lectures, or they can take T.O.P.S. courses as refreshers.

Late start: There are excellent opportunities under T.O.P.S. (see p. xl) for late starters to take technician training, especially in TV and radio servicing and other electrical/electronic specializations.

Part-time: Not very much at the moment, but it is likely that experienced technician engineers could make such arrangements (though this would probably not be possible everywhere).

Further in-formation Engineering Careers Information Service, 54 Clarendon Road, Watford WD1 1LY
Training Services Division (for T.O.P.S. courses), Ebury Bridge Road, London SW1 8PY

3. Crafts (Machine-Shop Crafts – Motor Mechanic – Electrician)

Entry quali-fications Average ability in mathematics, science (*ex*cluding biology), technical/practical subjects (*ex*cluding domestic science). Employers normally test applicants' aptitudes. Maximum age: normally 17 (but see T.O.P.S., p. xl). Many ask for C.S.E. Grade 3 maths.

The work Engineering craftsmen do skilled work and need sufficient theoretical knowledge to understand the principles behind the operations they carry out and to solve basic problems. Craftsmen work in all branches of engineering, and may be in charge of semi- and unskilled workers. Certain crafts or 'trades' (e.g. toolmaking) are practised in most industries, others are more specialized (e.g. marine engine fitting). Most prospective craftsmen are apprenticed to one trade. Some of the commonest trades are:

1. MACHINE-SHOP CRAFTS

(a) *Toolmaking*: a highly skilled trade, involving the use of precision machinery and tools to make jigs, gauges and other tools used in production work. Apprentices may start in the toolroom, or they are upgraded from other trades.

(b) *Toolsetting*: setting up of automatic or semi-automatic machines (such as capstan lathe) for use by machine operators in mass production.

(c) *Turning*: operating lathe, which machines small numbers of articles very precisely.

(d) *Milling*: using a revolving tool to machine pieces fixed in position.

(e) *Jig-boring*: highly skilled work in which very heavy articles are machined to a high degree of precision.

(f) *Grinding*: obtains a very accurate finish by removing small amounts of metal with rapidly revolving abrasive wheels. It is also used to sharpen tools.

2. FITTING

Fitters, whether working in mechanical, electrical or electronic engineering, combine the basic skills of the machine-shop craftsman with the ability to use hand tools. In production work they may assemble cars, generators, TV sets etc.; on customers' premises – private houses, factories, offices, etc. – they carry out maintenance and repair work: gas fitters install, service and repair gas-powered domestic appliances or industrial plant; marine engine fitters put together and repair ships' engines, etc.

Training for (1) and (2) Craftsmen serve a 3- to 4-year apprenticeship, preferably with a company which operates the Engineering Industry Training Board's Module training scheme. The first year is 'off-the-job', learning basic engineering processes such as machining, welding, electrical wiring and electronic assembly, followed by training in one or two skills, on-the-job, with day-release. Each module is a 'package of training and experience'; each module usually takes 1 year; 2 modules qualify for the Certificate of Engineering Crafts. Further modules may be taken either in a different skill, or in the same skill, either updating it (for example learning to use new machines or processes) or becoming more highly skilled. Additional modules lead to endorsements of the Certificate and may lead on to *technician* training (see p. 178).

About 95% of engineering craftsmen now train the E.I.T.B. way. Others learn a craft by attending either day-release or (if this is not granted) evening classes, for City and Guilds Certificate courses; but without the initial off-the-job training it is difficult, if not impossible, to progress in modern engineering.

3. MOTOR MECHANIC

Most specialize as either *Light Vehicle Mechanic*, working on cars and vans, or as *Heavy Vehicle Mechanic*, working on trucks, buses, coaches, etc. Both kinds work *either* in garages to which vehicles are brought for servicing or repair *or* for organizations owning fleets of vehicles. Organization of work varies according to type and size of garage/workshop. For example, in a small roadside garage a mechanic might deal with customers direct and then carry out whatever servicing/repair is required; in a large garage a reception engineer or service manager (who may or may not be a promoted mechanic) would instruct the mechanic what to do. Mechanics occasionally take a mobile repair van to a broken-down vehicle. Work varies from quick and easy repairs to long jobs involving diagnosing faults and doing complex repairs, possibly calling on the help of colleagues with special skills, for example, auto-electricians (a specialization with its own apprenticeship).

In workshops where organizations' fleets of vehicles are serviced, mechanics have contact mainly with other mechanics and there tends to be a hierarchy; in repair/service garages there is more contact with the general public and less of a hierarchy.

Workshops and garages are usually noisy and often cold and, naturally, the work involves getting dirty.

Training for (3)

Normally 4-year apprenticeship with day-release *either* for City and Guilds Certificate *or* for the T.E.C. awards (see p. xv). While T.E.C. programmes have rather higher training objectives (and may make it easier to add additional skills to the basic ones), job and promotion prospects are equally good for apprentices taking the old-established City and Guilds Certificate. There are also some 'integrated' off-the-job (block-release) and F.E. College course schemes. It is highly advisable to take an apprenticeship rather than just a job in a garage (though the latter may be better paid to begin with). Once trained, it is possible to switch to another type of mechanics' work.

4. ELECTRICIAN

She may work in private houses, offices, etc., or in workshops repairing electrical goods. She may work for general building firms, for manufacturers of electrical goods on repair in the workshop and in customers' premises, and she may be self-employed, doing servicing and repair jobs, mainly on customers' premises.

Training for (4)

Apprentices working in workshops of large organizations normally follow the E.I.T.B. apprenticeship scheme (see above), but those engaged in domestic repair and installation work, working for general building contractors or small firms of electricians are unlikely to do so at present. They usually attend day-release (or only evening classes), and learn by working as skilled electrician's 'mate'. It is important to work for the City and Guilds Certificate, which normally takes about 4 years.

Prospects

Vary from one geographical area to another, and depend on economic climate. But intending craftsmen are usually eventually able to find an apprenticeship in the trade of their choice or in a related one.

Craftsmen with good exam results may be able to go on to Technical training.

Pay: Low during training, later medium to occasionally high (see p. xxiii).

Position of women

There are at present very few women indeed in any type of craft except hairdressing. Girls account for only about 2% of apprentices in manufacturing industry and 0·3% in the construction industry. (While about 40% of boys enter crafts apprenticeships on leaving school, only about 7% of girls do so, and over 80% of these go into hairdressing!) There are certainly still many employers who find good reasons for not taking girl apprentices, but others now take them gladly (largely, probably, because they realize that any girl who wants to take craft training is really keen to do so). The engineering industry, especially large employers, and the E.I.T.B. are genuinely trying to attract and train more girls.

There is every reason why women should and could succeed in the trades boys train for, but only girls with the right temperament will enjoy the work (and, incidentally, ease the way for the girls who will follow in their pioneering sisters' footsteps). To enjoy entering what is still a virtually all-male preserve, girls need considerable self-confidence and self-sufficiency: it can be lonely being the only woman in a workshop or on a construction site, or in the canteen. And it can be daunting, when, for example, calling on a household to repair a TV set, to be greeted with amazement. Girls who have taken up welding, carpentry, TV repairing, etc., all say that very few colleagues, or customers, are hostile, but that one has to be prepared to be considered a 'bit odd' and/or a very special person indeed.

Promotion prospects for women are still unknown, but it is likely that girls must not only be good craftsmen, but also have special leadership qualities if they are to be made chargehand and foreman, with responsibilities for male workers. However, anyone who feels she has been passed over for promotion unjustifiably, should consult the Equal Opportunities Commission (see p. xxviii).

Career-break: Craft training must not be interrupted, but once fully trained, a break should not present any problems, though opportunities for employment vary from area to area and returners might have difficulties in areas where there are unemployed young people.

Late start: Maximum age for apprenticeships normally 17, but adults can train, by full-time course, under T.O.P.S. (see p. xl) for a large variety of skills, for example TV repairing, electronic wiring, welding, plumbing.
Part-time: Not normally at the moment.

Further information   Engineering Careers Information Service, 54 Clarendon Road, Watford WD1 1LB
Road Transport Industry Training Board, Capital House, Empire Way, Wembley HA9 0NG

Related careers   *Agriculture and Horticulture – Art and Design – Building Crafts – Engineering Technician – Printing – Surveying Technician*

NOTE 1: There is a vast variety of crafts for which apprentice training (and T.O.P.S. courses) are available – from cabinet- to watchmaking, baking to welding, shoe-repairing to woodworking. There is no room in this book to list them. Consult careers service, and job centres.

NOTE 2: The microchip is making traditional skills and trades obsolete. So traditional apprenticeships – inflexible content, age of entry, duration – are becoming obsolete too. The whole question of how best to train people when technologies are changing established procedures and processes throughout manufacturing and other industries is being re-thought. In the meantime, some companies may offer their own updated training schemes. If such schemes lead to T.E.C., City and Guilds or other recognized qualifications, they are as useful as apprenticeships once were (and they probably take a shorter time to complete). If they do not lead to recognized qualifications, check with Careers Office or relevant I.T.B. before accepting 'traineeship'.

ENVIRONMENTAL HEALTH OFFICER

Entry quali- 2 A-levels and 3 O-levels including English language, a mathematics
fications subject, 2 science subjects. Also *graduate entry*.

The work Environmental Health Officers work for local authorities (see Local
Government, p. 255). They are concerned with the prevention of
disease and the enforcement of regulations designed to secure healthy
living and working environments. They are responsible for:

(1) *Food*: Inspecting places where food is stored, prepared (including
slaughterhouses), sold or served, to check that it is hygienically handled
at all stages. Officers check cleanliness of equipment, washing facilities
for staff, the state of the staff's overalls, etc. They also make spot-checks
on different foods, taking away samples for bacteriological examination
and chemical analysis. In cases of food poisoning officers trace the
source of the trouble, which involves a good deal of detective work.

As well as visiting restaurants, shops, warehouses, etc., environmental
health officers also check food at fairs, exhibitions and stalls. Some
E.H.O.s work for food manufacturers, ensuring efficient and clean
handling and transporting of food, and investigating new technologies.

(2) *Housing*: An officer has powers to enter and inspect homes unasked
if she 'has reason to believe that the premises are not fit for human
habitation'. In most cases she calls only if there has been a request for
advice. She helps to decide whether the premises should be repaired or
modernized, or whether they are only fit for demolition. She must be
able to discuss health and structural questions on equal terms with
experts and to advise landlords and tenants, including those in overcrowded slum property, or owner-occupiers wishing to modernize their
houses. Officers also check on conditions and facilities for caravan and
houseboat dwellers.

(3) *Places of work*: Officers check on satisfactory working conditions:
sanitary arrangements; overcrowding; temperature; ventilation; lighting; provision of seating in shops; closing hours; hours of work for
juveniles. The extent of duties varies, and overlaps with Factory
Inspection (see p. 188).

Environmental health officers are also responsible for implementation
of anti-pollution legislation.

An officer spends more than half her time visiting, inspecting, discussing suggested improvements, etc.; desk work consists mainly of record-keeping and report writing.

Prospects   Good.
       Pay: Medium to high (see p. xxiii).

Training   *Either*: For the Diploma awarded by the Environmental Health Officers' Education Board: 3-year sandwich or 4-year day-release course. Arrangements are made for students to get experience of work not carried out within their authority's area; for instance, students in suburban areas go elsewhere to see factories, caravans, etc.
       Or: 4-year sandwich degree. Syllabus includes the basic sciences as applied to environmental health (control of infectious diseases and of vermin, for instance); physical aspects of housing (dilapidations, unfitness); public cleansing; water supply; drainage, sewerage and sewage disposal; procedures under Housing Acts; hygiene of buildings (standards of heating, ventilation and lighting); food (hygiene and inspection), etc.

Personal   Interest in people's living and working environment; ability to take
attributes   decisions; sufficient self-confidence to go where one is not necessarily welcome, to be firm when necessary and to discuss complicated problems intelligently.

Position   Only a minute proportion of women. Applications from women are
of women   increasing very slowly. However, this is one of the careers where legislation and changing attitudes should help a lot: there never was any discrimination at the *entry* stage, but, largely because women were assumed not to be able or willing to do the rough parts of the work (slaughterhouse and unfit-for-human-habitation dwelling inspection), women did not qualify for promotion – not having had all-round experience. Now women cannot be barred from that part of the work.

Late start: Not much opportunity for on-the-job training, but possible with pre-entry degree training.

Career-break: Should be no problem if you have kept up with developments.

Part-time: Not at the moment, but it should be possible to organize it in this type of work.

Further in-   The Environmental Health Officers' Association, 19 Grosvenor Place,
formation   London SW1X 7HU

| **Related careers** | *Factory Inspector – Food Technology – Housing Management – Trading Standards Officer* |

NOTE: In Scotland education requirements and duties are slightly different.

FACTORY INSPECTOR

Entry quali-
fications
Honours or post-graduate degree (any subject); *or* ordinary degree, T.E.C. Higher Award or equivalent in a scientific or technological subject, plus at least 3 years' experience in industry, preferably in production or similar department. All candidates must have at least O-level mathematics.

The work
A factory inspector is responsible for seeing that the standards required by the Health and Safety at Work and similar Acts are observed in factories and various other places of work. She deals with people as well as with technological problems. She used to be entirely concerned with physical conditions at work, but in 1975 the Health and Safety Executive was set up, and her responsibilities widened. She is now also concerned with the social and psychological implications of technological developments (for example, what leads to, and what situation or innovation diminishes, job satisfaction), and with the effects of industrial hazards – such as toxic waste disposal – on the public.

Her duties are varied. She advises employers on methods of safeguarding health from dust and fumes given off in industrial processes; she checks heating, ventilation, safety of equipment used and standards of hygiene, and she investigates accidents and their causes. Occasionally, she may conduct legal proceedings for which she collects the necessary evidence, prepares the case, and gives evidence. If at all possible she effects changes by persuasion and advice rather than legal action.

She visits places of work at fairly regular intervals, but it is up to her to decide which places need frequent visits and which do not, and she plans her own working day.

There is nothing desk-bound about this career. The work involves gathering first-hand information on conditions in factories, on construction sites, etc. Only about 1 day a week is spent in the office, when the inspector consults with her colleagues, writes up reports and reads technical literature; it is also part of her job to advise industry on new processes and equipment and on the lay-out of new factories.

Prospects
Fair. Factory inspectors are needed in many parts of the country.
Pay: High (see p. xxiii).

Training
2 years on-the-job, but including a 6-month full-time course for Diploma in Safety and Hygiene, as well as other shorter courses.

Personal attributes   Self-reliance; interest in technical matters and in people; diplomacy; ability to get on well with all kinds of people; fitness; initiative; ability to take responsibility; ability to communicate easily; self-confidence to work in male-dominated environments.

Position of women   10% of factory inspectors are women; too few apply. As the work is done in almost entirely male-oriented settings, women have to be willing to face occasional surprise or opposition when visiting factories, and have probably to be better qualified, in terms of work experience and personality, to get promoted on equal terms with male colleagues. However, the Inspectorate genuinely wants more women to apply.

Career-break: In theory, women who keep up with developments should be able to return, but work is not always available everywhere, and generally only in cities.

Late start: Over 30s likely to be accepted for training only if they have had extensive industrial or other relevant experience.

Part-time: None at the moment, though in theory no reason why it should not be possible to arrange small 'caseloads'.

Further information   Health and Safety Executive, Baynards House, 1 Chepstow Place, London W2 4TF
Civil Service Commission, Alencon Link, Basingstoke, Hampshire

Related careers   *Engineering – Environmental Health Officer*

FASHION

Designer – production manager – sketcher, stylist, cutter, assistant designer, assistant designer-cutter, pattern-cutter, pattern-grader – fitter – hand – sample machinist. FASHION SIDELINES: lingerie, corsetry, swimwear, shoes and knitwear – paper patterns – theatrical costume design – embroidery – millinery

Entry qualifications Vary according to the type of training from none to degree.

The work There is a good deal of confused thinking about careers in fashion, which is an industry, not an art. Very few designers create original models or launch a new line which shakes the fashion world. The majority spend most of their time and talent on translating famous designers' ideas and on adapting last year's best-sellers to suit this year's mood, and on producing clothes which are marketable and economic to manufacture.

The industry falls into overlapping sections: haute couture – now a tiny section; 'up market ready-to-wear' – medium-sized; mass production – a vast field; and an uncategorizable group of young determined designers who do not fit into the traditional pattern of the industry.

Haute Couture

Houses show twice-yearly collections. No more than about two dozen copies of any one garment are made; each is cut and made up individually, almost entirely by hand. In the workrooms where this is done, the hierarchy is usually assistant designer, fitters, hands, junior assistants and learners.

A few designers/dressmakers work on much the same lines as couture, except that staff consists of only one or two hands and garments are sold only to individuals, not retailers.

Up-market ready-to-wear

Follows couture trends. Garments are made individually with a considerable amount of hand-work, but graded into stock sizes and sold in limited quantities at home and abroad.

Mass production

Adapts high fashion within limits set by mass-production methods, costing and mass-appeal. Garments are sold in thousands at home and abroad. They are cut by machine, hundreds at a time, and made up with a minimum of hand finishing. By far the largest sector.

Many houses within each of the three categories now produce several types of collections, each under a separate name with its own style and price-range, each collection designed for a given market. Usually each of these collections has its own design team.

Young designers

Usually art and design graduates, with exceptional drive and determination, who set up on their own, with very little capital, possibly working from their homes, often a few friends working together and employing a few 'outworkers'. They usually make trendy clothes for men's, women's or unisex boutiques; some open their own boutiques; a few get some orders from enterprising store buyers; the majority give up after a few years (often heavily in debt). Only the exceptionally lucky, talented and hard-working survive. They either join an established house (but continue designing under their own name) or find financial backing to enlarge and put their business on a sound footing.

The best career opportunities are in the design rooms of wholesale and mass-production houses. Here sample garments and prototypes are worked out before garments go into production.

Working conditions vary. Generally the larger the firm the better the premises, pay, organization, and the atmosphere is less dependent on the designer-employer's temperament, but creative opportunities may not be great.

Different types of jobs:

1. DESIGNER

Titles give little indication of a job's creative content and status. An assistant designer or a pattern-cutter may have more scope in one firm than a designer in another in which the head of the firm has the creative ideas and employs the designer merely to interpret and modify his/her own sketches, or to carry out decisions taken jointly by a team including fabric buyers, production, and marketing specialists.

The designer's job always involves a variety of tasks but it varies enormously according to the size and organization of the firm for which she is working. Few designers spend much time creating styles and trends. Instead, the majority are 'creative technologists', using their creative ability and technical expertise to incorporate trends and their firm's 'hand-writing' into garments which sell on a given type of market (for example, trendy, classic, classy, young, elegant). Most designs are an amalgamation and adaptation of ideas from various sources; perhaps a sleeve the designer thought up herself; a skirt-front featured in a foreign magazine; a pocket-flap seen in a shop-window abroad, a collar sketched roughly by the head of the firm. The skill of the designer shows in how brilliantly she can adapt last year's best-seller to look entirely new, while incorporating features which made it a best-seller.

Designers may do their own *pattern cutting*, which combines ingenuity – saving cloth yet retaining the design's essential features – creative ability and technical knowhow. They may also make working drawings of their own or someone else's designs, cut sample garments, drape and pin them on dress-stand or model, and make necessary adjustments to improve appearance or facilitate manufacture.

Designers work closely with *production managers* (see below) and must understand and be able to use the latest production processes and management principles.

Each garment is costed to fall into a given price range. This may involve working out a compromise, minimizing, for example, the number of operations and components while keeping the maximum similarity between the original conception of the garment and its eventual prototype for, say, 30,000 copies.

When a designer goes to dress-shows in Rome or Paris – by no means all do – she decides whether to buy an (expensive) toile (a draft model tacked up in muslin) for the wealth of its ideas, or whether she can memorize such details as the cut of a sleeve, the position of a dart in relation to the arm-hole, etc. (sketching is not allowed at dress-shows). Her job may include choosing – on her own or jointly with the buyer or merchandise director – the materials for forthcoming collections. This is a challenging task: she has to visualize the potentialities and limitations of materials in design terms, and to evaluate the properties of new fibres in production terms.

Designers work under many constraints, which is challenging, but is entirely different from drawing pretty sketches and either leaving others to translate the idea into something that is marketable, or making it regardless of the cost. That kind of designing is done by only a very few geniuses. Most jobs in fashion combine technical and creative elements – only the proportions of the two vary.

2. PRODUCTION MANAGER

They are a fairly new breed of fashion experts. Work varies as much as, or even more than, designers'. They know exactly what each piece of manufacturing equipment can do; how to adapt garment design to the equipment's limitations; how to change details so as to reduce the number and complexity of operations needed to complete a garment and yet retain as much as possible of the designer's concept. For example, they may suggest a change in the shape or construction of a pocket or collar to ease the production process.

Whether the designer or the production manager decides finally on the detailed construction of a garment varies. In practice, a designer's success is ultimately judged by the profitability of her designs. She is therefore likely to take note of the production manager's suggested modifications even if she is, theoretically, not forced to do so (which, however, she might be).

The production manager is in charge of working out and managing production flow systems – ensuring that the manufacturing process, once it is broken down into a number of operations, will work smoothly, without bottlenecks, and keeping all the operators and equipment evenly busy. In houses which design and manufacture for the boutique trade, production management is particularly tricky as rush orders for short-run designs have to be fitted in at frequent but irregular intervals; the twice-yearly collection system does not apply here.

Production managers must be thoroughly conversant with constantly developing manufacturing technologies, with cutting and sewing-room organization techniques, with quality control methods. They may also be concerned with labour relations and other personnel matters (see Personnel Management, p. 338, Production Management and Production Engineering, p. 166), especially if – as is usual in the clothing trade – the unit is too small to have a personnel officer. In large units there are production supervisors under the production manager.

3. SKETCHER, STYLIST, CUTTER, ASSISTANT DESIGNER, ASSISTANT DESIGNER-CUTTER, PATTERN-CUTTER, PATTERN-GRADER

Their work may be what the titles imply but exact functions and responsibilities depend on the size and type of firm and on the director's temperament and talent. A director of a small wholesale firm may theoretically do the designing him/herself, but in fact may give only a rough sketch to his/her 'assistant designer' or cutter who produces a workable design without getting the credit for having done so.

Pattern-cutting and the highly skilled (non-creative) pattern-grading can be stepping-stones to work with more creative content or to production management.

4. FITTER

The work possibly varies even more. One fitter may be entirely in charge of a workroom, organizing the work and seeing the buyers. Another may work on improvements to the original design before it is put into production. In retail stores and shops a fitter's job is again different. She is in charge of all the alteration work, but does no designing. In this job there is considerable contact with the public.

5. HAND

In couture and retail and in sample workrooms, a hand distributes work to the junior assistants and learners and does the most skilled parts of garment-making herself. The work is very important but not creative; again it may be a stepping-stone.

6. SAMPLE MACHINIST

Exactly what the title implies: she runs up prototypes and samples and often suggests simplifications. Can also be a stepping-stone, but rarely is.

Fashion Sidelines

1. LINGERIE, CORSETRY, SWIMWEAR, GLOVES, SHOE AND KNITWEAR DESIGN

Competent but not necessarily brilliantly creative women have more chance of finding responsible, semi-creative jobs in one of the less known offshoots of fashion: lingerie, corsetry, swimwear, children's wear and especially shoe and knitwear design. This is part creative, part production technology work.

2. PAPER PATTERNS

Designs are adaptations and simplifications of current fashion. Designers must be particularly highly skilled technically, and must be able to design patterns for various types of garments, though some specialize in one type of pattern, such as children's wear, or 'couture' patterns, particularly simple ones, etc.

Designers with a flair for public speaking sometimes visit schools and women's organizations, to give talks on fashion and dressmaking.

3. THEATRICAL COSTUME DESIGN

This is design and dressmaking plus historical research. The sixteenth-century dress or the war-time uniform must be accurate and the material must be suitable for its special purpose. For films or television the garments are not required to last but they must look right under the cameras. For the stage, dresses must be of particularly tough materials. Most of the work is done by specialist firms under the supervision of the designer of the show. Theatrical costume designers often merely fill in details and work to designs they are given. Only occasionally are they asked to 'dress' a show.

Film and television studios have their own art departments where costume supervisors and wardrobe mistresses are in charge of hiring, making, adapting, and maintaining costumes (see Broadcasting, p. 82). There are far more people who wish to do theatrical design than there are vacancies, but there is scope for exceptionally talented and highly trained designers.

4. EMBROIDERY

Machine-embroidery is extensively used in most sections of the fashion industry. Embroiderers usually learn on-the-job, and some eventually do simple embroidery designing. Most designing, however, is done by fashion designers who specialized in embroidery during their degree course. There is considerable scope for embroiderers, not so much for designers.

5. MILLINERY

(a) *Model Millinery*
Model hats are hand-made in workrooms attached to fashion stores, boutiques, etc. A model is rarely repeated more than thirty times. A worker spends up to 3 days making one hat from start to finish. The designer, called 'the milliner', is in charge of design, workroom organization, and of buying the materials. She may also be boutique owner.

(b) *Mass Production*
Hats are mass-produced by machine, with the minimum of hand-finish. Mass-production firms buy originals from model milliners. 'Copyists' then adapt them to mass-production methods and price-range. Organizing production is highly skilled work, demanding knowledge of fashion production (see above).

'Copyists' also produce some designs of their own, incorporating the current fashion trends. Millinery is a declining industry.

Prospects   *Design*: Good only for those with outstanding talent and realistic, thorough training (see below). There is a surplus of designers who have had long but out-of-date, out-of-touch training. Such designers have little hope of jobs, though they can become dressmakers working for private clients – a lonely job – or fitters in store and shop workrooms (which is *not* creative work).

Production Managers: Good if well trained.

The fashion industry is getting more streamlined and more highly capitalized. Small houses are being taken over by large organizations which are businesses first, creators of beautiful garments second. To set up on one's own requires exceptional talent, business acumen – and capital.

Pay: Varies enormously, according to ability. No general rule.

Training   In theory, it is possible to train in a workroom, learning by working and watching. In practice, full-time college training is highly advisable today, and is becoming essential as more new fabrics are produced, each with its own limitations and possibilities, and as production methods and machinery become increasingly more sophisticated: for example some garments are now heat-sealed rather than sewn, pattern-grading is computerized; designers must know what machinery can and cannot do with new materials, and how materials will react to given manufacturing processes. Designers and production managers must also understand marketing and general business aspects of fashion design, production and sales.

No particular type of qualification necessarily leads to a particular kind or level of job; the ultimate value of a course depends largely on 4 factors rather than on the qualification it leads to:

(a) The college must have good connections with industry so that students may work in or at least regularly visit design rooms and factories.

(b) The college must have up-to-date equipment.

(c) At least some of the staff must be working part-time in industry – to know what is happening in this fast-changing field.

(d) The syllabus must include production management and technology as well as design. It does not matter whether the course is held in an art school, polytechnic or technical college.

Various types of courses may and may not fulfil these conditions.

1. Degree in Art and Design, Fashion/Textiles Specialization
For details of degree, see Art and Design, p. 60.

2. B.Sc. (Hons.) in Production Technology

4-year sandwich degree course at Brunel University with Clothing Studies option in years 2, 3 and 4. Candidates need 2 A-levels including mathematics and preferably a physical science, plus 3 O-levels.

3. C.N.A.A. degree BA (Hons.) Clothing Studies

4-year sandwich course at Manchester Polytechnic. Entry requirements: 2 A-levels and 3 O-levels, including mathematics and a science.

4. Courses for the Clothing and Footwear Institute Examinations Parts I and II

Candidates should have 2 A-levels and 3 O-levels, including an English and a mathematics or science subject. Courses are planned in collaboration with industry; numbers of students are kept down to the number of skilled staff which the industry can absorb. Courses take 4 years, including 1 year in the industry. The syllabus includes knowledge of materials, design, anatomy, translation of two-dimensional materials into a three-dimensional form, pattern construction, cutting-room and sewing-room organization and management; production management, work study, marketing; personnel management; basic engineering principles. Candidates must submit a thesis based on their industrial experience.

Clothing and Footwear Institute examination courses put more emphasis on production management; degree courses more on design, but degree holders can eventually take jobs in which production management plays a more important part, and Clothing and Footwear Institute students can specialize in design. Having studied production management in depth they are qualified as designers in mass production fashion manufacture (where there is by far the greatest scope) rather than in couture.

Associateship of the Clothing and Footwear Institute (gained by passing its examinations), plus 3 years' industrial experience, confers 'degree equivalent' status for teaching purposes: useful at the return-to-work stage.

5. 3-year B.E.C. Higher award (see p. xvii) with Fashion option

1 A-level and 3 O-levels.

6. Regional or College Diploma courses

Entry qualifications vary between none and 2 A-levels. Course takes 2 or 3 years.

The usefulness of a course depends on the 4 factors mentioned above.

Candidates are advised to visit the college, ask detailed questions about the course content, connection with industry, and type of work now done by former pupils. Syllabuses vary. Many courses specialize. A few highly specialized courses are of the same value as the degree or Clothing and Footwear Institute examination; for example, courses in knitwear and lingerie and shoe design at Leicester.

(It is worth noting that the Royal College of Art post-graduate courses, for which competition is extremely stiff, accept more students from non-degree courses, i.e. college or regional diploma or Clothing and Footwear Institute courses, than from degree courses.)

7. City and Guilds Certificate Courses

In various aspects of garment manufacture. Craft and Advanced Craft courses cover practical work; technician courses cover supervisory duties. Full-time courses vary in length, normally lasting 1 year for each certificate.

Courses are planned on progressive 'bottom to top' lines; school-leavers without any leaving certificates but with practical ability can advance from one Certificate course to the next and may even, in theory, eventually go to the Clothing and Footwear Institute courses. Students without school qualifications are therefore not necessarily permanently barred from high-level courses.

For students who go straight into industry after leaving school, there are *part-time* courses leading to the same certificates. Normally, part-time students take 2 years over each Certificate course.

Students can also start with a full-time course for a year or two and then continue attending part-time classes while working in the industry.

NOTE: It is important to ensure that a part-time course is *vocational*. Some City and Guilds and other courses are intended for people who merely want to learn enough to make their own clothes. These courses are no use whatever as career preparation. Part-time training *very* rarely leads to design jobs, but may lead to *cutter*.

8. One-Year Full-time Course in Fashion Merchandising

At the London College for the Distributive Trades. Entry qualifications: 4 O-levels in theory; in practice, because of competition for places, 2 A-levels are usually necessary.

The course is geared to retailing, and covers properties and performance of textiles, colour and design, display, accounting, customer relations, retail organization, evolution and psychology of fashion. Students spend 1 day a week working in a variety of stores and boutiques. They also do 'projects' which involve research and writing up research results.

See also Fashion Writers' course (Journalism, p. 224).

9. *Workroom and Factory Training*

No educational requirements; there are now hardly any apprenticeships. *Workroom* and *factory* training are quite distinct and lead to different work:

Workroom training, 4–5 years, learning making-up by hand and sewing-machine. This *may* eventually lead to design-room work, but *not* to designing; or, in retail, to fitter. The individual has to make herself noticed so that she is given a variety of jobs and not left to sew in sleeves or do hems for years. Hardly any day-release; ambitious workers must go to evening classes.

Factory training teaches mass-production methods. With evening classes it may lead to senior posts, including that of cutter and to production management, but not to design-room work.

Personal attributes

For top level designers: visual imagination and creative genius; exceptional business flair or a partner with business flair or unlimited capital; the power to make customers trust their judgement; a flair for sensing what people may be persuaded to buy next year and for making staff work devotedly; technical ability; absolutely unshakeable faith in their own talent; determination to overcome apparently insurmountable obstacles; (ability to draw beautifully is *not* necessary); lynx-eyes and a photographic memory for details once seen.

For others: visual imagination and colour sense; a good deal of creative talent but willingness to subdue this to the technical and economic necessities of design for a popular market; finding satisfaction in creating something which is firstly saleable and secondly artistic; adaptability; ability to work as one of a team; some manual dexterity; dry hands; good feet; self-confidence; ambition; determination.

For production management: as above, plus interest in the technology of fashion, and organizing ability.

Position of women

TOP JOBS

1. *Designers*: In women's up-market ready-to-wear and mass-production an increasing proportion of designers are women; but while there are lots of male designers in women's fashion, no woman has yet succeeded in men's fashion (which is big business too, now).

2. *Production Managers*: *Very* few women at the moment; more would be very welcome, because women production managers are more likely to want above all to work in fashion and choose production management as a way in. Male production managers tend to drift into fashion production as a production management job.

Career-break: (1) *Designers*: Depends on how established before break. (2) *Production Management*: Probably no problem for women who have had good experience before the break. Changing technologies can easily be coped with by well-trained production managers.

Late start: Depends on talent and drive: competition from young college-leavers is very stiff.

Part-time: Not normally, except as freelance designer, or, *very* occasionally, as relief (holiday) cutter, etc.

Further in-
formation
Clothing and Allied Products Industry Training Board, Tower House, Merrion Way, Leeds LS2 8NY

The Clothing and Footwear Institute, Albert Road, Hendon, London NW4 2JS

City and Guilds of London Institute, 76 Portland Place, London W1N 4AA

Related
careers
Art and Design – Broadcasting – Journalism – Photography –
Public Relations

FLORISTRY

Floral make-up – buying – outside work – hotel florist

Entry quali- No specific requirements, but English language, art or science C.S.E. or
fications O-level advisable.

The work There are, broadly, four aspects:
1. *Floral Make-up*: consists of wiring, 'mossing and de-thorning'
bouquets, wreaths, sprays, and a wide range of set table-decorations.
Wiring a presentation bouquet or making a set piece may take anything
from an hour to a whole day. Set pieces are usually made from sketched
or detailed designs. For bouquets, makers-up are normally given the
flowers and then use their own imagination.
  The majority of florists work on making-up. Some combine this
backroom work with selling in the shop; others who work in small shops
or on their own also do the buying. The buyer often has to start work
at 5 a.m. Making-up is usually done in damp, cool rooms, and the
conditions are adjusted to suit the flowers rather than the staff. The
work is hard on the hands, and most of it has to be done standing up.
But the atmosphere in flower-shops is usually friendly.
2. *Buying Flowers*: from markets or market-gardeners, requires a
knowledge of market prices at various times of year and of the revival
powers of wilted flowers.
3. *'Outside Work'*: involves regular trimming, watering and generally
keeping in good order the window boxes of office blocks and official
buildings, making and arranging table decorations for private banquets;
and flower work in hotels, exhibition halls, etc.
  Outside work is often done at odd times depending on the type of
work. Flowers may be needed just before a banquet, and window-boxes
in busy streets may have to be watered late at night when the traffic is
less heavy. The florist on outside work meets a great many people and
sees many different houses, hotels, and exhibitions.
4. *Hotel Florist*: a minority of experienced florists are employed by
hotels and catering firms, etc., to run the 'flower side'. This is done
either single-handed or as an organizer with a staff to do the actual
making-up. The florist is part of the hotel staff and meets colleagues and
guests from all over the world. Hotel work involves long irregular hours
with early mornings and late nights.

Prospects   Fair. There is plenty of work in making-up, but other jobs are not easy to find. Experience and capital are essential for setting up on one's own. *Abroad*: Occasionally.

      Pay: Low to medium (see p. xxiii).

Training   *Either* 3- to 12-month courses at private floristry schools (expensive, grants not usually given);

Or as trainee with part-time (evening usually; day-release rarely) study for City and Guilds Certificate Parts 1, 2 and 3;

Or full-time 1- or 2-year courses (only a few available) for same City and Guilds Certificates;

Or (one only) 3-year full-time O.N.D. in Floristry and Flower Production at Welsh College of Horticulture.

      The Society of Floristry holds annual examinations for an Intermediate Certificate and a Diploma in Floristry. No specific training, but to be accepted for examination candidates must hold *either* City and Guilds Stage 2 Certificate with credit or distinction, or the O.N.D.

Personal attributes   Nimble fingers; patience; good health (no tendency to chilblains); visual imagination; good colour sense; organizing ability for managerial posts; a friendly manner for shop, outside and hotel work.

Position of women   An almost all-female profession.

Career-break: No problem.

Late start: Difficult to get traineeship, but full-time courses may qualify for T.O.P.S. grant (see p. xl).

Part-time: Good opportunities.

Further information   City and Guilds of London Institute, 76 Portland Place, London W1N 4AA

Related careers   *Agriculture and Horticulture – Art and Design*

HAIRDRESSING

Entry quali- No special qualifications.
fications

The work Both men and women work in men's, women's and unisex salons.

All hairdressers are on their feet almost all day. If well trained they can choose whether to work in an elegant salon, where the pay and tips are higher but the work probably harder, or in a small suburban hairdresser's, where they earn a little less but where the atmosphere is likely to be more relaxed.

Apart from cutting, shampooing, tinting and styling, a hairdresser may also look after and order stores, keep the appointments book, do simple book-keeping, make out bills, measure clients for and 'dress' wigs, switches, and other kinds of 'made-up' hair. Wig-making is expanding, but wigs are made in special workrooms, not by hairdressers.

Prospects Fair but depend on locality and economic conditions. There are also a few jobs in hotels, on ships and in television studios (see Broadcasting, p. 82) for experienced hairdressers.

There is scope everywhere abroad, except in the United States. Resorts in most tourist countries welcome experienced hairdressers who speak the relevant language. Hours in holiday places are long, but the pay is good. As there is always a slack time between the winter and summer seasons, it is difficult to get a permanent job abroad.

Pay: Low to very high (see p. xxiii).

Training There are 3 ways:

1. *3-year indentured apprenticeship*
supplemented by day-release and some evening classes. Formal apprenticeships are taken in salons approved by the British Hairdressing Apprenticeship Council. Such salons undertake to see to it that apprentices are properly taught, and given day-release. Good salons spend 1 night a week teaching cutting, scalp massage, tinting, etc.

At college, apprentices are taught hygiene, the nature of hair, and some chemistry, tinting and bleaching, the rudiments of wig-making. At the end of the training, apprentices sit for City and Guilds examination.

2. 2-year full-time course at colleges of further education

The courses are recognized by hairdressing associations as the equivalent of an apprenticeship, and also lead to the City and Guilds examination. They cannot, of course, give the same opportunities for learning how to deal with clients. Technical college courses are the first choice for anyone too shy to ask questions and who finds it hard to pick up facts for herself.

Both day-release and full-time college courses deal with men's and ladies' hairdressing.

3. 6- or 12-month course at private hairdressing schools

Pupils from private schools cannot normally sit City and Guilds examination. Most schools' own diplomas are not recognized by the majority of hairdressers. Fees at private schools are high. There is no legal need for hairdressing schools to register or be licensed, and some give very poor training.

Anyone who joins as a 'junior' or as a 'shampoo-girl' on a proper salary will usually be too busy to learn and is not entitled to the type of teaching given to an apprentice. However, though this method of learning is frowned upon by many hairdressers, some juniors who start in good salons where there are regular weekly 'practice nights' do eventually get good jobs. Only when registration of hairdressers becomes compulsory will all hairdressers have to train at recognized schools or as apprentices.

Personal attributes Fashion flair; some artistic ability; a friendly, outgoing personality; an unruffled manner and pleasing appearance; dexterity; good health, especially strong feet.

Position of women The top salons now welcome female stylists as they once only welcomed men.

Late entry: Difficult to get apprenticeship and college vacancy.

Career-break: No problem. Many hairdressers work from home, taking on a few private clients.

Part-time: Plenty of scope.

Further in-   Joint Training Council for the Hairdressing Industry, Crossroads House,
formation   165 The Parade, Watford, Hertfordshire

Related   *Beautician – Model-making*, p. 58 – *Window Display*, p. 58
careers

HEALTH SERVICE ADMINISTRATION

Entry quali- For membership of Institute of Health Service Administrators: 2 A-
fications levels, 3 O-levels including English or English Language, mathematics
and a science.

The work In 1974, the hospital, general practitioner and community health services
were welded into one administrative structure. Health service administration now covers a far wider field, and offers more scope for
administrators' individual skills, qualities and preferences than did its
predecessor, *hospital administration.*

Health service administrators are the non-medical staff responsible
for the general management, coordination and smooth running of all
services provided by staff, from clerk to consultant, cook to G.P. The
work is varied and includes decision-making based on up-to-date
management techniques and principles; the planning of future requirements (human and material); financial forward planning; as well as
responsibility for maintenance of buildings, purchase and control of
supplies and equipment, personnel management, and for the organization of support-services such as laundry, catering, domestic work and
transport.

Individual administrators' functions vary according to specialist skills
and interest as well as according to the level of the administrative
structure at which they work. For example, at the 14 Regional Health
Authorities' offices, administrators are primarily concerned with forward planning, and with assessing needs and priorities of the 90 smaller
Area Health Authorities, which administer services in the 90 areas. The
day-to-day managing is done by administrators at the 205 'Districts',
and in hospitals, health centres and family practitioner committee
offices. Specialist administrators (see **Training**) are more likely to work
at 'Area' and 'Region' levels. At grass-roots level, administrators have
some contact with patients. There is scope for those who want to meet
the public, making appointments, checking in arrivals, dealing with
queries and complaints, and for those who prefer backroom work –
which nevertheless also helps to improve the patients' lot.

NOTE: Health Service structure is about to change but administrators'
work will basically remain the same.

Prospects   Fair but depend on current levels of public expenditure.

Pay: Medium to high (see p. xxiii).

Training   Membership of Institute of Health Service Administrators used to be the normal route to top jobs. There is now a trend for specialists with professional qualifications – in, for example, chartered secretaryship, personnel, information systems, management, accountancy – to go into health service administration. Specialist qualifications are as useful as Membership of the Institute of Health Service Administrators. Candidates who are interested in one aspect of administration can therefore train for the appropriate qualification; those who are not sure which field interests them most or who know they will want to stay in the Health Service, can train for Membership of the Institute of Health Service Administrators. There are various trainee schemes:

1. For graduates and those with equivalent qualifications (organized by the National Staff Committee in association with the King's College Fund, Nuffield Centre, at Leeds, Manchester and Birmingham Universities):
(a) 27-month training scheme for I.H.S.A. examination.
(b) 40-month training in financial administration leading to the Institute of Public Finance and Accountancy examination.
2. For those with 2 A-levels and 3 O-levels: 3- to 4-year regional schemes, leading to various professional or I.H.S.A. examinations.
3. For those with at least 4 O-levels or B.E.C. award (see p. xvii): occasional regional schemes of varying length.

Staff may also attend short courses on specialist subjects, e.g. in computing, or in supply, designed to develop potential for promotion to higher posts; administrators' Development Courses provide management training for trainees and other staff in the 23–35 age-group. At more senior levels, staff may attend multidisciplinary management courses.

Personal attributes   Efficiency; adaptability; the ability to discuss complicated issues with specialists at all levels; organizing ability; tact and diplomacy.

Position of women   Still far fewer women than men in senior administrative jobs, but now almost half of all I.H.S.A. students are women. Women still have to be more highly motivated than men. For promotion it is usually necessary to move around to get varied experience.

Career break: Should be no problem. Some area health authorities are 'considering' *refresher* in-service training. However, promotion prospects are restricted in practice when competing with colleagues who have gained wider administrative experience. Seniority, rather than 'life experience', counts in Health Service administration.

Late start: Women over 30 who work in, or have worked in, the N.H.S. may become I.H.S.A. students with lower than normal entry requirements. For *Graduate* Training Scheme the upper age limit is 30. Specialists in accountancy (see p. 1), chartered secretaryship (see p. 131), personnel management (see p. 338), supplies (see Purchasing, p. 384) and work study (see p. 502) can go into health service administration up to about 50.

Part-time: Occasional opportunities; no reason why women administrators should not suggest job-sharing schemes.

Further information

National Staff Committee, Department of Health and Social Security, Hannibal House, Elephant and Castle, London SE1 6TE

Institute of Health Service Administrators, 75 Portland Place, London W1M 4AN

Related careers

Company Secretary – Institutional Management, p. 106 – *Secretarial Work*

HOME ECONOMICS

Entry quali- None laid down; depends on **Training** (see below).
fications

The work   Home economics is basically domestic science updated to take account
of the needs of present-day consumers, whether they are shoppers,
providers of home creature comforts, or family units with special
problems, e.g. they might be one-parent families, immigrants who have
no knowledge of wise buying in this country, or simply poverty stricken.

Home economists work in various settings: industry, social services,
public relations, consumer advice, the retail trade. There is nothing
clear-cut about the professional home economist's work: people with
related kinds of training may do the same, or similar, jobs; and qualified
home economists may branch off into related fields such as catering,
marketing, journalism.

The majority of home economists work in manufacturing industry on
development, quality control, promotion and marketing of products,
appliances and equipment used, or services provided in the home.
Before new or improved food and washing products, dishwashers,
cookers, central heating systems, etc. are put into production, home
economists discuss details of design and performance with engineers,
scientists, designers, marketing people. They act as link between users
and products, and put the customers' point of view; they test prototypes
in the laboratory under 'ideal conditions', and they also use them in the
same way as the housewife might – being interrupted in their work and
not always following the instructions as they should. For instance, they
test whether a new type of fat creams easily enough, even if kept in the
fridge too long and if clumsily handled; how a washing machine behaves
if switches are turned on in the wrong order, or how easily a new cooker
cleans when it is really dirty. As a result of laboratory and 'user' tests,
alterations are often made before a product is put into production.

For manufacturers and for gas, electricity and solid fuel suppliers
they work as 'home service advisers' (titles vary). They visit consumers
in their own homes: this may be a straightforward 'after sales service';
more often it is to investigate a complaint, maybe about a central
heating installation which is not working properly. This requires the
home economist to be able to diagnose the fault and perhaps then to
explain tactfully that the instructions have not been followed. Increasingly they are involved with educating the public in the need for, and

methods of, energy conservation (for example, home insulation and other fuel-saving devices).

The work combines dealing with laymen who have much less technical knowledge, and with experts who have very much more.

Under the heading *'customer relations'* or *'marketing'*, work involves writing clear, concise user-instructions for explanatory labels and leaflets which accompany fish-fingers, freezers, synthetic fibre carpets, babyfoods, etc., as well as dealing with inquiries and complaints correspondence.

Home economists also identify demand for new products or changes in existing ones. This may involve field work – interviewing potential customers in their homes (see Market Research, p. 18) and thinking up innovations which could *profitably* be marketed.

In the *media* – magazines, newspapers, TV and radio – home economists prepare features and programmes: they cook and cost elaborate as well as very cheap dishes, or arrange and cost domestic interiors which are then photographed and described, or demonstrated on TV.

In local authority *social services departments* home economists may advise low-income families on budgeting and general household management; and they may run the home-help service and advise on the efficient running of the authority's residential homes.

In *hospitals* home economists become domestic administrators at top management level.

They may also work in the Trading Standards Department (see p. 497) in the consumer advice services.

Experienced home economists can work as freelance consultants: firms may wish to research and/or promote a new product and need a home economist for a particular project rather than permanently. For example, home economists worked as freelances on metrication, writing explanatory leaflets; changing recipes and equipment, etc.

Prospects Depend very much on economic conditions; though the combination of technical knowledge and understanding of family and consumer needs can be useful in a variety of jobs, competition for jobs is very keen indeed. Jobs tend to be concentrated in cities. Greatest scope probably in food and domestic appliance manufacturing.

Pay: medium (see p. xxiii).

Training No particular qualification leads to any particular type of job. It is possible for anyone with basic approved training or related training (see Catering, Institutional Management, p. 106) and the right experience and personality ultimately to do as well as a graduate. But the more thorough the training, the wider the scope of job.

(1) *For candidates with at least 2 A-levels:*

(a) Home Economics degree (either at university or at the reorganized colleges of education (see Teaching, p. 489). Mathematics and a science O-level may be required; no specific A-levels.

(b) Degrees in related subjects, such as Nutrition, Food and Management Science, Hotel and Catering Administration. Usually 1 A-level science requirement; chemistry at least at O-level.

(c) 2-year Diplomas in Higher Education (see Teaching, p. 490). Some offer home economics or related modules, which can then lead to further home economics or teaching or other professional training.

(2) *For candidates with 1 A-level and 4 O-levels*, including an English and a science subject (and, usually, mathematics), 3-year course for *Home Economics Diploma*. (In practice 2 A-levels may be necessary.)

Degree and Diploma syllabuses include varying amounts of: food and materials science; nutrition; social studies; administration; home management; business and marketing studies. Courses normally include a period of practical work in industry/institutions.

(3) For candidates with 4 O-levels, including an English subject: 2-year *Certificate in Home Economics* at further education college. Syllabus covers home management; social studies; food and nutrition; and in most colleges a number of optional subjects: recipe development; fabrics and fashion; community services, etc.

(4) *For those with none to 4 O-levels*: City and Guilds part- and full-time craft-level courses in housekeeping and catering (unlikely to lead to home economics job immediately; more likely to lead to assistant in residential homes, hospitals). Syllabus similar to Home Economics Certificate, but geared to work in residential homes, hospitals, etc., rather than to industry.

Personal attributes

Practicality and organizing ability; interest in consumer affairs and in streamlining housework. *For top-jobs*: ability to understand both consumers' and manufacturers' point of view; ability to communicate easily both with more highly qualified professional and with often poorly educated, possibly illiterate, consumers; a liking for working with and for women.

Position of women

This is a virtually 100% women's occupation. Industrial and media employers of home economists tend to think of customers for whose benefit home economists work as housewives or women. Anyone who feels strongly about equality might not fit into many of the jobs done by home economists.

Late start: Mature entrants are welcome on all courses and should not have more difficulty than young entrants in getting work, as their own experience in bringing up a family is useful in this field. 1-year general housecraft courses qualify for T.O.P.S. grants (see p. xl); 2-year courses are sometimes shortened to 1 year for mature entrants.

Career-break: Should be no problem at all.

Part-time: Not normally, but see paragraph about *Freelance Consultants* above, p. 210.

Further in- **formation**	The Secretary, Association of Home Economists, 307 Uxbridge Road, London W3 *Craft-level courses from autumn 1981*: City and Guilds of London Institute, 76 Portland Place, London W1N 4AA

Related **careers**	*Catering – Dietitian – Public Relations – Teaching (Housecraft,* *p. 491) – Trading Standards Officer*

HOUSING MANAGEMENT

Entry quali-
fications

2 A-levels, including English language, and 3 O-levels *or* B.E.C. National award in Public Administration or T.E.C. award in Property Management and Housing Services. Considerable graduate entry.

The work

Traditionally, housing managers are responsible for the administration, maintenance and allocation of accommodation let for rent. Since the early 1970s their scope has expanded enormously and it is still expanding. It now also includes, for example, the running of Housing Aid Centres; the administration of rent rebate and rent allowance schemes; housing research and the formulation of housing policy. The majority of housing managers and housing assistants work for local authorities; a growing number work for housing associations and a few for private property owners.

Day-to-day housing work adds up to an unusual combination of dealing with people, using technical knowledge and getting out and about. Duties include interviewing applicants for homes; visiting prospective tenants in their homes to assess their housing needs; inspecting property at regular intervals and arranging, if necessary, for repairs to be carried out; dealing with tenants' complaints about anything from noisy neighbours and lack of play facilities for children to leaking roofs or lack of maintenance. Rent collecting, which used to be the most important and time-consuming task, is dying out: most tenants now take or send rent to the housing office. But as soon as a tenant falls into arrears, the housing assistant still visits. As rent arrears are often the first sign of social distress, housing management is a preventive social service; there is a considerable element of social work in housing management; staff work closely with social workers. For example, if a housing assistant notices a disabled person's or an unsupported mother's need for help, she alerts the social services department. She herself might help, for example, if a family who move from a one-room hovel into their first adequate home need advice on how to budget for new furniture.

Housing staff try to establish or maintain good tenant–landlord relationships and try to forge a conglomeration of dwellings into a community. To this end they may try to involve tenants in managing their block of flats or estate, or they may set up tenants' management committees. In Housing Aid Centres, housing staff advise on any problem related to housing, from how to cope with an eviction order or how to get a rent allowance, to where to apply for a mortgage.

At senior level, the work involves top-level general and financial management using modern management techniques; the purchase of properties; the allocation of accommodation (which is the most onerous task); research into general housing needs and into such questions as 'How can we retain the neighbourliness of the slums in new developments?', 'What is a good environment?', etc.; advising architects and planners on social aspects of siting, design and lay-out of new developments.

Many housing managers prefer to stick to day-to-day management throughout their careers, because they enjoy dealing with people.

In local authority departments which administer thousands of dwellings, staff usually specialize in one aspect of the work at a time. In housing associations, which manage a smaller number, one housing assistant or housing manager may deal with everything concerning a number of tenancies. While this makes for more variety of day-to-day work, there is usually more scope for promotion in local authorities.

Prospects   Good normally but depends on current level of public expenditure.
Pay: Medium (see p. xxiii).

Training   1. The traditional method: on-the-job with day-release for the Institute of Housing Professional Qualification. Students are given experience in the various housing functions and may be seconded for a time to a housing association (or to a local authority if they are training with a housing association). Training takes about 3 years, less for graduates. The syllabus includes building construction and maintenance (to a standard which any interested woman can cope with whether technically-minded or not); landlord and tenant law; town planning and other relevant law; organization of social services and local government; estate records and accounts.
2. Degree in Housing Studies, which covers the wider social aspects of housing and includes some social administration; it leads to total exemption from the Professional Qualification.
3. Social science degrees and diplomas which lead to partial exemption from the Professional Qualification.
4. For housing association work only: any degree or professional qualification, and learning on-the-job – not necessarily for the Institute of Housing qualification.

Personal attributes   Getting on well with all types of people; an interest in social problems, and in planning; tolerance; ability to be firm; physical fitness and agility, for such tasks as climbing into roofs and examining drains; indifference to being out in bad weather.

**Position
of women**

The proportion of women and men entering housing is fairly even, but of over 400 local authority housing managers in 1978 only 18 were women (see Local Government, **Position of women**). This situation is likely to change; there is no reason whatever why women should not do better. They do very well in housing associations.

Career-break: Returners are usually welcome, but depends on level of unemployment.

Late start: Late entrants welcome in theory, but training vacancies are often difficult to find for mature entrants. Untrained mature entrants often do the same work as trained younger people, without the chance of promotion. More opportunities in housing associations where aptitude and relevant work, as well as 'life experience', are more important than qualifications.

Part-time: Fair opportunities.

**Further in-
formation**

The Institute of Housing, 12 Upper Belgrave Street, London SW1

**Related
careers**

*Environmental Health Officer – Local Government – Planning –
Surveyor*

IMMIGRATION OFFICER

**Entry quali-
fications**
2 A-levels and 3 O-levels in approved subjects, one of which must be English or English language, or promotion from the Clerical Officer grade (see Civil Service, p. 125). In practice, though this is not an official requirement, usually fluency in a foreign language. Many candidates are *graduates*.

The work
Immigration officers are responsible for checking passports and credentials generally of persons arriving and departing from sea- and airports. They are responsible for carrying out regulations governing the entry of persons to this country. The work can be tricky and distasteful when officers have to ask searching questions to try and ascertain personal details from arrivals, however sympathetic they may feel towards the individual they have to question; in the interests of upholding the law, officers may have to be suspicious and thus possibly embarrass the innocent in order to catch out the guilty. When necessary they have to take harsh action and refuse entry to would-be immigrants or visitors. (Senior officials take final decisions.) However, most of the time the work merely involves routine checking of documents.

The atmosphere at ports and airports is always lively (and noisy). Immigration officers meet large numbers of people – each usually very briefly.

Prospects
Apart from promotion to chief immigration officer at a port, opportunities exist for promotion to higher executive officer and other posts in the Civil Service. In addition, after at least 2 years' experience, immigration officers can become administrative trainees and go up the administration ladder (see Civil Service, p. 121).

Pay: Medium to high (see p. xxiii).

Training
Given after entry, largely on-the-job.

**Personal
attributes**
Aptitude for foreign languages; interest in current affairs; patience, tact and courtesy; quick judgement in order to make accurate assessments of people after a short interview; ability and willingness to stand the pressure of enforcing what may appear harsh regulations.

**Position
of women**
Women have only recently been able to become Immigration Officers. About 12% are women.

Further in-   See Civil Service, p. 130.
formation

Related   *Civil Aviation (Ground Staff) – Civil Service*
careers

INSURANCE

**Entry quali-
fications**
Either B.E.C. National award (see p. xvii); or 2 A-levels and 2 O-levels, including English at either level and one A-level to be in one of the following: English, Mathematics, Geography, History, a foreign language, Natural Science, Economics, Public and Economic Affairs, British Constitution, Surveying, Accounting, Sociology, Law.

Also *Graduate entry*.

The work
Insurance is a method of compensating for losses arising from all kinds of misfortunes, from the theft of jewellery to the loss of a ship at sea. It is based on the principle that many more people pay regularly into a common fund than ultimately draw from it, and thus the losses of the unlucky few may be made good. The organizers of the system are the Insurers, i.e. the insurance companies or Lloyds' underwriters. Lloyds itself is not an insurance company, but a society whose members transact business as individuals, or as individual companies.

It is usual to specialize in one of the main branches of insurance: marine, aviation, life and pensions, property, accident, motor liability and reinsurance, although transfers are possible.

Insurance *brokers* act as intermediaries, bringing together the insurers and those who wish to be insured.

In the office, risks are assessed by the underwriting department, and according to the degree of hazard, a premium is agreed upon. A contract is drawn up based on the premium, and arrangements are made for the premium to be paid regularly. When a claim is received, losses are assessed to determine the sum the sufferer should be paid in fairness to all parties.

Other jobs involve visiting clients. *Inspectors* have a good deal of independence: they are responsible for obtaining new business and ensuring that existing clients' cover is adequate in changing circumstances. *Outside claims officials* are responsible for inspecting damaged property.

Prospects
Prospects of promotion are good only for people entering with A-levels, H.N.D. or degree in Business Studies. There are increasing opportunities, particularly for graduates, in specialist fields such as insurance law.

Pay: Medium (see p. xxiii).

Abroad: Possible in theory. There are branches of insurance in most parts of the world.

Training

1. *On-the-job*: with day-release for 3 years (evening study is also necessary) for associateship of Chartered Insurance Institute, followed by one year (approximately) for Fellowship C.I.I., or for B.E.C. Higher award. This leads to partial exemption from C.I.I. examinations, and leaves options open for work in other commercial fields.

2. *Pre-entry*: Degree in Business Studies with insurance options, *or* full-time or sandwich B.E.C. Higher award. (See pp. xvii, 265.)

Personal attributes

Some mathematical ability; a liking for paper work; ability to grasp the essentials of a problem; sound judgement; determination and a certain amount of push; tact; a persuasive confidence-inspiring manner; ability to communicate with people, often in difficult circumstances.

Position of women

Well under 10% of qualified, but 25% of student, members of the Chartered Insurance Institute are women. The tradition of men in senior jobs is still strong in this industry and women have to be very determined and very good indeed to get to the top. No problem at middle-level jobs.

Career-break: Previously qualified returners are usually welcome if they have kept up with developments. Retraining on an *ad hoc* basis.

Late entry: Possible, some relaxation of minimum qualification, but training vacancies might not be so easy to find. Upper age limit in practice 30.

Part-time: Few opportunities.

Further information

The Careers Information Officer, The Chartered Insurance Institute, The Hall, 20 Aldermanbury, London EC2

Related careers

Accountancy – Actuary – Banking – Computers – Stock Exchange

NOTE: From 1982 the Fellowship examination will be more difficult: non-graduates may take more than a year training for it.

JOURNALISM

Newspapers – Magazines

Entry quali- *Newspapers*: 5 O-levels including English language for traineeship, but
fications nearly all school-leaver entrants have at least 1 A-level, most have 2;
one-third of entrants are graduates. For pre-entry course: 2 A-levels.
Magazines: Depends on editor; for pre-entry course: 1 A-level, 4 O-
levels.

The work Journalism covers a variety of jobs in a variety of settings (or 'media',
which really should be 'media of communications'). Broadly, the main
job groups are *reporter*; *correspondent* or *specialist writer*; *feature writer*;
news editor; *editor*; *freelance*. Division of duties depends on paper's size
and organization.

Newspapers

Virtually every journalist starts as trainee-reporter. *Reporters* cover any
kind of event: from council or Women's Institute meeting to political
demo, fire, or press conference for visiting film star or foreign statesman.
Reporters 'get a story' by asking questions and listening to other
journalists' questions and interviewee's answers at press conferences, or
in one-to-one interviews with individuals. For such interviews, reporters
have to do some preliminary 'homework' – for example to interview a
trade union secretary or famous novelist requires some background
knowledge.

Reporters must compose stories quickly, sometimes dictating them
over the phone, sometimes typing them in a noisy office. Accuracy,
brevity and speed are more important than writing perfect prose:
reporting is a fact-gathering and fact-disseminating rather than creative
job.

Occasionally, reporters may be on a particular story for several weeks,
researching the background and/or waiting for developments. They
work irregular hours, including weekends.

SPECIALIST REPORTER OR CORRESPONDENT

'Hard news' is broadcast more quickly than it can be printed; to fight TV and radio competition, newspapers have developed 'interpretative' or specialist reporting. Specialists' titles and precise responsibilities and scope vary; the aim always is to interpret and to explain news and comment on events, trends, causes and news behind the news. The number (and the expert knowledge of) specialists varies according to the type and size of newspaper. On the whole, only the nationals have specialists who concentrate entirely on one speciality; on other papers and in news agencies, reporters with a special interest in a particular field (or several) may do specialist along with general reporting. The main specializations are: parliament and/or politics generally; industry; finance; education; foreign news; local government and/or planning; social services; sport; science and technology; agriculture and food; motoring; fashion; women's/home interests; theatre; films; broadcasting. Financial correspondents tend to be economics graduates, science correspondents are science graduates, but education correspondents are not normally teachers: there are no hard-and-fast rules about how specialists acquire their specialist knowledge (and how much they need).

NEWS EDITOR

Journalists with organizing ability may become news editor, controlling reporting staffs, allocating stories to individual reporters and attending senior staff's daily editorial conferences. It is an office job and normally involves no writing. The title usually applies on daily papers; titles and organization of work vary considerably from one paper to another.

SUB-EDITORS

Sub-editors do the detailed editing of copy; they re-write stories to fit in with required length, re-write the beginning, and may 'slant' stories. They write headlines and, in consultation with night or assistant editor, may do the layout of news pages. On large papers there are several specialist subs. Subbing is team-work and entirely desk-bound; it always has to be done in a hurry.

FEATURE WRITERS

Usually experienced journalists who can write lucidly and descriptively on any topic; but specialists may also write features. Reporters may combine reporting with feature writing.

COLUMNIST

Like feature writing, a job for experienced journalists; there are specialists, for example financial or consumer affairs columnists, and general columnists. The work requires a wide range of interests and contacts.

LEADER-WRITERS

Leaders may be written by the Editor, or specialist correspondent, or other experienced journalists.

EDITOR-IN-CHIEF, ASSISTANT EDITOR, DEPUTY EDITOR

Editors (including departmental editors) are coordinators, policy-makers. The number of top jobs, and the amount of writing editors do, vary greatly: some editors write leaders on specific subjects, some write in crises only; some on a variety of subjects, others not at all.

The amount of freedom an editor-in-chief has to run the paper the way she wants to depends on the proprietor; policies vary enormously.

There is no set promotion structure on newspapers. Some journalists do all or several types of newspaper work in succession in preparation for senior editorial jobs (subbing is a vital step on the ladder), others become heads of departments (finance, fashion, home affairs, chief sub, etc.) fairly quickly. Many remain reporters.

Titles, functions, and division of labour are not consistent throughout the industry and often change with a change of editor-in-chief or proprietor.

Magazines

Broadly there are two types:
(1) Trade, technical, professional and 'house' journals, geared to a particular profession, trade or organization.
(2) 'Consumer' magazines: they cater for all types of leisure interests and include women's, teenage and hobby magazines and comics.

On (1) journalists work closely with experts in the particular field of which they must have/develop some understanding. They write features, report developments, and re-write experts' contributions. Magazine work, however specialized, can be a way into newspaper work – especially for graduates with writing ability and experience of absorbing facts who want to skip the apprenticeship (see **Training**).

Consumer magazines employ feature writers, sub-editors and departmental editors more than reporters, but organization varies enormously. Consumer magazines also use freelances more than do newspapers. Editors' work includes originating feature ideas and selecting and briefing outside contributors, both freelance journalists and specialists who are not journalists.

FREELANCE JOURNALISM

Freelances are either 'generalists' – feature writers who write on any subject – or specialists. On the whole, only experienced journalists with staff experience, and particularly those with specialist knowledge which is in demand (technology, consumerism, child development, education, for example) succeed.

Specialists – teachers, engineers, lawyers, with writing ability and topical ideas – also do freelance journalism as a sideline, but this is becoming more difficult.

Prospects (all journalism) On newspapers reasonable only for exceptionally determined and talented people, as the market is shrinking; better on trade and technical magazines. Work on a journal dealing with one particular subject, whether physiotherapy or municipal affairs, is good experience and a stepping stone to more general journalism. There is limited scope in broadcasting (see p. 73) for experienced reporters. Science and engineering graduates have reasonable scope on the increasing number of publications which deal with various aspects of science and technology and which try to attract both specialist and lay readers.

Pay: Medium to high (see p. xxiii).

Training NEWSPAPERS: either:

1. *Direct entry traineeship*: After 6 months' probation, it takes 3 years for entrants with 5 O-levels; 2½ years for entrants with 2 A-levels; 2 years for graduates. Maximum age normally 24; exceptionally 30. Editors often prefer school-leavers to graduates. Acceptance depends largely on paper's policy and candidate's suitability, rather than on academic qualification. Candidates must apply direct to editors of *provincial* (including suburban) dailies and weeklies. The London-based nationals do not normally take trainees. (When applying for traineeship it is advisable to submit samples of work done: an article specially written for the particular paper, which shows the Editor that the

applicant has identified the paper's style, is better than work done for school or university paper, though that can be sent too.)

During training trainees attend in-house or block-release courses. Trainees must pass the National Council for the Training of Journalists' proficiency test. Subjects studied: English usage; relevant law; public administration; shorthand; interpretive reporting (interviewing, fact-gathering methods, etc.); current affairs; sub-editing skills. (Graduates do not have to study all subjects.)

Papers are supposed to offer trainees a 'schedule of experience', which should cover work in all departments including production, but this is by no means always forthcoming. Training tends to be best in newspaper groups which run in-company training schemes jointly with the N.C.T.J.

Even if training is bad, it is very difficult to 'break indentures' or switch employers; it is therefore advisable to find out as much as possible about the training before accepting a traineeship.

2. *One-year full-time pre-entry* course (maximum age 20, i.e. non-graduates only): 2 A-levels required.

About one third of entrants to newspaper journalism now take such courses, at colleges of further education. Courses shorten subsequent apprenticeship by several months, but a traineeship is at least virtually guaranteed on satisfactory completion of the course. A few candidates are sponsored by newspapers; the majority are accepted after having been interviewed by the N.C.T.J., to which applications must be made.

Or:

3. *Post-graduate* course at the Centre for Journalism Studies, Cardiff University and at the City University, London. Graduates from these courses also have to start as trainees, but they take the N.C.T.J.'s proficiency test after only 1 year's training.

Theoretically it is not possible to get on to a London-based national newspaper without provincial paper traineeship. However every year a few, perhaps 2 or 3 (*not more*) exceptionally gifted graduates manage to go straight from university on to a national newspaper. They tend to be economists or scientists, accepted because of their specialist knowledge. (See also *Late start*.)

MAGAZINES

There is one 1-year pre-entry course, mainly intended for consumer magazine journalists, at the London College of Printing (entry requirement: 1 A-level, 4 O-levels); one 1-year Fashion Writer's course at the London College of Fashion (entry requirements: A-level English and O-level French, German or Italian); but entry to magazine journalism is not organized; entry depends on specialist knowledge and/or writing skill.

Personal attributes

The different jobs demand different talents and temperaments, but all journalists need a feeling for words, the ability to express themselves lucidly and concisely; wide interests; an unbiased approach; a pleasant easy manner so that shy inarticulate people will talk to them easily; a certain presence so that busy, important people do not feel they are wasting their time answering questions; powers of observation; ability to sift the relevant from the irrelevant; ability to absorb atmosphere and to sum up people and situations quickly; an inquiring mind, great curiosity; the ability to become temporarily interested in anything from apple-growing to Zen Buddhism; resourcefulness; resilience; tact; willingness to work very hard; punctuality; a fairly thick skin (interviewees can be rude). *For senior jobs*: organizing ability.

Position of women

Newspapers
While the proportion of women apprentices has increased considerably over the last few years (45% in 1980), their share of senior jobs has increased very little indeed; yet there is no shortage of applicants (as there is in some other careers where women do badly). Women have no more difficulty than men getting apprenticeships, but there seems to be discrimination at subsequent levels (on newspapers, not magazines). Women also still tend to have 'women's stories' allocated to them. They are not given the varied experience (city page writer; foreign correspondent; assistant to news editor; sub-editor, etc.) which is vital for top jobs. However, this is slowly changing, especially on provincial papers.

Women still have to be considerably better journalists, more determined and more undauntable than their male colleagues, to get beyond middle-level jobs.
Magazines: No problem.

Career-break: Near-insurmountable problems as reporter on newspapers. Only well-above-average women who had proved their value to the paper before the break have much hope of returning after several years away. Many women turn to freelancing or edit, on a freelance basis, small organizations' or professional magazines: this is almost a cottage industry and badly paid. Fewer problems for feature writers, sub-editors.

Few problems on magazines.

Late start: Specialists, especially scientists, engineers, teachers, etc., can go into specialist journalism. A small number (either sex) in their late twenties are taken on for traineeship.

Part-time: Mainly as freelance. A few openings on trade journals, usually a few days a month rather than regular part of day.

Further in- **formation**	National Council for the Training of Journalists, Carlton House, Hemnall Street, Epping, Essex

Related careers	*Advertising – Broadcasting – Information Work – Photography – Public Relations*

LANDSCAPE ARCHITECTURE

Entry qualifications
Vary according to training, but for Membership of Landscape Institute: 3 O-levels, 2 A-levels, including a mathematics or a science and an English subject. The other subjects must include either geography, history or a foreign language. See **Training** for graduate entry.

The work
A landscape architect is concerned with the planning and design of the outdoor environment. Working with architects, civil engineers, planners or landscape contractors, she is called upon to minimize the aesthetic damage done to the scenery by, for example, industrial development or new housing estates. She plans factory sites in country areas and determines how best to blend new highways into their surroundings so that they are as unobtrusive as possible. She works on land reclamation, tree preservation, and the control of mineral workings. She designs layouts for open spaces, anything from spacious grounds for new hospitals to small private gardens, play and recreation grounds. She may site and design picnic areas in country parks or lay-bys on motorways.

She is responsible for inviting tenders from contractors, supervising the subsequent work, seeing that it is carried out satisfactorily and within a fixed budget. She is also responsible for ordering the right type of plants to achieve the desired appearance at all times of the year: this means balancing the amount of maintenance available in a public park, for example, with the amount of maintenance needed by the particular plant. Her knowledge of horticulture must be extensive.

Some landscape architects set up in private practice, or work for landscape or horticultural contractors, but the majority are employed by ministries, new town corporations and local authorities. In the latter, they are responsible to planning officers or architects, with less freedom than in private practice to carry out their own designs.

Prospects
Fair. The demand for qualified landscape architects is growing as the need to make the best of our remaining countryside is becoming more widely appreciated. Some opportunities in E.E.C. countries.

Pay: Medium to high (see p. xxiii).

Training
Either:
1. 4-year full-time course at a school of landscape architecture, attached to a university or polytechnic.
2. Architectural or town planning course (see pp. 46 and 356), followed

by a university diploma or certificate course in landscape architecture, either 2 years full-time or longer part-time.

3. At least 5 years at evening classes in preparation for the Landscape Institute's examinations, while working in the office of an architect, landscape architect or planning consultant or department to gain practical experience. The syllabus covers: basic design; horticulture; landscape architecture.

Alternative method of entry:

The title 'landscape *architect*' can be misleading. Unlike architects who put up buildings and who must be registered before they may use the title 'architect', landscape architecture is not a profession in the sense that only people with certain qualifications may use the title. There is no rigid division between landscape or garden *designers* and landscape *architects*.

Training courses in landscape architecture are limited, but it is possible to get into landscape architecture/design by training in a variety of allied disciplines, such as, for example, geography, geology, planning, soil science, plant sciences, rural environment studies, art and design, horticulture, and then learn on-the-job, working in a landscape architect's office. Initial training should preferably be at degree level, but there is always some limited scope for people with a flair for design and horticulture who are willing to combine some practical work with designing. This overlaps with gardening/garden design. See Horticulture, p. 24. Some private courses, which do not lead to membership of the Landscape Institute, are available.

Personal attributes

Visual imagination; flair for design; a keen interest in design and in horticulture; a knowledge of how people live in town and countryside; ease of expression, both in drawing and writing; the ability to work well with other people; a good business head (for private practice).

Position of women

Women were among founder members of the Institute. Now about 20% of members and between ⅓ and ½ of students are women – considerably more than 10 years ago. There has never been much discrimination in this career. The long training has kept the number of women low.

Career-break: Women who have kept up with developments should have no problems, but few have returned so far.

Late start: As vacancies on landscape architecture courses are scarce, young applicants are given preference, but see alternative method of training (which, however, is even longer).

Part-time: Occasional opportunities in employment; possibility of running small consultative practice – but part-time work likely to be sporadic rather than regular.

Further in- The Secretary, Landscape Institute, 12 Carlton House Terrace, London,
formation SW1

Related   *Agriculture and Horticulture – Architectural Technician –*
careers   *Architecture – Art and Design – Planning*

LAW

Barrister – Barristers' Clerk – Justices' Clerks' Assistant – Legal Executive – Solicitor

BARRISTER

Entry quali-fications

Degree (any subject).

The work

Barristers plead in courts and give advice on legal matters in Chambers (the term used for barristers' offices). They are consulted by solicitors on behalf of their clients: they do not normally see clients without a solicitor being present. Barristers clarify points of law and use their critical judgement in deciding what legislation and what precedents are relevant in any particular case. Their expertise helps clients, but barristers are first and foremost concerned with points of law, not with helping individuals: their relation with clients is far more formal than that of solicitors.

Barristers normally specialize *either* in *common law*, which includes criminal work (the greatest proportion: it covers any case of law-breaking, however minor the offence), divorce, family, planning and commercial law; *or* in *chancery* work, a much smaller branch which covers conveyancing, trusts, estate duty, taxation, company law.

In *common law* the emphasis is on pleading in court ('advocacy'); in *chancery* on work in Chambers, drafting 'opinions' and advising. *Common law* work appeals, therefore, more to people who enjoy verbal battles and the court's somewhat theatrical atmosphere; *chancery* work appeals to those who enjoy the challenge of intellectual problem-solving.

Common law barristers usually join one of the 6 'circuits' into which England and Wales are divided for legal administration purposes; they may then plead in provincial courts as well as in London.

Prospects

Good only for barristers with very good contacts and/or exceptional determination. The Bar is a small (about 4,410 practising members) club-like community. Organization and procedure have not changed for centuries, which causes problems. Barristers still practise their profession only under traditional constraints: they *must* practise from a 'tenancy' in Chambers, the Bar's professional accommodation which, in London, should normally be in one of the 4 Inns of Court (they are rather like non-resident Oxbridge colleges; the bar student must join one of them at the beginning of her training). In recent years the number of barristers has increased enormously, with scarcely any more tenancies being available; yet a newly-qualified barrister has to find Chambers which will offer her a tenancy. This depends entirely on contacts and luck: there is no system of allocating tenancies.

Unlike other professionals, a barrister may not go into partnership nor be employed by another barrister: once in practice, a barrister is, financially, on her own. She must wait for briefs by solicitors or be given work by the *barristers' clerk* (see p. 234) who 'distributes' work which comes to the set of Chambers rather than to a particular barrister in the Chambers. Barristers at first often supplement their income by coaching, or other work, unless they have enough money to live on for the first year or so. Many barristers never attempt to practise at the Bar (others try to, but cannot get into Chambers or get work); instead they become legal advisers in industry, or in local or central government. Such work is usually more easily available. It is far less precarious than the Bar, and in industry and commerce can lead to board-level jobs, but the work is not as varied as, nor has it the glamour of, being at the Bar.

The Civil Service offers a variety of jobs: barristers work in ministries as legal advisers; in the Lord Chancellor's Office on the administration of the courts; with the Law Commission which keeps English law under constant review; in the Law Officers' Department which advises the government on points of domestic and international law; in the Office of the Parliamentary Counsel on drafting legislation and parliamentary motions – this work involves attending sittings of both Houses; or as Justices' Clerk, advising the lay Justices (J.P.s) in magistrates' courts. Justices' Clerks have close day-to-day contact with the public.

Barristers, after at least 7 years' practice, are eligible for appointment (by the Lord Chancellor) as Chairmen of Industrial Tribunals. These Tribunals deal with unfair dismissal, redundancy payments and other matters relating to employment generally. Under the Sex Discrimination Act they also now hear complaints from persons who believe they have been discriminated against in terms of equal pay, promotion, acceptance for a particular job and other employment matters. Chairmen are appointed to regional panels and sit on Tribunals within a given area. Appointments can be full-time or part-time (i.e., some lawyers carry on with their practice as well).

In the E.E.C. countries and elsewhere abroad barristers may work as legal advisers. There is no equivalent in the E.E.C. and hence no mutual recognition of legal qualifications.

Pay: Very low to start with. Medium to very high later (see p. xxiii).

Training   The structure has changed. Training now consists of an *Academic Stage* and a *Vocational Stage*.

The *Academic Stage* replaced the traditional Part I Bar Examination. To complete this Stage, students either take a 'Qualifying Law Degree', which is basically one which covers the 6 'core' subjects (see Solicitor, **Training**, p. 239), or they take any degree, followed by a 1-year full-time course and a new 'Diploma in Law' examination. Holders of the solicitors' C.P.E. (see p. 240) may be exempt, at the Council of Legal Education's discretion, from the Bar's *Academic Stage*.

Law degree courses vary greatly in emphasis on particular aspects of law. All include the 'core subjects', but it is important to relate content to one's interests and plans: for example some courses concentrate more on international and/or E.E.C. law; some on family and welfare law; some on tax and/or company law; some are geared more to private practice, some more to public service. Consult C.R.A.C. *Degree Course Guide*, see p. xliii.

The Vocational Stage remains the responsibility of the Council of Legal Education. Courses, which last about 1 academic year, are held at the Inns of Court School of Law and the College of Law. All prospective barristers must *take* the Vocational Stage examination. But attendance at a course is compulsory only for those who intend to practise in Chambers, i.e., not for barristers who intend to become advisers or assistants in industry, local or central government, etc. However, it is advisable to attend a course and become qualified to practise at the Bar (which means plead in the courts). Vocational Stage training includes some specialization in a particular branch of law, for example landlord and tenant, hire purchase and sale of goods, local government and planning, family law. It also includes instruction in pleading in court and drafting. Students may no longer repeat subjects in the Bar examination which they have substantially covered in their degree studies.

After having passed the Vocational Stage examination, barristers who want to practise at the Bar must complete a year's 'pupillage' in Chambers (for which they have to pay around £100); during the last 6 months of that year they may 'accept instructions' from solicitors, which means they may be able to earn a little.

All Bar students must join one of the 4 Inns of Court and 'keep terms' by dining in the Hall of their Inn a certain number of times. The purpose of this is to make contacts with practising barristers and to be initiated into the traditional ways of the Bar.

Scotland: Training and organization differ. English qualifications do not entitle to practise at Scottish Bar and vice versa.

Personal attributes

A confidence-inspiring personality; power of logical reasoning; gift of expression; a quick brain; capacity for very hard work; tremendous self-confidence; some acting ability, or at least a sense of drama and relish for verbal battles in front of critical audiences; physical stamina; a good voice; resilience; for women: indifference to seeing male colleagues, even if less able, get on better.

Position of women

Entrenched attitudes and methods of working make this one of the most difficult professions for women to succeed in. Sex discrimination legislation made it – theoretically – impossible for Chambers to admit only a quota of women or none at all (which was the situation till 1976), but discrimination is difficult to prove as there are no established criteria – such as examination results, etc. – according to which pupils are taken on and tenancies granted to applicants. (Women have no problems getting into the Civil Service and industry or commerce.)

Once in Chambers, a *far* greater proportion of women than men concentrate on 'small work' (minor criminal cases) because that is all they can get. 9 out of 423 Q.C.s (Queen's Counsels) are women, and it is from Q.C.s (successful barristers) that the higher judiciary is chosen. There are 4 women High Court Judges among 75 men. The proportion of practising women barristers was about 4% in 1970, and about 10% in 1980.

Only 3·6% of applications to the Lord Chancellor for appointment to Industrial Tribunals are from women (which is a fraction higher than the proportion of women actually appointed). The Lord Chancellor's office says there has been no noticeable increase in applications from women since the passing of the Sex Discrimination Act (and Tribunals' extended scope).

In the last 10 years 2 Bar Council committees have looked into the position of women barristers; neither has achieved anything much. The existence of discrimination was however admitted. In 1978 the second committee sent a letter to all Heads of Chambers 'reminding them of the need to conform with both the letter and the spirit' of the Sex Discrimination Act.

Women barristers' earnings still lag far behind their male colleagues' (even in the case of women barristers with unbroken full-time careers).

Career-break: There are problems in keeping a tenancy while not working at all. Women barristers have to try and reduce their workload rather than have a complete break of more than a few months, unless they had built up a successful practice before the break, or have a very sympathetic Head of Chambers. (See Civil Service, p. 130, for opportunities for returners; in industry and commerce, arrangements vary.)

Late start: Over-25s may be admitted to the Diploma in Law examination but they probably have to study 2 years, taking 8 subjects. There are provisions for mature entrants with relevant experience/qualifications to study part-time or by correspondence course. There are difficulties getting pupillage and tenancy.

Part-time: As practising barrister, under-employment rather than regular part-time which is impossible to arrange; there may be opportunities as legal adviser in industry.

Further in-formation	Council of Legal Education, 4 Gray's Inn Place, London WC1R 5DX
	Scotland: Faculty of Advocates, Parliament House, Edinburgh EH1 1RF

Related careers	*Accountant – Civil Service – Legal Executive – Solicitor*

BARRISTERS' CLERK

Entry qualifications	3 O-levels including an English subject.

The work	This small profession has changed little over the past 100 years or so. Barristers' clerks 'manage' Chambers and the barristers working in them (see Barristers, p. 230). The *senior clerk*'s job is a unique mixture of power-behind-the-throne and humdrum clerking. She negotiates fees and other matters relating to briefs coming to Chambers with solicitors (from whom the briefs come). Clerks play a particularly important role in 'building up' young barristers: some briefs come to Chambers rather than to individual barristers and it is the senior clerk who decides which of the young barristers is to be given the brief.
	Senior clerks usually have junior clerks who make tea, carry barristers' books and robes to court, type Opinions and Pleadings. There is no career-structure and *no hope whatever* of progressing to becoming barrister, but as senior clerks get a commission on all their Chamber's barristers' earnings they often earn more than some of the barristers for whom they are clerking.

Prospects	Keen competition for openings.
	Pay: Very poor for junior clerks; high to very high for senior clerks (see p. xxiii).

Training　　On-the-job, with lectures. Clerks now normally take the Barristers' Clerks Association examination, after 4 years' clerking.

Personal attributes　　Self-confidence and presence; tact; willingness to tackle any kind of menial office job; respect for tradition and the established professional and social pecking order, in which barristers are a long way above clerks; interest in the law.

Position of women　　About 23% of clerks, but only about 10% of senior clerks are women. Very few women apply for Senior Clerks' jobs. See Barrister for male-oriented atmosphere at the Bar.

Career-break: Return to work would be *very* difficult.

Late start: Upper age for starting is normally 20; but women who worked as legal secretaries can switch to clerking at any age: i.e. barristers are not willing to train late entrants; secretaries would know what clerks' duties are.

Part-time: Limited opportunities, and none for Senior Clerk. (No logical reason for this.)

Further information　　Barristers' Clerks Association, Lamb Building, Temple, London EC4 7AS

Related careers　　*Civil Service – Legal Executive – Secretarial and Clerical Work*

JUSTICES' CLERKS' ASSISTANT

Entry qualifications　　Since 1980: 3 O-levels; many enter with higher qualifications.

The work　　Justices' Clerks' assistants work in the Justices' Clerks' department attached to magistrates' courts; they are employed by local authorities. Departments range in size from 3 to 90 staff. Assistants recruited into the general grade carry out general office duties and usher people to and from the courts – many of whom are anxious, some difficult. As the assistant progresses, she may prepare warrants, licences for betting offices and public houses, make out orders and notices to people who have been fined, supervise the receipt and payment of maintenance money and help prepare the court accounts. Later she may sit in court with the Justices' Clerk and take notes on cases and depositions of witnesses. Senior assistants may become Court Clerks and stand in for the Justices' Clerk in the Magistrates' courts.

Prospects
Fair for first jobs. Promotion may be fairly slow, depending largely on assistants' willingness to move to another office. There is no possibility of promotion to *Justices' Clerk*.

Pay: Medium (see p. xxiii).

Training
On-the-job training with some short residential courses. For promotion to Court Clerk (minimum age 22, and at least 2 years' service): 3-year part-time courses at some polytechnics, plus short residential courses.

Personal attributes
Interest in law and court procedures; a conscientious approach to office work; ability to deal discreetly and sympathetically with the public; good figurework for accounting.

Position of women
Approximately half are women.

Career-break: Possible.

Late start: Quite common.

Part-time: Very unlikely.

Further information
The Home Office, Whitehall, London SW1A 2AP

Related careers
Barristers' Clerk – Legal Executive – Police

LEGAL EXECUTIVE (formerly Managing Clerk)

Entry qualifications
4 academic O-levels.

The work
A legal executive works for a solicitor in much the same way as a junior executive works for a managing director: she is responsible for a strictly limited section. The solicitor is in overall control, makes contact with

clients and lays down policy. The legal executive often specializes in one particular branch of the law – probate, conveyancing, litigation, company law, etc. She works out the details as they apply in each particular case – looking up references in law books, preparing documents, interviewing witnesses, and conferring with clients on points of detail. In small practices, or when managing a branch office, she may also be involved with the whole spectrum of work.

Although she cannot speak in open court, she appears before Registrars or Masters of the High Court or in the County Court on summonses in the course of proceedings. She may also appear before a Judge in Chambers or before a magistrate.

Prospects   Fair, but the proportion of assistants to senior legal executives is not very encouraging. A legal executive may have to wait for a senior member of the firm to retire before she gets promotion. There is no prospect of promotion to solicitor, but the Law Society grants some exemptions from its exams to Fellows of the Institute of Legal Executives (see Solicitor, p. 238). This is therefore a career for those who are interested in law but unable to become solicitors.

Pay: Low to high – according to type and size of solicitor's practice and seniority (see p. xxiii).

Training   On-the-job, together with part-time training at day-release and/or evening classes, or by approved correspondence course, for first the Associate and later the Fellowship examination of the Institute of Legal Executives. The Associate examination is usually taken during the first 3 years' work in a solicitor's office or a legal department, and the Fellowship examination during the next 5 years. However, candidates do not need to attend courses during the whole of the 8 years it takes to qualify. The syllabus includes general legal subjects and practice and procedure, and allows for specialization in one branch of the law.

Personal attributes   Sufficient powers of concentration to detect relevant details in a mass of complex documentation; patience and perseverance; self-confidence and ability to discuss matters with all types of people from criminals to judges.

Position of women   This used to be an all-male profession; now 40% of Associates of the I.L.E. are women, and about ⅔ of students. However, solicitors tend to be conservative, and women legal executive students have to have more drive than men to get the breadth of experience which is essential for passing exams and getting promotion.

It is possible to prepare for the I.L.E. exams while being employed as clerk or secretary: many women have done this, in the hope of getting a more responsible job once they have passed the exams.

Career-break: Should be no problem for women who keep up with legislative changes.

Late start: Over-30s do not need the O-levels; many secretaries decide to become legal executives only after having been legal secretaries for many years.

Part-time: Some opportunities for jobs and also for training.

Further information The Institute of Legal Executives, Ilex House, Barrhill Road, London SW2

Related careers *Barrister – Barristers' Clerk – Company Secretary – Solicitor*

SOLICITOR

Entry qualifications Since 1980: a degree or high A-level grades, i.e.2 A-levels (min. B and C) at one sitting or 3 A-levels (min. C at one sitting, B and 2 Cs at two sittings). O-levels to include English.

The work A solicitor is a confidential adviser to whom people turn for legal advice and information in a vast variety of personal and business matters. As everyday life becomes more complex, the solicitor is increasingly asked to help in matters where common sense, wisdom and an objective approach are as important as legal knowledge. Whenever possible a solicitor tries to settle matters out of court. When lawsuits are necessary, she represents her client in the lower and county courts. In the High Court (and at assizes) she briefs counsel (see Barrister, p. 230). But it is always the solicitor, not the barrister, who discusses problems with her clients.

Solicitors tend to specialize in, for example, company law; in taxation, conveyancing or in what is called 'heavy commercial work'; in E.E.C. or international law; or in family law – divorce, custody of children, etc. In recent years some solicitors have begun to specialize in social welfare law and/or women's rights (sex discrimination legislation has increased scope and demand here), and also in consumer legislation.

There is no need to specialize to the exclusion of all other types of work: very much depends on the type and organization of the partnership a solicitor joins. About 80–90% of solicitors are in private practice. A small proportion work in neighbourhood law centres, usually in poor areas, where they deal largely (but not only) with social welfare and tenancy matters. It is also possible to set up on one's own and wait for clients to come, but this requires capital and contacts.

A solicitor interested in the law, rather than in people *and* the law, may become a legal adviser in the Civil Service (see also Barrister, p. 230 these jobs are open to barristers and solicitors) or in local government, or in commerce and industry, where the work involves vetting contracts and other documents and general advising. There is more security than in private practice, but there may be less variety. More time is spent in discussion with other professional people and less in meeting members of the public, but there are the usual advantages of working in large organizations.

Solicitors can now become judges after many years' experience.

Prospects　Fair. It is not always possible to get exactly the kind of work envisaged, where one wants it, but solicitors have so many kinds of work to choose from that they are likely to find something congenial. Lawyers – barristers and solicitors – of at least 7 years' practice are eligible for appointment (by the Lord Chancellor) as Chairmen of Industrial Tribunals. These Tribunals deal with unfair dismissal, redundancy payments and other matters relating to employment generally. Under the Sex Discrimination Act they also hear complaints from women who believe they have been discriminated against in terms of equal pay, promotion, acceptance for a particular job and other employment matters. Chairmen are appointed to regional panels and sit on Tribunals within a given area. Appointments can be full-time or part-time (i.e. some lawyers carry on with their practice as well).

Solicitors may work as legal advisers abroad, but cannot set up in practice.

Pay: High to very high (see p. xxiii).

Training　Training now consists of an *Academic Stage* (replacing the old Part I examination) and a *Second (Vocational) Stage* (replacing the old Part II examination). These are the training methods:

1. Taking an 'approved' (by the Law Society) law degree which means one that covers the 6 'core' subjects: Constitutional and Administrative Law, Contract, Torts, Criminal Law, Land Law, Trusts. (For differences in course emphasis and content see Barrister, p. 232.) Law graduates then go on to the *Second Stage*. This comprises a 1-year full-time course at a College of Law or Polytechnic, for the Final Examination,

and 2 years' service under articles. Total training thus takes at least 5 years and 9 months.

2. Graduating in any subject, and then taking a 1-year full-time course at a College of Law or Polytechnic which covers the 6 core subjects and leads to the 'Common Professional Examination' (the title is confusing as, since the solicitors' change of policy on entry requirements, the barristers have abandoned the 'Common' (with the solicitors) examination and have their own 'Diploma in Law' instead). Students then take the Finals course and examination and serve under articles exactly as do law graduates, except that they may serve the 2-year term of articles *before* the Finals course. The total training thus takes at least 6 years and 9 months.

3. For non-graduates over 25 who have a professional qualification or work experience acceptable to the Law Society: taking a 2-year course for the C.P.E. in up to 8 subjects. They then complete the Second Stage like graduates.

4. For school-leavers and non-graduates under 25: taking a 1-year full-time course for the Solicitors' First Examination (S.F.E.) which covers 4 core subjects. They then serve under articles for 5 years, taking remaining core subjects, plus 2 others, by part-time or correspondence course. They then take the 1-year Final course and examination and serve the last 18 months under articles.

5. Fellows of the Institute of Legal Executives (see p. 236) must pass, or obtain exemption from (in up to 3 subjects), the C.P.E., then *either* attend Finals course and take examination *or* serve 2 years under articles before taking Final examination.

6. Holders of the Justices' Clerks' Assistants' Diploma (see p. 236) must pass or obtain exemption from the C.P.E.; then complete the Second (Vocational) Stage.

Holders of the barristers' Diploma in Law (see p. 232) are admitted to the solicitors' Second Stage, so it is possible to start training for the Bar and then switch to solicitor-training (but there are very few Diploma in Law vacancies).

NOTE: Training under articles varies greatly. In specialized firms clerks do not get the breadth of experience required for choice of work later; and in some firms clerks are used as general assistants rather than trainees (i.e. having work criticized; sitting in on principals' discussions with clients, etc.). It is important to investigate what training is given before accepting articles.

Level of pay bears no relation to the training given: some firms which provide excellent training pay a lot better than others which use articled clerks as general dogsbodies.

Personal attributes

Capacity for absorbing facts quickly; logical reasoning; ability to see implications which are not obvious; ability to come to grips with an intricate problem; a good memory for facts and faces; tact; patience; clear and concise expression in writing and in speech; sound judgement of character; an understanding of human behaviour; a personality that inspires confidence.

Position of women

About 40% of trainees now entering into articles, and 27% of those finally qualifying, are women. A large proportion of women solicitors then go into the Civil Service, industry and commerce, local government, etc. Only 8% of solicitors holding Practice Certificates are women; and most solicitors employed in private practice, and all full partners in practice, *must* hold such Certificates. While the proportion of women qualifying as solicitors has increased about threefold in the last ten years, the proportion holding Practice Certificates has only just doubled.

Women occasionally encounter difficulties getting articles, especially with the type of firm in which they can gain wide experience, so they have to be more determined than men to have equal chances of getting fully qualified. But the situation has improved in the last few years.

There are some firms still, especially those doing important commercial work, which prefer not to have women partners, but other firms welcome women colleagues. It seems that old-fashioned senior partners often *imagine* that clients would object to women solicitors, but in fact clients very rarely do so; once in practice, women solicitors are readily accepted by clients.

Only 3·6% of applications to the Lord Chancellor for appointment to Industrial Tribunals are from women (which is a fraction higher than the proportion of women actually appointed). The Lord Chancellor's office says there has been no noticeable increase in applications from women since the passing of the Sex Discrimination Act.

Career-break: No problem for women who keep up with legislative changes. The Association of Women Solicitors is running occasional *refresher courses*.

Late start: Entrants over 25 are allowed, at the Law Society's discretion, to take the C.P.E. by part-time or correspondence course; G.C.E. requirements may be relaxed.

Part-time: reasonable opportunities, mainly in private practice, but not necessarily very regular work/hours (also on Industrial Tribunals).

Further information   The Law Society, Law Society's Hall, 113 Chancery Lane, London WC2A 1PL

Association of Women Solicitors, c/o The Law Society (address above)

Scotland: Law Society of Scotland, Law Society's Hall, 26–27 Drumsheugh Gardens, Edinburgh EH3 7YR (training in Scotland differs from that in England and Wales)

Related careers   *Accountant – Barrister – Civil Service – Justices' Clerks' Assistant – Legal Executive – Training Standards Officer*

LIBRARIANSHIP AND INFORMATION SCIENCE

Chartered Librarian – Information Scientist

The division between *Chartered Librarian* and *Information Scientist* is now blurred (the two professional bodies, the old-established Library Association and the much younger Institute of Information Scientists, held their first joint conference in the autumn of 1980 to discuss a possible 'joint future'). Job titles often owe more to tradition than to logic. For example, a scientific learned society is likely to employ a 'librarian' who is a scientist and therefore able to cope with specialized inquiries. A multinational corporation's 'information department' is likely to be run by an 'information scientist' or 'information officer' or 'director of information' who might well be a Chartered Librarian.

Librarians and information scientists serve the same basic purpose: they organize and make available published material (printed or, increasingly, computerized, 'electronically-published' material on video cassettes, etc.). They also know how to ferret out information which is not readily available. In theory, the information scientist is more likely to be a specialist in the subject her special library/information department deals with and is more concerned with analysing the information; the librarian is more likely to be an organizer and communicator of general published information. In practice, titles are used arbitrarily, and the difference between the two jobs is mainly one of emphasis, working environment and proportion of time spent on different aspects of the work.

Computerized information storage and retrieval systems are becoming more widely used in all types of libraries – including public ones – and information departments. 'Data banks' (electronic versions of reference books, catalogues and other items of information) can now be connected to terminals in hundreds of locations. Introducing and making the best use of these new chip-based information-disseminating inventions is an important aspect of both chartered librarians' and information scientists' work. The term '*informatics*' is beginning to be used for all aspects of electronic information storage, retrieval, dissemination systems, and their implications and their physical development. Informatics specialists are expected to understand the technical side of computer application to information work. At the moment, informatics specialists are usually electronics or computer experts with an interest in library/information work. But this is such a new, unorthodox and rapidly changing job area that librarians/information scientists with an interest in and understanding of electronics could well go into 'informatics'.

Training for the two overlapping careers could be, but is not necessarily, identical; it is advisable therefore to look at the careers together and then to consider their different characteristics.

1. CHARTERED LIBRARIAN

Entry qualifications

Degree. See **Training**.

About 60% work in public libraries; about 30% in academic/educational establishments (schools, colleges, universities, research organizations, medical schools); the remainder work in industrial and commercial concerns' 'information departments'/'special libraries' (see Information Scientists).

The public library service generally is trying to get rid of its image as a stuffy old-fashioned institution; libraries are extending their 'information point' role and act as advice centres. Librarians have to know what services – social, consumer, commercial, entertainment – are available and how people can use them. So while librarians must of course be interested in books, they must equally be interested in the community's social and economic activities. Organization of individual library services varies in detail.

A *Chief Librarian* is always in charge of a Central Library, branches, and the various activities organized by the service. The Chief Librarian, with her Deputy, is responsible for buying books; how much freedom she has to use the limited cash as she thinks fit depends on the local authority's Library Committee, and on the Chief Librarian's strength of personality.

Each branch is run by a *Branch Librarian* who may or may not be a subject specialist. (In a large library service there are also 'group librarians' in charge of several branches.)

Specialist librarians advise on the purchase of books within their speciality, and they usually do 'extension work'. The *music specialist* organizes record evenings and perhaps recitals; the *science specialist* organizes 'projects' for children (jointly with the Children's Librarian) and lectures and exhibitions for the general public and for students; the *literature specialist* organizes poetry readings and may liaise with local dramatic societies. All specialists take part in projects to reach 'new' library users.

The *Cataloguer* does classifying and indexing of new stock and she evaluates new computerized systems; there are many, and views on their relative advantages and disadvantages differ. Electronic information storage, classification and retrieval systems, making distant – and often vast and specialized – library services' stocks accessible to local readers, are revolutionizing libraries. Systems are changing fast, and so is the cataloguer's role; it increasingly overlaps with that of the Reference Librarian.

The *Reference Librarian* deals with inquiries on a vast variety of subjects. Some are straightforward queries, answers to which are available in reference books; others need research. Reference Librarians now often try and make their services known to the local business community; for example exporting or manufacturing firms have to know about political and economic conditions of countries to which they may want to export, and the Reference Librarian can provide the necessary information. 'Electronic search' equipment is increasing the Reference Librarian's scope enormously – and also the need for her to understand what developing information technology can be used and in which ways.

The *Children's Librarian* is responsible for the choice and arrangement of her stock. She organizes a wide range of 'extension activities', such as story afternoons, puppet clubs, scrapbooks for exchange with children's libraries abroad, discussion and review afternoons (when the children review books for their own and younger age groups), and all sorts of activities which help children to appreciate books and library services. She liaises with schools and may help to stock school libraries. She co-operates with teachers on special 'projects', and she may be asked to teach children how to use libraries and reference books. Of all specialists, the Children's Librarian has the greatest freedom of action. She does not normally become a branch librarian but concentrates on her speciality either in a branch or, later, in charge of the whole children's library service.

The *Readers' Adviser* (titles vary) helps readers who cannot find their way around or who want to investigate a particular subject. She also acts as a guide to the varied library facilities, and shows readers how to use the catalogue (especially the new computerized ones).

Prospects   Limited. Library services are affected by public spending cuts, and new technologies used for cataloguing and such routine work as sending out 'overdue' letters are reducing the numbers of assistants needed.

Training   *Either* 3-year (a few 4-year) degree course, *or* 1-year post-graduate course, *or* 2-year post-Dip. H.E. course; all lead to membership (after several years' practical library experience) of the Library Association.

Course titles, as well as emphasis on different aspects of Librarianship/Information Science vary enormously; titles do not necessarily show where course emphasis lies. On some 'Librarianship' courses, new information technologies are given as much course-time as on some 'Library and Information Science' courses. Prospective students are advised to study course prospectuses carefully before choosing a particular course. Some courses prefer students to have worked as a trainee or assistant in a library before starting the course.

Personal attributes

Wide interests; curiosity; ability to make the first approach to diffident people, and a liking for superficial contact with large numbers of strangers; patience with their tastes and questions; a good memory (a photographic one is a help); a methodical approach; a logical mind; organizing ability. For Children's Librarian, an insight into young minds; the ability and patience to interest the less enthusiastic child. There are many different facets of library work and therefore room for people with only some of these qualities.

Position of women

The ratio of men to women in librarianship is 4 to 6, with a far greater proportion of men in senior jobs.

Career-break: As there are more newly qualified librarians than there are jobs, there may well be difficulties.

Late start: No age bar in training or jobs, but see **Prospects**.

Part-time: Few opportunities in public libraries at the moment, but no reason why two people should not share one job. Some scope in educational libraries.

2. INFORMATION SCIENTIST

Entry qualifications

Nothing rigidly laid down but generally a degree or similar qualification, preferably in a scientific/technological subject. A broad-based degree is usually more useful than a specialized one. See **Training**.

The work

As a career in its own right information science is fairly new. As it is no longer possible for the individual scientists, engineers, economists or indeed experts in almost any field to keep track of all the new information relevant to their subject, a growing number of industrial concerns and research organizations have set up information departments (also called 'special libraries'). An information scientist collects, indexes and classifies material. This involves scanning but not necessarily reading a large number of journals, papers, handouts, etc. Information scientists also abstract information and circulate it to those members of their organization to whom it might be of interest. In fact an information scientist is the link between (a) information that is available somewhere and (b) the person who wants it, or who would find it useful if he knew it existed. The information officer does not necessarily wait to be asked for information; her duties may include keeping specialists up to date with relevant information as it becomes available. She may also have to do research in other libraries and obtain information by telephone or correspondence.

Information scientists, unlike librarians, are expected to have sufficient specialist knowledge to be able to discuss the subject their organization is dealing with in some depth.

The work increasingly involves dealing with or organizing computerized information storage and retrieval techniques and equipment (see Computing, pp. 134, 243).

Some information scientists (and librarians) are involved in developing the wider use of 'viewdata' systems. With these new computer-based devices, information provided by government, and by commercial and professional organizations, can be 'called up' to appear on television screens or on special visual display units in libraries, offices, etc. Information can be continuously updated by the suppliers – so the information scientists and librarians may have to re-think their traditional cataloguing systems.

Information departments vary in size: some are streamlined, run by highly qualified people; others were started in a haphazard way. Industrial information departments are normally in London and industrial areas; but a number of the government ones, such as the one for the Atomic Energy Authority, are in the country. The work is sometimes very rushed, and information may be urgently required after office hours. Status varies: some information officers are considered as essential to their organization as the experts themselves; others do not rank so high.

Prospects   Good for scientists and engineers; fair for economists and other specialists with added information scientist qualifications.

Pay: Medium to high (see p. xxiii).

Training   (1) and (2) lead to the widest choice of jobs:

1. Science or engineering degree or T.E.C. Higher award followed by a 1-year full- or 2-year part-time post-graduate course in information science.

2. Degree in information science (or studies) which combines theory of information dissemination, storage and retrieval techniques; communication techniques; library organization, etc. with science studies. *Any*

2 A-levels may be acceptable, but G.C.E.s must include a science and a mathematics subject and a language other than English.

3. Degree in library studies.

4. An economics, business studies, or social science degree followed by a post-graduate course in information science or studies.

5. Assistant in an information department and taking a part-time course in information science.

6. Experience as reference librarian in public library (see above, p. 245).

A reading knowledge of a foreign language is useful, especially one that is not widely studied, such as Chinese or Russian.

Personal attributes   Great curiosity; an interest in a variety of related topics without the desire to delve too deeply into any one; a methodical approach; a high degree of accuracy; a pigeon-hole mind which retains apparently irrelevant information; staying-power for long, possibly fruitless search; a friendly manner which induces busy experts to answer queries willingly and helpfully; resourcefulness; interest in electronic information systems.

Position of women   As in all new professions where there is no tradition to break down, women have equal opportunities.

Career-break: Should be no problem, if well qualified. T.O.P.S. grants available for short courses which, though not intended as *refresher courses*, can be used as such.

Late start: Opportunities mainly for science and engineering graduates who can top up their existing qualifications with specialist training.

Part-time: Some opportunities for people with specialist qualifications and/or experience.

Further information   Education Officer, A S L I B, 3 Belgrave Square, London SW1
Education Officer, Library Association, 7 Ridgmount Street, London WC1E 7AE
Institute of Information Scientists, Harvest House, 62 London Road, Reading RG7 5AS
A S L I B, 36 Bedford Row, London WC1R 4JH

Related   *Archivist – Bookselling – Museum work – Publishing*

LINGUIST

Bi-lingual secretary – interpreting – translating – teaching – B.B.C. – Diplomatic Service – industry

There is no such career as 'Linguist' as such: a knowledge of languages on its own does not lead anywhere special. Apart from teaching, it is useful only if combined with either technical-scientific and/or almost any other specialist knowledge, or with secretarial skills, or with extremely exceptional talent. In almost any professional area from archaeology to zoology languages can be useful.

Main Possibilities

Entry quali-fications

1. *Bi-lingual secretary*: normally 4 O-levels, including a modern language and an English subject.

2. *Interpreting*: complete command of at least 2 foreign languages.

3. *Translating*: complete command of at least 1 foreign language plus specialist knowledge.

4. *Teaching*: see p. 485.

5. *Information Work*: see Information Scientist, p. 246.

Note: For language degree, O-level Latin is often required.

1. BI-LINGUAL SECRETARY

The work   (see Secretarial Work, p. 424.)

2. INTERPRETING

The work   *(a) Conference Interpreters*

At international conferences, interpreters do both 'simultaneous' and 'consecutive' translating. Simultaneous work demands, apart from 100-per-cent proficiency in 2 languages, a talent which even the most down-to-earth conference organizers call 'magic'. A simultaneous interpreter must relay the meaning of a phrase, in near-perfect style, almost instantaneously, and automatically. The technique can be perfected *only* if the inborn gift is there. Consecutive translating is only very little less difficult.

A conference interpreter invariably translates *into* her own language; she is expected to have complete command of 3 of the official languages (i.e. those used by United Nations Agencies), namely English, French, Spanish, Chinese, and Russian. In practice, this usually means that as well as French and German an interpreter has one of the more unusual languages.

Some interpreters are employed by international agencies; others are freelances and are booked for a particular conference. Most of the year is spent travelling from New York to Geneva, Paris and London, living in hotels. The life may be luxurious, but it is extremely hectic, with very long irregular hours. Most conference interpreters now are specialists.

(b) Specialist Interpreters

Have some specialist knowledge (such as engineering, physical science or economics), plus proficiency in a foreign language, and usually do translating as a main job, interpreting as a sideline (see below, translating on a freelance basis).

(c) General Interpreters

Most of them take foreigners around London. They are very few in number. Most of them are accredited guides (i.e. they need a considerable historical knowledge of London or other places) and are on the books of hotels and travel agencies for occasional assignments – it is a pleasant sideline, but not a career in itself.

Some also work for industry, for the courts and for conference organizers.

Prospects   Poor, except for the exceptionally gifted, and exceptionally lucky. Most successful interpreters are men, and competition for the very few jobs available is very keen. Far more interpreters than jobs.

Pay: High to very high (see p. xxiii).

3. TRANSLATING

The work   Translators must be able to translate idiomatically and to write lucidly and concisely – being bi-lingual is not sufficient. They translate into their mother-tongue, unless it can be shown that another language has wholly taken the place of this as a language of habitual use.

They need a very good general education and specialist knowledge of preferably a range of subjects. Most translations have some specialist content – contracts require some legal knowledge; scientific articles some understanding of the subject-matter; specifications (for construction work, of anything from ships to atomic power stations) need some technical knowledge. Translators often have to discuss phrases and technical jargon with engineers, scientists, lawyers, etc., to get the sense absolutely right; translating is therefore often teamwork.

Government departments, and industrial, commercial and research organizations often have translating departments, which employ specialists in particular fields, and sometimes non-specialists, who have, for instance, Chinese or Arabic, as well as 1 or 2 of the more usual languages.

Translating agencies employ specialists, and people who have unusual languages, often on a freelance basis. They like to have on their books a large number of people with widely different specialities and languages, on whom they can call at a moment's notice.

There is much rushed deadline work in translating, especially for freelances.

Prospects　　Good only for those with specialist technical/scientific knowledge and/or unusual languages.

Pay: Medium to high (see p. xxiii), but varies enormously according to specialist knowledge.

Abroad: Fair opportunities, but depending on other special qualifications.

4. TEACHING

Work and prospects　　(See Teaching, p. 485, for details.)

Language teachers are in demand and language teaching methods are changing, so there is much interesting experimental work at all educational levels, from primary school to universities.

Other Possibilities

1. B.B.C.

Most of the work in the foreign language section is done by nationals of the various countries; very few linguists are employed and those need thorough political and economic knowledge of the country concerned. Monitors listen to and précis broadcasts in over 30 languages. The work is very intensive and it is shift work. Few openings.

2. DIPLOMATIC SERVICE

Proficiency even in several foreign languages is no entry qualification on its own (see Civil Service, p. 126).

3. INDUSTRY

Complete fluency, together with thorough knowledge of social institutions and economics of the country concerned, *and* a specialist qualification in *anything*, from accountancy to engineering, science to marketing, may lead to jobs in companies with offices abroad.

Personal attributes (for linguists generally)

These vary according to the job, but all linguists must have an agile mind, interest in current affairs, a knowledge of cultural and social structures not only of their own country but of any country in whose language they specialize. They should be willing to take responsibility, for even in comparatively subordinate jobs (such as a secretary's) they may be the only person equipped to judge the correctness of a translation; they need the ability to concentrate for long stretches and to work well with others. Conference interpreters also need a calm temperament, exceptional physical stamina and the ability to snatch a few hours' sleep at any time.

General language training

1. 1- and 2-year full-time diploma courses at further education colleges

Candidates need 1, sometimes 2, A-levels, including 1 in a foreign language, and another language to at least O-level. Course content varies but is likely to include economics; social structure of the countries concerned; commercial practice; overseas marketing; interpreting technique.

2. C.N.A.A. or university degree

The content and approach of individual degree courses vary considerably; in some the approach is academic, the emphasis on philology and literature; others, particularly C.N.A.A. degrees, are more practical in content, and prepare students for work in commerce and industry by including more about the economy, the institutions, and the social climate of the country concerned. A number of degrees – university and C.N.A.A. – combine a language with a branch of engineering or science, or with such subjects as economics, international relations or law, or marketing.

3. Post-graduate courses

These courses are usually at polytechnics. Some are for scientists who need to know a language; others for linguists who want to be interpreters and/or translators.

4. Living and working abroad

This is usually in addition to and not instead of (1) and (2), and an *au pair* job on its own is not enough. It should be supplemented, or followed by, one of the courses for foreigners at various foreign universities. These last from 2 weeks to several terms; there are also some part-time classes, mainly in capital cities.

Note: The Institute of Linguists holds examinations in interpreting and translating, but it does not organize (or advise on) training. Examinations are at 5 levels: the Preliminary and Grade I Certificates are intended for those who study at evening classes or by radio or television, for pleasure and perhaps to be able to make themselves understood on holidays abroad. They are not for candidates who want qualifications which might help to get a job.

The Grade II Certificate is roughly equivalent to A-level, but more practical and less academic in content. It is suitable for day-release and secretarial students and 6th-formers.

The Intermediate Diploma is awarded to students who have practical knowledge of a language and who will probably have had 2 years' post-A-level part-time study, or taken a full-time course, studied abroad, and/or been in a job such as bi-lingual secretary or abstracting in a special library.

The Final Diploma is awarded to students who can use the language to 'near native' standard in communication between educated people with considerable knowledge of the political and cultural scene of the country where the language is spoken; and who also have either special knowledge of a particular subject (perhaps trade with the country concerned) or a special ability such as technical translation to near-professional standard. There is also a Translator's Diploma examination.

Certificates and Diplomas have no official standing in the way that a Higher National Diploma or Degree has; the Intermediate and Final Diplomas are, however, recognized as proof of competence to a certain standard.

The Institute of Linguists does not run courses, but many courses at polytechnics and colleges (and some schools) prepare students for these examinations.

Position of women

Rather more men than women are professional translators and interpreters, but women who do have the right knowledge and aptitude do well; women tend to be better than men at languages, but they fall down on the necessary specialist knowledge which usually requires long training.

Career-break: Unless very well established, return might be difficult for *interpreters*, as competition very keen. *Translating*: No need to give up all contacts while raising family.

Late start: Translating possibly; interpreting unlikely.

Part-time: Theoretically, there should be a good deal available as translating and interpreting are so often done by freelances. However, more linguists are seeking work than are needed and much of the work has to be done quickly – which means it is not regular part-time work, but a few days' or weeks' rushed full-time work every now and then.

Further in-   For courses abroad: individual embassies
formation   Central Bureau for Educational Visits and Exchanges, 55a Duke Street, Grosvenor Square, London W1
Institute of Linguists, 24a Highbury Grove, London N5 2EA

Related   Careers in which a knowledge of languages leads to better jobs:
careers   *Air Stewardess – Beautician – Civil Service – Hotel Work*, p. 103
– Information Officer – Scientist – Secretarial Work – Teaching – Travel Agent

LOCAL GOVERNMENT

Entry quali-
fications

Entry is at all educational levels; increasing proportion of *graduate* entry.

The work

Local government officers carry out the policies laid down by the elected local councils and are responsible for administering local services. Services are organized in departments; normally each is run by a person with relevant professional qualifications. (However, there is a tendency for a Chief Executive to be in overall charge of the multi-disciplinary team of heads of departments. She may have any type of professional qualification, but must be a top-flight administrator and coordinator, and must enjoy public functions – she has to attend many.) Departmental staff have relevant professional, administrative, technical or clerical qualifications or skills. Education, libraries, social services, planning, architecture, housing, legal, municipal engineering, finance, are the main departments. Not all local authorities provide all services.

Local government was reorganized a few years ago. Small authorities are now merged into fewer, larger ones. This has meant improved career structures within individual authorities. While in the past it was usually necessary to move to another authority for promotion it is now quite normal to be promoted within an authority, though this may still mean, in the case of large authorities, having to commute, or move, to another part of the authority's area.

Local Government in England and Wales is structured in tiers. At the top are 6 Metropolitan (large urban conurbations) and 47 Non-Metropolitan County Councils; the second-tier authorities are 36 Metropolitan and 333 Non-Metropolitan District Councils. (London is a special case, with the Greater London Council as the top tier and 32 London Boroughs and the City of London as the second tier.) Top-tier authorities' powers tend to be wider than the second tier's: for example, education and social services and overall planning are top-tier responsibilities. However, in some cases top-tier (County) authorities delegate powers to second-tier authorities. Housing and some planning functions may be shared by top- and second-tier authorities. The division of functions is very complicated indeed, but by and large there is more 'grass roots' involvement with the community at second-tier level; but top-tier authorities may offer better decision-making scope. It is quite common to move from second- to top-tier authority and vice versa in the course of one's career, so there is no need to decide at the outset on preference for either type of authority; but it is important to inquire into a particular job's scope.

Careers fall into 3 main groups: firstly those that can be followed both inside and outside local government, the most important ones being: accountancy, architecture, computers, engineering, horticulture, librarianship, law. Secondly, those that are entirely or largely local government careers, the most important ones being: planning, housing management, environmental health, social work, education (teaching, careers guidance), trading standards (consumer protection). (See individual sections.) Thirdly, there is Administration.

Senior staff attend council and committee meetings and advise on and discuss policy with elected councillors. Although there are many similarities with the Civil Service, local government service gives more opportunity of seeing the effects of one's work. Whether it is social work, building schools, or keeping the files which deal with playgrounds, the work is closely linked with the life of the community.

Facilities for further study are good. Day-release is usually granted for courses leading to qualifications, whether G.C.E. or professional. Officers may be seconded to full-time courses.

There is a tradition of 'upward mobility' in local government; many senior professional posts are today filled by people who qualified entirely by studying part-time by day-release and evening class. However, as more and more children go on to full-time training, recruitment policy is changing. It is still *possible* to start at 16 with a few O-levels and to study part-time right up to professional qualifications. But this is now very rare indeed. Entrants are usually qualified in their chosen profession if it is one of those which can be followed both outside and inside local government. If they want to follow one of the mainly administrative careers, they start as trainees, with the necessary G.C.E. passes.

There is very good scope in *general administration*. Administrative officers do committee work, supervise and organize the day-to-day running of departments, introduce and implement modern management techniques. They work closely with their professional colleagues – social workers, architects, housing managers, etc. – and relieve them of administrative duties, at which professional experts are not necessarily any good.

Staff are divided into Divisions. However, no two authorities are *exactly* alike in organization.

Structure by Entry Qualifications and Training – England and Wales

Entrants with fewer than 4, sometimes 5, O-levels start in the *Clerical Division*. The higher their entry qualifications, the higher the starting 'grade'. For some jobs secretarial or other skills may be demanded. All clerical staff are encouraged to work for qualifications. Opportunities to progress to administrative work (and into the Administrative and Professional Division) are good.

Entrants who have not made a career decision at the time of entry are encouraged to get to know the various services and the varied career opportunities open to them.

In the *Technicians and Technical Grade* there is wide scope to work as draughtsman, architectural, engineering or laboratory technician (see relevant entries). Entrance requirements vary but are usually at least 3 O-levels.

Entrants with at least 5 O-levels but sometimes A-levels or degrees start in the *Administrative and Professional Grade*. Many entrants are fully or partly qualified professionally.

Administrative officers may – but need not – specialize in the administration of one particular department. The work thus offers opportunities to people who would like to work for example in social service, surveying or planning, but do not want to become professional specialists.

Training   Trainee administrators enter with 4 O-levels and 2 A-levels and then take either a 4-year post-entry training by day- and block-release for the Diploma in Municipal Administration; or the B.E.C. Public Administration Certificate (see p. xvii); or they enter with a degree – any subject – and take either the D.M.A. or other qualifications such as the Diploma in Management Studies (see Management, p. 263); or they may be sent on post-graduate courses in, for example, computer techniques, social or financial administration or personnel management. Graduates with a degree in social administration are particularly likely to get quick promotion.

Scotland and Greater London Council

In Scotland work and qualifications required do not differ substantially from those in England and Wales.

Greater London Council structure:

 Clerical officer 1: no entry qualifications.

 Clerical officer 2: 5 O-levels, including English language.

 Executive officer: no recruitment; promotion from clerical officer. (A-level clerical officer entrants are promoted to executive officer very quickly.)

 Administrative officer: entry with degree.

 Plus large number of professionals – architects, surveyors, planners, etc.

Prospects Limited at the moment by public expenditure cuts.
   Pay: Medium to very high (see p. xxiii).

Personal Depends on the particular type of work. *For all jobs*: interest in local
attributes affairs; *for purely administrative work*: ability to deal with people;
   capacity for picking out the relevant facts from a mass of detail;
   organizing ability; ability to work as one of a team. At senior level:
   willingness to carry into effect decisions taken by councillors whether
   one agrees with them or not.

Position Women do well in the various careers (see separate entries) up to
of women middle level, but only very few reach the top (see Planning, Social
   Work, etc.). The President of the Society of Chief Executives stated
   publicly in 1976: 'This (the small proportion of women in top jobs)
   simply will not do, and we, the Chief Executives, are the only people
   who can do something about it.' (Out of 487 chief executives then, 2
   were women. There was only 1 in 1980.) He advocated a 'deliberate
   policy of promoting more women to senior posts'. So far no such policy
   has been implemented.

   It is probably true that fewer women than men are willing to move
   from one local authority to another to gain the breadth of experience
   required for top jobs (but – as they see little hope of getting to the top
   anyway – they do not have men's incentive to move).

   Career-break: It varies from one local authority and one profession to
   another. No bar on returners, but no encouragement given either.

   Late start: See individual career entries. General administration entrants
   normally under 28; but older candidates with relevant commercial/
   public service/industrial experience are now also accepted.

   Part-time: See separate career entries. None in general administration,
   so far.

Further in- Town Hall or Council office
formation National Joint Council for Local Authorities' Services, 41 Belgrave
   Square, London SW1
   County Hall, London SE1 7PB

Related *Civil Service*
careers

MANAGEMENT IN INDUSTRY AND COMMERCE

Entry quali-
fications
Nothing specific (see **Work** and **Training**), but in practice, a degree or professional qualification is essential for senior management, and 4 O-levels for middle management.

The work
This is a vast and confusing field, with vague terminology. Management is not a career in the usual sense, but an activity, the purpose of which is to make the best use of available resources – human, money, material, equipment – in order to achieve a given objective. Managers, with the help of people working for them, decide how to achieve given objectives, and then get things done: management consists largely of enthusing subordinates into doing things as efficiently as they – the managers – would wish to have done them themselves.

One aspect which applies to all types and levels of management is communication: managers are said to spend between 70 and 90% of their time talking to people, in conference, on the phone, in one-to-one discussion. That applies whether a manager manages a whole or part of a department store; an international sales force; a large export department or a small section of one; an engineering workshop; or a manufacturing company.

Management is not normally a career for which one trains from scratch, like, for example, architecture or plumbing. Virtually all managers started as specialists in something (even if they always intended to manage rather than 'do' whatever they specialized in). Anyone who controls the work of other people 'manages'; therefore most people as they rise in the job hierarchy spend more time on managing than they did at first, and less time doing whatever they originally trained for (this does not necessarily apply in professions like architecture, teaching, medicine, but even there it does, or can, to a certain extent, at the very top of the tree).

If one's aim is management in business, the careers to choose are 'business functions', such as accountancy (p. 1), production (Engineering, p. 166); purchasing and supply (p. 384); marketing (p. 270); personnel (p. 338); shipbroking and freight forwarding (p. 384) or one of the so-called 'management services', which are: operational research (p. 325); computers (p. 134); work study (p. 502). Confusingly, engineering (p. 163), though not a business function, leads to senior management often more quickly and surely than any of the business functions. It deserves to be considered as a way into senior management in both industry and commerce much more than it is.

Levels of management: There is no very clear distinction between junior, middle, and senior management; rising from one to another does not necessarily depend on gaining further qualifications (although such qualifications are very useful indeed and often essential; having got them does not automatically lead to the next step on the management ladder).

Most people who choose a management career think of senior, and general, managers – but they are the smallest management section.

Junior managers are the easiest to define. A junior manager is usually responsible for controlling the work of a number of people who are all doing the same work – usually work in which the junior manager is trained (or at least which she is able to do) herself. For example a foreman fitter is a skilled fitter; a typing pool supervisor a typist; a factory production line supervisor has worked on the production line (though possibly as a graduate engineer gaining experience). Junior managers organize the flow of work, and sort out minor problems (often including their subordinates' personal ones). In the office of, say, an export department, a junior manager might be responsible for ensuring that documentation relating to goods for one or two countries is dealt with correctly; on the shop-floor for one or two production lines, which might mean about 100 people. Junior managers are also the link with middle management.

Middle management spans a wide range of jobs and levels of responsibility. The step from junior to middle management is the most crucial on the management ladder: while junior managers are responsible for people all doing the same kind of work, middle managers are responsible for coordinating a number of junior managers who are all doing slightly different jobs. This means that a junior manager who wants promotion must usually first broaden her experience and 'move sideways' before moving up. This experience-broadening is part of 'management development' (see Personnel Management, p. 338) and should be built into managers' training, but in very many firms young managers have to plan their own career-paths rather than rely on the personnel manager to do it for them. This is partly what makes 'management' such a difficult career to plan: it is not necessarily qualifications, but experience – and luck, drive and initiative – which matter.

The majority of managers remain middle managers always, gradually taking responsibility for a wider range of activities or for bigger departments. For example a sales manager in charge of a regional sales force is a middle manager and remains so even when she becomes responsible for a larger sales force, or a more important – in cash-terms

– region. A manager in charge of a mail order firm's dispatch department, responsible for a large sum of money and for the firm's reputation for reliability, is a middle manager, and she might still be a middle manager when she oversees the dispatch *and* the packing departments. However, in another firm she might be a senior manager: it depends on a firm's organization, and their interpretation of what senior management *is*.

Anyone responsible to the Board is definitely a senior manager: all heads of departments – personnel, production, finance, marketing, etc. And coordinators, the general managers (all former specialists), are senior managers. They base important planning and policy decisions on information and advice from specialist senior managers.

Some terms used in management jargon:

Line Management: A line manager is the manager in charge of whatever the organization's principal activity and main purpose is. In a manufacturing industry it is the production manager; in retail it is the store manager; in an air freight charter company it is the person selling aircraft space. (The term 'line' is apparently derived from 'being in the firing line' – the line manager is the one who tends to get shot at when things go wrong.)

General Management: A general manager coordinates the work of several specialist departments (or functions), for example personnel, production, accountancy, etc. She is usually a specialist in one of the functions for which she is responsible, which one is immaterial.

Executives and Managers: The distinction is vague. Broadly, managers are responsible for controlling other people's work, which executives are not necessarily: for example, a legal adviser is a senior executive, but not a manager. But middle or senior managers may also be called executives.

Managers and Administrators: Again the distinction is vague. What is called management in industry is often called administration in the public sector. The terms are often interchangeable (in terms of activity), but 'administrators' are more likely to be concerned with the smooth running of a department or organization without making any changes; whereas 'managers' are expected to choose the most efficient (or 'cost-effective') of various alternative routes to achieve an objective. Management implies more decision-making. But as in the whole of the management field, different people mean different things by the same terms.

Prospects   Management covers such a vast range of jobs that it is impossible to generalize. However, there is a shortage of good managers in manufacturing industry. Engineers with management ambition and potential particularly are wanted in most industries. There is a shortage of production managers (see p. 166), of purchasing and supply (see

p. 384) and of export (see International Marketing, p. 270) specialists. However, jobs may not be available where they are wanted; it depends on economic conditions.

Pay: Medium to very high (see p. xxiii).

Training   This is not neatly structured as it is for the professions. No specific qualifications entitle the holder to any level or type or title in management. Usual ways of qualifying for:

1. *Senior Management*
(a) A specialist qualification (see **Work**, above), for example in accountancy (p. 1); engineering (p. 163); law (p. 238).

(b) 4-year sandwich degree in Business Studies. Courses include practical experience in industry or commerce (or public authority) which gives students an insight into the real world of work and enables those who do not enjoy the atmosphere, or find the pace too exacting, to change to some other graduate career. Employers welcome Business Studies graduates because they have had work experience, know what to expect, and have a basic understanding of business.

Sandwich courses come in two versions: 'thick sandwich' students normally spend 2 years at college, then 1 year in paid and supervised work experience, with a final year at college (but some students start with a year's practical work). 'Thick sandwich' students are usually sponsored. They spend their work experience period with their sponsor and normally get a job with their sponsor after graduating. 'Thin sandwich' students usually divide their first 3 years between college and work experience and spend the whole final year at college. They are not sponsored and spend work experience periods in a variety of work environments. They gain a wider range of experience, but do not acquire so much in-depth knowledge of any particular aspect of business. Neither type of sandwich course is 'better' than the other, though people who know exactly what kind of work they want to do eventually may prefer the sponsored 'thick sandwich'. Colleges (usually polytechnics) normally run *either* 'thick' *or* 'thin' sandwich courses – not both kinds – so choice of course may be narrowed down by preference for either 'thick' or 'thin' sandwich. There are also some part-time Business Studies degrees, mainly for people in relevant employment, though occasionally people who have had previous relevant experience may be accepted. These courses can then be useful for people who want to return to or switch to a business career while still in other employment. Recently 'mixed mode' courses have started – students combine 1 or 2 years' full-time study with 2 or 3 years' part-time study.

Business studies syllabuses vary greatly. All provide a systematic introduction to management and to the various business functions; most courses specialize in a particular branch or management function – for example, marketing or international marketing; industrial relations; export management; manpower planning; finance; organizational behaviour, etc. Some courses are more suitable for people interested in, for example, 'human resources management', others for those interested in business economics/finance; or in transport management, a growing field. Titles alone do *not* precisely describe a course's emphasis. Students should study the C.R.A.C. Course Guide, C.N.A.A. *Directory of First Degree and Dip. H.E. Courses*; *Which Degree*, and individual course prospectuses.

Entry requirements: Normally any 2 A-levels and 3 O-levels, including English and maths. Only a few courses require A-level maths; and a few (those which specialize in international marketing or European business administration) a modern language. Most courses accept the old O.N.D./C. and the new B.E.C. National awards (see B.E.C., p. xvii) in lieu of A-levels. Mature candidates may be accepted with experience in lieu of qualifications.

(c) Any degree. Over the last few years one-third of all graduate vacancies notified to the graduate careers advisory services were open to graduates from *any* discipline (the two-thirds which specified disciplines most frequently specified a technological subject, with Business Studies degrees next in order of preference).

(d) *Post-graduate Training* (includes post-relevant professional qualification and often post-B.E.C. Higher National award – see below). Post-graduate courses fall into two main groups:
(i) Courses in general management; and (ii) courses leading to specialist qualifications such as personnel management, international marketing, transport, or production, or export management, etc. Both types of courses can be either full-time, or part-time while in relevant employment.

General management courses are more likely to be full-time. The best-known courses are at the graduate business schools in London and Manchester, but there are a great number of others, attached to universities and polytechnics, which are equally valuable. Courses last 1 or 2 years; many are for graduates who have been in employment for from one to several years (they are called 'post experience', and, exceptionally, managers who are neither graduates nor B.E.C. Higher award holders, but just very able, may be accepted). Courses lead to M.Sc., M.B.A., M.Phil., in Management Sciences, in Administrative Management, in General Management, in Industrial Management. Titles do not necessarily indicate the particular course emphasis; prospective students should look at C.R.A.C. *Graduate Studies* and at course prospectuses.

The C.N.A.A. Diploma in Management Studies is the largest single management training scheme. Courses are available at about 90 polytechnics and colleges. The 2-stage course structure is very flexible – the D.M.S. can take 6 or 12 months full-time; or 2 or 3 years' day- or block-release or evening study. As the two stages are usually separate units, it is usually possible to switch from one mode of attendance to another; for example, take stage 1 by evening study only, then get sponsored by an employer or T.O.P.S. (see p. xl) for a full-time stage 2 course. The scheme is intended primarily for people with a few years' middle-management experience: 45% of D.M.S. students are between 28 and 35; 25% are over 35; only 5% are under 24. Entry qualifications are *either* H.N.D./C., degree, equivalent professional qualifications; and, often, mimimum age 23, *or* minimum age 27 with at least 4 years' relevant experience in lieu of academic qualifications.

All D.M.S. courses update students' knowledge of management techniques and aim to improve their management skills. Most courses also specialize either in a 'management function' – for example, personnel; export marketing; production management; or in an 'operational area', for example, recreation/leisure management; transport management; public administration; education administration. Like other vocational training (rather than academic education) courses, D.M.S. course contents are constantly changing to meet employers' and students' changing requirements.

The D.M.S. is useful for people who want to return to work after a gap: for example, women who used to be senior secretaries and then left work to raise a family.

Recently some Business Studies degrees, post-graduate and post-experience courses have started offering options in 'small business' management, for people who want to work in small firms or who want to set up and run their own small show.

2. *Below degree-level training, likely to lead to middle management*
B.E.C. (Business Education Council) Higher National Diplomas or Certificates (Diplomas cover a wider range of subjects than Certificates). Higher National Diploma courses are usually 2 years full-time or 3 years sandwich. Higher National Certificates are usually taken by day- or block-release while in appropriate employment (see Employers' Training Schemes, below). *Entry qualifications*: 1 A-level (some courses require 2, or 1 passed and another studied) and 3 O-levels, including English language and maths; for a few courses, 1 modern language *or* B.E.C. National award (see below). Mature entrants may be accepted with business experience in lieu of qualifications. All B.E.C. courses teach business basics and students all study what are called 'Central Themes':
(a) money – basically financial consequences and implications of

decisions taken; (b) people: how to get on with and manage them; (c) communication – overlaps with (b) and broadly means making sure everybody in an organization understands what others are doing and why. It involves explaining actions and proposals clearly, in writing and verbally; (d) numeracy – overlaps with (a) and involves learning how to 'quantify' plans, problems and situations, and developing an analytical approach. B.E.C.'s 'Central Themes' approach should enable students to be flexible and able to adapt to the different kinds of jobs everyone is likely to be doing throughout their working lives.

On top of the 'Central Themes', B.E.C. students specialize in one of four main career groups; each group has 'core modules', plus 'option modules' to suit each student's (and local employment) requirements. The four B.E.C. groups are:

Business Studies (B1) (a confusing title as it also applies to B.E.C. courses generally): covers non-specialized work in wide range of commercial, manufacturing and service organizations. Options include personnel work; stock control; data processing; transport management; purchasing. B1 is a suitable choice for students who want to go into small or medium-sized organizations, where functions are not as specialized as in large ones, and for those who are not sure exactly where their interests lie.

Finance (B2): students specialize in financial occupations within organizations, in insurance, banking, building societies, etc.

Distribution (B3) for students who want to go into wholesale, retail, mail-order; or into distribution in large manufacturing concerns. Most B3 courses are part-time for people in relevant employment. Distribution courses are not as widely available as the others. Distribution students can take a General Business Studies course and add Distribution options.

Public Administration/Public sector (B4) for students who want to work in local and central government; public utilities (electricity, water authorities, etc.); health service administration, police, etc. (For the vague distinction between Management and Administration, see p. 261 above.)

B.E.C. Higher National awards may lead to complete, and certainly to partial, exemption from relevant professional bodies' intermediate examinations; for example, B.E.C. Finance H.N.D. normally leads straight to the Institute of Bankers' and Chartered Institute of Insurance's final examinations. There is a tendency for more and more professional bodies in the commercial field to accept B.E.C. Higher National awards in lieu of their own former stage 1 or intermediate examinations. (The advantage from the students' point of view is that they can postpone narrow specialization till they know more about all the related specializations, and that they can more easily switch specializations in mid-career.) For range of B.E.C. H.N.D. specialization, see *Compendium of Advanced Courses in Colleges of Further and Higher Education*.

3. *Qualifications likely to lead to junior management* (at least in the first instance; they can be stepping stones to middle management)
B.E.C. National Diploma (2 years full-time or 3 years part-time) or National Certificate (at least 2 years, possibly 3, by day- or block-release while in relevant emploment). *Entry qualifications*: Normally 4 O-levels including an English subject and one proving numeracy (preferably maths), or B.E.C. General Award (see Secretarial/Clerical Work, p. 430) at credit standard. Students study the 'Central Themes' (also called 'core modules') and two 'option modules' for the National Certificates, six for the National Diplomas. National Diplomas and Certificates may lead to partial exemptions from professional bodies' exams (not from final ones) and are accepted by many professional bodies, and for many degree courses, in lieu of A-levels.

Employers' Training Schemes: Many firms (mainly large ones) and nationalized industries run training schemes. Entry is at various levels either for training, with day-release, for a professional qualification, or, for professionally qualified people – in whatever subject, but specially accountancy or engineering – as 'graduate trainee' or 'management trainee'. Schemes vary enormously in content, quality and usefulness to the trainee. In some firms, trainees learn only how to be of use to that particular organization, in others they get a thorough training in industrial management. Detailed research is necessary; the term 'management trainee' does not necessarily indicate training for management. Increasingly, large organizations especially take only, or mainly, graduates for training schemes likely to lead to senior or even senior–middle management. Retail chains are the exception – they often groom A-level entrants for top jobs.

Personal attributes
Numeracy, business acumen, the ability to get on well with and be respected by people at all levels in the hierarchy; natural authority; willingness to take the blame for subordinates' misdeeds; self-confidence; unflappability in crises; organizing ability. *For senior management*: an analytical brain; ability to see implications and consequences of decisions and actions taken; ability to sift relevant facts from a mass of irrelevant information; enjoyment of power and responsibility; a fairly thick skin to cope with unavoidable clashes of temperament and opinion.

Position of women
Women are faring worse in industrial/commercial management than in the professions. 41% of the total workforce are women, but only 2% of

managers. Of the British Institute of Management's 65,000-plus members – all in at least senior–middle management – only 1·4% are women, and the vast majority of these are in service industries like retail or catering rather than in wealth-creating manufacturing; and in personnel rather than in 'sharp end' functions like production or financial management. Yet manufacturing industry is desperately short of *good* managers, and for today's 'participative' management style establishing and maintaining good personal relationships with a wide variety of types of people is considered one of the most important management qualities. Women are supposed to be 'good with people', so it is illogical that so few are managers. As industry now realizes that it cannot afford to waste half the nation's management potential simply because it happens to be held by females, several research projects (and many conferences) have been funded in recent years by government and industry to find out (a) why women are making such slow progress in industry (it is not just discrimination; it is clearly more complicated than that), and (b) what can be done to get more women managers. (In 1979, 8,334 men and only 1,756 women went from university into industry.)

An 'in depth' research project was carried out at Ashridge Management College and identified (or, perhaps, confirmed?) that there are three basic and interrelated reasons why women do badly in this traditionally male area:

1. *Organizational causes*: Traditional career paths were designed for men, and have not been adapted to take account of women's different requirements and life pattern.

2. *Assumptions* which do not stand up when tested: for example it is still widely believed that women management trainees/graduates leave their first employer sooner than their male colleagues, and before they have 'paid off' the money invested in their training. But this is not so. Statistics show that women leave to have babies after about 7 years; men switch companies after between 5 and 7 years. The chairman of a big company said at an Industrial Society Conference in 1980 that he would much rather lose a manager because she was about to have a baby than because he/she was going to work for a competitor.

Another false assumption: women's alleged worse absentee record. Women employees *as a whole* take more time off, but the lower the level of responsibility, the higher the level of absenteeism; *far* more women have lowly jobs, so far more take time off. At middle and senior management level, women's record equals men's. Other assumptions which research has disproved include: women are more emotional at work; men do not want to work for women. Broadly, research has proved that discrimination founded on false assumption persists, but is getting less.

The third and most intractable reason why women do badly in

management lies in *women themselves*: their attitudes, aspirations, qualifications. Women lack confidence and ambition; they need to do more strategic career-planning than men and in fact do less. This ties up closely with (1) above – career structures planned for men: in most companies young men are *assumed* to want to go up the ladder – their careers are almost automatically 'developed'; they are sent on courses and given broadening experience which fits them for promotion. Women have to *ask* for 'career development', to be sent on courses and given broadening experience (this applies at all levels of management, especially junior management). Women therefore have to be much more highly motivated in order to try as hard as men do automatically.

Women find themselves in two kinds of chicken-and-egg situations: (a) if they push themselves forward, they are dubbed aggressive – and that is unacceptable in women managers. If they do not push themselves forward, they are far less likely than men to be given the training/experience essential for promotion. (b) Women have few 'role models'. As so few women are in top jobs, few girls know, or know of, anyone with whom they can identify; whom they can emulate. They feel they will not be promoted anyway; so they do not try. They do not try, so they do not get promoted.

Women are also less likely than men to have the kind of qualifications which help to get on in management: 2% of women but 21% of men university students started technology-based degrees in 1979; yet about two-thirds of graduate jobs in industry are for people with such degrees. About four times as many men as women choose business management studies degrees (though any A-levels are acceptable). Far fewer girls than boys have the sort of qualifications which enable them to start at the bottom on the shop-floor, and get day-release for technical qualifications which can then lead to supervisory work and junior management.

The Ashridge research project also found that women's careers 'take off' later than men's. Only when the employer *and the woman herself* seem sure that she will take her career seriously will she be given, or press for, appropriate training.

The most important, though not startling, proposal for attracting more women into industry and commerce is that career structures must take account of women's 'broken career-pattern'. No blueprint for action has been produced, but, almost by stealth, forward-looking companies are quietly setting precedents: they are making *ad hoc* arrangements for women managers to return after a few years' break (the statutory maternity provisions have not helped much: most women managers want to take a longer period off work). Arrangements for working part-time, often two or three days a week, or term-time only, rather than short (school-hours) days, are being tried out.

The *average* woman in management still has more problems than the *average* man. For above-average women prospects are now good: their talents are needed. All the big companies stress that 'recruitment ratios reflect application ratios': not enough women graduates have the confidence to apply for management training.

Career-break: see above. Various plans for helping women resume their careers are in the early discussion stages. For example, it has been suggested that 'returners' should have an 'industrial tutor' or 'mentor' – someone in the organization (not necessarily a woman) who helps her pick up the threads. Then there are various courses 'returners' can take – for example, the Diploma in Management Studies (see **Training**). T.O.P.S. grants may be available. A large variety of post-graduate courses exists and they would all welcome more women. For instance, at the London University Graduate Business School in 1980, only 17% of applicants were women, but 24% of those accepted were women (which is a rise of 9% in 2 years!) – so a higher proportion of women than of men applicants were successful. However, still only 3·3% of the Business Graduates Association members are women – the proportion has changed very little since the early seventies.

Late start: see above – post-graduate courses. A few companies, so far mainly in retail and in catering, are encouraging women of 30-plus to become management trainees. Candidates are expected to have a degree, or professional qualification, or relevant experience which is usually selling or secretarial; but a few companies realize that women who have managed a home, family, voluntary work and/or hobbies of some kind have in fact been 'project managers', i.e. they know how to bring different strands together.

Part-time: Few opportunities at present; possibly more in future.

Further information No one specific information point; see various business functions and:
Business Educational Council, 168–173 High Holborn, London WC1
Department of Education and Science for leaflet on Diploma in Management Studies
Universities' and polytechnics' prospectuses
C.R.A.C. Course Guides; *Which Degree*

Related careers *Accountancy – Computers – Engineering – Marketing – Operational Research – Personnel – Purchasing and Supply – Shipbroking and Freight Forwarding – Work Study*

MARKETING AND SELLING

Consumer goods marketing – industrial marketing – international marketing – selling
– export research

Entry quali- Nothing specific; for Institute of Marketing's qualification: 2 A-levels,
fications 3 O-levels including English. Considerable *graduate* entry.

The work Marketing is a vague term, used loosely to cover a range of activities.
Different establishments interpret the term differently, and titles vary
enormously – brand manager; product manager; development manager;
marketing executive; marketing manager, export manufacturing manager, etc. Titles do not necessarily indicate any particular level of
responsibility or scope.

The Institute of Marketing defines the purpose of marketing as
follows: 'Marketing is the management process responsible for identifying, anticipating and satisfying customer requirements profitably' – at
home and, vitally important, abroad.

In other words, marketing is the key to profitability in business and
Britain's healthy export trading position; marketing people (sometimes
called 'marketers') find out what customers want or can be persuaded
to want, at what price, and then relate potential demand to the
company's ability to produce whatever it is, get it to the 'point of sale',
and do all that profitably.

Marketing involves researching the market and analysing research
results – which involves devising and organizing surveys and interpreting
the results; discussing results with accountants, production, distribution
and advertising people. Marketers may suggest the company adapt its
existing products to cope with the competition's better products, or
with changes in buying habits, or they may think up a totally new
product and help to develop and launch it, or they may introduce a
better after-sales service.

All these activities have always been carried out in business, but as
business has become more complex and professionalized, with decisions
being based on researched facts and, above all, figures rather than
guesswork and experience, the 'marketing function' has become a
'business profession' and even a degree subject.

Marketing is often split into *consumer goods marketing*; *industrial
marketing*; and *international marketing* (which could refer to either, and
is part of the export business).

In all these activities, marketing involves several types of work:

detailed research to establish customers', and potential customers', needs, and potential needs: what type of customers, where, might buy at what price, with how effective an after-sales service, etc. Whether it is yet another washing powder or, in industrial marketing, a new piece of office machinery or computer, a new magazine or a food product, the procedure is basically the same. In *Industrial Marketing*, an engineering or science background is useful, but people switch from one kind of marketing to another. In *International Marketing*, a thorough understanding of other nations' cultural as well as social and economic set-up is vital (and of course speaking the relevant language). Perhaps the most crucial among several other marketing activities is *sales forecasting*. How many cars with what particular features will country X be willing to buy in 2, 5, 10 years' time?

Marketing people must always base their conclusions on researched social and economic trends, which include statistics – though marketing has a glamorous image, the basis of it is the correct interpretation of statistics.

Though the majority of marketing people work in large, often multinational, companies, increasingly medium and small companies are separating the marketing function from general business management.

Selling is both a career in itself, and an essential part of (and the best way into) marketing. The two are closely linked: if 'marketing' puts products on the market, 'sales' disposes of them.

There are different kinds of selling – and various ways of categorizing sales staff. A useful division is between consumer goods selling, and specialized selling. In consumer goods selling (this totally excludes retail and door-to-door selling), sales representatives, or reps, sell to wholesalers and/or, more usually, to retailers. Selling to retailers involves 'merchandising', which means helping the retailer to maximize sales, by promotion campaigns, suggesting ideas for improving shop display, etc. Reps may also advise retailers on new sales techniques, shop display, etc. There is a hierarchy in consumer goods selling, with the field sales supervisors and area sales managers in charge of reps, and sales managers and directors at head office directing the whole sales operation.

Speciality or technical or industrial selling is usually done by staff with technical background and perhaps production management experience (see p. 166). The speciality selling process differs totally from consumer goods selling: purchasing decisions are made not by shopkeepers or store buyers, but technical and financial experts. To effect one sale may take months of negotiations, and extensive after-sales service. Speciality sales staff do not necessarily sell only standard products – whether it is a large piece of machinery or machine tools –

they may agree for their company to modify a product or produce a 'one-off' piece of equipment.

A sales rep may form part of a team, or be the only rep in the firm. She may have a 'territory' in this country which may require her to be away from home for several days most weeks, or it may be a territory near home – it depends on the kind of product (how many potential buyers there are within an area). Export sales executives of course travel extensively.

Prospects Depend on economic climate – but companies vary in the importance they attach to marketing: some firms cut down marketing staff when business is bad, others expand it, believing that poor marketing in the past caused poor business performance; this applies particularly to international marketing. As exporting is becoming more and more essential for economic survival, international marketing is becoming a vital function in many more businesses. Marketing people also have good prospects of going to the top in general management.

Pay: High to very high (see p. xxiii).

Training There are various ways into marketing – the most usual way to start is as sales rep. Production (see Engineering, p. 163) people often move into marketing (which is usually better paid). Many graduates go straight into marketing as assistants.

While working as trainee or whatever the title, marketing staff can take part-time courses for the Institute of Marketing's Certificate and Diploma examination.

Pre-entry training is either by Business Studies degree with Marketing option; or by specialized marketing degree. These degrees either link marketing to a specific area such as chemicals or textiles or engineering; or concentrate on international marketing and export. An engineering or science degree is a good way into speciality selling.

There are also B.E.C. Higher awards (see p. xvii) with marketing and export options.

Personal attributes *Marketing*: A high degree of numeracy and of business acumen; a little gambling instinct; self-confidence; ability to assess the effects of events; ability to stand perhaps unjustified criticism when forecasts turn out wrong, due to unforeseeable causes; social awareness and interest in social and economic trends; ability to communicate easily with colleagues and clients, whatever their temperament and their degree of expertise.

Selling: Numeracy; extrovert personality; ability to establish instant rapport with people; judgement; sensitivity for gauging right approach to customers; indifference to the occasional rebuff; enjoying being alone when travelling; willingness to be away from home a lot.

Position of women

This is an area in which personality counts more than qualifications. Women have good prospects if they fit the employer's idea of what the 'right type' for any particular job is. In other words, they still have to be better, and more highly motivated, than the men with whom they compete. In export marketing their scope is limited because employers fear that in many countries saleswomen and women negotiators are not acceptable. Graduate women stand much better chances than school-leavers, who tend to be offered secretarial jobs 'with a view to progressing in marketing', and then do *not* progress. Graduate sales reps who are good at their job say they are at an advantage: they tend to be noticed and 'trained up'. So far, however, there are very few women sales directors (except in cosmetics, etc.). Potentially it could be a promising area. Especially in specialized *selling*, more women would be genuinely welcome in many organizations. Companies say that not enough women graduates apply. The proportion of female graduates *accepted* is slightly higher than that of males accepted. Probably women who do apply are more highly motivated. It is too early to say, however, what women's promotion prospects to senior sales management positions are.

Career-break: It is not likely that in this competitive field it will be easy for any but the best and most determined women to return to what is essentially still a young and a men's career. Women with technological or science degrees or experience stand the best chances in industrial marketing.

Late start: Not advisable to start from scratch, but women with technological or business qualifications might switch to marketing.

Part-time: Only in backroom research – very few openings indeed.

Further information

Institute of Marketing, Moor Hall, Cookham, Maidenhead, Berks, SL6 9QH

Related careers

Advertising – Management in Industry and Commerce – Public Relations – Retail Distribution

MEDICINE

General practice – community medicine – hospital service – research and teaching – industrial medicine

Entry quali-fications
Precise requirements vary between medical schools but usually 3 A-levels, in chemistry, physics and biology or zoology or mathematics, lead to exemption from the 'First M.B.' course (which most medical schools do not run now). But applicants with other good A-levels, even if entirely on the arts side, may be offered a place on condition that they obtain 3 good science A-levels (i.e. they are offered a conditional place 1 or 2 years ahead). 2 O-level sciences and O-level mathematics are essential for this conditional acceptance.

Doctors can work in a variety of settings:

1. GENERAL PRACTICE (Family Doctor)

The work
This absorbs almost half of all those who qualify. The vast majority work in contract with the National Health Service. They may also take private patients; but these account for a very small proportion of the general practitioner's work.

A G.P. spends from 2 to 5 hours holding surgeries on weekdays and visits patients when necessary. She must be available for emergency calls at all times or arrange for someone to stand in for her. The majority of G.P.s work in some form of partnership, either with a doctor whose surgery is nearby, or with one or several doctors in 'group practice', sharing premises and the services of a secretary-receptionist, and possibly of a nurse and/or health visitor or social worker. Such arrangements solve the problem of isolation which used to affect single-handed young G.P.s who missed discussion with a colleague.

G.P.s spend much time discussing patients' personal problems which are often the real cause of symptoms. Perhaps the main difference between general practice and hospital work (working in medical specializations) is that general practitioners 'treat the person, not the illness'. The therapeutic value of 'talking to the doctor' is great; general practitioners must be as much interested in helping people cope with their problems as in medical science.

In many areas there are now part-time hospital appointments for general practitioners. This enables G.P.s to combine general practice with specializing in one aspect of medicine. These G.P.s' hospital jobs are *not* 'training posts' (see below, *Post-graduate Training*).

Prospects   Vary from one geographical area to another, but good on the whole. British qualifications are recognized in Eire, most Commonwealth countries and in E.E.C. countries.

   Pay: Medium to high, depending on size of practice (see p. xxiii).

2. COMMUNITY MEDICINE (formerly Public Health)

The work   Community medicine is primarily concerned with preventive medicine. It deals with health problems as they affect whole communities and particular geographical, occupational and age groups. For example, inhabitants of certain areas may need attention because of air pollution dangers; workers in certain industries may need regular checks because of occupational hazards; schoolchildren, expectant mothers, the old and the handicapped need special provision.

   Community physicians' work also includes the overall administration, planning and development of the 3 branches of the health service (environmental health, personal health, community care); the development of comprehensive information; and health education services. Community physicians also act as advisers to local authorities, which retain responsibility for running school, environmental and some personal health services.

   Environmental health covers infectious disease control and prevention (regular immunization and special immunization campaigns); food and other hygiene inspection; prevention of insanitary conditions in restaurants, shops, housing (including overcrowding); control of noise nuisance and air pollution. The day-to-day work is carried out by environmental health officers (see p. 185).

   Personal health services cover provision of ante-natal, post-natal and child health clinics; midwifery; home nursing, district nursing services (see separate entries); care of handicapped children.

   Community care covers provision for the care of the mentally ill and subnormal who live at home or in hostels; support in the home by social workers; day centres for the elderly and handicapped; social clubs; hostel accommodation and organization; cooperation with local voluntary organizations in the mental health field.

Prospects   This is an expanding field, but job prospects are affected by public expenditure cuts.

   There is some confusion about the similarities and differences between the new community physicians' work – and therefore prospects – and that of the traditional local-authority-employed public health doctors. Amongst the latter were many women who staffed clinics; this provided excellent opportunities for part-time work. But the new community medicine specialists, by definition, are concerned with groups rather than individuals. Clinics are not likely to be staffed by *community medicine* specialists, but by G.P.s or by specialists in paediatrics, geriatrics, etc. There are opportunities for part-time sessional clinic work, but for that *community medicine* is not the speciality to choose. Mature entrants (returners) are very welcome.

Pay: High (see p. xxiii).

3. HOSPITAL SERVICE

The work   At the top are consultants who have specialized in a particular field of medicine, such as child health or obstetrics or surgery. There are over 40 specialities. Training under the consultant, and doing most of the day-to-day routine work, are senior registrars, registrars, and house officers. Most of them are studying for various specialist examinations. Students usually decide on a particular specialization during their general medical training, not before.

Prospects   Vary greatly from one speciality to another. In many fields there are far more senior registrars than there are consultant vacancies. Prospects are good only in 'shortage' specialities, such as geriatrics; child psychiatry. Consultants may take private patients, but private practice makes up a very small proportion of the work of all but a minority of consultants.

Pay: Low to very high for a consultant (see p. xxiii).

4. RESEARCH AND TEACHING

The work   Research into new forms of treatments and new drugs and their effects is done in hospitals, research establishments and drug firms. Doctors can, and usually do, combine clinical and scientific work, but there are also research appointments, often including some teaching, for those who are interested in the scientific side of medicine rather than 'patient contact' (see Science, p. 400).

Prospects   Fair.

Pay: Medium to high (see p. xxiii).

5. INDUSTRIAL MEDICINE OR 'OCCUPATIONAL HEALTH'

The work   Industrial medical officers give medical check-ups to employees and work with personnel departments. They also do research into occupational health, studying the effects of diverse environmental conditions on health and efficiency of the staff.

Prospects   Fair.

Pay: High (see p. xxiii).

Abroad (all doctors): To work in E.E.C. countries, it is essential to speak the relevant language fluently. The developing countries do not offer as much scope as is generally supposed, but there are some opportunities, mainly in paediatrics, obstetrics, and preventive medicine.

Training   Doctors must obtain a 'registrable qualification'. There are several, each signified by different initials; all are essentially of equal value.

The basic course takes 5 or 6 years. It usually falls into 2 parts. The first is the *pre-clinical* course, which lasts 2 years and covers anatomy, physiology and biochemistry. The work consists of lectures, laboratory work and a great deal of reading. The *clinical* course lasts 3 or 4 years. Students are attached to a succession of consultants in different specialities (firms). They have contact with patients, take case histories and, under supervision, make diagnoses and give treatments. The clinical course is extremely hard work, with little spare time.

Before students get their registrable qualification they must spend a 'pre-registration year' as full-time resident junior house-officer in hospital. (At this stage they start earning.)

Post-registration training is essential, very hard work, and rather haphazard. Everybody has to arrange their own succession of hospital 'training posts', each training post has to be 'accredited' as such by the relevant Royal College (for example a training post in surgery has to be accredited by the Royal College of Surgeons). Post-registration training in a succession of accredited training posts as house officer, registrar, senior registrar takes from 3 to over 10 years (it depends mainly on the specialty chosen). During this period of full-time work, doctors study for specialist examinations.

In 1982, post-graduate training for principals in *general practice* becomes compulsory. It will consist of 2 years in a variety of full-time hospital and community medicine posts, and 1 year as full-time trainee in general practice (or the equivalent on a part-time basis). Doctors without this post-graduate training may still be employed as assistants, locums or deputies.

Personal attributes

The ability to take responsibility and to make vital decisions after weighing up all the relevant factors; self-confidence; conscientiousness; resourcefulness; the energy and stamina to work hard for long and often irregular periods; great powers of concentration; above-average intelligence; good health.

Especially for general practitioners and the hospital service: patience with people unable to express themselves clearly; sympathy without emotional involvement; understanding of and liking for all types of people and tolerance with human weaknesses.

For research: patience for long-term projects and an inquiring mind.

Position of women

Proportions of women as practising doctors:

General Practice: 16%

	Consultants in:	*Registrars* in:
General Surgery	0·8%	4%
Paediatrics	16%	35%
Obstetrics and Gynaecology	12%	17%
Psychiatry (child and adolescent)	9%	55%
Psychiatry (mental handicap)	25%	33%
Geriatrics	9%	9%

Present training patterns (see post-graduate training), established long before there were many women doctors, fit in very badly with women's dual role. Yet almost 40% of entrants to medical school in 1979 were women, and by the mid-80s the proportion is expected to be 50%. The male/female proportion of entrants to medical school reflects that of applicants very fairly: there is no discrimination at the entry stage, but indirect discrimination is built into the traditional training and employment pyramid.

If a profession's structure is unsuitable for half its members, that structure must change. The Medical Women's Federation has fought for years for more part-time post-graduate training posts. Late in 1979 the D.H.S.S. issued an important Memorandum which stated: 'It is important that optimum use is made of all our doctors and dentists including those only able to work part-time for domestic or other reasons. It will be particularly important to provide posts for women doctors and dentists who wish to complete their training or to work part-time while they raise their families.' The D.H.S.S. action was not taken in order to be fair to women, but to reduce the wastage among expensively trained women doctors who give up work/further training in their thirties. Changes are particularly important when general practitioners also have to do post-graduate training.

The Memo gives details of arrangements agreed between the D.H.S.S. and the profession, which should make it 'neither easier nor harder to obtain a post in a given specialty' for people who can train only part-time.

Implementation of the D.H.S.S. proposals – i.e. the setting up of part-time training posts and their 'accreditation' as training posts – still depend on regional health authorities' and the various Royal Colleges' willingness to adapt existing training patterns. It is highly likely that part-time posts will be available mainly in shortage subjects (for example, geriatrics, paediatrics, psychiatry, radiology) rather than in prestigious specialties where competition is very keen even for full-time training-post applicants.

The D.H.S.S. Medical Manpower Division is monitoring the new scheme. If regional health authorities and Royal Colleges do not increase part-time training posts, it will 'reconsider the situation'.

Once qualified, women specialists probably have no more difficulty getting full-time consultants' posts than men (i.e. it depends on their specialty and the part of the country in which they want to work); but there are at present very few part-time top jobs, and in specialties where full-timers are expected to be on call 24 hours a day (surgery or obstetrics for example), far fewer women than men can compete. Experiments with job-sharing and similar arrangements have shown that part-time schemes can work well.

In *general practice* women can choose whether they want to work part- or full-time. Most practices today very much want a woman partner.

Career-break: Some attempt has been made to adapt career patterns to women's needs. Under the D.H.S.S.'s Doctors Retainer Scheme, women who, because of domestic commitments, work less than 2 sessions a week, and who intend to return to medical practice when they are more free again, receive an annual retainer of £130 (1980). In return, they undertake to keep up their Registration, to read a professional journal, attend at least 7 'education' sessions a year, and take at least 12 paid service sessions a year.

It is possible (though complicated) to do the *post-registration training* (see above) in part-time training posts, but it is almost impossible to resume training if the break was made *before* completing the pre-registration year as resident junior house officer.

Refresher courses: With the help of the Medical Women's Federation and Postgraduate Dean's committee, *ad hoc* arrangements can often be made.

Late start: Individual medical schools vary in their policies on accepting mature candidates, so one has to inquire from several before giving up – if determined to start; it becomes very difficult if over 30. Length of training is not normally reduced even for qualified nurses or people with other related qualifications.

Part-time: See **Position of women**.

Further information   The British Medical Association, B.M.A. House, Tavistock Square, London WC1

Medical Women's Federation, Tavistock House North, Tavistock Square, London WC1

Related careers   *Dentistry – Nursing – Occupational Therapy – Ophthalmic Optician*, p. 328 – *Orthoptics – Osteopathy – Pharmacy – Physiotherapy – Science – Social Work – Veterinary Surgeon*

NOTE: Applicants who fail to get a training place should decide whether what attracts them to medicine is dealing with people, or the scientific aspect. Such careers as nursing or physiotherapy do not offer comparable scope. Another science which may lead to medical research may be a more satisfying second choice than one of the auxiliary medical careers.

MERCHANT NAVY

Engineer officer – deck (navigating) officer – radio officer – catering officer – assistant purser – children's hostess – nurse – stewardess – ship's doctor

Entry quali-fications   *Engineer, Deck and Radio Officers*: normally 4 O-levels including mathematics, English and physical science. *Catering Officer*: T.E.C. Hotel and Catering Operations (but see **Training**).

The work

1. ENGINEER OFFICERS

They are responsible for ship's engines including heating, pumps, etc. They ensure that the ship sails smoothly and efficiently; supervise repairs at sea and overhauls in port. When on watch, the engineer monitors the engines, now usually done with computerized equipment. Modern ships' engine-rooms are clean, airy and contain a mass of electronic equipment. They have nothing in common with old-fashioned boiler-rooms.

Engineer Officers are in charge of and responsible for the work of engine-room staff; so managing people is part of the job, as of all ships' officers.

2. DECK (NAVIGATING) OFFICERS

They navigate the ship. In port they are responsible for efficient loading and unloading, which involves both mathematical and common-sense problem-solving, especially in ships which carry a variety of cargo, simultaneously or in succession. They are responsible for controlling large numbers of seamen; in port they may negotiate with stevedores and others concerned with loading and unloading.

Deck Officer is a step on the ladder to becoming Captain or Master.

3. RADIO OFFICERS

They maintain communications between ships and between ship and shore. Systems vary according to size and age of ship, from morse to satellite-assisted transmitters. They may also operate radar, close-circuit TV and depth-sounding apparatus. In highly automated ships – most of the supertankers and container ships – there may also be an Electronics Officer, who could be either an engineer or a radio officer.

4. CATERING OFFICER (called Purser or Hotel Manager on passenger liners; sometimes Chief Steward on tankers, etc.)

Responsible for purchase, storage, preparation (supervision) of food, meal service, maintenance of accommodation. On liners, they are also responsible for passengers' banking, information and entertainment services.

Training   1. *Engineering Cadets (trainee officers employed by shipping company)*
(a) With 4 O-levels to include mathematics, physical science and English: 4-year course for T.E.C. Diploma and Higher Diploma. A few opportunities exist for those with less than the above qualifications to follow a (possibly longer) T.E.C. Higher Certificate course. All cadets take D.O.T. Class 4 Certificate examination at the end of the training.
(b) With A-level mathematics and physics studied, and a pass in one of them: 3½-year sandwich for H.N.D. Mechanical Engineering (Marine) or T.E.C. equivalent.

2. *Navigating Cadets (trainee officers employed by shipping company)*
(a) With 4 O-levels including mathematics, physics and English: about 3½ years for T.E.C. Diploma in Nautical Science, leading to D.O.T. Class 4 and Class 3 Certificates.
(b) With A-level (subjects as above): 2½-year 'accelerated cadetship' leading to D.O.T. Class 3 Certificate.
(c) With 2 or 3 A-levels (1 in physics or mathematics) and 3 O-levels: B.Sc. Nautical Science, 5- to 6-year sandwich course.

3. *Radio Officers (employed normally by radio companies)*
Unlike cadets they must get their qualification, the General Radio-communications Certificate, *before* going to sea. They need O-levels in mathematics, physics and English and then take a 2-year basic Certificate or, more usually, 3-year full-time course for the City and Guilds Final Technician's Certificate and the Department of Trade Radar Maintenance Certificate.

4. *Catering Officer*
Boys start as Catering Rating. Women are not accepted at National Sea Training College for catering training; they start higher up the ladder with Hotel and Catering Operations T.E.C. award (see p. 108).

Other Opportunities at Sea (very limited):
5. *Assistant Purser*
Must be over 21, have good shorthand/typing, a foreign language, 4 O-levels.

6. *Children's Hostess*
Must be R.S.C.N. (Registered Sick Children's Nurse, see p. 307) or teacher.

7. *Nurse*
Must be experienced S.R.N. (see p. 303) and over 26.

8. *Stewardesses on ferries and passenger liners*
Employment largely seasonal, experience of domestic work in hotels and a foreign language useful. Not a career with prospects.

9. *Ship's Doctor*
Newly-qualified doctors often work as ship's doctor for a few months. So far *very* few women, but on vessels with adequate accommodation theoretically no bar.

Prospects and position of women

There is a large turnover of crews: many officers who can use their training on shore do so after a few years at sea. However, conditions at sea have changed dramatically. The bulk of merchant navy tonnage now consists of tankers, supertankers, container ships and other bulk-carriers. Over half of these vessels are less than 5 years old, and living conditions for crews are far better than they used to be (and still are on passenger liners). Everything is being done to minimize boredom and irritation which tends to arise when groups of people live and work together in a close community. Vessels now often have single or double cabin accommodation, TV rooms, spacious lounges. Life at sea in modern ships is a mixture of modern technology and traditional hierarchy. Modern vessels have family accommodation so that officers can bring their wives. It is on ships with this type of accommodation that most women officers and cadets sail.

There are some female *ratings*, but as most deck and catering ratings are trained initially at the Sea Training College, where girls are not admitted, female ratings can only enter the Merchant Navy by applying for a *job*, not for training. Their hopes of promotion to Petty Officer and beyond are slim. However, girls are being recruited as *Deck Officer Cadets* by a number of companies and a few are being considered as *Engineer Cadets*. There have been women *Radio Officers* for some years. More women would be welcomed as Deck, Engineer and Radio Officers. *Catering Officers* have rather less scope, mainly because the majority of Catering Officers come up through the ranks, after training at the Sea Training College.

In November 1980 the first woman got her Master's Certificate which qualifies her to be Master – Captain – of a foreign-going vessel. There are now about 100 women Deck and Engineer Officers in the British Merchant Navy – more than in any other Western merchant fleet.

Pay: Medium to occasionally high (see p. xxiii).

Personal attributes	Self-sufficiency, as being the only, or one of two or three women among large groups of men, can be lonely; indifference to standing out in a crowd and therefore being constantly 'on show'; practicality; resourcefulness; ability to supervise and control men at work; gregariousness; willingness to take orders and accept one's place in the hierarchy, coupled with ability to take responsibility and make instant decisions.
Further information	British Shipping Careers Service, 30/32 St Mary Axe, London EC3A 8ET
Related careers	*Services – Shipbroking*

METEOROLOGY

Entry quali-fications
Scientific Officers: A degree in mathematics, electronics, physics (as single subject or with meteorology) or computer science or a T.E.C. Higher award (see p. xv) in applied physics or a mathematical subject.

Assistant Scientific Officers: At least 4 O-levels including English Language and mathematics or physics or general science. Many have better qualifications.

The work
The Meteorological Office is responsible for weather forecasts for the Forces, Civil Aviation, the Merchant Navy and government departments, public corporations, local authorities, the press, television, radio, industry, as well as the general public. It also does research.

1. SCIENTIFIC OFFICERS

They do mainly mathematical and physical research (see *Science*, p. 404). A few supervise weather forecasting.

2. ASSISTANT SCIENTIFIC OFFICERS

They do a variety of jobs. At airfields they read meteorological instruments, record the information and then pass it to Air Traffic Control (see p. 113) for transmission to aircraft, and, in international code, by teleprinter for national and international use. They plot weather maps and graphs and answer telephone inquiries as well as pass on warnings of impending bad weather to such bodies as local authorities and others who need such information. They also do statistical and computational work. They must be prepared to work anywhere (often in isolated locations) in the United Kingdom, and move when required. They must work unsocial hours if necessary. They may have to do shift work.

Prospects
Competition for vacancies is very keen. Once in, there are reasonable prospects for promotion if a higher qualification in a relevant subject is gained. (Day-release is granted.) There are now also a few opportunities for experienced meteorologists (A.S.O. grade) outside the Civil Service, to supply oil rigs with forecasts.

Pay: Medium to high (see p. xxiii).

Training
Initial training at residential Meteorological Office College is 4 weeks for Assistant Scientific Officers; up to 5 months for Scientific Officers. On-the-job training is also given.

Personal attributes   Self-sufficiency; the ability to work in a team; great interest in science.

Position of women   At the moment the ratio of men to women is 11 to 1; among new entrants it is about 4 to 1; but the majority of women are only qualified to enter as Assistant Scientific Officer.

Career-break: Women are eligible for re-instatement (see Civil Service, p. 129), though need for mobility and to work unsocial hours prevents most mothers from returning. Also weather forecasting and reporting procedures are changing all the time and potential returners must have kept in touch through extensive reading and attending lectures.

Late start: Age limit for Scientific Officers is 30, for Assistant Scientific Officers 26.

Part-time: A few opportunities for women to work part-time temporarily, on the expectation that they will return to full-time work when commitments permit.

Further information   The Secretary, Meteorological Office, Met 0 10 Recruitment, London Road, Bracknell, Berkshire, RG12 2SZ

Related careers   *Science*

MODELLING

Fashion – advertisements

Entry quali-fications	No educational requirements.

1. FASHION MODELLING

The work A 'live' model, or showroom or house model, is employed on a permanent basis by wholesale, retail or couture houses, or works as a freelance. A *photographic model* is booked for photographic and film sessions; she is normally freelance. These two fields overlap.

(a) *Live model*

The designer usually 'builds' his/her originals on models who have to stand for hours while cloth is being draped and pinned. Modelling clothes to customers involves changing outfits at top speed – and yet looking cool and perfectly groomed. Freelances are busy only for a few weeks each in spring and autumn when the trade shows its collections to press and buyers. Then models have to rush from one show to the next.

(b) *Photographic (fashion) model*

The photographic fashion model may work in cramped studios; in August she may swelter in heavy tweeds; in December she may pose by the sea in a bikini. She dashes from one appointment to another, carrying all accessories she may possibly need – she usually has to provide her own. She has irregular meals. There is the very occasional Mediterranean cruise or flying visit to a foreign city when exotic backgrounds are used for a magazine fashion feature, but these usually come the way of top models only.

Prospects *Live model*: She may earn less than the photographic model, but her working life is longer – if she keeps her figure.
Photographic model: There are rarely more than a dozen top models at any time, and only the most versatile, who can virtually change their whole appearance and personality to meet changing fashion trends, last more than a few years; photographers then start searching around for new faces.

Some lucky and intelligent women eventually get jobs as fashion consultants or commentators, in public relations, in retail stores or on magazines; a few remain – or come back later – as 'older' or 'mature' models, for whom there is a small but steady demand. Men usually start modelling a bit later in life than women. They should qualify in some other work first, to which they can return if their 'type' goes out of fashion or they get too old.

Pay: Low to very high (see p. xxiii).

Entry and training

Women: Entry is through a good model agency. Most run their own courses for both live and photographic modelling – showroom, television and film make-up; how to wear and show clothes; how to walk; how to pose for the cameras. Training may consist of 14 or 18 lessons either alone, or in a group with other girls. Evening sessions are available for women who sensibly decide to continue their present job while training.

It is essential to choose agency-schools carefully: one sign of a good one is that it rejects applicants who show little chance of succeeding in this highly competitive and over-glamorized field. Good schools turn down well over half the applicants. Applicants should ask searching questions about the type of work now done by previous pupils, and the proportion of pupils who have succeeded as full-time models.

There is a 1-year full-time course at the London College of Fashion. Girls must have 3 O-levels and must be between 5 ft 6 ins and 5 ft 8 ins. Syllabus includes English, German, French, anatomy and hygiene, knowledge of materials, business studies, salesmanship, history of costume, model training, an appreciation of clothing manufacture, millinery and accessories, hairdressing and beauty culture.

Men: Male models do not need special training – agencies can see from a snapshot whether a man has modelling potential. If he has, the agency will teach him the necessary tricks of the trade. Male models should be about 6 feet tall and have a chest size of 38 inches. They should be older than women when they start.

Personal attributes

Shape and looks currently fashionable; for photographic models, good bone structure. A strong feeling for clothes and the moods which go with them – the casual air for tweeds and sportswear, the regal air for furs and jewellery; the faculty for lending glamour to even the dullest clothes, in fact, some acting talent; a flair for fashion trends, to be always ahead with the newest hair-dos, make-up, etc.; iron constitution; total reliability; visual imagination; unwavering self-confidence; indifference to being turned down by photographers; adaptability; infinite patience; perseverance; ability to remain calm and keep smiling and to appear interested, however bored or tired.

2. MODELLING FOR ADVERTISEMENTS

The work Female advertising models, who appear in press advertisements, mail order catalogues, on posters, in commercials and advertising films, are not as a rule the same as fashion models – unless the advertisements are for clothes, or possibly jewellery and cosmetics. Male models combine fashion and advertising (press, etc.). Teenage models usually come from drama schools. In TV commercials and films the work is now nearly always done by actors and actresses (i.e. Equity members, see p. 13).

Television commercials are made under film studio conditions, and may take anything from half a day to several days to make. Most of the time is spent waiting while shots are 'set up'. The actual 'takes' are done quickly, but each one may be repeated over and over again.

Prospects Even if successful, a short working life, especially for women. If a model is put under exclusive contract for one product, and appears in advertising campaigns to promote it, she may earn as much as £15,000 a year and become famous; but because her face has become associated with one product, she will not be used for another product for some time afterwards.

Pay: Low to very high (see p. xxiii).

Training With an agency-school which specializes in camera work. However, training is not essential; having a set of photographs taken (which may cost up to £150) and hawking it round to photographers and advertising agencies is just as likely to lead to success.

Personal attributes Much the same as for photographic fashion models; but instead of impersonal stylized elegance, vivacity and a natural manner. Actual measurements, especially height, not as important as in fashion modelling; for advertising films (commercials mainly), acting talent.

Career-break: There are some jobs for 'mature' models, but fewer even than for young ones.

Late start: Not recommended for women – see *Career-break.*

Part-time: Most work is part-time, except for top models.

Further information No central organization.

Related careers *Acting – Advertising – Fashion – Journalism – Photography*

MUSEUMS AND ART GALLERIES

**Entry quali-
fications**

For assistants: In theory 4 relevant O-levels plus reading knowledge of at least 1 foreign language; most have far higher qualifications.

For conservation officers and technical assistants: A science degree and/or art-school training (not necessarily at degree level, depending on the work).

For assistant keepers and research assistants: A relevant good honours degree, or diploma in art history, plus a reading knowledge of at least 1 foreign language. Specialist knowledge may, in exceptional cases, be acceptable as an alternative qualification.

Degrees in subjects such as English literature, or languages, do not normally lead to museum work.

The work

Professional museum staff are usually called keepers or curators. Duties vary according to type and size of museum or art gallery. Most of the work, except that on the technical side, is concerned either directly or indirectly with helping the public to understand and enjoy the exhibits, and to induce more people to visit the museum. The work is by no means only backroom research; it is a combination of research, administration, and public relations. It may not involve direct contact with people, but it is certainly concerned with their interests.

The traditional museum skills are *research, classification, conservation* and *identification*: a new museum skill is *communication*. Museums and art galleries are trying to shed their image of solemn shrines devoted to earnest study of art and history; they are becoming more welcoming places which visitors want to go on visiting and which fit into children's learning-by-discovery process (see Teaching, p. 485). Saturday clubs, junior centres, weekend seminars and various other 'participation' schemes are run for children by museum education officers (titles vary). Many of these are experienced teachers with a flair for showmanship (and for controlling children in a free-and-easy atmosphere). Individual schemes vary greatly and include, for example, studios for art and craft work; making and playing with replicas of old toys; examining scientific instruments; 'acting out' or thinking up stories about paintings on show; joint projects with local history, archaeology, conservation societies, as well as with local radio stations, or local authority planning and architects departments.

In some museums a good deal of time is spent answering the public's questions, both personally and by letter. Objects brought in for identification may range from live insects to old paintings and pieces of pottery dug up in the garden.

Conservation officers work on the restoration, repair, protection and conservation of exhibits. Senior conservation officers are scientists by training, art historians by inclination: their work is a unique combination of scientific work, art appreciation and knowledge of art history. Senior conservation officers may research into new methods of conservation. The practical work is done by artists, technical assistants, or craftsmen who had art-school training but not to degree level.

Most large museums are staffed by Civil Servants. In local authorities' small museums, qualifications required vary.

Prospects   Not good. There is great competition for few vacancies. Promotion to senior posts is slow, and may require moving to another museum.

Pay: Medium (see p. xxiii).

Training   *After* entry into museum work:

(a) On-the-job with tutorials and short courses, for the Museums Association's Diploma. Syllabus covers museum administration, collection, preservation, preparation and storage techniques. Studies are related to the branch of museum work in which the student specializes, such as art, archaeology, ethnography, natural history, etc.

(b) If mainly concerned with conservation and restoration: Part-time day-release for Museums Association's Certificate which is in 2 parts: (i) City and Guilds Science Laboratory Technician's Certificate; (ii) course on museum techniques which is recognized by Museums Association.

(c) Technical assistants doing purely practical work may take the Museums Association's Technical Certificate after 3 years' work.

Before entry into museum work:

(a) Post-graduate (any degree) courses in Museum Studies, which lead to partial exemption from Museums Association's Diploma.

(b) Institute of Archaeology's (London University) degree in Conservation (normally chemistry at A-level required). Syllabus covers applied chemistry, archaeological draughtsmanship, photography, conservation technology, recording systems, care and restoration of pictures.

There is a waiting-list for vacancies; applicants frequently go into museum laboratories as juniors and take this course later. It may then be possible to take it in 2 years instead of 3.

Personal attributes   Intellectual ability; a love of knowledge for its own sake; organizing ability; visual imagination; a lively curiosity; an understanding of laymen's interests and tastes.

Position of women

The ratio of men to women is about 6 to 4 amongst assistant keepers and keepers, but there are very few women museum directors.

Career-break: This would delay promotion.

Late start: No objection in theory: entry requirements to Museums Association's Diploma might even be relaxed, but young entrants likely to be taken in preference for junior jobs.

Part-time: No (though there is no reason whatever why this should not be possible).

Further information

Museums Association, 34 Bloomsbury Way, London WC1A 2SF

Local museums

Related careers

Archaeology – Archivist – Art and Industrial Design – Information Officer – Librarian

---

MUSIC

Performing – teaching – music-technology – music therapy – administration – musical instrument technology

**Entry quali-
fications**

Acceptance at music colleges depends on performance at audition. For performers, except for singers, intensive musical training must have started at 14 at the latest.

For teaching, see p. 485. For degree courses at least 2 A-levels and 3 O-levels, with, usually, A-level music.

1. PERFORMING

The work

Many professional performers teach part-time, because there are more qualified performers than there is work. The provincial and the B.B.C. symphony orchestras normally employ orchestral players on a full-time basis; the London-based national orchestras are made up largely of freelance musicians who are, however, booked regularly, for series of concerts and possibly tours as well, rather than for individual concerts. Section leaders are often employed on a contract basis.

Most freelance musicians, however devoted to serious music, are glad to work as 'session players' on TV commercials, film background music and other light music recording sessions, etc. A violinist may play in a concert at the Festival Hall on one evening and the following day in a TV jingle recording session. However, few serious musicians are able to satisfy the requirements of the 'pop' recording managers.

A freelance musician has to fit in work as it comes. The work may fluctuate from 14 hours a day over a long period, to no work for many weeks. Long practice at home is always necessary. TV, radio, live concerts or recording sessions are arranged well in advance, and accepting bookings requires careful judgement. Once a date is booked, it is unwise to break it, even if a better engagement is offered.

The musician's work is physically exhausting, and may include travel over long distances, combined with rehearsals and nightly performances, often in cold or overheated halls. An engagement for a season with a ballet or opera company may involve 5 performances a week with as many rehearsals, and practice at home. The atmosphere amongst musicians is usually friendly, although the competition is keen.

Part-time teaching, either privately or in schools, gives many freelance musicians a supplementary income. However, it is often difficult to fit in performing engagements with teaching.

2. TEACHING

As the main job this is quite a different career. Teachers are employed in primary and secondary schools. They teach music either full-time in one school, possibly with a second subject, or part-time in various schools, and/or youth clubs and evening institutes run by the local education authority.

There is scope for imagination and initiative. The music teacher's main job is to promote interest and enthusiasm, as only a few pupils take music examinations. She may start an orchestra, or record evenings; organize record libraries, visits to concerts, etc.

3. MUSIC-TECHNOLOGY

The application of science and technology – mainly electronics – to the faithful reproduction, and indeed the creation, of sound is an area which until now invariably needed 2 experts: the musician and the sound engineer. Now, a music-technologist is emerging. She combines the jobs of artistic director, or producer, and of the sound engineer; she works for broadcasting or recording companies.

Prospects   *Orchestral performing*: Not very good at the moment. It is estimated that only about 1 in 10 of music students who finish their full training (itself restricted to the good students) eventually makes a living as a performer. Only one in many hundreds becomes a soloist. Good luck is nearly as important as talent.

Singing: A good deal of evening and week-end work in cities which have choirs.

Pianists: Particularly poor performing prospects because they are restricted to solo-playing or accompanying. *String players*: better numerical opportunities in orchestras.

Pop, folk and jazz: A short career for most performers.

Teaching: There is still a shortage of music teachers in some areas.

Composing: Not a career in the usual sense. Those who have the talent need a full musical training as well.

Music-technologist: It is too early to say; broadcasting and record companies have not yet got used to the new breed of professional; music-technologists so far have started usually as technologists rather than as music-technologists – i.e. they work under a musical director/producer. However, it is highly likely that they will find it easier to climb the recording engineer ladder, and that they will be able either eventually to work as producer/sound engineer, or switch to music-producing.

Pay: *For performers*: Depends entirely on ability and luck. *For teachers*: Medium (see p. xxiii).

Training

Either 3–6 year full-time graduate course at a college of music; the period of training need not be decided at the outset. Students choose *either* the teaching *or* the performing course after the first year, but it is sometimes possible to switch from one to the other later in the course.

The syllabus normally includes a principal subject and a second study subject. Instrumentalists play two instruments. Singers may either take an instrument as a second study or they may take speech training, or speech and drama. Other subjects included are music appreciation, theory and history of music, aural training, choral and opera study, orchestra practice, and often a language.

Or a B.A. in Music. Most degree courses are largely academic and theoretical. At some universities music can be taken as a subject in a general arts degree, or in conjunction with electronics or physics, leading to work as music-technologist in recording studios and T.V.

To teach music in schools, courses must be followed by 1-year course of professional teacher training (see Teaching, p. 485). At some colleges of education (see p. 489) music can be taken as a main subject in a B.Ed. course. Instrument teachers do not necessarily need professional teacher training.

Personal attributes

For Performers: Apart from outstanding talent, the qualities of perseverance, resilience, courage, and indifference to setbacks; the ability to work as one of a team; a pleasant manner; good health; very wide musical interest; good sight-reading speed; willingness to work outside the musical field between engagements. *For Teachers*: As for teachers (p. 491), plus creative imagination and initiative.

4. MUSIC THERAPY

This is a small field. Music therapists work with physically or mentally handicapped children and adults. Music can contribute to the development and treatment of handicapped and maladjusted people in various ways – by helping to relax their bodies and minds as a mental stimulus, and as an emotional outlet. Autistic children, for example, and severely withdrawn adults, who do not respond to any other form of activity and cannot form relationships, often benefit greatly from listening to, and making, music.

There is a 1-year full-time post-graduate course in music therapy. Candidates must have at least a 3-year full-time musical education or must be experienced musicians. Music therapy is rarely a full-time career: music therapists are employed on a sessional basis, i.e. part-time, usually.

5. MUSIC ADMINISTRATION

There is much more to running an orchestra, opera house, festival or regional music or arts centre, than most prospective musicians (and audiences) realize. Music – or indeed other arts-graduates with exceptionally wide musical knowledge – may take the Arts Administration course (see Art and Design, p. 64) and become administrators employed by an orchestra or similar set-up. Music administrators' specific responsibilities and degree of decision-making varies; but they are always responsible for organizing the orchestra's affairs, from transport to publicity; finance to personnel matters. They must combine exceptional organizing ability; flair for public relations and programme-building. Though they would not normally be entirely responsible for programme-building, they often have to persuade artistic decision-makers to include the right amount of popular items in programmes to ensure the necessary minimum of 'full houses' during a season. Music administrators need not be performers; in fact most of them are good administrators who happen to be very musical.

6. MUSICAL INSTRUMENT TECHNOLOGY

For musical young people who want to learn a craft, there is some limited scope in *musical instrument technology*, which means repairing and making musical instruments. There are 3-year courses leading to college certificates and a 4-year T.E.C. Diploma/Higher Diploma course for 16-year-olds with, normally, 3 G.C.E.s, preferably including mathematics and any craft subject. Students usually specialize, after the first year, in 1 of 5 specializations: piano (including tuning); early keyboard instruments; violin, viola and violoncello-making; fretted instruments (lutes, guitars). All these specializations are craft-work-shop-based; the fifth specialization is electronics, related to the manufacture and repair of musical equipment – it is electronic-lab based and requires ability to cope with physics. The latter specialization has probably the best prospects.

There is a steady demand for *piano tuners*. Training is *either* as above in musical instrument technology, *or*, for those with fewer qualifications, there are apprenticeships with 3-year block-release for City and Guilds certificate in String Keyboard Instrument Manufacture (i.e. pianos and harpsichords).

Position of women

About 10% of Musicians Union members are women (and virtually all professional performers are Union members); but normally more than half of music students are women. Women orchestral players were barred until very recently from several of the well-known orchestras (with the exception of harpists), and even now the proportion is below 10%. Women musicians have suggested that auditions should be held with performers playing behind a screen so that the sex of the players is not known. However, the suggestion has not been widely taken up, if at all, and women still appear to be discriminated against – though it is probably impossible to prove discrimination.

Career-break: It is unlikely that performers can resume orchestral playing after a long gap unless they kept up with serious daily practice; but there should be no problem returning to teaching.

Part-time: *Performing*: work as freelance is possible in many areas – but work tends to be sporadic rather than regular part-time; and it includes unsocial hours, of course (but see session players, p. 293). *Teaching*: part-time should be possible, but not necessarily exactly where one wants it.

Further information

For early training: Local Education Authority music adviser.
For music colleges: Department of Education and Science, Elizabeth House, York Road, London SE1 7PH; Scotland: Scottish Education Department, St Andrews House, Edinburgh 1
Music Therapy: British Association for Music Therapy, 48 Lanchester Road, London N6
Association of Musical Instrument Industries, 16 Dickerage Road, Coombe Hill, Kingston, Surrey.
London College of Furniture, 41 Commercial Road, London E1

Related careers

Broadcasting – Dancing – Teaching

NURSERY NURSE/NURSERY OFFICER

Nursery classes and schools – infant schools – social services departments' day and residential nurseries – private nurseries – hospital – private nanny

Entry quali- None laid down for National Nursery Examination Board's Certificate,
fications but majority of colleges demand at least 2 O-levels, and many entrants
have more. (See **Training** for Diploma's 5 O-level requirements.)

The work Nursery nurses care for children under 7. Unlike Registered Sick
Children's Nurses (see p. 307), nursery nurses are primarily concerned
with healthy children (they are now often called nursery officers), but
in this context 'healthy' may include 'disturbed' and also physically and
mentally handicapped.

Nursery nurses' functions cover very much more than physical care
and supervision of young children. It is known today that young children
learn through play and through communicating with other children and
with adults, and that they must receive adequate stimuli and individual
attention to ensure their healthy intellectual, emotional and social
development. When the nursery nurse reads to children, talks to them
individually, discusses, say, their painting efforts, and generally helps
them to enjoy nursery activities, she is in effect doing 'indirect teaching'.

Nursery nurses work in various settings:

1. *Nursery classes and schools* (for 3 to 5s) and *infant schools* (5 to 7s),
run by local education authorities. Nursery nurses help organize play
activities, read to and play with children. Usually 1 nurse is responsible
for a small group of children. A qualified nursery or *infant teacher* (see
p. 486) is normally in charge.

2. *Day nurseries* run by social services departments for under-5s (mainly
3 to 5s) who are at risk socially, physically or emotionally, and for
children whose mothers have to go out to work or for other reasons
cannot satisfactorily look after them during the day. There are now
very few places for children whose parents merely think that nursery is
a Good Thing: such children either go to private day nurseries (which
also employ nursery nurses) or play groups, which usually cannot afford
paid staff.

As day nursery children are often disturbed, work can be very demanding. Occasionally staff may involve mothers in the nursery's activities – largely to help mothers understand the children's needs and development. Staff may also do unofficial 'casework' (see Social Work, p. 446). This aspect of nursery nursing is new and *ad hoc*. It suits people who want to work with children *and* adults, and it may be a preparation for over-25s' professional social work training (see p. 453).

3. *Residential nurseries*, also run by social services departments, for under-5s who cannot be looked after at home; they are 'in care' either short-term because of mother's illness, a new baby, temporary homelessness, etc., or long-term because of family breakdown, mother's death, etc. Whenever possible, healthy young children in long-term care are placed in foster-homes, so that a relatively large proportion of those in residential care are disturbed, or physically or mentally handicapped, and they may have behaviour problems: for example be disruptive, bad-tempered, unresponsive.

Usually, each nurse is responsible for her own small group – it may be only 2 or 3 children. Staff try and establish a family atmosphere. (Residential nurseries may be housed in a small family house, on an estate.) Staff do not have to live in, though they usually have to be on duty and sleep in some nights.

4. In *Hospital*, nursery nurses look after babies in maternity wards and, on children's wards, they amuse and feed children; actual nursing is done by State Registered nurses (see p. 303).

5. About 18% work in *private families*. This work has changed considerably over the last few years. Nannies no longer work only in families where the mother has too many social engagements to look after her children herself, but more often for families in which both parents go out to work. They may work a 5-day week as 'daily nannies', but hours are usually longer than office hours.

A variety of working patterns is emerging: some nannies take charge of a young child all day, and then in between the end of the school day and a parent's return from work (and perhaps during school holidays) they may look after several school children whose parents share the nanny's salary. Other nannies work 2 days for one family, 3 days for another – if the mothers concerned are themselves part-timers and only need part-week nannies. Work in a family differs from that in institutions in that nannies are on their own: nobody to ask for help in emergencies, and much of the time no other adult to talk to. The work is both more responsible, and lonelier. It may also be less hard work, and it may involve travelling with the family, and regular free weekends.

6. A very small proportion work on liners, in hotels and holiday camps as *children's hostess*.

Prospects   Daily nannies: good. Local authorities staff: not very good at the
moment (1980) because of public spending cuts.

Promotion prospects are good only for the exceptional and determined; the ratio of junior to senior staff is unfavourable. Also, it is
planned that in future day and residential nurseries may be run by social
workers, not nursery nurses, though nursery nurses are still being
appointed 'matrons'.

Good opportunities abroad for *experienced* nannies.

Pay: Medium (see p. xxiii).

Training   1. The usual method (minimum age 16): 2-year courses at colleges of
further education for the National Nursery Examination Board's
Certificate (essential for all local authority and hospital work). Students
must find a college place in the first instance: the college organizes
practical experience. They spend three-fifths of their time in college,
two-fifths working with children in residential and day nurseries, nursery
and infant schools. All students gain practical experience with children
of ages spanning at least 4 years (i.e. not necessarily the whole age-
range). The syllabus includes the study of care and of the social,
emotional, physical and intellectual development of children from 0 to
7; children's social, emotional and physical needs to ensure normal
development; causes and manifestations of social and emotional deprivation; causes of and dealing with physical and mental handicap and
disturbed behaviour; importance and significance of play, companionship, communication; promotion and maintenance of health (including
nutrition and prevention and control of infection); organizing play
activities (which includes things like making toys from egg-boxes, etc.);
patterns of family life and social institutions – and changes in both; how
the social services work; and, usually, English, arts and crafts, some
general studies. (See also *Preliminary Certificate in Social Care*, p. 454.)

2. 18–24-month courses at the 3 private Association of Nursery Training
Colleges (see p. 301). Students must be at least 18; most look after
children privately, to make sure they like the work, in between school
and college. Private colleges prepare students for the N.N.E.B. examination and for their own diplomas. Residential nurseries are attached
to the private colleges. Private college training costs between £2,000 and
£4,000. Local education authority grants are rarely given.

Students at private colleges, with at least 3 O-levels, including an
English subject, take the Nursery Nurse Diploma Examination held by
the Royal Society of Health, but for all local authority work the
N.N.E.B. Certificate is *more* important, though entry qualifications are
lower.

3. 1-year Advanced Certificate. Students need 3 years' experience,

N.N.E.B. Certificate and 5 O-levels. The course equips students for work with severely physically or mentally handicapped under-7s.

Personal attributes

A way with young children; patience; imagination; willingness to take responsibility and to work hard at chores; ability to work well in a team; interest in mental, social and physical development of children.

Position of women

Virtually 100% women's occupation; no reason at all why this should remain so – men would be welcome on courses and in jobs.

Career-break: No problem for women who are able and willing to work long day and residential nursery hours.

Late start: It is difficult for mature students to get training places: special courses for mature students are being phased out, largely because most mature students, once trained, were unwilling to work the long hours required and were unable to travel long distances to where school jobs were available. But see *Part-time*.

Part-time: Little opportunity in social services department nurseries and in infant nursery schools and classes; but growing opportunities as daily nanny – working for women who are themselves working part-time.

Further information

National Nursery Examination Board, Argyle House, 29–31 Euston Road, London NW1

Association of Nursery Training Colleges, Chiltern Nursery Training College, 20 Peppard Road, Caversham, Reading, Berks.

Local authority education or social services departments.

Related careers

Nursing – Social Work – Teaching

NURSING

State registered nurse – registered sick children's nurse – state enrolled nurse –
registered mental nurse – registered nurse for the mentally subnormal (mental handicap
nurse) – occupational health nurse – community nurse – health visitor – midwife

The work 'Nursing' covers a range of jobs which vary widely in terms of levels of
responsibility, professional qualifications required, environment worked
in. There is therefore scope for people with widely differing aims,
interests, abilities. Some nurses, for example, concentrate entirely on
practical bedside nursing; others manage whole hospital groups' nursing
services (jobs which equal top executives' in industry in terms of power,
pay, and responsibility). Then there is scope for people interested in the
impact of new technologies on nursing procedures; for those interested
in psychiatry; in the sociological and psychological aspect of patient-
care, or in preventive medicine in the community. Nurse-training can
also lead to jobs not directly concerned with the care of the sick, both
in and outside the hospital (for example specialist publishing; management and administration).

Nursing is *not* a second-choice career for people unable to get into
medical schools (or put off medicine by the long training). The two
professions are complementary and suit people with very different aims
and personalities. A vital difference is that the doctor's contact with the
patient is fleeting and episodic, while the nurse must establish and keep
up a relationship with the patient (this applies even to nurses who after
a few years' ward-nursing opt for other specializations). Nurses are
team workers, doctors are not. The doctor/nurse relationship has
changed greatly in recent years. The extent of change depends of course
on personalities and seniority of nurses and doctors in each case, but
there is generally today much more joint decision-making, and more
mutual respect for the other's function. Within each of the specialist
nursing professions there are again opportunities for working in a
variety of environments.

I Nursing In Hospital

Entry quali- Minimum age for training 18; 17½ in Scotland (see Bridging the gap,
fications p. 312).
State Registered Nurse; *Registered Sick Children's Nurse*; *Psychiatric*

Nurse: *either* O-levels in 2 subjects, 1 of which must be English or Welsh language or English literature or history, and proof of attainment of a satisfactory standard in 5 other subjects; *or* 3 O-levels, one of which must be English or Welsh language, English literature or history; (City and Guilds Foundation Course in Community Care counts as *one* O-level); *or* General Nursing Council's own educational test. However, in practice the vast majority of students have more than the minimum G.C.E. qualifications.

State Enrolled Nurse: no specific requirements, but the majority have some O-levels or C.S.E.s.

District or Home Nurse: State Registration or State Enrolment.

Occupational Health Nurse: State Registration and 5 O-levels.

Health Visitor: State Registration and 5 O-levels.

Midwife: minimum age 20; S.R.N. or R.S.C.N., or 5 O-levels.

Also graduate entry. See **Training**.

General, sick children's, State Enrolled and psychiatric nurses work mainly in hospitals; occupational health nurses, home or district nurses, midwives and health visitors work mainly in the community and tend to work more independently, away from the sheltered hospital atmosphere.

Prospective nurses can ask local hospitals to show them round, or even spend a day in the various types of hospital, to see for themselves.

1. STATE REGISTERED NURSE – S.R.N.

The work   An S.R.N. spends varying amounts of time on 'bedside' or 'practical' nursing: making beds, dealing with bed-pans and bed-baths, taking temperatures, generally making patients comfortable. For this part of the work she needs above all sympathy, patience, basic nursing skills.

She needs extensive knowledge for a variety of highly complex, responsible tasks. These include: administering a vast array of drugs in the right dosages and understanding what side effects to watch out for; using highly sophisticated machines on the wards and in coronary and other intensive care units; keeping records on patients and knowing at all times what changes if any have occurred in her patients' condition; organizing the ward team; discussing patients' condition with relatives and doctors; helping distressed patients to come to terms with their situation; trying to allay anxious patients' fears. She may have to decide whether a patient's condition warrants sending out an emergency call for the doctor, and she may suggest in discussion with the doctor that the medical social worker (see p. 448) should come and help sort out a patient's domestic problems. She also helps with the teaching of nurses in training.

Since April 1980, nurses work a 37½ hour week (or 75 hour fortnight).

They have to work nights, but senior nurses are often able to arrange regular working hours, especially in out-patient clinics, or on night duty.

Duty rosters are normally known well in advance. Nurses now can live out, and most do so.

The atmosphere in hospitals varies considerably. The old-fashioned disciplinarian nursing officer is fast disappearing (there are no longer any 'matrons': titles have changed twice in the last few years; senior nursing officers are now called 'Miss' or 'Mrs X', their nursing officer-title (Senior, Chief, Divisional, etc.) depends on the size of the hospital and their responsibilities within the administrative area).

Nursing officers in charge tend to be much younger than they were even 10 years ago, many are married (and quite a few are male). Whatever their age, most treat nurses as responsible adults and do not impose any petty rules. All prospective nurses are interviewed by senior nursing staff. There is no reason why this interview should not be a two-way discussion with the applicant asking questions about regulations, duty rosters, recreational facilities, study programmes, etc. Applicants are usually shown round the hospital by a student nurse of whom they can, and should, ask questions about atmosphere and work. They should also ask about the programme of clinical experience as this may involve quite a lot of moving about from, say, an acute hospital in London to a psychiatric hospital in Surrey to a geriatric hospital somewhere else. The amount of moving about varies from one school to another.

Prospects Fair in most areas, at all levels of responsibility. At the top of the hierarchy, nurses, jointly with doctors and administrators, are now responsible for running hospital and community health services (see Health Service Administration, p. 206). Staff nurses can choose whether to stay on the wards, or to go into teaching, administration or clinical specialization.

On the wards, in *clinical nursing*, responsibilities are extending as treatments become more sophisticated, requiring nurses to have technical skills and theoretical knowledge of a high professional order.

Clinical nurses can become specialists in theatre work, intensive care units, children's or geriatric nursing, and do research into new techniques and procedures. Specialist nurses may be in charge of numbers of specialist wards or units within a group of hospitals and act as clinical consultants to junior staff and colleagues.

Nurse-teaching is a vitally important nursing specialization suitable for nurses interested in teaching skills and training methods and organization. Nurse-tutors take various courses which academically are at university-lecturer standard and so are at the same level in the hierarchy as Nursing Officers in charge of a group of hospitals.

The third specialization is as *nurse-manager*. She is not as much directly concerned with patient-care as with the smooth and efficient running of a complex organization. The work resembles management in commerce and industry; a large number of people carry out a variety of vital, interrelated activities which have to be coordinated. These 'managers' may have greater job-satisfaction than managers at that level in industry, because the end-product is the well-being of patients. Nurse-managers normally take a succession of management courses, some of them general senior management courses, attended by managers from industry as well; the principles of management are the same, whatever the organization to be managed. Managers work in the hospital and in the community.

Nurses who want to move out of hospital can become *health visitors*, *occupational health nurses*, *community nurses*, *midwives*, or work for general practitioners' group practices. There are also opportunities for nurses with several years' experience, in the Services (see p. 433), in health education – lecturing to schools, various clubs, etc., and doing research in nursing or in medicine; in journalism and in the Civil Service, and in agency nursing.

Pay: Medium (see p. xxiii).

Abroad: S.R.N. qualifications are now accepted in the E.E.C. and most other countries.

Training   The basic three-year training takes place at about 250 schools of nursing, which are based on hospitals. The broad curriculum is laid down, and the individual schools' 'training programmes' are approved by the General Nursing Council which is in charge of nurse education and training. Training must now include several weeks each in psychiatric, geriatric, obstetric and community nursing (i.e. nursing outside the hospital). (Until 1979 nurses' training included only two of these four specialties.) Organization of individual training programmes varies from one hospital to another. Ideally student nurses should be students first and nurses second. While it is generally agreed that nurse training must always be on-the-job, the success, and the method with which schools solve the dilemma of their dual responsibility – to patients and to students – varies greatly.

It is quite illogical that, while prospective degree students carefully consider where to study their subject and finally choose after having studied 'course comparison guides' and university or polytechnic prospectuses, nurses tend to choose where to train rather haphazardly and to go by the advice of someone who trained years ago. Prospective nurses should at least consult the Directory of Schools of Nursing, write for a number of prospectuses and visit several schools before making their final choice.

Nursing as a degree subject

It is envisaged that about 5% of nurses in future should be graduates (this proportion has not been reached yet). There are now about 15 courses which lead to a degree either *in* Nursing plus State Registration, or to a degree in the social or the natural sciences *as well as* State Registration. Nursing as a degree subject is still in the experimental stage and the two ways of graduating are on trial. The main differences between the two types of degrees are (a) the Degree *in* Nursing is shorter – it takes about four years, and (b) all students on the course are going to be nurses. The degree which combines nursing with another subject (a) takes four and a half to six years; (b) it qualifies students in a specific degree subject other than nursing and thus leads to two qualifications; (c) nurses study together with students who are not going to be nurses. (The drop-out rate among nursing degree students is around 14% – the normal degree studies drop-out rate; compared with more than double the drop-out rate from traditional (often haphazardly chosen) nurse training.)

Three part-time (day/block-release) degrees in nursing for qualified S.R.N.s started in 1979; and there are eight shortened (2-year) courses for graduates with 'relevant' degrees. It is up to individual nursing course directors to decide what is a relevant subject – but it is normally one which includes social or natural sciences.

Graduate nurses are not necessarily promoted more quickly – they start as staff nurses like other S.R.N.s, but their dual qualification widens their opportunities in nursing and outside it. A graduate nurse is eligible for any 'graduate job' where degree subject is not specified (and that covers one third of all graduate jobs in industry and commerce).

Likely Changes in Training

Training may change in the next few years. Nothing is definite yet, but proposals include lowering of minimum age to 17; *all* entrants, regardless of entry qualifications, to start with common 18-month Certificate course; post-Certificate courses to lead to variety of Registration and post-Registration qualifications and specializations; more degrees in nursing.

Personal attributes   Common sense, practical bent; sympathy for the sick and the old without sentimentality; an interest in medicine without morbid curiosity about illness; sensitivity coupled with a certain amount of toughness so as not to get too emotionally involved; organizing ability; patience; a sense of humour to put up with the inevitable occasional short tempers and difficult people; ability to know when to be firm – and how to be firm but not rude; powers of observation; initiative; ability to take responsibility one moment and to do exactly as told the next; good health.

2. REGISTERED SICK CHILDREN'S NURSE – R.S.C.N. (Paediatric Nursing)

Entry qualifications See p. 302.

The work The work is much the same as for the S.R.N., plus keeping children amused and dealing with relatives. Nursing sick children in hospital is both more rewarding and more arduous than nursing adults. A large proportion of children get well, but many R.S.C.N.s work with mentally or physically handicapped children. Modern wards are run to resemble home conditions as much as possible. Visiting is now usually allowed at all times; rigid tidiness and regimentation are frowned upon. Work under these conditions is very hard and requires a good deal of organizing ability.

Prospects Fair. Jobs for children's nurses are not as readily available as they used to be: children's health is much improved, and also hospitals now discharge children more quickly than in the past.

There are very few jobs on liners, in hotels, as air stewardesses, as nannies at home and abroad, in boarding schools and as local education authority school nurses.

Pay: Medium (see p. xxiii).

Training In England and Wales the separate training for R.S.C.N.s has been stopped. There are a few 3-year R.S.C.N. courses in Scotland, but these will be phased out, too. In any case, for some years now jobs above staff nurse have been open only to nurses with dual S.R.N./R.S.C.N. qualification. There are now 2 good ways of training for sick children's nursing: (1) a combined 3/4-year course for S.R.N./R.S.C.N.; (2) a 13-month post-registration (i.e. post-S.R.N.) training for the Register of Sick Children's Nurses.

Personal attributes The same as for the general nurse; plus extra patience and a way with children. A sick children's nurse must be able to talk to children on their own level. Many of the best children's nurses come from big families. Good powers of observation are essential, as small children cannot explain their ailments.

3. STATE ENROLLED NURSE – S.E.N.

Entry quali-fications Minimum age 18; Scotland 17½. No laid-down requirements, but many hospitals impose their own.

The work State Enrolled Nurses undertake routine nursing duties of a standard no less high than that of their Registered colleagues, but different in the range of functions performed and the degree of responsibility.

They do most of the bedside or practical nursing, in fact most of the work generally thought of as the essence of nursing: giving immediate attention to patients' well-being. Their work is complementary to that of the S.R.N., though it requires less medical knowledge and carries less responsibility.

The work of S.E.N.s often overlaps with that of S.R.N.s; especially, but not only, with that of student nurses. Their working hours and conditions are exactly the same as those of S.R.N.s. They share S.R.N.s' social facilities, dining rooms, nurses' homes, etc.

S.E.N.s can also specialize in Mental Handicap Nursing and in Mental Illness Nursing (see p. 309).

Prospects Good in most areas. There are opportunities for promotion to Senior Enrolled Nurse for those who have been on the Roll for at least 3 years. A Senior Enrolled Nurse's responsibilities are similar to those of the staff nurse who is a State Registered Nurse. A wide choice of post-enrolment training courses prepares the S.E.N. for specialized work, including work in district, psychiatric or geriatric nursing. In fact S.E.N.s have scope in the whole field of clinical nursing careers, but not in teaching, administration, and health visiting. (No opportunities abroad.)

Pay: Medium (see p. xxiii).

Training S.E.N.s train for 2 years *either* in general *or* in one of the two kinds of psychiatric nursing (see below and p. 311). Training is almost entirely practical, on the wards. Pupils watch, are told what to do, and then do it. In the second year there is an 'assessment': senior hospital staff observe and assess the way pupils carry out their duties; the only written test is a simple one taking about 1¼ hours. S.E.N.s in training are called 'pupil nurses'. S.E.N.s who want to become S.R.N.s usually take another 2 years' training.

Nursing Auxiliaries do not take any systematic training or examinations. They assist nurses in most hospital wards and clinics. They can work full- or part-time.

Personal attributes Above all a wish to look after other people and to do things for them; a practical nature; the ability to get on well with all kinds of people and to work well as one of a team; good health.

4. PSYCHIATRIC NURSE

There are two separate Registers:
1. Registered Mental Nurse (R.M.N.), which is nursing the mentally ill.
2. Registered Nurse for the Mentally Subnormal (R.N.M.S.), which is nursing the mentally backward. It is now usually called Mental Handicap Nursing (M.H.N.).

Entry quali- As for S.R.N. (see p. 302).
fications

The work   1. *Nursing the Mentally Ill (R.M.N.)*

Nursing patients who have suffered a breakdown, but who in the majority of cases will recover. This form of nursing differs very much from general nursing. It differs, too, from most people's picture of it, and from what it was like even a few years ago. In recent years there have been great developments in the treatment of mental illness and in mental hospital atmosphere generally. The number of violent patients has drastically decreased; the proportion of geriatric patients is increasing.

Most psychiatric patients are up and about all day. Many go out to shop, to visit friends, some even to work. Others walk about and busy themselves in the hospital's often extensive recreation rooms, workshops and gardens. Very few wards are locked.

Ninety per cent of patients are 'voluntary' (now called 'informal'). Most patients stay for only a few weeks, though some come back fairly regularly for further treatment. As most mental illness takes the form of an exaggeration of our normal moods of depression, elation, or aggressiveness, patients tend to be much the same as anyone else in behaviour and appearance.

Nurses do little physical nursing, except in geriatric wards and for patients with physical complaints. Psychiatric nursing is often less *physically* exhausting than general nursing, but emotionally it is more demanding.

For many patients an important part of their treatment lies in the contact with a friendly nurse. The inability to 'communicate' with other people is part of most mental illness: nurses help a great deal towards patients' recovery by talking to them and, above all, by listening.

In good psychiatric hospitals the atmosphere is relaxed and informal. Patients and staff live in a friendly so-called 'therapeutic' community with nurses establishing and maintaining personal relationships as an essential part of the treatment. Patients are treated as individuals and are encouraged to share with the staff responsibility for running wards and for the active social life of the hospital. The aim is always to minimize the institutional atmosphere.

At informal meetings with staff the patients are encouraged to discuss and even criticize treatment, to talk about their difficulties and to help each other with their problems. At staff-only meetings, after ward-meetings with the patients, even the most junior nurse has a chance to discuss patients, treatments and new methods with consultants and senior staff.

In many hospitals there are joint wards for male and female patients; male and female nurses cooperate in their care.

Psychiatric nursing can of course sometimes be harrowing. Nurses must always remember that their patients' selfishness or childishness is a symptom of their illness. Teamwork among the staff helps a great deal, and during their training nurses learn to recognize and handle the emotional aspect of their work.

There are an increasing number of day-hospitals for patients well enough to live at home but still in need of contact with nurses, occupational therapy and perhaps psychiatric treatment.

Most hospitals work on shift systems and staff know well in advance when they will be free. Nurses may live out, but as psychiatric hospitals are often in country areas this is not always practicable. Nurses' homes are usually comfortable; each nurse has her own room. There are normally no petty restrictions; nurses are treated as responsible people. Staff come from all over the world, and the staff's social clubs are polyglot. Recreational facilities are usually good; occasionally licensed premises are provided for staff.

Often nurses do not wear uniform, to emphasize the 'normal' atmosphere. The atmosphere in psychiatric hospitals is far more democratic than in general hospitals. The proportion of male nurses is much greater than in general nursing.

Prospects Very good. Psychiatric nurses can also work outside the hospital, in community care, visiting patients who live at home, and at day-hospitals and centres.

Pay: A little higher than S.R.N. (see p. xxiii).

Training Minimum age for training 18; Scotland 17½.

The 3-year course is organized much like the S.R.N. general training (see pp. 305–6). The syllabus covers: human development and behaviour from infancy to adulthood, deviations from normal behaviour, human biology, psycho-physical disturbances; physical illness and bedside nursing; the principles and practice of psychiatric nursing; psychology and enough elementary psychiatry to understand patients' symptoms and treatments; organization of day-care centres and community care, nursing care of the mentally and physically sick; the art of listening, 'counselling', nursing care in relation to physical methods of treatment such as drugs, neurosurgery.

One of the degree courses (see above) leads to R.M.N. nursing.

Personal attributes

Curiosity about what makes people behave as they do; emotional stability; patience and perseverance; the ability to listen well and to be genuinely concerned without becoming emotionally involved; interest in outside work to keep a sense of proportion; a sense of humour; a gregarious nature; good physical and mental health.

2. Nursing the Mentally Subnormal (R.N.M.S.)

Mentally handicapped patients are 'backward'; their mental development has been arrested either before birth or at an early age.

The work

Mentally handicapped (the term now used in preference to 'subnormal') patients are cared for in special hospitals. Some stay there all their lives, but the tendency today is to provide hostels and day-centres so as to enable as many patients as possible to live outside the 'institutionalizing' hospital atmosphere. This means that patients *in* hospital tend to be the more severely handicapped. It also means that nurses can work in hostels and day-centres for the mentally handicapped, as well as in hospital.

Nurses help patients to develop as far as their capacity allows. For example, it is an achievement in some cases to teach a patient to dress and feed himself; others can be taught to do domestic or other simple tasks, go out to work, and live at home.

Most mentally handicapped persons behave like happy children. The majority become devoted to those who look after them and understand their ways. Showing love and affection is a great part of this type of nursing.

The emphasis in these hospitals is on creating a home-like atmosphere. Patients spend their days in extensive recreation grounds, and are taught and occupied in the hospital's schools, handicraft rooms, and gardens. Some of the older and fitter patients help both the younger ones and those with physical handicaps who have to be fed, helped to walk, or even carried.

Prospects

As for R.M.N.
Pay: A little higher than S.R.N. (see p. xxiii).

Training

Training is organized very much like that for S.R.N. (see pp. 305–6). The syllabus is similar to that for nursing the mentally ill, but with special emphasis on mental handicaps, and on physically handicapped children and adults. The nurse gradually gains experience with patients in different age groups, from babies upwards. She works in the nursery where children learn play-occupations such as painting, doing simple exercises to music, and she works with adults.

There is also a course (3 years 9 months) leading to Mental Subnormality Nursing and to the Diploma of the Central Training Council for Teachers of the Mentally Handicapped. These teachers teach in training centres and hospital 'schools' for the mentally handicapped. (The Diploma is *not* a professional teaching qualification.)

For candidates with 2 A-levels and 5 O-levels there is a new 5-year course which leads to dual qualification as teacher and as nurse for the mentally subnormal. Students can then choose, later, whether to teach or nurse. They might, but need not, specialize in remedial teaching in schools.

It is also possible to take a 13-month post-registration course for the Register of Nursing the Mentally Subnormal. One degree course leads to R.N.M.S. (see p. 306).

Personal attributes

Affectionate nature; a practical approach; patience; gentleness; interests unconnected with the work; ability to be genuinely concerned without becoming emotionally involved. Those who like looking after small children and animals often enjoy this work.

NOTE: There are also 'Nursing Assistants' in both branches of psychiatric nursing. They help with the practical work of keeping patients occupied and can work full- or part-time. They do not have systematic training.

BRIDGING THE GAP

The time between leaving school and starting training can be spent looking after children or doing the kind of work which brings school-leavers into contact with people. Working as a shop assistant, in a factory or in a hairdresser's, for example, might be valuable.

There are also pre-nursing courses at some further education colleges, lasting 1 or 2 years. Subjects studied include English and arithmetic, human anatomy, physiology, community care and basic nursing skills. Courses include visits to hospitals, to give some idea of the atmosphere.

Some hospitals still run nursing cadet schemes for young people waiting to take up nurse training. They attend a further education college 1 or 2 days a week; in hospital, they help mainly with child patients on the wards and in the clinics. (These schemes are on the way out. Prospective nurses prepare themselves more usefully by working outside the hospital.)

II Nursing Outside the Hospital

1. OCCUPATIONAL HEALTH NURSE

Entry quali- Normally 5 O-levels, plus S.R.N. training (see pp. 305–6); exceptionally
fications S.E.N. training plus experience.

The work The occupational health nurse works in factories, stores or wherever there is a large number of employees. The work is above all preventive. She advises on diets, keeps an eye on the disabled, discusses worries with those who ask her to, deals with accidents and sudden illness. She gives regular minor treatment, such as injections and dressings, and advises both on health problems generally and on those peculiar to a particular industry, e.g. skin or respiratory diseases caused by certain types of work.

She usually keeps medical records of all employees and assists at the medical examination of prospective employees. She often arranges for such ancillary services as chiropody, eye-testing, physiotherapy. She may discuss safety measures on the shop-floor with management, shop steward and factory inspector (see p. 188).

She works closely with the personnel department. If an employee's work is deteriorating, she helps to find the psychological or physical cause. For those with physical disabilities she helps to find suitable jobs. She discusses work satisfaction problems generally, from canteen facilities to staff holidays, from the rearrangement of desks or work-benches in the toolshop, to the rearrangement of duties in the typing pool and overtime arrangements on the shop floor.

In large concerns there may be a medical department; more often there is one occupational health nurse working under the personnel director or the visiting medical officer.

Unlike other nursing jobs, normal office hours usually apply. O.H.N.s usually belong to firms' social and sports clubs, and generally benefit from any available welfare facilities.

Prospects Occupational health departments are expanding. There is scope for both State Registered and for experienced State Enrolled Nurses. The jobs are mainly in industrial areas.

Pay: Medium (see p. xxiii).

Training S.R.N. training (pp. 305–6) followed by a 6-month full-time non-resident or longer day-release course leading to the Occupational Health Nursing Certificate. The syllabus includes industrial organization, factory and allied legislation, toxic hazards, psychology and occupational health nursing techniques.

Applicants for this course must have had good experience in out-patient and accident and emergency departments.

Personal attributes   As for general nursing, with a special interest in industrial health, safety problems, and human relationships at work. The ability to work independently and to discuss matters easily both with workmen and management is essential.

2. DISTRICT OR HOME NURSE (now often called Community Nurse)

Entry quali-fications   S.R.N. training or S.E.N. training plus experience (see pp. 305–6, 309).

The work   The home nurse undertakes skilled nursing duties for patients not ill enough to be in hospital but needing nursing care. She visits acute and chronically ill patients in their own homes and gives injections, changes dressings, makes beds, takes temperatures, and washes patients. She visits elderly people at regular intervals to keep an eye on them and possibly bath them. She also helps permanently disabled patients to learn to use new aids, and advises relatives on routine nursing tasks. When necessary she puts people in touch with social workers or gets in touch with them herself.

Home nurses cooperate closely with local general practitioners, who advise on whom to visit and the treatment required, and with hospitals. Hours are fairly irregular, with evening visiting. As there is a tendency for patients to be discharged from hospital as early as possible, home nurses are undertaking more and more technical nursing procedures, such as changing dressings for post-operative patients, taking out stitches.

In small, tight communities, the home nurse is a well-known figure and is consulted on many problems which have no direct bearing on her work.

Prospects   Much as for S.R.N.s. Home nurses may choose the kind of district they wish to work in: whether to be constantly on call in a country area as the only nurse, or to be one of several nurses on a duty-rota in an urban district. There are good chances of promotion to senior administrative posts.

Since the reorganization of the Health Service and the bringing closer together of hospital and community nurses (which includes health visitors and midwives), home nurses may, for example, do some out-patient or other clinic sessions in hospital. This means they have both the independence of the home nurse and the companionship and chance to talk shop which hospital work offers.

Pay: Medium (see p. xxiii).

Training

The basic S.R.N. training followed by a 6-month non-residential course for Certificate in District Nursing. The training consists mainly of learning how to adapt hospital nursing techniques to nursing under possibly primitive home conditions, the nursing of illness met infrequently in hospitals, the teaching of home care to patients' relatives; the organization, scope and availability of the social services.

State Enrolled Nurses may take a special, longer course and have to satisfy the authorities that they are suitable for the work. Most S.E.N.s in Home Nursing are over 30.

Personal attributes

As for general nursing, plus organizing ability. The home nurse must wish to work independently and to use her experience and ability in the community, rather than in the sheltered atmosphere of the hospital. She should be resourceful, friendly, and a good listener. She needs a wide interest in the community in which she lives and works, and tolerance of other people's way of life. She should know when to be critical and when to accept her patients' own standards of cleanliness, etc., as the best they can achieve.

Position of women

NURSING GENERALLY: About 1 nurse in 10 is male. A disproportionate number of senior jobs are held by men; this is not only due to discrimination: because of demographic changes (more men than women in below 35 age groups, hence fewer spinsters), there are now not enough unmarried women to fill the top jobs, which are too time- and energy-consuming for most women with children.

For a profession which has traditionally relied on single, dedicated women to fill senior jobs, there has been surprisingly little discussion on how to reorganize the job-structure so that married women can more easily combine their two roles.

Career-break: Should not present any problem (but see above). *Refresher* training arrangements vary from place to place. If none is available, local Health Authorities could be asked to make arrangements. There are also various post-Registration courses which enable S.R.N.s to take up one of the specialized types of work.

Interrupted training: Students who did not finish their S.R.N. training before the career-break have to ask the General Nursing Council whether they may resume where they left off, or have to start training again from scratch. The length of the 'gap' largely determines how much training has to be repeated.

Late start: Nursing schools and hospitals welcome mature entrants; but over-30s are usually advised to take the 2-year S.E.N. training.

Part-time: At the moment there are fair opportunities up to staff nurse. At ward sister level, part-time starts to be difficult. However, as *some* ward sisters successfully run their wards on a part-time basis, it is obviously possible to do so. It is illogical that full use is not made of retired nurses who would gladly return to work part-time. With some prodding from nurses themselves, more senior jobs (both in clinical nursing and in administration) should be available. Also, 'Nurse Banks' now operate successfully in most parts of the country. Nurses who cannot work regularly 'go to the bank'. They notify the days and times they could work, the senior nurse concerned then says whether or not the bank nurse is needed for any of these times. The bank nurse may also be approached if there is a staffing crisis to see if she would be free to help out. There is no contract of employment and the scheme operates rather like a nursing agency. Many nurses with domestic responsibilities prefer this loose arrangement to regular part-time work.

Occupational Health Nursing: Men are beginning to train for this. Older entrants are very welcome; there are good opportunities for S.R.N.s (and in certain circumstances, with extra training, S.E.N.s) to train for occupational health nursing. Courses may be available under T.O.P.S. (see p. xl).

Part-time training: 3-year S.E.N. courses widely available, but only one or two S.R.N. and psychiatric courses. Again, as it is *possible* to train nurses part-time, more opportunities *could* be created if there were strong demand.

Further information (all nursing)   Nursing and Hospitals Careers Information Centre, 121/123 Edgware Road, London W2
Nursing Officer, Area Health Authority (address from local phone book)
Occupational health nurse: Royal College of Nursing, 1a Henrietta Place, London W1

Related careers   *Health Service Administration – Medicine – Police – Prison Service – Social Work*

---

3. HEALTH VISITOR

Entry quali-   5 O-levels plus S.R.N. training with midwifery or obstetrics.
fications

The work   Health Visitors are professionals in their own right. They organize their
own work.

The purpose of health visiting is the prevention and early detection
of physical and mental ill health. Health visitors give health care advice,
identify the need for and if necessary mobilize other sources of help.
The important difference between health visitors on the one hand and
nurses and social workers on the other is that the latter meet clients
only when something has gone wrong.

The health visitor visits all new-born babies and their families as a
matter of routine. She gives practical advice to young mothers at home
and in clinics and checks the child's development. She tries to see all
under-5s every few months. Usually that is all that is needed. However,
her home-visits may act as an 'early warning system', she may notice
signs of stress or disorder before these develop into problems. For
example, a young mother who gave up the companionship at work just
before the child was born may feel lonely, and guilty for not being a
radiant mother; the health visitor helps by discussing her feelings and
by suggesting ways of coping with the problem. Other matters which
might develop into problems but for the health visitor's early advice are
older children's health or behaviour, or marital difficulties.

Health visitors also visit patients recently discharged from hospital;
mentally ill or handicapped people who are cared for at home; the
elderly; anyone who may be referred to them by social workers, doctors,
a neighbour even. They also provide health teaching on a variety of
subjects in many settings.

In all cases, health visitors are concerned with the family as a whole,
not only the ill or disturbed member of the family. They may be based
in doctors' practices, or work from health centres or offices, or from
home. They are employed by local Health Authorities (see Health
Service Administration, p. 206). They work very much more independently than nurses.

Prospects   Good; demand in most areas. Also opportunities to go up the nurse-
administration ladder, and in health visitor teaching after one year
course.

Pay: Medium (see p. xxiii).

Training   For S.R.N.s with midwifery and 3 months' obstetrics experience: 1-year
full-time course. Subjects include: social aspects of health and disease;

psychology; social studies (with special reference to the family as a social institution); organization of statutory and voluntary services.

Personal attributes   Interest and belief in preventive medicine and social advice; understanding and sympathy with social pressures and with people, whatever their temperament, background, life-style, competence; desire and ability to use expertise in the community and to work independently rather than in the sheltered hospital atmosphere; tolerance; patience.

Position of women   This was a female occupation till recently; now there are some men. It is too early to say whether, as in nursing, a disproportionate number of men will aim at the administrative and teaching posts, and also whether men will be acceptable as advisers to young mothers.

Career-break: No problem.

Late start: Fair opportunities for S.R.N.s; possible to start the whole training, up to about 30. T.O.P.S. awards (see p. xl) for post-S.R.N. course. Some G.C.E. requirement relaxations.

Part-time: Good opportunities.

Further information   Council for the Education and Training of Health Visitors, Clifton House, Euston Road, London NW1 2RS

Related careers   *Medicine – Nursing – Social Work*

---

4. MIDWIFE

Entry qualifications   5 O-levels including English language, or special entry test, but see **Training**.
Minimum age 20.

The work   A midwife gives ante- and post-natal advice and instruction and delivers babies. It is her job to take full responsibility for the actual delivery in straightforward cases, and to call the doctor in case of complications. She also looks after the health of the mother and child for the first few weeks after the child's birth.

Most deliveries now take place in hospitals and therefore most midwives now work – or are based – in hospitals, and combine hospital and domiciliary work. They are also responsible for hospitals' 'special care nurseries' and babies' intensive care units where premature and sick babies are looked after. This work involves using highly sophisticated equipment.

Domiciliary midwives deal mainly with ante- and post-natal care. Midwifery often involves dealing with women's post-natal depression. Generally there is now more emphasis on the psychology of child birth in midwifery work than even a few years ago. For example, midwives are very much involved in the hospital-versus-home-confinement debate.

A small number of midwives work in private maternity homes or in private practice, attending the patients of non-N.H.S. doctors.

Prospects Depend on training: good for midwives who are S.R.N.s. They can also work in E.E.C. and other European countries, in U.S.A. and in the developing countries and the Commonwealth.

Pay: Medium (see p. xxiii).

Training Three methods (almost all new entrants now choose the S.R.N. training – it leads to wider choice of opportunities):

1. S.R.N. training (p. 305) followed by 12-month midwifery training.
2. Training for State Enrolled or for Nursery Nurses (see p. 308 and p. 300) followed by about 18 months' midwifery training.
3. Minimum age: 20. 2-year full-time training for the State Certified Midwives Certificate. Pupil midwives do deliveries under supervision in hospital conditions, receive theoretical instruction in midwifery and in the care of the infant, and learn basic nursing techniques. Practical training includes at least 3 months' experience with a district midwife. This is the most crucial training period. Pupil midwives learn how to manage without hospital facilities and how to adapt often unsatisfactory home conditions for a safe delivery. It is, however, extremely difficult to find a training vacancy.

No time is lost and much useful experience gained by taking a midwifery course after nurse training.

Personal attributes Much as for S.R.N. (see p. 306) and for home nurses (p. 314), with of course a special interest in babies. Willingness to work very irregular hours, and the ability to snatch sleep at any time of day, are essential.

Position of women Almost 100% women's profession at the moment, but under the Sex Discrimination Act, arrangements were made for men to be trained at 2 training centres. So far only very few have trained.

Career-break: No problem; *refresher courses* are available; 1-year training (i.e. for S.R.N.s) is normally available under T.O.P.S. (see p. xl).

Late start: Good opportunities, both for qualified nurses and to start from scratch.

Part-time: Good opportunities – no part-time training.

Further in- Central Midwives' Board, 39 Harrington Gardens, London SW7
formation And as on p. 316.

Related *Health Visitor – Nursery Nurse – Nursing – Social Work*
careers

OCCUPATIONAL THERAPY

Entry quali- 1 (in practice often 2) A-level, 5 O-levels including a science and an
fications English subject. Also *graduate* entry.

The work Occupational therapists treat patients suffering from physical or mental
disorders by whatever form of training or activity is likely to contribute
to their recovery.

The therapist receives guidance from the patient's doctor on the
'objective' of the treatment, which means the degree of recovery the
patient may be expected to achieve. She then plans the treatment to suit
the individual patient, taking into account his physical, social, economic,
and psychological circumstances.

The main branches of the work, which often overlap, are:

1. REHABILITATION OF PHYSICALLY DISABLED PEOPLE

For work: this often involves cooperation with physiotherapists. For a
man with severe hand injuries, for example, the occupational therapist
and the physiotherapist together work out a scheme of gradual retraining
for a specific job.

The occupational therapist usually gets in touch with employers to
make sure that patients are trained for work which is locally available.

For independence: to lessen the psychological effect of their disability,
special gadgets may have to be designed for patients. A partially
paralysed woman, for example, may be shown in a specially built
hospital 'kitchen' how to cook from a wheelchair, possibly using long-
handled saucepans. Men and women learn how to dress by using special
gadgets to put on shoes and take clothes off hangers, etc.

(a) *Teaching handicapped children*
The children are taught to feed themselves, to play, and to walk, possibly
with special aids.

(b) *Visiting patients at home*
An old lady who recently left a geriatric ward may be visited to see how
she manages her disability, with the special attachments to her chair
and cooker.

(c) *Occupying bedridden and long-stay patients in hospital*

Activities range from embroidery done in bed, to woodwork or making Christmas decorations. Some of the work in hospital workshops is done for payment under contract with outside firms.

2. REHABILITATION IN PSYCHIATRIC HOSPITALS, AND IN THE PSYCHIATRIC DEPARTMENTS OF GENERAL HOSPITALS

Work is done in cooperation with psychiatric staff (see Psychiatric Nursing, p. 309). The occupational therapist works out a 'social programme' for each patient. Severely disturbed patients may have to be coaxed into taking some interest in the world around them and in their own appearance. Some may need encouragement to talk at all, others may be helped by a visit to the hospital's hairdressing salon, or by a walk in the hospital grounds.

The second step may be encouraging the patient to socialize. Group activities are organized by patients with the help of the occupational therapist and range from whist-drives, dances, and play-readings to outings to the seaside.

Art therapy (see also Art and Design, p. 62) may also be done by the occupational therapist, though artists may help with this work.

The next step for the patient coaxed back from apathy is to help her become independent. The occupational therapist may run a special 'flat' in the hospital where patients housekeep and invite staff and other patients to tea. Patients about to leave hospital need help in adjusting to the world outside, and the occupational therapist may take them out shopping, to a job centre or even an employer. She helps to organize work done by patients in hospital garden, kitchen, and workshop. It is also her job to find firms willing to place contracts for work to be done by patients. It is important that patients should work with a purpose, and not just be aimlessly occupied.

The occupational therapist may choose the setting in which she wishes to work. This may be a mental hospital where, in a 'therapeutic community' setting, she takes part in research projects on new methods of treatment; in a general hospital with or without a psychiatric ward. It may be a day-hospital for mental patients; a hospital for spastic children; an orthopaedic hospital; an industrial rehabilitation centre; a child guidance clinic; or a prison. About 20% of occupational therapists now work with local authority social services, visiting people at home and running, or helping at, day-centres.

The occupational therapist is always an important member of the team of professional people helping patients to return to normal health.

Her day-to-day work is very responsible since she usually works on her own, even in large hospitals where there are several other occupational therapists.

Prospects Fair. Public spending cuts have reduced opportunities, but there are shortages in some areas. Qualifications are recognized in the Commonwealth, most other English-speaking countries, and in the U.S. There are some opportunities in the E.E.C. for those who speak relevant languages.

Pay: Medium (see p. xxiii).

Training 3–3½ years full-time at an occupational therapy school. About 1 year is spent working in different types of O.T. settings.

The emphasis in training has shifted from the mainly craft teaching to psychological aspects of the work. The syllabus includes anatomy, physiology, psychology, medicine, surgery (theoretical only), and psychiatry. Under 'occupational techniques' come practical work such as 'self-help' (which is concerned with helping disabled patients back to independence in everyday life), organizing recreational and cultural activities, art and craft work, and the theory and underlying principles of occupational therapy for physical and mental disabilities.

NOTE There is now at the Central London Polytechnic a part-time day- and block-release degree course for *qualified* occupational therapists, physiotherapists and remedial gymnasts in employment. It is useful for people who want to do research and/or explore the possible advantages of joint training for the various 'therapies' professions. It is also likely to be useful for people who want to practise in E.E.C. countries where similar professionals take degree-equivalent qualifications. It should also be noted that other 'professions supplementary to medicine' – dieticians and speech therapists – either have to or can take degrees.

Personal attributes Organizing ability; the ability to explain things clearly to all types of patient; adaptability and judgement to find the right approach to psychiatric patients; resourcefulness, patience, cheerfulness, good powers of observation; some dexterity; an interest in practical work, and a fairly strong scientific bent.

Position of women At the moment an almost all-female profession, but men are now encouraged to join.

Career-break: No problem. *Refresher courses* available.

Late start: Good opportunities up to 40, some G.C.E. concessions;

shortened training occasionally possible for related professions such as nurses, psychology graduates.

Part-time: Good opportunities.

Further information   College of Occupational Therapists, 20 Rede Place, London W2 4TU

Related careers   *Physiotherapy – Psychiatric Nursing*, p. 309

OPERATIONAL RESEARCH

Entry quali- Degree in a subject requiring numeracy; such as mathematics, engi-
fications neering, natural sciences, economics, statistics, computer studies;
business studies

The work Operational researchers apply mathematical and statistical methods to
the solving of organizational and management problems. They set up a
'mathematical model' of the system they intend to improve, incorporating such factors as risk and chance in given situations, following
different courses of action. They can then predict, and compare, the
outcome of alternative decisions. This technique enables management
to base its plans and decisions on something more reliable than hunch
and experience. Even if there is no one perfect solution in a given
situation, operational researchers can forecast in which aspect one
course of action will produce different results from another. Operational
research is used in any field in which a number of variables have to be
taken into account in decision-making – and this covers virtually the
whole world of work – industry, government, commerce. (Operational
research is a 'management service' (see Management, p. 259).

For example, in planning a chain of supermarkets, shopping 'peaks
and valleys' cause problems: to avoid check-out queues completely on
Fridays and Saturdays would mean allocating vast amounts of floor-
space and staff to check-out positions, which would be idle most of the
week. Operational research workers examine the variables which affect
the cost-effectiveness of various levels of expenditure on staff, equipment, floor-space for check-out positions and balance it against what
they work out is an acceptable level of queueing (i.e. what length of
queue will customers put up with before they go to the competition?).

Other problems in which Operational Research measures and then
balances various factors include levels of stock to be carried in the
supermarket; sorting out public transport problems or hospital waiting
lists; allocating resources among competing projects in a manufacturing
company. Or, if a set of products can be manufactured in a number of
factories spread over the country, 'O.R.' workers determine where how
much of each product should be manufactured to minimize production
and delivery costs.

The attraction of Operational Research is that it deals with problems
which affect everyone in the community and that it enables operational
research workers to work in whatever type of environment appeals to

them. Operational research combines working closely with people at all levels and in most areas of an organization (invariably a large one), either extracting information or discussing research results, with concentrated desk-work.

Prospects

Good. This is an expanding field, but jobs tend to be available mainly in cities.

Pay: High (see p. xxiii).

Personal attributes

Numeracy, logical and analytical mind, ability to get on well with people at all levels within an organization and to explain complicated matters clearly. There is also room, however, for backroom-research types.

Training

Either: (1) degree which includes operational research in, for example, economics, business studies or computer studies; *or*: (2) post-graduate operational research course. Pre-entry training is usually followed by on-the-job training with in-house or outside short courses.

Position of women

As in all new career areas, where there is no tradition to break down, women who try to get in do very well, but relatively few women – even of those who have the right first degree – have tried to get into O.R., possibly because its mathematical content tends to be over-emphasized, and its 'communication-content' under-emphasized.

A very small proportion of applicants to post-graduate O.R. courses are women; more would be welcome.

Career-break: Should be no problem for those who keep in touch; updating courses available to all operational research workers can be adapted as *refresher courses*.

Late start: Only for women with suitable degree and industrial experience.

Part-time: Not at the moment, but might be possible on a project basis, for experienced people.

Further information

Operational Research Society, Neville House, Waterloo Street, Birmingham B2 5TX

Related careers

Actuary – Computers – Engineering – Insurance – Management in Industry – Mathematics (see Science)

OPTICAL WORK

Dispensing optician – ophthalmic optician

All opticians must be registered with the General Optical Council.
There are two kinds of careers for opticians:
1. Dispensing optician, who supplies spectacles, contact lenses and other optical appliances;
2. Ophthalmic optician, who also tests eyesight and prescribes whatever spectacles are necessary.

1. DISPENSING OPTICIAN

Entry qualifications
4 O-levels including mathematics, or physics, and English, plus 1 other subject.

The work
Dispensing opticians do not do any sight-testing or other eye-examination. They interpret the prescription of the ophthalmic surgeon or optician and use complex apparatus to measure for, fit, and supply spectacles, contact lenses, and artificial eyes. All such work requires calculations of distance and angles, etc. Equally important are the selling and 'cosmetic' aspects of the work. Dispensing opticians discuss with patients (a term opticians use in preference to customers) which type of frame is the most flattering in each case.

Most dispensing opticians also deal with other types of optical instruments, supplying apparatus to ophthalmic surgeons, opticians and laboratories, and selling sunglasses, opera glasses, microscopes, etc. to the general public.

Dispensing opticians can also get managerial jobs in 'prescription houses' (firms which make lenses to prescription) and in firms of dispensing opticians which manufacture optical instruments.

Prospects
Excellent. A dispensing optician usually starts as an assistant but later may manage a shop, or practice, in which ophthalmic opticians or surgeons do the eye-testing.

Dispensing opticians have at least as great a variety of jobs and settings to choose from as ophthalmic opticians. In relation to their educational qualifications and the length of their respective trainings, they do better financially – a dispensing optician manager may in fact earn more than a practising ophthalmic optician.

Pay: In hospital: low to medium; in commercial employment (which includes sight-testing opticians' practices or shops): medium to high (but longer working hours than in hospital). (See p. xxiii.)

Training   *Either* (and recommended): a 2-year full-time course at a technical college, plus 1 year's practical experience.

Or: 3 years' work as a trainee with a dispensing optician, plus theoretical instruction, either part-time day-release or, since part-time classes are very few, by correspondence course, with some attendance at a college.

Both methods of training lead to the qualifying examinations for Fellowship of the Association of Dispensing Opticians and membership of the Faculty of Dispensing Opticians.

The syllabus covers optical physics, the anatomy and physiology of the eye, the interpretation of ophthalmic prescriptions, the necessary measurements and adjustments for frames, and the recording of facial measurements. The full-time course includes business practice.

Position of women   Steady increase of women entrants over last few years; now women account for over 50%. They do extremely well; many are in charge of high-street shops staffed by men.

Career-break: No problem: but *refresher courses* were discontinued because of poor response.

Late start: No problem.

Part-time: As assistant, yes; not as manager.

2. OPHTHALMIC OPTICIAN

Entry qualifications   2, in practice 3, A-levels selected from physics, mathematics, chemistry, and biology or zoology, plus 3 O-levels which must include an English subject. Some universities insist on A-level physics. Physics may be required at O-level if not offered at A-level.

The work   The main duties of an ophthalmic optician are examining eyes; measuring vision defects with the help of optical instruments; and working out lens-prescriptions for short- or far-sightedness and astigmatism.

Ophthalmic opticians do not treat patients with diseased eyes. If they find something is wrong which spectacles cannot cure, they refer the patient to an ophthalmic surgeon. They are concerned with optics, not with medicine; their work is essentially scientific, not medical, but they are taught to treat the human being, not simply a pair of eyes. The work combines dealing with people (without getting to know them) and applied science.

Ophthalmic opticians work either in general practice, doing mainly sight-testing, or in hospital, where they see more intricate eye conditions and assist ophthalmic surgeons with investigations and treatment of eye disease, and with research.

General practice may mean seeing patients in 'rooms' – possibly in the optician's own home; it may mean managing and/or owning an optician's shop and doing all the dispensing work as well; and frequently it means doing the ophthalmic work in a shop managed and/or owned by a firm of ophthalmic or dispensing opticians which owns several shops.

Prospects   Very good.

Pay: High (see p. xxiii).

Training   3 years for a B.Sc. degree plus 1 year's clinical experience in paid employment (in Scotland 4-year C.N.A.A. degree course).

In 1980 the three former professional bodies, the Worshipful Company of Spectacle Makers, the British Optical Association, and the Scottish Association of Opticians, were amalgamated into the British College of Ophthalmic Opticians. This is now the examining and registering body for ophthalmic opticians. The syllabus includes physical optics, optical instruments, anatomy and physiology, abnormal and pathological conditions of the eye, refraction (all subjects which are covered in the degree course).

Personal   An interest in physics and mathematics; patience; manual dexterity; a
attributes   liking for meeting a flow of new people; a confident manner especially with old people and children; organizing ability; and for dispensing work: an interest in salesmanship and the fashion aspects of spectacle frames.

Position   Women have been accepted for a long time and have no problems
of women   getting good jobs. The proportion is still only 17% of qualified
(ophthalmic   practitioners, but 45% of students.
work)

Career-break: If one has kept up with developments, no problem.

Refresher courses: Updating courses available for all ophthalmic opticians.

Late start: This is a long training and courses are oversubscribed, therefore only applicants with up-to-date knowledge of science likely to be accepted. But there should be no problem getting jobs.

Part-time: Fair opportunities.

Further in-formation	The Association of Dispensing Opticians, 22 Nottingham Place, London W1M 4AT The British College of Ophthalmic Opticians, 10 Knaresborough Place, London SW5 0TG Faculty of Dispensing Opticians, Apothecaries Hall, Blackfriars Lane, London EC4
Related careers	*Orthoptics*, p. 331

ORTHOPTICS

Entry quali- 5 O-levels and 2 A-levels, including English language, mathematics and
fications a science subject.

The work Orthoptists work directly under ophthalmic surgeons, for whom they
diagnose and treat squints and related eye defects. Patients are often
children, some no older than 6 months; ingenious apparatus has been
designed for use with those old enough to follow instructions. Orthoptic
treatment is basically a process of re-training areas of the brain
concerned with vision and focusing which are not functioning properly.
The orthoptist uses her judgement, in cooperation with the ophthalmic
surgeon, in deciding which cases will benefit from treatment. Some
patients, especially children, attend regularly for several months and
should do exercises at home. It is up to the orthoptist to make the
treatment interesting enough so that patients do their exercises conscien-
tiously.

The great majority of orthoptists work in hospitals, some in school
clinics, a few with ophthalmic surgeons in private practice. The
orthoptist in hospital enjoys the facilities and companionship of working
in a community.

Prospects Good. Orthoptists can choose the type, size and location of hospital
that suits them. Many posts are single-handed, but in eye hospitals,
where there are several orthoptists, chances of promotion are better.
Excellent opportunities in teaching and research, after further training.
Little scope in private practice. British orthoptic qualifications are
accepted in most countries. Scope in Europe for women who speak the
relevant language.

Pay: Low to medium (see p. xxiii).

Training (For State Registration which is required in all jobs.) 3 years full-time
at schools attached to hospitals. Syllabus includes general anatomy and
physiology; anatomy and physiology of eye and brain; optics; diseases
of the eye and the principles of eye surgery; practice of orthoptics.

Students gradually gain clinical experience working with patients.

Personal A scientific bent; powers of observation, deduction and persuasion;
attributes understanding of people of all ages and temperaments; ability to work
as one of a team, and also independently.

Position
of women
This is still an all-female profession, but no reason why it should remain so.

Career-break: No problem.

Refresher courses: Short 'up-dating' courses.

Late start: This should be an ideal job for a mature entrant, but the orthoptists insist on normal G.C.E. qualifications and schools tend to prefer school-leavers; however, determined candidates in their 20s or 30s should try and fight these out-of-date attitudes.

Part-time: Excellent opportunities.

Further in-
formation
British Orthoptic Council, Norvic House, Hilton Street, Manchester M13 9WH

Related
careers
Dispensing Optician – Ophthalmic Optician

OSTEOPATHY

Entry quali-
fications
2 A-levels, including preferably chemistry and either biology or zoology; and 3 O-levels, English language to be included at either level.

The work
An osteopath uses manipulative methods of treatment for the correction of derangements of the bony and muscular structures of the body, and makes a special study of the spine in relation to health and disease. Osteopathy does not include the curing of organic disease but it covers the treatment of some organic functional disorders. The majority of patients need treatment because of stiff joints, slipped discs, etc. Patients are occasionally referred to osteopaths by doctors who recognize the value of osteopathic treatment for certain disorders, but the majority of patients come through personal recommendation.

Osteopaths are not recognized under the National Health Service because they do not have orthodox medical qualifications. The normal procedure is first to obtain experience as an assistant to an osteopath or at a clinic, then to start one's own part-time practice in addition, and perhaps finally to concentrate entirely on one's own practice.

Prospects
The profession is small, but interest in osteopathy is growing.
Pay: Medium to very high (see p. xxiii).

Training
4-year full-time course at British School of Osteopathy in London. The syllabus includes anatomy, physiology, osteopathic theory, practice and technique, diagnosis, pathology, applied anatomy, applied physiology, preventive medicine, biochemistry, dietetics and bacteriology. Students are then ready to take the qualifying examination, the Diploma of Osteopathy. Subject to character references, this enables them to become members of the General Council and Register of Osteopaths.

Personal
attributes
Confidence-inspiring manner; skilful, gentle, yet strong hands; physical strength; good health.

Position
of women
About 25% of osteopaths are women, and about 35% of osteopathy students. Experienced osteopaths, women and men, say that it is not a job for small and/or delicate women: they would find some of the work physically impossible. But on the whole women osteopaths have no problem getting patients.

Career-break: The vast majority of women osteopaths continue working part-time from home throughout their career. Post graduate refresher courses available.

Late start: Some relaxation of G.C.E. requirements if candidates considered suitable; shortened courses for people with relevant qualifications (e.g. physiology degrees, medicine). Late entrants have no difficulty getting patients once trained, but not more than 5 mature students a year are accepted for training.

Part-time: Very good opportunities.

Further information	British School of Osteopathy, 1–4 Suffolk Street, London SW1Y 4HG General Council and Register of Osteopaths at the same address

Related careers	*Medicine – Physiotherapy*

PATENT AGENT (Chartered) AND PATENT EXAMINER

Entry qualifications Science degree: fluency in French and German.

1. PATENT AGENT

The work This is a mixture of legal and scientific/technological work. A patent agent advises inventors, and others connected with inventions, on the validity and infringement of patents at home and abroad.

She makes 'searches' for clients to ensure that their inventions really are new, and prepares detailed specifications, descriptions and formulations of claims which 'cover' the invention. She files and negotiates the application for a patent on behalf of her client at the Patent Office. She assists in the creation of a patent, and may have dealings with its commercial application. She deals not only with patents for processes and articles, but also with 'Registered Designs' and 'Registered Trade Marks'.

The majority of agents specialize, for example, in chemical or mechanical inventions, electronics or in design and trade marks. Patent agents work in private practice, or for industrial organizations or government departments. It is usual to start as an assistant doing searches in the Patent Office and other libraries.

Patent agents' work has increased in scope and complexity since Britain joined the E.E.C. It now involves dealing with and thoroughly understanding E.E.C. countries' patent law and regulations; and it may involve travelling to E.E.C. countries to do searches and/or to negotiate. Fluency in both German and French is important.

Prospects Fair, both in this country and in the E.E.C.
Pay: Medium to high (see p. xxiii).

Training Since 1978 students have had to train for both the examinations of the (British) Chartered Institute of Patent Agents and for the new European examinations. Candidates who pass only the European examination may, at present, only practise before the European Patent Office (i.e. not in this country). When the standard of the European examination has been re-assessed and found to come up to the British C.I.P.A. examination standards, success in the European examination may lead to partial or full exemption from the British examination. Candidates for the European examination must train for four years with a European patent attorney at home or in another E.E.C. country. (For the British examination the training period is only three years, but as that period is too short for entry to the European examination, the British Institute's three-year requirement is in practice now meaningless.) The syllabus for both examinations covers British and European law and procedure, drafting and interpretation and criticism of patent specifications. Some of the documents dealt with are in French and German languages.

Personal attributes   Curiosity; an analytical mind; a good memory; a scientific bent; the ability to assimilate facts quickly and to reason clearly, both verbally and in writing; liking for concentrated desk work.

Position of women   Women make up 3% of Chartered patent agents and 20% of students, so numbers are increasing.

Career-break: Return only possible if legal and technological changes/developments kept up with. (No one seems to have returned yet.)

Late start: There are difficulties getting training vacancies.

Part-time: Very limited opportunities in employment, but possible to run small private practice, at least in theory, for experienced patent agents with good contacts.

Further information   Chartered Institute of Patent Agents, Staple Inn Buildings, London WC1V 7PZ

2. PATENT EXAMINER

Patent Examiners work in the Patent Office in London, and examine applications for patents. They are Civil Servants (see p. 121) and need to have a first- or second-class honours degree in a scientific, engineering, or mathematical subject, or equivalent qualifications.

An examiner's work involves detailed examination of the description of an invention; making a search through earlier specifications to ascertain the novelty of the invention; classifying and indexing the features of the invention; writing a report embodying her findings; and, if necessary, interviewing the inventor or his agent to discuss any objections. The work requires an analytical and critical mind. Each examiner works in a specialized field.

Pay: Medium to high (see p. xxiii).

Further in-   The Patent Office, 25 Southampton Buildings, London WC2
formation

Related   *Civil Service – Engineering – Scientist*
careers

PERSONNEL MANAGEMENT

Entry quali-fications For Institute of Personnel Management's membership examination: *Either* 2 A-levels and 3 O-levels and minimum age 20; *or* 2 years' relevant work experience and minimum age 23. About half of all entrants are graduates. See **Training** for alternative method of entry.

The work Personnel officers (titles vary and are not necessarily any indication of scope and level of responsibility) are part of the management-team. Their primary aim is the efficient utilization of human resources. The Institute of Personnel Management says emphatically that personnel management is not a job for people who 'want to work with people'. It is not the personnel manager's job to manage people, but 'to provide the specialist knowledge or service that can assist other members of the management-team to make the most effective use of the human resources – people – of the organization'.

Personnel management used to be considered an offshoot of social work; now, 'welfare' is just one of the 'personnel specializations'. The average personnel officer spends no more time in one-to-one discussions with individuals who need advice than do solicitors or accountants. Personnel management is however not yet a profession with as clearly defined responsibilities and body of knowledge as, for example, accountancy or law, but it is generally agreed that 'personnel' is a 'management function', like buying, marketing and production. Its challenge is to interpret conflicting views and objectives to people at various levels in an organization, some of whom have divergent interests.

Personnel officers are employed not only in industry, but also in hospitals, local and central government: the efficient use of human resources is equally vital to profit-making and to non-profit-making organizations. The range of jobs is very great indeed. In a large organization employing say 70,000 people, at several sites, a personnel director may have a staff of 70, some of whom specialize in one aspect of the work; in a small organization one or two people might do everything.

Main personnel specializations:

Recruitment, training and management-development: the latter means assessing individuals' potential, identifying and planning their career paths accordingly; this may include use of psychological testing and assessment methods.

Manpower planning: involves close cooperation with all levels of management as well as with recruitment and training colleagues.

Wage and salary administration: covers *job evaluation* (and equal pay administration) and involves detailed study of the tasks that make up individual jobs within the organization, in order to establish salary gradings. 'Wage and salary administration' sounds misleadingly like a desk-bound routine job; but it is one of the most non-routine specializations.

Industrial relations means above all establishing and maintaining lines of communication between an organization's various interest groups. It may involve discussing, with shop stewards and management, 'worker participation' schemes; implication of new legislation (of which there is a constant flow), or of mergers, or of installation of new machines. It is, probably, the most challenging of personnel specializations. *Safety and health*, sometimes called *employee services*, covers all welfare aspects, which used to be the main personnel function. It may now include personal counselling services; responsibility for canteens, etc., as well as sophisticated job satisfaction improvement schemes and cooperation with manpower planning and other personnel specialists.

Not all personnel departments necessarily divide personnel functions in the same way; there are many variations on the theme.

Personnel workers who want to get to the top must normally have had experience in several specialist fields, but in this developing profession there are few hard and fast rules. A specialist training officer in a large and/or progressive organization may have greater scope, responsibility and status (and salary) than a personnel director in charge of all specialist functions in another organization. It is impossible to generalize about career-paths, but it is probably best for those aiming at top jobs to get experience in large organizations, where they have the chance of working on a wide range of problems using a variety of personnel techniques.

Prospects   Fair for personnel officers with industrial relations experience and willingness to be mobile: many organizations with establishments in different towns expect personnel officers to move around the country. It is also quite usual to move from one employer to another, not necessarily remaining in the same type of organization, for example from factory to hospital, store to local government, etc.

Pay: Medium to high (see p. xxiii).

Training   A new examination structure has been introduced. It is divided into 3 stages. Stages 1 and 2 students either take a 1-year full-time course (mainly at polytechnics) or they study 3 years part-time, normally while in relevant employment (but see **Position of Women**). Stage 3 can only be taken while in relevant employment.

Entry requirements
B.E.C. Higher National award holders (see p. xvii) and graduates qualify for partial or total exemption from Stages 1 and 2 exams; the extent of exemption depends on subjects studied for previous qualification.

It is possible to prepare for I.P.M. exams by correspondence course, preferably, but not necessarily, while in relevant employment.

For people in personnel work who do not have any A-levels there is a Foundation course which leads to student membership of the I.P.M. and later to admittance to Stages 1, 2 and 3 courses. In other words, there is a possibility for people without the normal entry qualifications to catch up and qualify.

Graduates with a social/behavioural science degree or post-graduate qualification may get on well without I.P.M. qualifications. They must acquire the necessary knowledge (legislation, training techniques, industrial relations procedures, etc.). Many employers do not mind whether efficient staff have I.P.M. qualifications or not. However, qualifications *are* required by many employers and they are particularly valuable for women who want to return to work after the child-rearing gap.

Personal attributes
Lack of prejudice and a fair-minded approach; tact; detachment; a sense of humour, an understanding of people of all types, age, race and background, and the ability to gain their confidence and respect; organizing ability; a flair for seeing all sides of a problem and interpreting each side's point of view to the other; a good memory for names and faces; at least an absence of dislike for figure work, preferably a liking for it; interest in business management.

Position of women
There were proportionately far more women personnel managers in the past, when personnel work was largely concerned with welfare. As emphasis changed from 'dealing with people' to improving the efficient working of an organization, men took over top jobs and it became customary for women only to look after women personnel – i.e. women only remained in top jobs, if at all, in stores and other places where most of the staff were female. No figures are available (job titles give little indication of level of responsibility) but women are now definitely very much in the minority at head of department level, though many do well as training specialists and in small and medium organizations. There are very few women with industrial relations experience, which is essential for most senior jobs in large organizations. Some women have difficulty getting jobs in which to gain such experience, but others are unwilling

to move to where such jobs are – often in the industrial North and Midlands.

Career-break: Personnel workers are able to return to the work if they have kept up with legislation and other personnel work developments. They can take part-time courses or correspondence courses, mentioned in **Training**, to update their knowledge.

Refresher courses: None.

Late start: Employers welcome mature entrants who have had relevant experience in the past. I.P.M. courses may be available under T.O.P.S. for entrants with previous commercial experience.

Part-time: Very few opportunities, but recently some determined returners have convinced employers that part-time *works*.

Further information Institute of Personnel Management, Central House, Upper Woburn Place, London WC1H 0HK

Related careers *Careers Officer – Factory Inspector – Management in Industry – Retail Distribution*

PHARMACY

PHARMACIST: retail, hospital, research and industrial; PHARMACY TECHNICIAN

Pharmacist

**Entry quali-
fications**
Degree-course requirements including 3 A-levels in chemistry, physics or mathematics, and biology or botany or zoology. Maths at O-level, if not included in A-levels.

Pharmacists work in 3 distinct fields: retail, hospital, and industry. Students do not need to decide which branch of pharmacy they want to go into until after qualifying.

1. RETAIL PHARMACISTS (usually called 'chemists' – a title pharmacists discourage)

The work
The job combines, in a unique way, professional scientific work, running a business, and direct contact with the public.

The work includes: dispensing ready-made medical preparations on prescription and on free sale; making up prescriptions, and using potentially dangerous drugs – minute quantities have to be weighed with meticulous accuracy; keeping a poisons register and being responsible for the safety and correct storage of a variety of chemical substances and medical preparations; acting as a link between doctors and pharmaceutical manufacturers by being able to discuss developments and implications knowledgeably with both; acting as a link between doctors and customers by explaining the use and effects of drugs; when asked, giving advice to customers about minor complaints – and knowing when to send people to their doctor; selling toilet requisites and cosmetics; budgeting, buying, and generally managing a business on commercial lines.

Prospects
Fair. Pharmacists are now more often managers of pharmacies or of dispensing departments than owners of their own business. 'High Street' chemists' shops are declining in number.

Abroad: Qualified pharmacists can practise and get jobs fairly easily in some countries of the Commonwealth; mutual recognition of qualifications in E.E.C. countries will soon apply.

Pay: Medium to high (see p. xxiii).

2. HOSPITAL PHARMACISTS

The work Particularly suitable for those who are interested in the science of pharmacy. They dispense medicines to out-patients and to hospital staff for use in the hospital. As a rule, hospital pharmacists make up more of their own medicines than do retail pharmacists; they also take part in teaching pharmacy students and, occasionally, in research projects. There is some shift work.

Prospects There are more assistants' jobs in hospital than in retail pharmacy. There is room both for people who like contact with the public and for backroom types. Hospital pharmacists work in a community, with the opportunity of meeting people in similar jobs.
Pay: Medium (see p. xxiii).

3. RESEARCH AND INDUSTRIAL PHARMACISTS

The work Research pharmacists work in laboratories of pharmaceutical firms and other establishments, on the development of new drugs and the improvement and quality control of existing drugs. As in other scientific work (see p. 400), research pharmacists work in teams, often together with scientists from other disciplines. They also do desk jobs: they prepare data on new drugs for submission to the Medicines Commission, and for doctors. After some years in the laboratory, they may go up the general commercial management ladder. Those with a bent for salesmanship can become representatives, visiting doctors in their surgeries and in hospital, explaining products' special features, and then become marketing executives.

Industrial pharmacists work on the production of drugs (see also Production Management, p. 166).

Prospects There is scope for the quiet backroom type content with semi-routine work, for the team-leader with a bent for pursuing new lines of thought and for those who want to go into general management, marketing and, above all, pharmaceutical sales.
Pay: Medium to high (see p. xxiii).

Training 3-year degree course. The syllabus includes: *pharmacognosy* – the study of medicinal plants and animal and mineral sources of drugs; *physiology* – study of the structure and functions of the human body; *pharmacology* – the effect of drugs; *pharmaceutical chemistry; pharmaceutics* – study of the preparation of medicines; general principles in the practice of pharmacy in the 3 branches; ethics and laws governing pharmaceutical practice.

After 3 years' full-time study, graduates must obtain 1 year's pre-registration experience in pharmacy, which must include at least 6 months in retail or hospital practice before they are eligible to apply for registration as pharmaceutical chemists.

Personal attributes

For all pharmacists: A strong scientific bent; meticulous accuracy; a strong sense of responsibility; a calm, logical mind; ability to concentrate; organizing ability.

For retail and industrial pharmacists: A flair for business; ability to deal with semi- and untrained staff; a liking for people.

For research pharmacists: An inquiring mind; ability to work as one of a team; infinite patience.

Position of women

This is a very promising career for women; 30% of registered pharmacists are women (compared with 23% in 1969) and about 50% of students are women. Proportionately more women work in hospitals (where they have equal promotion chances) than in retail and in industry. But that is by choice: they are welcome as retail pharmacy managers (the majority of clients are women) and also in sales and marketing.

Career-break: Should be no problem. *Refresher courses* available (intended mainly for practising pharmacists, but useful for returners). In some cases the Department of Health will even pay costs of refresher course.

Part-time: Fair opportunities in retail and in hospital.

Further information

Pharmaceutical Society of Great Britain, 1 Lambeth High Street, London SE1 7JN *or* 36 York Place, Edinburgh EH1 3HU

Related careers

Medicine – Pharmacy Technician – Scientist (Biochemist, p. 406: Chemist, p. 405)

Pharmacy Technician

Entry qualifications

3 O-levels preferably including chemistry or another science (many colleges *insist* on chemistry).

The work Pharmacy technicians work in hospitals and retail pharmacies, where their work is similar to that of experienced, knowledgeable assistants in other shops. They deal with the public, selling goods, taking in prescriptions, etc. In retail pharmacies and especially in hospital pharmacies they assist with dispensing, helping to make up prescriptions, measuring liquid, counting out tablets, keeping stocks in good order. They are not allowed to make up prescriptions on their own or to sell poisons or goods supplied only on prescription.

Pharmacy technicians may choose whether to work in retail pharmacy or in hospitals; thus there is room both for those interested in selling, and for those who prefer a backroom job. Technicians always work under the supervision of a registered pharmacist in hospital, where they may have more scope for using their professional skill.

Prospects There is a steady demand for pharmacy technicians in hospitals and in retail pharmacies.

Pay: Medium (see p. xxiii).

Training As trainee with part-time day-release and/or evening classes for, usually, 2 years. This leads to the Society of Apothecaries' and to a City and Guilds' examination. Trainees with inadequate chemistry may have to take evening classes in this subject to be able to pass the examinations.

Syllabus includes general knowledge of drugs and their preparation and action; physiology; some physical and chemical properties; the principles underlying dispensing operations; a knowledge of the law governing the handling, storage and dispensing of preparations; the relationship between patient, medical practitioner, pharmacist and pharmacy technician. Practical work involves compounding preparations (after deciphering the doctor's prescription), weighing and measuring, and filtration and sterilization

There are private schools which run full-time courses, but local authority grants are not given for these because this training has no advantage over learning while employed.

A T.E.C. (see p. xv) Pharmacy Technician qualification is going to be introduced. It will be more comprehensive and more broadly based than present courses and may take longer to complete. It is likely that only hospital and industrial research technicians will take the new qualification; few retail pharmacy technicans are likely to get the necesssary day-release, nor do they need the wider knowledge acquired through T.E.C. courses. However, the T.E.C. qualifications will be specially useful for people who want to return to work after a break.

Personal attributes Meticulous accuracy; a scientific bent but not necessarily great academic ability.

**Position
of women**   The vast majority of technicians are women.

Career-break: Returners' opportunities depend on supply and demand position.

Late start: Depends on local supply and demand position. Entrance requirements may be waived; but school-leavers may be given preference.

Part-time: Fair opportunities.

Further information   Society of Apothecaries, Blackfriars Lane, London EC4
City and Guilds of London Institute, 76 Portland Place, London W1N 4AA

Related careers   *Retail Distribution – Science Technician*

PHOTOGRAPHY

PHOTOGRAPHER: Creative photography (general practitioners, advertising, fashion) –
press and photo-journalism – industrial and scientific – medical; PHOTOGRAPHIC
TECHNICIAN

Photographer

Entry quali-
fications
No definite educational requirements for photography as such. For the
Institute of Incorporated Photographers' Vocational examination: 4 O-
levels.
For the Professional Qualifying Examination: 2 A-levels and 5 O-levels,
see **Training**.
For medical photography: 4 O-levels.
For press photography: 4 O-levels and 1 A-level.
Most, but not all, London photographers are specialized, but in the
provinces one studio often does all types of work.

1. CREATIVE PHOTOGRAPHY

(a) *General practice*

The work
Approximately half of all photographers work in general photographic
studios found in most high streets. The bulk of their work consists of
portraiture, groups and commercial services. Portrait subjects include,
increasingly, pets; some photographers specialize in children.

Photographers prefer their subjects to come to the studio to be
photographed, because it is easier there to arrange the lighting.
However, there is an increasing demand for portraits in the home,
garden or workplace, especially in the case of children's portraits. The
'natural' portrait is much more popular today than the formal one. To
produce not just a good likeness, but a characteristic portrait, photographers must have considerable understanding of, and insight into, human
nature; they must be able to put sitters at ease so that their expression
is natural.

Weddings and other group photographs (e.g. sports and social clubs)
form another important part of the work. Wedding photography now
offers more scope for 'creative' pictures in a less formal style than it
used to. Commercial work is mainly for publicity purposes – for local
companies, estate agencies, architects, etc. who do not have enough
work to employ a staff photographer.

Prospects   Reasonable. One way in for the keen amateur is to help a busy studio
with Saturday weddings.
Pay: Medium to high (see p. xxiii).

(b) *Advertising*

The work   Very varied. Although advertising photographers may often be given
exact instructions about what to photograph and what effect to aim at,
they are also expected to suggest their own ideas for new angles. Many
advertisements are records of everyday life – whether it is of a child
eating breakfast, or a woman getting out of a car – and involve both
work with models and persuading ordinary people to agree to be
photographed.

Advertising photographs are taken either by the photographic departments of advertising agencies, by photographic studios (i.e. several
photographers working as partners, sharing darkroom and office facilities, or salaried photographers and assistants working for an employer),
or by freelance photographers. Most do some catalogue work; some
studios specialize in mail-order photography (and may be owned by the
mail-order company).

Prospects   This is the best paid and hence a very competitive branch; success
depends entirely on ability, efficiency and the right personality.
Pay: Medium to very high (see p. xxiii).

(c) *Fashion*

The work   Although advertising includes fashion photography, some photographers specialize in fashion. Most fashion photography is done by
specialist studios or freelances who are commissioned by editors, fashion
houses, or advertising agencies; they usually work under the direction
of a fashion expert.

Prospects   This is the most sought after branch and hence *very* difficult to enter.
Pay: High (see p. xxiii).

(d) *Photo-journalism (feature photography) and press photography*

The work   Photo-journalism is, essentially, telling a story in pictures, and therefore
a journalistic sense is needed. Feature photographers may work with
reporters as a team, or may be freelances, or work for studios. Only a
tiny minority are on editorial staffs. It is very varied work, and leads to
assignments at any time and in any place – photographing V.I.P.s at
home, or life in foreign parts, or schools at work – anything that makes
a story. Hours are irregular.

There is more hard, hurried work than glamour in newspaper
photography, which consists almost entirely of single news pictures. A

press photographer must be versatile in taking all kinds of subjects. On small provincial papers she may have to do the developing. She must know what makes a good news picture; be able to write an accurate caption; work well with a reporter; be very quick and often work under difficult conditions. Hours are irregular.

Prospects   Not good. The market for photo-journalism is small and getting smaller. Most work as freelances and may specialize, e.g. in travel. For press photography there are always more candidates than jobs. Some possibilities for photographers in other branches to sell work to newspapers or press agencies.

Pay: Medium to high (see p. xxiii).

2. INDUSTRIAL AND SCIENTIFIC

The work   This is the most varied branch of photography. Clients include manufacturing companies, research organizations, government departments, higher education establishments, the police and H.M. Forces. Examples of the work: making photographic progress reports in laboratories; recording the various stages of manufacturing processes; photographing building sites. Industrial photographers also take pictures for house magazines, exhibition stands and instructional purposes. Most of these photographers are salaried employees; some work as freelances or for studios (see General Practice).

Prospects   Better than in all above branches.

Pay: Medium to high (see p. xxiii).

3. MEDICAL

The work   Most teaching hospitals and medical research institutions employ medical photographers, who make still and cine records of work done in operating theatres and research laboratories, and of particular cases among patients. Photographers must not be squeamish.

As part of a team of hospital workers, medical photographers enjoy the comradeship and friendly atmosphere of hospital life. Of all careers in photography this is the least hectic, least tough, most companionable and worst paid.

Prospects   Good. There is some demand for medical photographers.

Pay: Low to medium (see p. xxiii).

Training   *All Photography*
Study can be part-time, while working as a junior in a studio, or, increasingly, full-time. The main courses are:

1. With C.S.E. or some O-levels, *either* 2-year full-time or 3-year part-time for City and Guilds;
Or full-time courses leading to college diplomas or certificates;
Or D.A.T.E.C. validated courses, 1–3 years (see pp. 60, 61).
2. With 4 O-levels (including English language, maths and a science), a full-time 2-year or part-time 3-year course in the photographic department of a technical or art college leading to the Vocational Examination of the Institute of Incorporated Photographers.
3. With 2 A-levels and 5 O-levels (including English language), a full-time 3-year or part-time 4-year course leading to the I.I.P. Professional Qualifying Examination.
4. With 2 A-levels and 3 O-levels, including chemistry, a degree in Photographic Science and Technology.
5. With 2 A-levels and 3 O-levels, several Photography or Photography, Film & Television or similar degree courses.
Several Art & Design degrees (see Art & Design, p. 53) have special photography options.
Press Photography
Either: 1-year pre-entry course organized by National Council for Training of Journalists (see Journalism, p. 224);
Or the N.C.T.J.'s 3-year traineeship (see Journalism, p. 223).
Medical Photography
With O-levels or preferably A-levels, or after general photography course, entry as trainee in a hospital medical photography department. Then either private study for I.I.P. Basic and Higher Medical Photography examinations *or* part-time or block release for Modules 1 and 2 of Institute of Medical and Biological Illustration, leading to the Diploma in Medical Illustration.

Photographic Technician

The work   The processing and printing of films is an extremely important aspect of photography and one in which backroom types are happiest. Most work nowadays is in colour and is increasingly automated (black-and-white film is still mainly processed on a 'hand' line). The work requires considerable concentration and technical knowledge, especially of the complex chemistry of colour film; without these skills a photographer's assignment worth hundreds or even thousands of pounds could be ruined. Technicians may take turns at all the jobs; processing, transparency-making, enlarging, printing and mounting, or may stick to one or two. Experienced technicians can learn more specialized skills, e.g. retouching, or making duplicate transparencies. Apart from laboratories which service professional photographers, there are 'photofinishing' companies which process film taken by amateurs (e.g. holiday snapshots).

Prospects

Good. There is a shortage of good technicians; there is a greater demand for technicians than for photographers. Photofinishing offers most openings to school leavers.

Pay: Medium to high (see p. xxiii).

Training

Usually starting as a junior or trainee in a photographic laboratory, and studying by day-release and/or evening classes for City and Guilds or D.A.T.E.C. (see p. 60) examinations. Alternatively, technicians can take one of the full-time courses.

Personal attributes

Needed by all photographers in varying degrees: Visual imagination; eye for detail and composition; patience; perfect colour vision; artistic sensitivity; creativeness; trust in their own judgement (photographers, unlike other craftsmen and artists, do not usually know whether they have done a good job or not until it is too late); good powers of observation; ability to work quickly, under pressure, surrounded by crowds – in all kinds of unfavourable circumstances; ability to work well with others while keeping to their own individual style; originality; unusual inventiveness (for advertising and fashion photography); business sense (for arranging appointments, sending out bills etc.), as very few can afford secretaries; willingness to 'sell' themselves; a manner which encourages people to co-operate.

Press photography: News sense; ability to remain calm and unmoved, however tragic or unpleasant the circumstances.

Medical photographers: A scientific bent; tactful and reassuring manner; total lack of squeamishness.

Technicians: A scientific bent; manual skill; an eye for detail; patience.

Position of women

There are now a fair number of well-known women photographers, although very few have reached the top in the advertising field. Women still have a little more difficulty than men getting in, especially to press photography.

Career-break: Depends on stage reached before the break and type of work done. Possibly difficult to return to best-paid and most competitive fields, but it should be possible to return to some kind of photography and/or to do some freelance work even while raising a family.

Late start: Press photography: upper age 20. A number of photographers have worked in other fields before taking up photography. The main drawback is poor salaries of trainee or assistant photographers.

Part-time: Fair opportunities, especially as freelances.

Further information	Institute of Incorporated Photographers, Amwell End, Ware, Herts SG12 9HN City and Guilds of London Institute, 76 Portland Place, London W1N 4AA Institute of Medical and Biological Illustration (I.M.B.I.), 27 Craven Street, London WC2
Related careers	*Art and Design – Broadcasting – Fashion – Journalism*

PHYSIOTHERAPY

Entry quali- 1 A-level and 5 O-levels including an English and 2 science subjects.
fications Minimum age for training 18. Most schools ask for 2 A-levels. Degree
course students: 2 A-levels and 3 O-levels.

The work A physiotherapist uses exercises and movement, electrotherapy, ultra-
violet light, short-wave diathermy, and massage to treat the injured, the
sick, and the convalescent of all ages for a large variety of conditions.

Chartered physiotherapists only treat patients who have been referred
by a doctor. Some doctors give exact directions for treatment. Others
state the 'objective' (the therapeutic aim); the physiotherapist decides
on the details of the treatment.

Patients too ill to be moved are treated in bed; others, such as post-
operative patients, may have to be helped to walk properly again. Post-
paralysis cases are taught to make their healthy limbs or muscles do the
work, as far as possible, of paralysed ones, and how to use partially
paralysed limbs.

The work can be physically strenuous as it involves lifting and
supporting patients, but physiotherapists learn to lift heavy weights
without strain. In fact 'lifting' is one of the things they teach: patients
needing treatment for strained backs are taught to lift correctly.

Some patients, mainly partially paralysed ones, do exercises in water
– the buoyancy helps them – and the physiotherapist works with them
in heated swimming pools.

Some patients are treated in groups, but most individually. In all
cases, the physiotherapist must use her judgement. She must know how
far to coax a patient into doing an uncomfortable exercise, and she
must adapt treatment to suit each patient. A physiotherapist uses tact
and encouragement together with specialist knowledge. She may have
to explain to a patient why it is important that exercises are done
regularly at home, to persuade children to cooperate; or to allay
patients' fear of electrical treatment.

The vast majority work in hospital physiotherapy departments. They
work the usual office hours, but may have to do some evening clinics,
'on call' night work and week-end duties.

Some specialize and work in hospitals for the elderly, in orthopaedic
or chest hospitals, or with disabled children only, in homes, hospitals or
in schools; or part-time in schools or maternity clinics.

There is also room for physiotherapists who do not wish to work only with the sick and injured. Some sports clubs employ physiotherapists (often part-time) to keep their members fit, and to treat minor injuries; large industrial and commercial organizations employ a physiotherapist to do largely preventive work: to see that typists' desks are the right height for comfort, health, and therefore efficiency; to show typists how to sit without strain; to teach sales assistants to relax while standing; to teach porters to carry without strain, and so on.

Prospects   Good. There is a world shortage of physiotherapists, especially of physiotherapy teachers.

An experienced physiotherapist can set up in private practice, treating patients either in her own treatment rooms or in patients' homes. But this needs good contacts with local doctors and capital to buy equipment and see her over the first few months. Qualifications are recognized in most countries *abroad* and physiotherapists can work their way around the world.

Pay: Medium (see p. xxiii).

Training   3 years full-time at training schools attached to hospitals and recognized by the Chartered Society of Physiotherapy.

For the first few months, training is entirely theoretical; after that it is a combination of theory and practice, treating patients under the supervision of trained physiotherapists. The syllabus includes physiology, anatomy, physics, movement, electrotherapy and manipulative procedures; conditions for which physiotherapy may be used; how to handle patients (both physically and psychologically).

The first physiotherapy degree course started at Ulster Polytechnic in 1976; it is expected that at least two polytechnics (North-East London and Sheffield) will start similar courses in 1981, and eventually physiotherapy, like dietetics, may become an all-graduate para-medical profession.

Degree course students are expected to have two science A-levels (or at least one *very* good science O-level and one at A-level). The syllabus will not differ basically from the present one, but there should be more 'thinking time' – less time will need to be spent on fact-learning if students enter with higher qualifications. Degree course students may also be able to spend a bit more time on the psychological aspect of their work, and they may study a particular relevant science in greater depth. The main difference between the proposed degree-method of study and the present one is that physiotherapy students will be able to mix with students generally.

For physiotherapists with at least 3 years' experience (some of which may have been some years ago): 1-year physiotherapy teacher training at technical teacher training college in conjunction with physiotherapy school. Training is jointly with other, specialist/technical, further education teachers. (See also Note on p. 323.)

Personal attributes

Enough interest in science and medicine to keep up to date with new developments; a sympathetic yet objective approach to the sick and disabled; ability to work as one of a team and to take responsibility; good health.

Position of women

The vast majority are women, but a disproportionate number of men are heads of physiotherapy schools, apparently because men more often take the additional physiotherapy-teacher-training.

Career-break: Returners are welcome; *refresher* training is usually arranged on an in-service, *ad hoc* basis.

Late start: Although it is known that mature entrants give longer service and are more highly motivated, many schools restrict the number of entrants over 20, and some will not take anyone over 30. However, G.C.E. entry requirements may be relaxed for late entrants and hospitals welcome mature entrants. Courses are shortened for occupational therapists, graduate nurses and other graduates with relevant degrees, and for remedial gymnasts and P.E. teachers.

Part-time: Good opportunities in many areas, though usually only at junior level: few departments promote part-timers, but this may change as the generation of unmarried heads of department is beginning to retire and the majority of young physiotherapists are married.

Further information

Chartered Society of Physiotherapy, 14 Bedford Row, London WC1R 4ED

Related careers

Hospital Technician – Occupational Therapy – Physical Education Teacher – Remedial Gymnast – Speech Therapist

---

PLANNING (Town and Country Planning)

Entry quali- For admission to studentship of the Royal Town Planning Institute: 2
fications A-levels and 3 O-levels including English language (or use of English),
mathematics, and history or geography or a foreign language.

The work Planners aim to reconcile the community's desire for a high standard of
environment for work, home and leisure with the conflicting demands
for land from industry, traffic, etc. They are concerned, in broad terms,
with civic design, land-use and transportation systems. The majority
work in local authorities, some in the Civil Service and some in private
consultancy firms.

The planning process may be broadly broken down into two separate
but interrelated functions:

1. SURVEY, ANALYSIS, AND RESEARCH

This involves devising, planning and conducting surveys of the structure,
functioning, wishes and needs of communities and the assessment of the
problems and aims of urban and regional development. Physical
planners' final plans are based on the outcome of these findings.

2. PHYSICAL PLANNING

This involves drawing up plans for urban, rural and regional development
and redevelopment and their implementation. When, for example, a
satellite town is to be built, or a twilight area pulled down and
redeveloped, planners draw up plans for new road networks (which have
to fit in with adjacent roads) as well as for the siting of housing, schools,
shopping precincts, open spaces, playgrounds, pubs, etc.

Each county (see Local Government, p. 255) is covered by a *Structure
Plan* which outlines planning policy for that area in relation to
neighbouring counties' Structure Plans. This is 'regional planning'. A
county council planner might collate and analyse information in order
to predict, for example, likely levels of need for transport, leisure
facilities, schools, if plan 'A', proposing plans for increased industrial
development, is implemented.

Structure Plans are mainly written policy statements. District planning authorities draw up *Local Plans*. These fit into a Structure Plan,

and go into much more detail. They consist largely of maps and drawn plans. A Local Plan would show, for example, streets which are designated conservation areas; or a plan for a town centre with a traffic-free shopping precinct. Local planners are also concerned with Development Control – dealing with planning applications from the public. Very broadly, there is more scope for improving the environment at Structure Plan level planning; more contact with the general public and such immediate environmental matters as closing roads to and re-routing traffic, rehabilitating old houses rather than pulling them down, at district council level.

Prospects They fluctuate with economic conditions and public authority spending levels. There are occasional openings for experienced planners in developing countries, mainly on a short-contract basis.

Pay: High (see p. xxiii).

Training 1. 4-year full-time or 5-year sandwich degree leading to exemption from the Royal Town Planning Institute's Final examination and eligibility for Membership subject to satisfying the practical experience requirements.

2. Post-graduates (any subject) can take a 2-year full-time or 3-year part-time course leading to exemption from the Royal Town Planning Institute's Final examination; or a part-time course leading to the R.T.P.I. Final examination.

3. Practical training as trainee in a planning office, with day-release and evening study for the R.T.P.I. examinations. Length of training at least 6 years, usually more.

4. Practical training as in (3) to First Professional examination, followed by 2-year full-time or 3-year part-time course. Length of training 5–6 years.

5. Full-time training to First Professional R.T.P.I. examination followed by traineeship and part-time day-release. Length of training 5–6 years.

Methods (3)–(5) are not recommended: drop-out and failure rates are high, and trainee vacancies are very difficult to get.

After 2 years' practical planning experience, candidates who have passed or been exempt from the R.T.P.I.'s Final examination qualify for election to Membership as Chartered Town Planners.

Note: Sociologists, geographers, economists, architects, and other specialists concerned with the various aspects of planning also work in planning offices on appropriate aspects of planning work. For work concerned with overall strategic planning problems and policy, however, a planning qualification is essential.

See also *Architectural Training* (p. 47).

Personal attributes   A keen interest in other people's priorities and way of life; powers of observation; creative imagination; some ability to draw; patience for painstaking research; the ability to work as one of a team as well as to take responsibility; interest in social and environmental developments.

Position of women   The ratio of women to men is improving, 7·2% of all qualified members and 16·3% of all student members of the R.T.P.I. are women. However, the proportion is rising; in 1979 the entry was 14·6% and 21·7% respectively. Women do well up to middle-level jobs; *very* few (2 in 1980) are Chief Officers in Local Government Planning Departments.

Career-break: Planning priorities and legislation change constantly, so planners must keep up with developments. There are 'mid-career' updating courses and seminars for all planners, which could be useful as *refresher courses*. Returners can also take additional courses, for example in traffic engineering/planning at the returning stage. But see **Prospects**.

Late start: Graduates with relevant degrees (geography, social science, engineering) could start post-graduate training. There is no specific upper age limit, but course vacancies are scarce and school-leavers are given preference.

Part-time: Not normally, but experienced planners may occasionally do freelance work.

Further information   The Royal Town Planning Institute, 26 Portland Place, London W1N 4BE

NOTE: T.E.C. (see p. xv) Certificate courses for people employed in town planning offices lead to technician-level work. In practice 4 O-levels including mathematics are required.

Related careers   *Architectural Technician – Architecture – Auctioneer – Cartography – Economics – Engineering – Housing Management – Landscape Architecture – Local Government*

POLICE

Entry qualifications
Minimum age 18½ (cadets from 16); minimum height for women 162 cm (5 ft 4 ins) approximately; for men 172 cm (5 ft 8 ins) approximately. No specific educational requirements; applicants with fewer than 4 O-levels, including English language and mathematics, take an entrance examination in these subjects. (Entrants without G.C.E.s may have difficulty passing the qualifying examination for promotion to sergeant; see **Prospects**.)

Also *graduate entry scheme*, see **Training**.

The work
Police work is a unique mixture of important decision-making, independence, teamwork, variety, and routine. The primary purpose of policing is the prevention of crime, not the apprehension and chasing of criminals. Police officers' uniformed, routine presence on the beat, as well as their presence in crowds or wherever trouble is expected, acts as a deterrent to (at least some) potential law-breakers.

Police officers start with 2 years on the beat. In most areas the 'unit beat' system now operates. Like the old village policeman, the unit beat officer tries to be known by and know people on her regular 'patch'. She has considerable say in arranging her working hours to suit the needs of her area; for example in a quiet suburb she might be around in the early afternoon when mothers fetch children from school and burglars get busy; in a 'rough' area she might be around at pub-closing time.

A typical 'unit' has 2 'resident' police officers; a detective constable and a panda may 'cover' 2 units. All these officers are in touch with each other and the station by personal radio. They can summon instant assistance and ask the station for information or advice.

While patrolling, police officers are on the look-out for missing persons, 'persons behaving in a suspicious manner', stolen and unlocked cars, and generally take note of – and may talk to the station about – anything which seems not quite right. Even when nothing happens, police officers are working.

After about 2 years, police officers may specialize (but it may take longer till a vacancy in the chosen specialization occurs). The main specializations are:

Traffic work, including mobile patrolling; vehicle inspection and giving expert evidence in court; jointly with local authority analysing causes of accidents and of traffic chaos, and working out improvement schemes. This involves research, negotiations, and operating computerized control systems.

C.I.D.: Occasionally includes working on big newsworthy crimes, but most of it is painstaking attention to detail, collecting and piecing together bits of apparently unimportant evidence. C.I.D. officers work closely with the uniformed branch (there is now much more interchange between the two branches than there used to be). The work also includes crime prevention (advising the public on how to make their homes, offices, cars, shops, etc. burglarproof); criminal records, 'scene of crime' and fingerprinting experts (see also Forensic Science, p. 419). C.I.D. officers do a lot of interviewing – not only of suspects, but also house-to-house inquiries covering whole areas.

Mounted branch, dog handling, river police are small specializations which appeal to people who choose the police because of the active, outdoor life; *Community relations* and *juvenile liaison* are specializations for those who choose the police because they want to help solve social problems. In fact most police work involves dealing with and trying to alleviate tensions in society.

From sergeant upwards, policing includes a considerable amount of 'man-management', ensuring as far as possible that every officer's special abilities and interests are made use of. The work also includes more paper-work and requires extensive knowledge of the law. For example when a suspect has been arrested and is brought to the station by the constable, the station sergeant (or possibly an inspector) is responsible for seeing that charges are correctly set out, the prisoner is formally charged and given whatever facilities he is entitled to (contacting his solicitor, for example).

Prospects   All promotion is from the ranks. Constables can take the Sergeant's exam after 2 years (it is a stiff exam, requires hard work, mainly in one's own time), and the inspector's (equally stiff) exam after 2 years as sergeant. (However, even after passing exams, promotion is not automatic: vacancies are not always available.) After inspector, promotion is on merit, without further exams.

By no means all constables try to become sergeants; there are a number of jobs for them apart from beat constables; for example becoming 'collator' – collecting and filing information relevant to the area and answering fellow officers' queries about anything from the name of a local vet to numbers of stolen cars (and details of missing persons).

See **Training** for fast promotion for *graduates*.

Pay: Medium to high (see p. xxiii).

Training
Men and women entrants train together, for 10 weeks, at residential regional training centres. Subjects include law; organization of and liaison with social services; courts and policing procedures. Realistic role-playing exercises are carried out to teach, for example, how to deal with traffic accidents, street fights, domestic disputes, hooliganism; how to take statements from shocked suspects. Training also includes some sociology and psychology to enable officers to understand the underlying causes of contemporary problems such as racial tension and vandalism, and how to deal with them. Self-defence and physical education play an important part in training.

After the 10-week course the officer is posted to a station. At first she patrols together with an experienced officer. For the first 2 years she is on probation. Throughout her career she attends specialist and/or promotion courses. Officers who show potential for senior rank may be sent on the residential 'Special Course' at Police College. This lasts 12 months; teaching is at university level. Promotion to at least superintendent eventually is more or less guaranteed.

Under a *graduate entry scheme*, selected graduates are accepted, with a near-guarantee of admission to the Special Course after their 2 years on the beat (which is essential grass-roots training). They are likely to be inspectors after about 6 years from joining, and promotion prospects after that are very good indeed.

Personal attributes
A sense of proportion and outside interests to avoid developing a biased view of humanity; a sincere but not too critical interest in other people's ways of life; understanding of and sympathy with human weakness; ability to combine sympathy with firmness; a sense of humour; an observant eye and a cool head; the ability to make quick decisions, shoulder responsibility and yet accept discipline; the ability to work as one of a team; physical courage; a liking for being out of doors in all weathers; good health (especially good feet).

Position of women
Ratio of female to male police officers is ·1 to 11, but almost half of police cadets are women.

Women have had equal powers and duties for a long time, but until recently they had their own promotion structure, apart from their male colleagues', and they tended to work largely with women and children. Now, they are totally integrated and compete for promotion and specialization on theoretically equal terms with male colleagues. It is too early to say how 'equal' their chances of top jobs now are, but it is quite likely that as a result of integration a smaller proportion of women officers will be promoted to senior jobs. They undoubtedly have to be above average in 'man-management' ability and have much more drive than men, to be put in charge of a busy station – which is usually an important step on the promotion ladder. Women will now not automatically do the social-work part of policing – dealing with women and children in trouble, and liaising with social workers – but many may well go on concentrating on this type of work. It is up to individual senior officers to decide how to make 'the best use of each officer's abilities', and many senior officers still consider women particularly suitable for the social-work aspect of policing.

As individual Forces' policy about promoting women police officers depends ultimately on the Chief Constable's views, women could ask for details about numbers of women and their distribution in the specializations and ranks before applying to any particular Force. There is no need to join one's local Force.

Career-break: Returners are welcome up to about 30; older returners' chances depend on Chief Constables' views (and shortage of young applicants). Chances better for sergeants and inspectors than for constables.

Late start: Normal upper age 30, but at Chief Constables' discretion whether to accept older candidates.

Part-time: No opportunities at the moment. (No reason why experienced officers should not try to change this situation.)

Further in- **formation**	Local police headquarters Police Recruiting Department, Home Office, Queen Anne's Gate, London SW1 Scotland: Police Recruiting Department, Scottish Home and Health Department, New St Andrew's House, St James Centre, Edinburgh EH13TF

Related **careers**	*Environmental Health Officer – Factory Inspector – Services –* *Social Work*

POLITICS

Member of Parliament – Agent

This is not a career in the usual sense; prospective politicians must first prove their ability in some other area before they stand any chance of attracting votes. Politics is included here simply because so many young people want to know how to get into it.

Entry qualifications
Part-time voluntary work in constituency parties or on local councils is the proving ground of loyalty and the essential starting point of any political career.

1. MEMBER OF PARLIAMENT

The work
There are 635 M.P.s. The House of Commons sits in the afternoon and evening for an average of 35 to 40 weeks a year. Sessions often last late into the night. An M.P. spends most of her time listening to and, if she wishes, participating in debate. Mornings are spent in committee (where much of the most important parliamentary work is done), answering constituents' letters, seeing visitors, researching. If at all possible, M.P.s spend a day a week or frequent weekends in their constituencies, holding 'surgeries', arranging and holding meetings. They must find time to attend social functions, open bazaars, be interviewed by the Press, TV, radio, and attend weekend rallies.

M.P.s are able (but are generally not encouraged) to carry on with some kind of job which can be fitted in with their busy parliamentary schedule; many are journalists, some lawyers, trade union officials, business people. M.P.s have very little free time indeed. Though vacations are long, they have to attend to constituency matters all the year round.

Prospects
Impossible to predict. In marginal constituencies an M.P. is very insecure; even in a safe seat the unexpected can happen at the next election; M.P.s may also fail to be re-adopted by their constituencies. Most M.P.s hope to hold office eventually, but only a small proportion ever do so. It depends partly on their ability and hard work, but also on luck – mainly whether their party is in office, and whether their views on particular issues are acceptable to the party leader.

Pay: Medium (see p. xxiii).

Selection and training   A candidate must normally have been a member of her party for at least 2 years. Many learn the business of politics – debating, dealing with constituents' problems, canvassing, collecting relevant facts, making speeches – by being (unpaid) local councillors. Prospective Labour candidates must be members of a trade union, if eligible.

The methods of selection are, with minor variations, basically the same for the three main parties: candidates can choose whether to put themselves forward as candidate for their local constituency only, or whether to apply to the central party organization to be put on a list of candidates for adoption wherever a vacancy occurs. In either case, candidates go through a number of selection interviews where they prove their knowledge of current affairs and their debating and speaking skills.

First-time candidates tend to be given hopeless seats to fight, so that they gain experience and prove that they have the enthusiasm needed to campaign successfully.

Personal attributes   Strong political faith and convictions; self-confidence; resilience; considerable debating skills; great physical stamina; willingness to work unsocial and long hours and to give politics priority over other interests/activities; thick skin to cope with personal attacks.

Position of women   Women M.P.s have numbered between 19 and 30 for many years now. Nothing like as many women as men put themselves forward as candidates, even though women are very active as voluntary party workers. The long hours, the need to be absent from home and the lack of crèche facilities make politics a difficult career for women with children and/or with husbands who are not equally committed to politics or at least to running home and family in their wives' absence. It is probably harder for women to be adopted in the first place: a woman candidate has to be of better calibre than a man to stand equal chance of adoption. There is no indication that women candidates fare worse than men in parliamentary elections (which may of course be due to the fact that women candidates generally *are* of above-average ability). All parties genuinely want more women M.P.s – as long as they are exceptionally good. Once in Parliament, women are very successful in terms of holding office in relation to their numbers, and they are very active on committees.

Late start: Maturity is an asset, but a woman candidate of 40 who competes for adoption with a man of 30 is probably at a disadvantage. It is very difficult for women to win: if they are very young, adoption committees fear they will have babies (which is more of a temporary hindrance in politics than in other work); if they are middle-aged, young men tend to be given preference.

2. CONSTITUENCY AGENT

The work Agents are paid or unpaid constituency officials (not all constituencies have paid full-time agents). An agent is responsible for efficient constituency organization, for checking electoral registers, for membership and fund-raising drives, for organizing meetings and M.P.s' visits and general local party matters. She normally has mainly voluntary helpers.

Selection and training Potential full-time agents must have worked for the party for at least 2 years. Before being eligible for appointment, Labour Party workers take a correspondence course and an examination for the Diploma in Electoral Law and Party Organization. Tory workers have a minimum of 15 months' training working with a qualified agent while taking the examinations for the Associate Membership of the National Society of Conservative and Unionist Agents. Liberal Party training is less formal, but their agents also have to learn relevant law and organization during a residential crash course.

Prospects There are not many posts, but all parties welcome more applicants. Promotion can be either to a key constituency, or to a regional or central office post. Agents' work is grist to the mill for anyone wanting to become an M.P. eventually, but a certain period of time has to elapse before an agent may stand as candidate in a constituency in which she was an agent.

Pay: Low to medium (see p. xxiii).

Personal attributes Much as for M.P.s, plus considerable organizing ability, and ability to make volunteers work hard.

Position of women In the Liberal Party, about half the agents are women, rather fewer in the other 2 parties, but this is entirely due to the proportion applying. There is no discrimination in this (usually badly paid) work.

Late start: No problem.

Part-time: Possible in theory; in practice part-time agents tend to be volunteers.

**Further in-   Local or central party organizations.
formation**

**Related   *Acting – Barrister – Economics*
careers**

NOTE: *On the fringes of politics: Trade union* organizer or researcher.
The majority of paid trade union officials are recruited from unpaid
union officials; but occasionally sociology, economics and other graduates are taken on as researchers, or possibly as organizers.

PRINTING

Entry quali-fications   See **Training**.

The work   Printing has been called the 'meeting place of art and science', but above all it is an industry. It uses a variety of technological processes to create a product of visual impact. The product may be books, newspapers, packaging, postage stamps, writing paper, record sleeves or reproductions of old masters: it is always a form of communication. Some printing processes are centuries old, but printing technology has changed enormously in the last few years and continues to change. For example, computer typesetting is now often used for text, and electronic scanners are used in the production of coloured illustrations. In many cases, alternative methods are available, and *production controllers* or *managers* (titles and precise functions vary) have to decide, with the client, on the most advantageous method in any particular case, weighing up such factors as relative speed, cost, quality.

Apart from working in printing production, technicians and technologists also work in research and development on new machinery, paper, inks.

Prospects   Very poor at craft level, a little better at technician, technologist and management levels.

Pay. High (see p. xxiii).

Training   Maximum age for craft apprentices 25 in theory, 17 in practice. Craft level entrants can go up the training ladder and eventually become managers or technologists, sales executives or production controllers. Entrants take courses according to their entry qualifications.

(1) Craft apprentices are trained for groups of printing crafts, but most of these are in the process of change as new technologies are being introduced. Entry qualifications vary slightly according to firms' particular requirements, which depend largely on types of new technologies. Basically, entrants need at least 3, more often 4, Grade II C.S.E.s; for some apprenticeships even 4 O-levels. Subjects should normally include mathematics, a science and, for some occupations/crafts, a practical subject like art or technical drawing; for others English and another science.

(2) Entry qualifications for craft and technician training overlap. With

4 O-levels including English, a science and mathematics, entrants can take a 2-year day- or block-release course for the T.E.C. Certificate (see p. xv) in Printing, followed by a 3-year sandwich course for a Higher T.E.C. award.

(3) With A-level mathematics, physics or chemistry and one other science among 4 O-levels, entrants can train for the Higher T.E.C. award, normally by a 3-year sandwich course.

(4) With 2 or 3 A-levels including at least one science (preferably chemistry), entrants can take a 4-year B.Sc. in Printing Technology.

(5) Art school training (see Art and Design, p. 60), with specialization in Graphic Design or Typography, can also lead to printing jobs.

Personal attributes

Depends on type and level of work, but generally some visual imagination; interest in machinery; practicality; some dexterity; indifference to being the only, or one of a few, women in an all-male setting.

For managerial jobs: organizing ability; ability to work under pressure; being a self-starter.

Position of women

This is one of the most traditional industries (especially newspapers). There now are a few women craft and technician apprentices, but women still meet prejudice on the shop-floor and have much greater difficulties getting apprenticeships than men. At the technology level there is no valid reason whatever why women should not succeed; they have no difficulty getting onto degree or T.E.C. Higher Diploma courses. Art school trained women are doing quite well in typography and production/design.

Career-break: Return to work is likely to be difficult because of technological changes and shortage of jobs.

Late start: Not from scratch; but design-trained women might try – none seem to have done so.

Part-time: No opportunities in printing: possibly as freelance typographer.

Further information

British Printing Industries Federation, 11 Bedford Row, London WC1R 4DX

Printing and Publishing Industry Training Board, Merit House, Edgware Road, London NW9

Institute of Printing, 8 Lonsdale Gardens, Tunbridge Wells, Kent TN1 1NU

Related careers

Art and Design – Engineering – Science – Publishing

PRISON SERVICE

Prison officer – assistant governor

**Entry quali-
fications**

Prison officer: minimum age usually 21.

No specific education requirements. Selection is by short written test and interview.

Assistant governor: minimum age 21.

No specific qualifications laid down, but in practice entry is with a degree or comparable qualification.

The work

This is basically social work, with the emphasis on training, not punishing, prisoners. The important aspect is dealing with people with problems, not just locking and unlocking cells. Staff, who are no longer called 'warders', are expected to take a personal interest in the prisoners, to talk to them as one human being to another and to help their rehabilitation by fostering their self-respect and gaining their co-operation. Prisoners are often in trouble through force of circumstances rather than real criminality, and day-to-day contact with firm but understanding officers is a vital part of their rehabilitation. Although some prisoners are abusive and violent, the majority are not disruptive and just want to finish their sentences as quickly as possible.

There are five different types of establishment: remand centres, mainly for young offenders and persons awaiting trial or sentence; local prisons, to which convicted prisoners are sent initially for assessment; training prisons, open, closed or maximum security, which have facilities for training prisoners in a range of skills; Borstals, which are training centres for juveniles between 17 and 21; and detention centres, which provide a tough regime for 14- to 21-year-olds serving shorter sentences than those in Borstals.

Prison work is, of course, often depressing but, like other types of social work, it can be very rewarding and is of real value to the community.

Staff accommodation is normally provided, but increasingly prison staff live out and receive an allowance in lieu of accommodation. Prison staff can either buy meals in the mess or cook their own. Work is inevitably on a shift basis.

1. PRISON OFFICERS

Daily routine varies from prison to prison. Prison officers must be willing to serve in any type of institution, although they have a certain amount of choice. They are concerned with the training, rehabilitation, control and routine supervision of prisoners at work in the kitchen, laundry, workshop, gardens or farm; in their cells; at exercise and during recreation. They escort individual prisoners to and from courts and hospitals and accompany visitors to the visiting room. They work as part of a team, together with medical staff, welfare officers and specialist instructors and teachers. They must see that prisoners who seem to have specific problems discuss these with senior staff. In certain establishments they may take part in 'group counselling' when a group of prisoners and staff discuss personal and general problems. Prison officers with a skill or trade (anything from engineering to art and craft) may become instructors.

2. ASSISTANT GOVERNORS

Some are promoted from prison officer but the majority are recruited from outside the Prison Service. Of these two thirds are new graduates. The selection board looks for candidates with a good understanding of social problems and modern methods of dealing with them. A degree in any subject or experience of management in a social setting (for example, personnel work, social studies, institutional management) is an advantage. The precise nature of the work depends on the type of establishment, but it is primarily managerial. The assistant governor is usually in charge of a 'wing' or 'house', and is responsible for managing inmates' general rehabilitation and welfare. She organizes, or helps to organize, work and leisure activities (lectures, concerts, etc.), keeps records of prisoners' progress and problems and is involved in parole matters.

Prospects   Very good. There is a shortage of prison staff at all levels. Over half of prison officers gain some promotion and they can climb up the ladder to assistant governor if they are able to absorb the necessary degree-level academic training. Assistant governors with exceptional ability may be promoted to prison governor. Promotion usually means transfer to another establishment.

Pay: Low to medium; high for governors (see p. xxiii).

Training   *Prison Officers*: 5 weeks in preliminary training at a prison or Borstal working closely with experienced officers, followed by 8-week training at a Prison Officers' Training School. Academic and technical instruction is given in subjects appropriate to the work, e.g. prison classification, dealing with people with problems, escort and court duties, supervision of inmates at work and play, security.

Assistant Governors: Entrants under 24 work for about 1 year as prison officers. Training during the first 2 years as assistant governor consists of practical experience alternating with theoretical training at Prison Service College. Subjects include psychology, sociology, social casework and group work, management, rehabilitation of prisoners.

Personal attributes

Leadership: this is difficult to define, but for example a young person who enjoyed taking an active part in organizing at school or youth club probably has it; a sense of right and wrong, without being censorious; a genuine desire to help people in trouble and the ability to understand and sympathize with people's failings without necessarily condoning them; the ability to find the right approach to all types of people; immense patience with people at their most unbearable; interests entirely outside prison work to help keep a sense of proportion; a friendly, naturally happy disposition.

Position of women

Prison officers work only with inmates of their own sex, but assistant governors can work with both sexes. As there are relatively few women's prisons, women assistant governors are more likely to serve in men's establishments than vice versa. Although far fewer women than men apply for assistant governor posts, a much higher proportion of those who do are accepted.

Career-break: No problem (if there is a local prison).

Late Start: *Prison officer*: Entry up to 49½. *Assistant governor*: Entry normally up to 35. A *few* people with relevant experience in other spheres are appointed above this age.

Part-time: Virtually none.

Further information

Home office, Freepost, London SW1E 5BX
Scotland: Establishment Officer, Scottish Home and Health Department, St Margaret's House, London Road, Edinburgh EH8 7TG

Related careers

Personnel Work – Police – Social Work

PSYCHOLOGY

Educational – clinical – occupational – social – experimental – psychotherapy – counselling

Psychologists are concerned with the systematic study of human behaviour. They must not be confused with psychiatrists, who are medically qualified specialists who give treatment to the mentally sick and disturbed.

Entry quali-fications Usually 2 or 3 A-levels, including at least 1 science or maths; maths and a science at O-level if not at A-level (requirements also vary according to whether the course leads to a B.Sc. or B.A.).

The work There are several specializations: educational, clinical, occupational, social and experimental psychology, but they all overlap. Educational and clinical psychology are the most well-established, with defined salary scales; occupational psychology is the most diversified, social psychology the least clearly defined, and experimental psychology, although probably the most specialized, overlaps most with the other fields.

1. EDUCATIONAL PSYCHOLOGISTS

They advise teachers, parents, doctors and social workers on children's and young people's adjustment and learning problems. Assessment involves sessions with the 'problem' child as well as, usually, its parents and teachers, and a thorough study of the subject's background and environment. Various established techniques, such as ability tests and 'personality schedules' are used. Treatment may include individual counselling sessions with child and/or parents and advice to parents and teachers on the 'management' of the problem. Apart from helping when problems have arisen, educational psychologists do preventive work, such as organizing in-service courses for teachers and social workers, talking to groups of parents, to 5th- and 6th-formers, and to youth clubs.

They are employed by local education authorities and work in school/county psychological services and child guidance clinics. They have considerable autonomy right from the start.

2. CLINICAL PSYCHOLOGISTS

They are concerned with helping handicapped people to make the best use of their potential. Therapeutic work is carried out with children and adults, in individual counselling sessions and in groups, in therapeutic communities (see Psychiatric Nursing, p. 309); at day-centres (see Social Work, p. 445), and in family groups. The wide range of problems treated includes physical and mental handicap; phobias (including children's inability to face school); neurological and obsessional disorders; sexual difficulties; reading and writing difficulties.

Clinical psychologists organize, coordinate and cooperate in vocational guidance for the handicapped, rehabilitation, training and retraining programmes for patients with physical or neurological and subnormality handicap. They set up systems for job analysis, assess and evaluate the work potential and the progress of patients. The broad types of therapeutic work undertaken are behaviour therapy, psychotherapy and counselling, rehabilitation and training. Most clinical psychologists work in hospitals, some in child guidance clinics. They work in close collaboration with neurologists, psychiatrists and other specialists.

3. OCCUPATIONAL PSYCHOLOGISTS

They study people as workers. They advise on how people can both enjoy and be efficient in their work by giving vocational guidance to both children and adults. They set up selection procedures for staff and develop training schemes. They also help in the organizing of work itself by devising new methods of doing jobs, and advise on the design of tools and machines so that they are easy to use. They also research into and advise on psychological implications of organizational structures and proposed changes, aiming at improving both job satisfaction and productivity (this is now called 'organizational psychology' and overlaps also with social psychology).

Occupational psychologists have developed techniques for collecting information from people about what they like doing and what they are good at, as well as what they find difficult and unpleasant. They match this information against that collected by detailed studies of the actual work involved in the jobs concerned.

They work in vocational guidance for industrial rehabilitation units; very occasionally in the careers service, research institutions for industrial firms, and for business consultants.

Other occupational/social psychology specializations are concerned with retirement: pre-retirement counselling and training and generally looking into problems connected with the growing proportion of retired people in the community; with mid-career changes necessitated by changes in job opportunities; with problems connected with women's changing career-patterns and aspirations.

4. SOCIAL PSYCHOLOGISTS

They are concerned with people in groups and with how groups can affect each other and the behaviour of individuals. They study what groups of people do or think – and why – in given circumstances, such as when they shop in supermarkets or when they vote in elections, and when they go berserk at football matches. They use interview and questionnaires to collect information from people in carefully planned surveys of groups and samples of people. They also study the structure and organization of various types of groups. It is the least clearly defined psychological specialization. The work often overlaps with that of the sociologist and the economist.

Social psychologists are employed by the government, in industrial and university research organizations, in market research and advertising agencies, and by industry, where they are mainly concerned with industrial relations.

5. EXPERIMENTAL PSYCHOLOGISTS

They help to solve a wide range of problems that affect people by applying both the accumulated psychological knowledge about people and the special experimental methods that have been developed to study human behaviour. These problems range from designing road signs that can be seen at speed, designing easy-to-use aircraft controls to prevent accidents due to pilot error, finding out how well older people can learn new jobs, developing clothing for special work, to planning houses, offices, and playgrounds for children. In all this work experiments are planned, information is collected and analysed, and conclusions are drawn to enable someone to make decisions that in some way affect people. As well as solving problems experimental psychologists are always trying to extend the scope of psychology by carrying out experiments to find out more about people and how the human brain works.

Experimental psychologists usually work in teams with other scientists; they are mainly employed in government research laboratories, in the Services and in universities.

6. PSYCHOTHERAPISTS

Psychotherapy is not a career to go into straight from school or university. Maturity and 'experience of life' are essential even to be accepted for training.

(a) *Adult psychotherapy*: 'Adult psychotherapists' help patients by 'talking through' their psychological or emotional problems. Patients include people who feel they need to gain a better understanding of their own personality, who have suffered bereavement or are depressed for other reasons, and people who are mentally disturbed or ill. There are various 'schools' of psychotherapy: the term is now used to cover different methods of treatment which vary greatly in depth, intensity and basic philosophy.

(b) *Child psychotherapy*: This is a form of treatment for children who suffer from behaviour disturbances which are psychological in origin. Psychotherapists must build up a good relationship with their patients – verbal communication usually has to be supplemented with playing, drawing, painting. Most children are seen individually; some are treated in groups.

Child psychotherapists work at child guidance clinics; young people's advice centres, where their patients are adolescents rather than children and the work involves listening and sorting out problems; and with educational psychologists in the National Health Services.

Prospects   *Psychologist*: There is a small but steady demand in all fields; postgraduate training is virtually essential for all types of jobs. A psychology degree plus professional training can also lead to Social Work (see p. 445) and to Personnel Work (see p. 338).

Psychotherapist: *Adult psychotherapy*: The demand, especially outside London, is growing, but this is a very small profession and opportunities in the N.H.S. are very limited indeed, so practitioners rely almost entirely on private patients. Good contacts with local g.p.s are essential. *Child psychotherapy*: Overall demand is growing, but although local education authorities and the N.H.S. need more child psychotherapists, expenditure cuts have severely affected job prospects.

Pay: Medium to high (see p. xxiii).

Training   3- (sometimes 4-) year degree course. The composition of the courses varies: some lead to B.A., some to B.Sc. Topics usually covered include: experimental study of such mental processes as thinking, learning and perceiving; animal behaviour, physiology of the nervous system; development of children; social relationships and their effects on personality; mental disorder; applications of psychology to the study of society, industry, and education; techniques of testing and experiment. Students also do a great deal of statistics, laboratory work, and often work with animals.

There is no need to decide what branch of psychology to specialize in till after the course. Post-graduate courses are essential:

Educational and *clinical* psychologists take post-graduate Diploma or Master's degree courses (possibly part-time or 'sandwich') which last 1 to 3 years. Those intending to take a post-graduate qualification in educational psychology must usually have at least 2 years' teaching experience.

Occupational psychologists normally take a 2-year full- or part-time Master's degree or Diploma course.

Experimental psychologists usually get 'in-service' training while working for a higher degree by doing research on a special topic.

Adult psychotherapists: Training varies according to 'school' of psychotherapy – there are several training organizations. All require students to have had previous qualifications and relevant experience, and all psychotherapists must undergo personal analysis (for which they must pay themselves).

The usual qualifications needed for psychotherapy training are:

(a) medical qualification: *or*

(b) psychology degree or a degree containing a substantial psychology component; *or*

(c) social work qualification or (exceptionally) counselling experience and qualification (see below); *or*

(d) teaching qualification and counselling experience.

Child psychotherapists: students must normally have a psychology degree and experience of working with children.

All psychotherapy training starts with a year's probationary work. If accepted for training, students then spend at least 4 years on intensive, time-consuming training. Training is a mixture of theory and practice. During the latter part of the training, students may be allowed to be paid for treating patients. There are a few salaried training posts, especially for child psychotherapists.

In practice, it therefore takes at least 4 years to qualify as psychologist and at least 8 years to qualify as a psychotherapist.

Personal attributes

A detached interest in individuals' and communities' behaviour rather than personal involvement; an interest in scientific method; the ability to work well on one's own and also to cooperate with people from different backgrounds; patience; numeracy.

Position of women

In psychotherapy women far outnumber men; in other specializations about 45% of professionally qualified psychologists and about 50% of post-graduate students are women. Far more women than men – about twice as many – take psychology degrees, but women then do not necessarily take further training. Women have no more difficulties in getting jobs than men.

Career-break: Depends on competition from newly-qualified people. There are (limited) opportunities to train as counsellor (see below).

Late start: Degree course entry requirements may be relaxed for mature students, who are welcome on degree courses, but proof of adequate knowledge of mathematics at least is essential, and the training is a very long one.

Part-time: Some employment opportunities.

Further in-formation   The General Secretary, The British Psychological Society, St Andrew's House, 48 Princess Road, Leicester LE1 7DR

Psychotherapy
London Centre for Psychotherapy, 19 Fitzjohns Avenue, London NW3
Tavistock Clinic, Belsize Lane, London NW3
British Association of Psychotherapists, c/o 121 Hendon Lane, London N3
Royal College of Psychiatrists, 17 Belgrave Square, London SW1X 8PG
Association of Child Psychotherapists, Burgh House, New End Square, London NW3

Related careers   *Personnel Work – Psychiatric Nursing – Social Work – Sociology – Teaching*

COUNSELLING: This is not usually a career in itself, rather an activity for people with certain skills, qualifications and experience. Counsellors listen to, and help clients cope with, personal problems. It is a form of psychotherapy but counsellors are not as highly qualified psychologically, and do not probe as deeply, as fully trained psychotherapists. Counselling is part of social workers', personnel officers', doctors' and teachers' jobs; very few people are employed entirely as counsellors, although some schools and other education establishments employ qualified teachers or social workers who have taken a counselling course; so do some voluntary organizations. The latter usually specialize in a type of 'client group', for example, people become marriage counsellors, student, youth or alcoholics' counsellors. Counselling of this type is usually done by volunteers or as a part-time job for a small fee. There are a few post-graduate counselling courses at universities and polytechnics or run by voluntary organizations, but there are far more qualified counsellors than job vacancies.

Further Information: British Association for Counselling, 1a Little Church St, Rugby CV21 3AP

PUBLIC RELATIONS

Entry quali- None are specified, see **Training**.
fications

The work A public relations officer (now often called 'public affairs' officer or executive) acts as a link between client and public; it is her job to present the client's image in more general terms than an advertising campaign. She provides factual stories about the client or his product to newspapers, magazines and television, thus keeping the product or the service in the news and creating a 'favourable climate or image'. She answers journalists' questions about her client's product, views or services, and may take journalists to see a client or his business. She arranges parties, exhibitions and other projects to 'put over' a client, and gives talks to interested groups – schools, women's organizations, etc.

She deals with inquiries (and also complaints) from the public.

Public relations officers work either in a public relations firm (several partners each with their own accounts and a shared office and staff), or in a public relations department of an advertising agency, or in separate press and public relations departments of individual organizations – from stores to public utilities and government departments. This last type of work is increasing. (The title here may be Information Officer.) More and more organizations employ staff to answer questions and generally to see that the public is informed about their functions and activities. Today, local authorities, trade unions, employers' federations, and professional organizations such as the British Medical Association employ public relations or information officers.

Prospects There is no security in p.r. work; far more people want to do this sort of work than there are opportunities.

Pay: Medium to very high (see p. xxiii).

Training School-leavers enter either as secretary in a public relations firm or department or via journalism (see p. 220), or with some specialist knowledge, for instance of engineering (see p. 163) or marketing (see p. 270).

Specific – not obligatory – training for students in relevant employment: part-time (mainly evening) study, for about 2 years, for the C.A.M. (Communications, Advertising and Marketing) Foundation's

Certificate. Syllabus covers public relations principles and practice; business organization; organization, technical and policy aspects of the media; communication principles and methods. The Certificate is followed by a further year's part-time study for the C.A.M. Diploma in Public Relations.

Entry requirements for the Certificate course are *either*:

2 A-levels and 3 O-levels; *or* B.E.C. National award (see p. xvii);

Or: 1 year's experience in a public relations office plus 5 O-levels;

Or: 3 years' experience plus employer's recommendation. (In other words, late developers and others who get no school qualifications can eventually catch up.)

The majority of p.r. people have not taken the C.A.M. training. Experience and aptitude are far more important than paper qualifications.

Personal attributes

Ability to get on exceptionally well with people of all kinds, whether hard-hitting journalists or timid members of the public; enterprise and initiative; good news sense; sense of salesmanship; a calm temperament; ability to write and speak well and persuasively; imagination; tact; ability to keep polite under provocation and/or pressure.

Position of women

Women do very well in p.r., some of the top jobs being held by women. This is one career area where starting as a secretary is a useful way in.

Career-break: No problem for women who were firmly established before the break. Many work from home, perhaps having only one client for a year or so then gradually increasing their workload.

Late start: Only advisable for women with special expertise, and even then jobs may be difficult to get.

Part-time: Some opportunities, especially working from home or for small, non-commercial (i.e. usually voluntary) organizations.

Further information

Institute of Public Relations, 1 Great James Street, London WC1N 3DA

Related careers

Advertising – Fashion – Information Officer – Journalism – Marketing – Secretarial Work

---

PUBLISHING

Editorial – production – marketing

Entry quali- In practice a degree or comparable qualification and/or specialist
fications knowledge/experience; art school training for some aspects of production.

The work Book publishing is an industry (one of the smallest in the country), not
a profession. It requires business acumen and an interest in marketing
(see p. 270) as much as creativity and literary flair. The function of
publishing has been described as extending the author's idea into a
finished book and getting it into readers' hands – in other words
publishing involves the organization of production and distribution as
much as literary effort.

Publishing houses vary greatly in size, from large ones with overseas
branches, producing hundreds of titles a year, to those run on a
shoestring with a handful of employees and a small yearly output. Some
publishers specialize in educational, scientific, art books, paperbacks.

All publishers select and commission manuscripts, design the appearance of the books, have them printed and bound, promote and sell the
finished copies, but the internal organization of houses varies. The
process is usually divided into 3 main departments (apart from the usual
commercial ones such as accounts). The division of work is more rigid
in some houses than others; in small houses everybody may have to do
anything that needs doing (a good way of learning).

The 3 main publishing departments or 'functions' are:

1. EDITORIAL

Main duties are selecting and commissioning manuscripts, getting
outside specialist readers' opinions, preparing MSS. for the printer;
liaising with authors, possibly suggesting changes; dealing with contracts, copyright, subsidiary rights (these may be separate departments).
Editorial departments also deal with new editions of existing books.

An editorial director or chief editor (titles and responsibilities
involved vary greatly in different houses) is usually in charge. Individual
editors may each be responsible for books on a special subject, or for a
range of subjects. The editor may initiate a book on a special subject.

select the author and deal with the project right through. The number of books one editor deals with at any particular moment varies according to type of firm and type of book, and so does the amount of contact the editor has with the author.

Editorial assistants or 'copy-editors' deal with 'copy preparation', checking facts and references, spelling, punctuation, and possibly doing some rewriting, proof-reading and correcting. Again, responsibilities and duties vary greatly. In specialist publishing, such as educational, scientific, or art, editorial assistants normally have a degree in a relevant subject. In general publishing, a graduate's degree subject is normally irrelevant.

2. PRODUCTION

The production department receives the edited manuscript and decides, in consultation with the editor, on the appearance of the book, on the shape, typeface, paper, illustrations, etc.; and it deals with printers, paper merchants, and binders, etc. Production staff require a knowledge of printing, book-production, typography and of costing and marketing. They usually employ typographers and picture researchers. Technical and textbook publishers may employ illustrators, but most artwork is commissioned from outside studios.

There are some training courses in book production and design and some vocational art courses which include book design and production (see Art and Design, p. 61).

3. MARKETING

In some ways the most important publishing activity, marketing or 'promotion' is responsible for planning, researching for, and preparing review lists, sales campaigns, writing 'blurbs', and for the representatives who call on bookshops, schools, libraries, etc. to give information on forthcoming books and to collect orders. This is a good department in which to learn how publishing works.

Prospects   Very limited opportunities, especially in general publishing; a little more scope in technical, scientific, educational. First editorial job is usually as editorial assistant ('assistant editor' may mean the same thing). It is usually necessary to move to another firm for a better job.

Pay: Low to medium (see p. xxiii).

Training   See under **Work**.

A few firms run training schemes. Pre-entry courses exist at a few polytechnics, but they are less useful than a degree.

Personal attributes Creative ability; interest in social and literary trends; ability to see books as a marketable commodity; some writing ability; critical judgement; common sense; resilience; good business sense; willingness to take responsibility and make decisions; ability to get on well with a wide variety of types of people.

Position of women There are far more male than female editorial directors and publishing house board members but women do well in 'senior middle' jobs, especially in Marketing, also as children's and educational book editors. Among copy-editors and editorial assistants women greatly outnumber men. Many women go into publishing as secretaries hoping to become editors; some do, although far more remain in junior editorial jobs.

Career-break: It should be possible (and it is advisable) not to give up completely, even temporarily.

Late start: Very difficult because of the competition from young graduates.

Part-time: Experienced proof-readers, copy-editors, editors may be able to do sporadic part-time work.

Further information Individual publishing houses

Related careers *Art and Design – Bookselling – Information Work – Journalism – Librarian*

PURCHASING AND SUPPLY

Entry quali-
fications
4 O-levels including English language and mathematics. Also consider-able *graduate* entry. No specific qualifications for mature entrants.

The work
The purchasing officer is responsible for ensuring regular supplies of materials, tools, components, equipment – anything other departments in her organization may require to function efficiently. This may be raw materials, office equipment, machine components. She searches out most suitable supplies and negotiates terms and delivery dates. She may have to decide, at times, when to agree to pay more than budgeted for in order to get supplies which are in short supply; this would probably be decided jointly with production manager and accountant. She is a vital link between the various departments which need supplies, and the suppliers – her success depends largely on maintaining good relationships with suppliers and on negotiating advantageous terms.

She may travel all over the world – and should be able to speak foreign languages; she must be aware of social, economic and political developments which might affect price levels and availability of supplies.

Purchasing officers work mainly, but by no means only, in industry, where purchasing is a 'management function'. They can switch from one type of buying to another: commodity knowledge is not vital as specialists give purchasing officers detailed specifications; for example, machine tools or electronic equipment can be bought by a purchasing officer who previously bought raw materials for a food manufacturer. However, many purchasing officers do stay in one type of buying, and a technical background (engineering qualification for example) is useful in many jobs.

Purchasing managers, in charge of departments, are also responsible for holding stocks, stores administration and possibly preservation of stocks (which may involve deciding how far forward supplies can be bought in), weighing up price rises and possible future shortages against possible spoilage and storage costs. They must be conversant with contract and negotiation procedures in this country and abroad.

Purchasing officers in the non-industrial sector are often called supplies officers and are concerned, for example, in hospital, with buying a vast range of equipment from beds to disposable towels; they work closely with medical staff. In education authorities they work closely with heads of schools and education officers.

Prospects   Quite good. Medium-sized organizations where buying used not to be
a specialist function now often employ purchasing specialists; purchasing is one of the functions which can lead into general management (see
p. 259).
Pay: Medium to high (see p. xxiii).

Personal   Numeracy; organizing ability; practical approach to problem-solving;
attributes   considerable business acumen and some gambling spirit; ability to
establish friendly relationships quickly; judgement to gauge the right
approach to individual suppliers.

Training   The Institute of Purchasing and Supply's Diploma is now becoming an
essential qualification for senior posts; study for it is by evening class
(rarely day-release) or correspondence course while in relevant employment. The majority of students study for Parts I and II of the Diploma
via Business Education Council courses; part-time, 2 to 4 years, full-
time 2 to 3 years, or sandwich (see p. xvii). Part III of the Diploma is
set by the Institute. Holders of Business Studies degree and equivalent
qualifications are eligible for exemption from Parts I and II. The syllabus
includes business procedures, buying methods, economics, statistics.
For Part III, students may specialize in Industrial Marketing; *or*
Structure, Planning and Control in Public Sector; *or* Commercial
Procedures and Techniques in Engineering and Constructional Con-
tracting; *or* Materials and Production Planning and Control.

Position   At the moment there are very few women indeed, but there is no logical
of women   reason for this – women have long been established as buyers for retail
stores, which is much the same kind of work. Women who have gone
into purchasing are doing well – a number are in engineering purchasing.
The main reason why there are so few women in this field is because
they don't know about it or imagine they need specialist knowledge.

Career-break: Should not present problems, but keeping in touch with
world economic conditions and commercial law is vital. Short Institute
courses can be used as *refreshers*.

Late start: Good opportunities. Part-time evening courses available;
women with previous clerical experience are welcome as assistant
purchasing officers. The I.P.S. Diploma and the Diploma in Management
Studies (see p. 263) are available under the T.O.P.S. scheme (see p. xl).
Graduates (any discipline) are granted substantial exemption from
I.P.S. exams and G.C.E. requirements for over-25s are waived.

Further information   Institute of Purchasing and Supply, I.P.S. House, High Street, Ascot, Berkshire SL5 7HU

Related careers   *Commodity Broking – Management in Industry – Quantity Surveyor – Retail Buying – Shipbroking*

RADIOGRAPHY

Diagnostic – therapeutic

Entry quali- 2 A-levels, 2 O-levels. English and mathematics *or* physics to be
fications included, at either level; *or* T.E.C. Sciences (see pp. 415–16).

The work Radiography has 2 branches: diagnostic and therapeutic.

1. DIAGNOSTIC RADIOGRAPHER

She works with medically qualified radiologists and takes X-ray photographs to assist doctors in diagnosing diseases and injuries. Doctors normally give only brief instructions: the radiographer is expected to know exactly how to use the X-ray apparatus, to understand the theory behind X-ray photography, and how best to photograph the relevant part of the patient's body. She therefore needs a considerable knowledge of anatomy, physiology and physics.

Normally she works in X-ray departments, but occasionally she takes X-rays during an operation, when it is particularly important to take quick, accurate pictures. She also works on the wards using mobile equipment. Unlike ordinary photographers, radiographers cannot rely on opportunities to 're-take'.

The diagnostic radiographer normally sees each patient only once or twice and will meet a large number of people on a rather fleeting basis.

2. THERAPEUTIC RADIOGRAPHER

She gives treatment by means of X-ray, radium and radioactive isotopes under the direction of a medically qualified radiotherapist. The latest advances of science are used to help cure disease, and the work involves using new and powerful substances and methods.

Treatment is often given to sick and worried patients, possibly over a long period of time. The therapeutic radiographer's duties are therefore twofold: firstly the actual treatment, and secondly establishing a friendly relationship with patients to give them confidence. The effect of radiotherapy is permanent: once given, it cannot be undone; the therapeutic radiographer's responsibility is heavy, and she must stick meticulously to the specialist's instructions. She needs extensive knowledge of human anatomy and physiology and of radiation physics.

Exposure to X-rays can be dangerous, but X-ray departments are equipped with safeguards which ensure that operators are not harmed in any way. Protective clothing is worn and operators are never within reach of the actual X-ray beams. The controls are operated from outside the treatment rooms so that the radiographer is never exposed to radiation; treatment rooms are lined with material which the X-rays cannot penetrate.

Prospects Good. There is a shortage of radiographers, especially diagnostic ones. The majority work in hospital. There are a few posts with specialists in private practice; these may be better paid, but the work is lonelier than in hospital. There are also some openings with mobile X-ray units. For both these jobs previous hospital experience is necessary. Radiographers can earn their living in most countries of the world, provided they speak the appropriate language. The College of Radiographers now also runs courses for qualified radiographers who want to work in such new areas as Medical Ultra-Sound and Nuclear Medicine, which are concerned with diagnostic and treatment methods for various diseases.

Pay: Medium (see p. xxiii).

Training 2–3 years full-time, at a training school attached to a hospital, for the College of Radiographers' Diploma, which is essential for employment. The first year is common to both types of radiography and includes physics, hospital practice, anatomy and physiology, some supervised practical work. During the second year diagnostic radiographers concentrate on radiographic photography; therapeutic radiographers on radiotherapy.

Students can take a further 18 months and acquire a dual qualification, but very few students do so.

Personal attributes A strong scientific bent; a steady hand and a sharp observant eye; a genuine liking for people and a desire to help the sick; a confident manner; patience; calmness; firmness and a sense of humour; ability to take responsibility and to work well with others; good health.

Position of women Until recently about 90% of radiographers were women; now there are 25% men. Men have a disproportionate share of top jobs.

Career-break: No problem, but re-training essential – extent depends on length of break (changes in procedures and equipment are drastic and rapid).

Refresher courses: Arranged on *ad hoc* basis, on demand; no organized ones.

Late start: Possible for women whose maths and physics are up to date.

Part-time: At the moment opportunities are limited, but there is no reason why work should not be organized on a part-time basis.

Further information   College of Radiographers, 14 Upper Wimpole Street, London W1M 8BN

Related careers   *Photography – Science Laboratory Technician – Scientist*

RECREATION MANAGEMENT

Managers/Administrators – Instructors

Entry quali- None laid down. In practice, for managers, professional qualification
fications and/or administrative experience; for instructors, P.E. teaching qualification or expertise in a particular sport plus flair for instructing.

The work This is a fairly new career. It has developed piecemeal as more sports
and leisure centres were established. Some local authorities set up
multidisciplinary leisure departments to cover indoor and outdoor
sports, the arts, community and children's play facilities, as well as
municipal entertainments and libraries. Most divide responsibilities
between two or more departments; often sports and leisure centres are
run as separate entities. Altogether there are now about 460 multi-
purpose sports centres. Local government is by far the largest employer
of recreation staff; others include the Sports Council, and company
sports and social clubs and some commercial leisure companies.

1. MANAGERS/ADMINISTRATORS

Job titles vary and can be misleading and do not necessarily indicate
levels of responsibility and scope for work. However, a recreation
department, or a large sports/leisure centre, usually has a director or
manager. Assistant managers are responsible for the operation of
particular amenities, e.g. swimming baths and the events organized in
the baths, all outdoor sports, or perhaps entertainments in the authority's parks. A large sports centre may have two deputy directors, one in
charge of organizing activities and the other in charge of administration
and finance. At the next level, assistant managers are responsible for
certain areas of the work, such as bookings (a centre may be used by
10,000 people a week), stores (1,000 pieces of equipment may be loaned
to users in a week), or supervision of the work of assistants and specialist
instructors. Supervisors or recreation assistants look after the day-to-
day running of activities, working in shifts to cope with the long hours
of opening.

The senior manager, whatever her title, is primarily an administrator.
She calls on assistants for specialist advice; for example, before
organizing musical events in the parks, she would consult a musician to

advise her on choice of programme and performers; before setting up judo classes, she would get judo experts' advice. A senior manager must be able to switch her attention instantly from, say, organization of an Easter parade or a miniature golf course to that of a nature trail; from reorganizing the booking system to hygiene and safety of a paddling pool. She must be a good publicist to attract all sections of the public – as one of the main reasons why local authorities spend money on providing leisure facilities is to attract young people who might otherwise, for lack of something better to do, vandalize property or annoy the neighbourhood in some other way with antisocial behaviour.

2. INSTRUCTORS

Some teach gymnastics, swimming and one or two other sports, some specialize in just one, say, judo or badminton. Instructors may work full-time or part-time on a sessional basis; some work part-time in two centres. Some start working as part-time evening instructors while doing another kind of job during the day, hoping to become full-time instructors. Some hire space in a sports centre in which to teach their own students, usually members of a club.

Prospects   Until fairly recently, this was very much a growth area. With rising unemployment the need for more sports and leisure centres is still generally accepted, but public expenditure cuts have affected centre developments. Local authorities vary in the priority they give to recreation facilities; some consider them a luxury, others believe they are essential. So jobs are not evenly distributed throughout the country.
    Instructors' jobs are usually easier to get than managers'.

Training   *Managers*
Entry and training are haphazard. A government committee is due to report on future recruitment and training. At present, posts are usually filled by people from administration in local government, or by physical education teachers or members of the Forces; some trainee posts exist in sports centres and larger recreation departments. It is still possible to switch from a clerical job, but most new entrants are expected to have or gain some kind of qualification. The main courses:

1. *With a degree in any discipline and some relevant experience*:
Either M.Sc. in recreation management, 1-year full-time; *or* Diploma in Arts Administration, usually 1-year full-time or 2 or 3 part-time; *or* Diploma in Management Studies (6 months full-time or a year part-time) with recreation management option.

2. *With 2 A-levels*:

Either B.Sc in Physical Education, Sports Science and Recreation Management, 2 years, or B.A. Combined Studies with relevant option, 3 or 4 years; *or* Diploma of Institute of Recreation Management, 2–3 years' modular course (while in relevant employment).

3. *With 1 A-level or equivalent*:
Either B.E.C. Higher Certificate in Management Studies for Recreation Management (only for those over 21 already employed in recreation); *or* B.E.C. Higher Diploma in Public Administration, with option in recreation studies (very few colleges offer this option).

Several of the professional institutes offer day-release or correspondence courses for people in relevant jobs. Completion of a course does not often lead to a management post straight away. It may be necessary to take a clerical post and be on the spot when a suitable vacancy occurs, or, for example, start as a swimming attendant or other sports centre assistant, or even by doing some unpaid voluntary work for one of the centre's specialist activities.

Instructors
Nothing rigid. Either sports training as above, or proof of proficiency in chosen sports; for example, for swimming instructors lifesaving certificates.

Personal attributes

Management: Good organizing abilities; practicality; ability to make different specialists work as a team; interest in the needs of all sections of the community; confidence in dealing with members of the public (even when they are impatient or boisterous).
Instructors: Teaching ability; enthusiasm; stamina.

Position of women

As there are no traditions, there are no barriers against the promotion of women to be broken down. Many women do well as instructors and as managers.

Career-break: Should be possible, but keen competition for jobs and the fact that it is a young person's field may cause problems.

Part-time: As specialist instructor.

Further information

Institute of Recreation Management, 200 Shorncliffe Road, Folkestone, Kent CT20 3PH
Institute of Baths and Recreation Management, Giffard House, 36/38 Sherrard Street, Melton Mowbray, Leicestershire LE13 1XJ
Association of Recreation Managers, Berry House, 41 High Street, Over, Cambridgeshire CB4 5NB

Recreation Managers' Association of Great Britain, 710b High Road, Finchley, London N12 9QD
Institute of Park and Recreation Administration, Lower Basildon, Reading, RG8 9NE
Individual sports organizations for instructors' work

Related careers   *Teaching – Local government – Horticulture – Museums and Art Galleries – Public Relations*

NOTE: The above organizations are discussing amalgamation and a new training structure.

REMEDIAL GYMNAST

Entry quali-fications
5 O-levels plus 1 A-level, preferably including a science subject. Minimum age for training 17.

The work
All physiotherapists (see p. 353) do some remedial gymnastics during their training, but the remedial gymnast does not train in physiotherapy. The remedial gymnast helps to rehabilitate patients by means of physical exercise. She devises particular exercises which will help restore strength to an individual muscle or group of muscles, or range of movement to an injured joint. Each case has to be treated in a special way. The work is varied and physically very active.

She works with individuals or groups in hospitals, in industrial rehabilitation centres, in the school health service, with spastic children. Much of the treatment of children is disguised as playing games. With adults, fencing or swimming and other forms of physical education are included.

Prospects
Fair; there is a shortage of remedial gymnasts but jobs are not necessarily available where they are wanted.

Pay: Medium (see p. xxiii).

Training
For State Registration, which is essential for most jobs, 3 years, including 2 years full-time at special colleges. The third year is spent in hospitals and is salaried. Syllabus includes anatomy, physiology, physical education, the principles and practice of exercise and recreational therapy, care of the mentally disabled. See note to **Training**, Occupational Therapy (p. 323).

Personal attributes
Great interest in sport and games; organizing ability; a liking for people of all types and the ability to win their confidence; very good health; a wish to help the sick and injured.

Position of women
This used to be an all-male profession; the ratio now is about 8 men to 1 woman.

Career-break: Return easy up to about 35. Some in-service *refresher training*.

Late start: Upper age limit 35. Physical education teachers and Services physical training instructors take a 24 months' course.

Part-time: Some opportunities.

Further information   College of Remedial Gymnastics and Recreational Therapy, Pinderfields General Hospital, Wakefield, Yorkshire
Society of Remedial Gymnasts, General Hospital, Northampton

Related careers   *Physiotherapy – Teaching (Physical Education, p. 492)*

RETAIL DISTRIBUTION

Buying – merchandising – staff management – store management

Entry quali- Nothing rigid; opportunities at all educational levels; considerable
fications *graduate* entry.

The work Retail distribution is one of the largest industries in the country. Career
opportunities at all educational levels are immensely varied. Retail is
also one of the very few fields in which progress to the top does not
depend entirely on passing examinations. However, the higher the entry
qualifications, the higher up the training and job ladder one can 'slot in'.
(See **Training**, p. 397.) The best opportunities are in department stores,
chains of shops or stores and in supermarkets. There are three main
types of organization, but each with many variations:
1. Buyers are given a sum of money to buy for the department which
they also manage.
2. A central buying department does the buying, often called 'selecting';
store managers work closely with central buyers and have a say in what
they sell – each store within an organization has a distinct character.
This applies mainly to firms owning several department stores.
3. Buying departments allocate merchandise to store, shop or department managers. This applies mainly to chains of stores and shops.
   Buying, selling, personnel and store management are the main retail
functions. *All* retail careers start with selling (see **Training**).
   A *buyer* bases her purchasing policy not just on flair and on what she
likes but on a methodical analysis and interpretation of past sales
records, on information supplied to her (or researched by her) about
possible changes in the composition of the buying public (for example
a new housing estate might mean more buyers in a certain income
group), and on economic forecasts. Only when she has these facts at her
fingertips does a buyer start the actual searching for merchandise, the
buying and using her flair.
   Buying itself involves choosing from wholesalers' or manufacturers'
ranges and prototypes at home and abroad. It also involves suggesting
to manufacturers how to modify certain lines; in some cases buyers –
especially those buying vast quantities for hundreds of retail 'outlets' –
may, jointly with the manufacturer and designer, work out new lines.
   In the past, 'commodity' knowledge (specific knowledge about one
type of merchandise – textiles, household goods, etc.) was a buyer's
most important asset and she would stick to her 'line' throughout her

career. Now managerial skills are much more important. A good buyer may now move up the career ladder within her firm, first to buying something on which more money is spent, and then into administration or into *merchandising* – which means ensuring that the right merchandise is at the right point of sale in the right quantities at the right time. This work involves thorough knowledge of the structure of retail distribution and business generally.

Many who go into retail because they hope to buy, enjoy the constant customer contact and stay in selling, which, at senior level, becomes store management. A good sales assistant soon gets her own 'section' (probably a few counters), then a small department, then a bigger one and finally her own shop or store. Responsibility at departmental and store management level includes working out yields per £ per foot of floor space; analysing last week's sales figures and changing goods displayed accordingly; re-allocating staff to different counters and sections where necessary.

Personnel or staff work in retail differs from other personnel management: management of sales staff means establishing and maintaining both good customer–staff relationship as well as good staff–management relationship. Reconciling the two requires skill and understanding in dealing with human relationships and behaviour as well as knowledge of retail organization principles and methods. The personnel department works closely with financial administration in working out how many staff at what salary a department can afford, and it is also usually responsible for staff training. Future personnel managers often start as staff trainers. Staff training, with mock-up sales departments, and including discussion of the psychology of shopping as well as the organization of retailing, is an expanding and varied field. All retail work means working very long hours.

Prospects   Good for those with at least 4 O-levels. Buying, store management, merchandising and personnel work may lead to general management (see p. 259). Retail experience can also lead to a job as sales representative (see p. 270).

Pay: Medium to very high (see p. xxiii).

Training   Recruitment and training systems vary according to type, size and policy of firm, but generally firms which offer good training schemes and prospects recruit trainees with 4 O-levels who then take B.E.C. Certificates (see p. xvii) by day-release. However, not all firms do have systematic training schemes, with day-release facilities. Those who want to get on should choose a firm which does take training seriously, as operation and management of retail outlets, whether super- or hypermarket, chain of small shops, department store or boutique, requires sophisticated knowledge of techniques, principles, methods.

Another point worth remembering when choosing a firm: it is easier to switch to a good job in a chain-store organization with a department-store training than the other way around. Chain-stores and supermarkets tend each to be organized in a specific way and to train staff to work according to their system; department-store training is usually more broadly based.

Usual organization of firms' training schemes:

With fewer than 3 O-levels: people enter as juniors, and are given some general, short 'in-service' training.

With at least 3 (in some firms 4 or even 5) O-levels, including English language and maths: people enter as junior trainees (titles given to entrants at the various levels vary) and are given what is often called 'circuit', or 'job rotation' training. This means experience in a number of selling and most behind-the-scenes departments, from dispatch to personnel and accounts. This experience gives them an understanding of store organization and helps them decide which department they want to work in.

Graduates and sometimes those with 2 A-levels: enter as 'management trainees'. They also get circuit training but it is shorter.

Each of the 3 levels of training schemes lasts between 12 and 24 months.

There are 'bridges' from one scheme to another, so that a 16-year-old entrant who shows aptitude may at 20 join a 21-year-old graduate on a management training scheme (and on appropriate Certificate courses), and then both girls' chances of getting to the top are absolutely even.

Full-time pre-entry training:

For entrants with at least 4 O-levels including English language and mathematics, or with B.E.C. General award (see p. xvii): 2-year B.E.C. National Diploma (Distribution).

For entrants with at least 1 A-level and 3 O-levels, or B.E.C. National award: B.E.C. Higher National Diploma (Distribution). B.E.C. Distribution courses cover general subjects such as accounting, communication skills, role of distribution in society, and usually a range of optional subjects. These may include introduction to marketing, consumer legislation, food retailing, merchandise display, buying, mail order, etc. Not all colleges offer all options. National Diploma students normally choose two options; Higher National Diploma students choose up to six.

For entrants with 2 A-levels and 3 O-levels: 4-year sandwich degree in Business Studies with Distribution/Retailing specialization.

See also *Fashion Merchandising* at the College for the Distributive Trades (Fashion, p. 198).

Personal attributes

Numeracy; an interest in both people and things – an important combination; objectivity, to be able to judge the relevance of one's own taste and gauge that of customers; flair for forecasting trends; good business sense; good memory; ability to train staff and delegate responsibility; an easy manner with every kind of person. But as there are so many kinds and levels of jobs, entrants with only one or two of these qualities should find suitable jobs.

Position of women

Considering that the vast majority of sales assistants are women, *very* few are in senior management. But, very slowly, women's opportunities are improving, and they are moving into all areas including store management. There are still very few in supermarket management; the reason given is that during training managers may have to hump heavy loads. However, with mechanical loading and unloading, there is very little work which is too hard for any but the most delicate.

To rise in any retail hierarchy, mobility is essential: experience of customers' buying habits in various areas of the country is essential, and it seems that women far more often than men refuse to move to broaden their experience. So women have to be more highly motivated than men to get equally far.

Career-break: Many companies encourage returners and provide *refresher* training.

Late start: Some companies positively welcome women of up to about 35 for management training, provided they are mobile. Previous work experience of some kind is an advantage.

Part-time: Plenty of opportunities as sales assistant, none at store management level. A few experienced merchandising and staff training specialists have shown that part-time or rather sporadic project work is possible. But it is very much up to the enterprising individual to create her own part-time opportunities.

Further information

Distributive Industry Training Board, MacLaren House, Talbot Road, Stretford, Manchester M32 0FP
Retail Distributors Association Inc., Palladium House, Argyll Street, London W1V 2LH
College for the Distributive Trades, 30 Leicester Square, London WC2

Related careers

Hotel Work, p. 103 – *Management in Industry – Personnel Work*

SCIENCE

Professional scientist – science laboratory technician – food science and technology – forensic scientist – medical laboratory scientist/technician

Professional Scientist

Research and Development – Analysis and Investigation – Production – Technical Sales and Service – Technical Writing.
Main branches: physics – cybernetics – mathematical sciences – chemistry – biological sciences – applied sciences – environmental sciences – forensic science – food science and technology.

Entry qualifications

Professional scientists normally need a degree, but the borderline between scientist and senior technician – T.E.C. Higher award holder (see p. xv) – is often blurred.

Precise degree course requirements vary from one course to another (consult C.R.A.C. *Degree Course Guides*). In general:

For *physics, cybernetics and applied sciences* degrees, A-levels must include physics and mathematics.

For some *mathematics* degrees, A-levels must include pure and applied maths.

For *chemistry* degrees, chemistry and physics and/or mathematics A-levels are preferred, but other combinations may be acceptable.

For *biological sciences*, biology, a physical science and mathematics are ideal; other combinations may be acceptable.

For *some* science degrees biology may only be accepted as a third A-level: if only 2 A-levels are offered they must both be in sciences more relevant to the degree subject.

In general – though there are exceptions – polytechnic and other non-university degree courses are more likely than universities to accept applicants with only 2 A-levels.

For T.E.C. Higher award (see p. xv) courses, one A-level and another subject studied at A-level. The A-levels do not necessarily have to be in a science, as long as the applicant has good science O-levels. But in the most popular careers, A-level science is needed. (See *Science Technician*, p. 413, for most careers for T.E.C. Higher award holders.)

The work   Scientists work in a vast variety of settings: in industry, the Civil Service, local government, museums and (rarely) art galleries, education, the health service. The nature of their work ranges from laboratory-centred 'boffin' research to 'people-centred' activities like teaching and technical sales (see below), 'profit-centred' work like industrial management, or 'people-and-technology-centred' work, like production (see pp. 166 and 402).

Work is usually divided into several types of activity, departments or 'functions' (this does *not* apply to Environmental Science):

1. RESEARCH AND DEVELOPMENT

Research is the lifeblood of science, enlarging existing knowledge and stimulating the growth of new branches. *Development* translates research findings into new – or improved – products and processes. The two overlap.

'*Pure*' research – increasing knowledge for its own sake – is carried out mainly in universities and research council laboratories. '*Applied*' or 'goal-oriented' research is done largely in industry, research council establishments and the Civil Service Science Group. But pure and applied research often overlap.

Most research is teamwork, with several scientists, often from several disciplines, and technicians, working under a team-leader. The work may be divided into projects; several scientists are then responsible for their own project within the overall framework.

Personal   Above-average intelligence; willingness to work patiently for long hours
attributes   (or even months) and persevere with tricky problems; creativity; ability to work in a team and to take decisions and stand up for them if things go wrong; ability to communicate findings effectively; great powers of concentration; stubborn persistence in the face of disappointing research results. Industrial researchers must be willing to change direction – at however interesting a point in their research – in the interests of the company's profitability.

2. ANALYSIS AND INVESTIGATION

Routine tests and investigations are carried out in all fields of science. In chemical *research*, for example, analysis of intermediate compounds enables scientists to keep track of chemical changes that are taking place. In manufacturing industry, the composition of both raw materials and products is monitored by analysing samples in *quality control* laboratories. In the food industry, regular checks are made on biological and chemical purity of foodstuffs. In pharmaceuticals the safety of drugs, beauty preparations and food additives is investigated. Before such products can be marketed, substances are tried out on experimental animals to see whether there are any toxic side effects. In the agrochemical industry, new fertilizers and pesticides are given field trials; the chemicals are used on experimental plots in various parts of the country – and sometimes overseas – so that scientists can determine how performance is affected by different soils and climates.

Many analytical techniques are automated; most routine testing is carried out by technicians (see p. 413). The professional scientist trains and supervises technicians, and initiates, organizes and oversees projects and researches into new experimental methods.

Personal attributes   Interest in applied science; methodical approach; patience; ability to organize other people and their work; ability to communicate effectively with highly specialized colleagues and with trainee technicians.

3. PRODUCTION (see also Engineering, p. 166)

The central activity in the manufacturing industry is supervising the people who operate the industrial plant. The production supervisor (titles vary) is a vital link in the chain of command from chargehand to production director, and between production and other departments. Her main function is to see that production runs smoothly. She spends much of her time on the factory floor. It may be noisy and dirty there, but not necessarily so: many factories are clean, quiet and airy, and working conditions can be pleasanter than those in many offices. Hours can be long and irregular, and they may include some shift-work – but this is by no means so in all plants. Production supervisors usually have a small office, but they spend little time in it. The work involves daily contact with other professionals and managers from other departments as well as with shop stewards, etc.

Personal attributes   Willingness to accept responsibility and take decisions; ability to keep calm in a crisis; leadership skills to motivate and organize plant operatives; practicality; ability to get on well with people at all levels in the industrial hierarchy; interest in the commercial application of science.

4. TECHNICAL SALES AND SERVICE

Two closely related activities: selling a science-based product and providing a technical back-up service for the customer. The product might be a sophisticated scientific instrument, an industrial chemical, a drug or a pesticide. The customer could be a research scientist, an industrial manager of a tiny or a large concern, a pharmacist or a farmer, i.e. a person with a lot of or no scientific knowledge. The technical saleswoman or 'rep' needs a thorough knowledge of the product, its uses and limitations. The kind of technical service a company provides depends on the nature of its products. A technical service scientist representing a plastics manufacturer deals mainly with customers who mould plastics into containers. She would investigate complaints and answer technical queries (and perhaps suggest new ways of using the material). She acts as a link between the research laboratories and the sales staff.

A representative for a pharmaceutical firm visits doctors and pharmacists and informs them about new drugs. She also provides feedback to her company on doctors' opinions of its products. In agricultural service industries reps may sell fertilizers, pesticides, animal health products to farmers and give advice about how they should be used (see Agriculture, p. 26).

Representatives are usually given a 'territory'; its size depends on what they sell and whether a country area or town: some reps may be away from home all week; others come home every night. Many work from home and only go to the office occasionally.

Personal attributes Outgoing personality; liking for meeting a succession of people; a thick skin for the occasional rude customer; sensitivity to gauge the right approach (long-winded, brief, aloof, friendly, etc.); ability to communicate facts effectively to customers who may be much more, and may be much less, knowledgeable than the rep herself; self-sufficiency for possibly long hours of lone travelling.

5. TECHNICAL WRITING

A technical writer assembles a package of scientific or technical information for a particular readership. The work is often done on a contract basis; specialist firms hire out technical writers to client companies for the duration of a particular writing project. This may concern, for example, a set of handbooks and instruction manuals to accompany a complex piece of electronic equipment which is being marketed by an electronics manufacturer. Two 'packages' may have to be written: one in simple language for operatives or chargehands who have only to know how to operate the equipment; and another package aimed at technical managers who want to know more technical details and may need to be able to repair or adjust the equipment. In the pharmaceutical industry, writers prepare 'case histories' of new drugs (experiments done, etc.) for submission to the Committee on Safety of Medicines.

Technical copywriters (see Advertising, p. 17) may write promotional material for science-based products. This is an expanding field, particularly in electronics, engineering generally and pharmaceuticals.

Personal attributes   Wide scientific/technological interests and knowledge; an inquiring mind; ability to search out information and sift the relevant – for the particular purpose – from the irrelevant; ability to explain complex matters lucidly and concisely; a scientific grasshopper mind, to switch from one type of subject to another; liking for desk work.

The Main Branches of Science

1. PHYSICS

Physics – the study of matter and energy – lies at the heart of science. It is closely related to chemistry; *chemical physics* – the study of materials and molecules – is a subject in its own right. *Biophysics* – the physical properties of living matter – has assumed greater importance as biological knowledge has grown. *Engineering* and *materials science* are 'applied' aspects of physics. So the physicist, who always has a sound mathematical background, has a wide choice of occupations and settings in which to work.

Most industrial openings occur in engineering and related industries – especially in electronics, telecommunications and computing; other opportunities exist in chemical and allied industries, oil industry, public utilities (gas, electricity, Post Office). In the Civil Service physicists work on problems ranging from design of naval ships to recycling industrial waste. (See also *Biomedical Engineering*, p. 170.)

The *medical physicist*, one of a team of specialists concerned with the diagnosis and treatment of disease, uses radiotherapy and diagnostic radiology, radioactive isotopes, electronic devices and many other physical methods to help doctors cure patients. In *occupational hygiene*, physicists help prevent damage to people's health by monitoring potential hazards from radiation, dust and other sources in working environments. (See also Environmental Sciences, especially *geophysics* and *meteorology*.) There are very limited opportunities for physicists (and for mathematicians) to branch out into *astronomy*. Research into such aspects of astronomy as satellite communications systems or the structure of the universe is done at government, university, and some commercial telecommunications (i.e. electronics) research laboratories. In *computer* design and manufacture, physicists play an important part.

2. CYBERNETICS

The original definition of cybernetics as 'control and communication in the animal and the machine' now extends to activities as different as landing a man on the moon, and using 'natural enemies' to kill pests. In a cybernetic system – such as a thermostat keeping a room at constant temperature – one thing controls another which reacts on the first to form a feedback loop. Since feedback processes operate in man-made control systems as well as in economics and biological systems, the term cybernetics is interpreted differently by people in different scientific spheres.

Cybernetics courses with a strong technological slant – containing such topics as feedback control theory and computer technology and application – are particularly suitable for a career in computer-based automatic systems (those used in navigation and air traffic control, for instance). Courses with a strong theoretical element – including the mathematical theory of cybernetics, artificial intelligence, biological and human cybernetics, for example – could lead to a career in computer design, systems analysis, operational research or planning.

The cybernetic aspects of industry – such as computer technology and applications – are expanding enormously.

3. MATHEMATICAL SCIENCES

Mathematicians – pure and applied – are much in demand. They work in commerce – in finance and in actuarial work (see Actuary, p. 15) for example – in science-based activities and in computers (see p. 134).

In the manufacturing industry and in the Civil Service they may work on translating problems into mathematical terms (making 'models'), working out solutions and then expressing the results in non-mathematical form. Sometimes the mathematical models are so complex that a special technique called *numerical analysis* is used to solve them. Some mathematicians specialize in numerical analysis; others become expert in operational research (see p. 325).

Statisticians – including mathematicians who have specialized in statistics – work in industry, in medical and agricultural research, and in the Civil Service, on the design and analysis of experiments. In market research statisticians establish the demand for goods and services by collecting, analysing and interpreting information.

4. CHEMISTRY

Chemistry – the study of the composition of substances and their effects on one another – forms the basis of, for example, the manufacture of general chemicals, pharmaceuticals, foodstuffs, paints, textiles, detergents, petrochemicals, plastics, agrochemicals, paper, cosmetics and many other products. Openings also occur in other manufacturing industries, public utilities, Atomic Energy Authority, etc.

Chemists in the Civil Service Science Group and in research councils are concerned mainly with new materials for roads; building; food preservation; pollution studies; forensic science (see p. 419), agricultural and medical research. A few chemists work in museums and art galleries as picture restorers.

5. BIOLOGICAL SCIENCES

Biology can be subdivided into 4 major disciplines – the study of: plants (*botany*); animals (*zoology*); micro-organisms (*microbiology*); chemistry of living matter (*biochemistry*). More specialized biological sciences deal with particular groups of living organisms – viruses (*virology*) and insects (*entomology*) for instance, and with particular biological processes such as the functioning of the body's organs (*physiology*) or the mechanisms of heredity and variation (*genetics*).

(a) Botany and Zoology

Most opportunities occur in the public sector – mainly in the Civil Service Science Group, agricultural and medical research, and in conservation. A small number of biologists work in the health service, for water authorities and museums. In industry there are limited opportunities in pharmaceuticals and agrochemicals.

The most marketable aspects of botany and zoology are those related either to medical and pharmaceutical research (such as parasitology and physiology), or to agriculture and horticulture (such as plant pathology and entomology). Opportunities in *marine and freshwater biology* and *general ecology* are very limited.

(b) Biochemistry and Microbiology

Biochemists and microbiologists have much better career prospects than botanists or zoologists; there is a steady demand from industry (mainly food and pharmaceuticals), from medical research, the Health Service, specialist research organizations and, to a lesser extent, agricultural research and the Civil Service Science Group.

A *biochemist* working for a pharmaceutical company might study the action of a new drug on experimental animals or (helped by a microbiologist) investigate biochemical aspects of the production of antibiotics by fermentation. *Hospital biochemists* work alongside medical colleagues and technicians as members of a team; they supervise routine biochemical testing (see Medical Laboratory Science, p. 420), do research, and may also teach clinical biochemistry to doctors and nurses.

Microbiologists often specialize in bacteriology and virology and become experts in plant or animal diseases. In the food industry and in environmental health laboratories they check samples for pathogenic microbes and investigate spoilage. In oil companies they explore ways of producing synthetic protein by feeding bacteria with the by-products of petroleum refining.

(c) *Biotechnology*

Biotechnology, or industrial biology, is the application of biological principles to industrial and environmental problems. Biotechnologists investigate and try to counteract the harmful effects of man-made products and processes on the natural environment; for example some pesticides, apart from doing the job for which they were created, have proved harmful to other creatures.

There are several aspects of biotechnology. Bio-deterioration, for example, is concerned with the deterioration of foodstuffs, building materials, and some synthetics, which is caused by organisms affecting these substances. Environmental biotechnology investigates and controls, for example, the pollution of water by lead pipes and of the atmosphere from lead in car exhaust fumes.

Biotechnologists also play an important part in the production of foodstuffs of which the world is running short; for example, they are working on the production of 'single cell proteins' – a much less wasteful source of protein than existing ones.

This is a specialization for biologists who are interested in working in industry rather than in pure research.

6. APPLIED SCIENCES

'Applied Sciences' covers *metallurgy, materials science* and specialist subjects such as *paper, textile, rubber, plastics technologies*. Materials science is a relatively new subject which includes elements of *metallurgy* but deals also with polymeric materials (plastics and man-made fibres), and other composite materials, together with ceramics, glass and natural fibres.

For metallurgists and materials scientists most opportunities occur in engineering and allied industries, mainly metal manufacturing and electronics. Plastics, textiles, paper and rubber industries have traditionally recruited graduates in physics, chemistry and engineering and specialists in the various specific technologies. But there are now good opportunities for materials scientists to use their interdisciplinary approach in these industries, as well as in the newer ones concerned with composite materials: polymers reinforced with glass or carbon fibre, for example, and others still in the experimental stage. Materials science leads to a wider choice of job than paper, rubber, plastics and other technology specialization.

Applied scientists, whether one-technology specialist or materials scientist, are in short supply.

7. THE ENVIRONMENTAL SCIENCES

The environmental sciences are fashionable. Concern with pollution, dwindling natural resources and threatened plant and animal species has given a fresh impetus to the scientific study of the environment. *Conservation* and *ecology* (the study of how plants and animals interact with their natural surroundings), together with *meteorology, oceanography, geology* and *geophysics*, are important environmental subjects.

Environmental science is often (and best) a *post*-graduate specialization: scientists take a first degree in a traditional subject and then either graft on an appropriate post-graduate course or get trained by employers in environmental aspects of their subject. *Meteorologists* and *physical oceanographers* usually have degrees in physics or mathematics; biologists normally specialize in ecology before becoming conservationists. *Geology* graduates are the exception: they can go straight into geological work without further training. *Geophysicists* usually build their specialist knowledge on a foundation of physics, geology or engineering. But there is an increasing number of first degree courses in environmental subjects – either joint honours (such as physics and meteorology) or broad-based integrated courses in *environmental sciences*.

(a) Geology and Geophysics

Geology is the study of the structure and history of the earth; *geophysics* is concerned with its physical properties and, in particular, with the application of physical techniques to solve geological problems. Geologists locate, and then extract, oil, natural gas, minerals, useful rocks and underground water in the earth's crust. The first stage of exploration often entails making a geological map of a region and then following this up with an aerial survey to provide greater detail of the terrain.

Geophysical techniques are widely used in geological exploration. In *seismic surveying*, for example, shock waves from a small underground explosion set off by geophysicists bounce off the rock layers and are recorded by instruments. By analysing the data with a computer, geophysicists can unravel the underlying geological structure.

Geologists and geophysicists are employed by oil companies, the mining industry, the Institute of Geological Sciences (part of the

Natural Environment Research Council – N.E.R.C.), by specialist contractors and consultants, and the Civil Service Science Group. Geologists also work for civil engineers who construct dams, reservoirs, roads, etc.; for the Nature Conservancy Council; and, a few, for museums.

Field geologists often work in remote parts of the world, under difficult conditions.

(b) Meteorology and Oceanography (see also Meteorology, p. 285)

Meteorology and oceanography – concerned with the atmosphere and the oceans – are closely related. The physics and dynamics of atmospheric and oceanographic processes have much in common; the oceans exert a powerful influence on the weather. At honours degree level, *meteorology* and *physical oceanography* are highly mathematical; numerical methods are widely used in modern weather forecasting.

The Meteorological Office also carries out research into such topics as the physics of cloud formation and energy exchange between atmosphere and oceans. Scientists are usually involved either in *forecasting* or in *research*.

Research in *physical oceanography* is undertaken at the Institute of Oceanographic Sciences (part of the Natural Environment Research Council – N.E.R.C.). Topics include studies of waves, tides, currents and general circulation of ocean water. N.E.R.C. also investigates the ecology of deep-water organisms, the composition of the sea-floor, *marine biology* subjects. *Oceanographic* work is done partly in the laboratory and partly at sea.

(c) Conservation

Nature conservation used to mean protecting unusual plants and animals and their habitats. Now, many human activities have an environmental impact. Crop protection chemicals, for example, can upset the balance of ecological systems. If herbicides are used to control aquatic weeds, dead plants consume oxygen while decaying. As a result, fish and other organisms may die through lack of oxygen. A pipeline laid across country may disturb plant and animal life around it; an opencast mine may leave a permanent scar on the countryside. Modern conservationists, recognizing the importance of protecting flora and fauna, are concerned with the wider problems of preserving the countryside as a whole.

The *Nature Conservancy Council* is responsible for conserving the wildlife and physiographical features of Great Britain. The Council manages over 100 National Nature Reserves and several thousand Sites of Special Scientific Interest, and advises farmers, landowners, local authorities, industrialists and others on conservation matters. Scientists (mainly botanists, zoologists, geologists and geographers) are employed as Assistant Regional Officers. The Nature Reserves are run by Wardens (often non-graduates) who are experienced conservationists. Research is carried out by the Institute of Terrestrial Ecology under the aegis of the Natural Environment Research Council.

See also Computer Scientist (p. 134).

Prospects generally

These vary considerably from one branch to another and they may change from one year to the next. Physicists are in greatest demand (mainly in the expanding electronics industry, see p. 165), but mathematicians, cyberneticians and some applied scientists are also in great demand, followed by chemists, biochemists and microbiologists. Botanists, zoologists and environmental science graduates are least in demand. However, scientists can often switch to another, related field.

The question whether a broad-based or a specialized degree leads to better prospects is impossible to answer in a general way: it depends on an individual's adaptability, motivation, specialization, on changing economic circumstances and on technological developments.

Prospects in the various types of work or *functions* vary mainly according to economic climate. In research and development, cutbacks tend to bite much earlier than in production and analysis and investigation. Technical writing and technical sales are expanding functions. However, scientists only specialize in a subject *after* graduation. (But some degree subjects are more likely to lead to one function, some to another: for example *applied* scientists are much more likely to be in demand in production than, for example, botanists, and a broad-based integrated course is not likely to lead to research.)

Scientists often start in laboratory work (*research and development; analysis; investigation*) and then move into *production, technical sales and service,* or *writing*; or they may use their science background in *marketing* (see p. 270); in *information work* (p. 246) or in *patent agency* (p. 335) or *operational research* (p. 325). Physics and mathematics *teachers* are much in demand: prospects for other science teachers are reasonable (in schools: higher education teaching prospects are bleak).

A science degree is not necessarily a vocational qualification, though it is so often believed to be just that. It is a way into all kinds of 'graduate jobs' – in industry, commerce, the Civil Service. Most employers of graduates welcome science graduates and arts graduates alike (except of course for specific professions); many even now prefer graduates with a scientific/technological background, because their special knowledge *might* be useful in management, and in explaining scientific facts and developments to their scientifically illiterate colleagues: and in any case, science graduates' minds are as trained as arts graduates' – and it is very often the 'trained mind' which employers want when they employ graduates.

Career prospects are generally much better for graduates who have at least a reading knowledge of a foreign language (at the moment especially German or Russian). Anyone who wants to work in E.E.C. countries must be fluent in the relevant language and/or have specific experience. Short-term contracts possible in developing countries.

Pay: Medium to high (see p. xxiii).

Training

Normally a university or C.N.A.A. degree. Science courses consist either of a detailed study of a single subject, with supporting ancillary subjects, or of a study of two distinct disciplines in a joint honours course, or of a cluster of several related disciplines, such as biological sciences. There is a continuing need for specialists, but a 'generalist' scientific education possibly leads to a wider choice of jobs (though it may have to be topped up with post-graduate study); its built-in flexibility enables the scientist to change direction if, for example, that should be desirable or necessary after a career-break, or because supply and demand in a specialization have changed.

For *research* a first or upper second honours degree is required.

Most C.N.A.A. degrees are 4-year sandwich courses, with a year spent at work. This may be an advantage to people who want to go into industry: their experience of the work situation during their training reassures employers that the applicant at least knows what a working environment is like.

T.E.C. Higher awards (see p. xv) or Dip. H.E.s may occasionally lead to good jobs, but normally these qualifications lead to senior technicians', not to professional scientists' jobs. The distinction between scientist and technician is often blurred.

However, T.E.C. Higher award students may complete their professional training by taking a further 1-year full-time or 2-year part-time (day-release) training for the Graduate Membership of the Royal Institute of Chemistry's examination, which is of graduate standard. There are several equivalent professional Institutes and examinations in other branches of science.

Once in a job, training, or at least learning, continues. This may or may not lead to a further qualification.

Position of women

The number of women scientists remains relatively small; the proportion of women taking science degrees is rising more slowly than the proportion taking science O- and A-levels (and *that* is rising slowly). A far greater proportion of women than of men with 3 science A-levels is trying to get into medicine – the most competitive of all disciplines –

than into other science-based degree courses. Industry would welcome more women scientists in research, as well as in technical sales, marketing, production (see pp. 166, 142). In 1979 about 13% of students starting physics courses and just over a third starting chemistry courses were women. Almost equal numbers of men and women students (i.e. a larger *proportion* of women) are taking botany degrees for which there is very little demand on the job market. In choosing their science-based degree courses, women do not seem to plan ahead as realistically as men do.

Career break: Return only possible if one has kept up with developments, and even then some areas, such as research and development, would probably be difficult to get back to. But it is possible to use a science degree to switch to technical writing or information work (see p. 246) or teaching (science teachers are still in demand).

Late start: Degree course requirements in terms of O-levels and A-levels may be relaxed, but candidates' knowledge of maths and science has to be up-to-date; many late entrants first take evening classes, to freshen up their school sciences, etc.

Part-time: Not many opportunities at the moment, except in technical writing (and then it is spasmodic rather than part-time) and in physics and mathematics teaching (see p. 485).

Further information   Biochemical Society, 7 Warwick Court, Holborn, London WC1R 5DP
Royal Society of Chemistry, 30 Russell Square, London WC1B 5DT
Institute of Biology, 41 Queens Gate, London SW7
Institute of Mathematics and its Applications, Maitland House, Warrior Square, Southend-on-Sea, Essex SS1 2JY
Institute of Physics, 47 Belgrave Square, London SW1X 8PY
Institute of Cybernetics, Kingston Lane, Uxbridge, Middlesex
Association for the Promotion of an Institution of Professional Geologists, Department of Geology, Imperial College, London SW7 2BP
Civil Service Commission, Alencon Link, Basingstoke, Hants RG21 1JB
Nature Conservancy Council, 19–20 Belgrave Square, London SW1X 8PY
Natural Environment Research Council, Alhambra House, 27–33 Charing Cross Road, London WC2H 0AX

Science Technician

**Entry quali-
fications**

Nothing rigid. They vary according to the job to be done and to colleges'
requirements; from a mere interest in science and basic numeracy to 1
science A-level and another one studied at A-level and 4 O-levels
including another science, mathematics and English language. (The
Civil Service requires 4 O-levels including a science, mathematics and
English language.) For Technician Education Council (T.E.C.) awards
(see p. xv) the minimum entry qualifications are theoretically 3 C.S.E.
Grade 3 in appropriate subjects. Many colleges, and employers, believe
that students need higher qualifications to be able to cope with
technician jobs and courses (see **Training** for people with lower
qualifications).

The work

Laboratory technician, assistant, technical assistant, research assistant,
scientific assistant, technical officer, assistant scientific officer are all
titles used to describe people who perform science-related procedures
and techniques under the overall supervision of scientists. As scientific
investigations become more complex laboratory technicians become
more important. They are essential team-members rather than unskilled
bottle-washers. Their tasks range from mundane routine to new work
which overlaps with that of professional scientists (see Science, p. 400).

There are 5 main settings: *industry*; *higher education*; *schools*; *Civil
Service*; *hospitals*. *Animal technicians* may work in all of these settings.

INDUSTRY

Very varied work falls into two broad categories: *quality control*, and
research and development.

In *quality control*, of production of chemicals, detergents, plastics,
cosmetics and other manufactured goods and in the food processing
industry, the technician tests, for example, the purity and/or nutritional
value of foodstuffs. In the pharmaceutical industry she helps with tests
on drugs and medicines. In electronics, technicians may test computer
circuitry or the quality of television and radio components (their work
overlaps with that of *Engineering Technicians*, see p. 175).

In *research and development* technicians assist scientists with all types
of research (see Scientist, p. 401). They may use new equipment and
help modify it and they adapt standard procedures to suit particular
experimental work.

HIGHER EDUCATION ESTABLISHMENTS

Technicians work in science faculties, in research institutes and medical schools. They prepare work for lectures; and they help with research.

Technicians may prepare specimens for lectures in microbiology, histology, zoology, botany or geology, using for example techniques for culturing bacteria, or prepare thin sections of rocks or fossils for microscopical study, etc. In a chemistry faculty the technician is concerned with the assembly, care and maintenance of apparatus, and the preparation of bench reagents used for demonstration and experiment. She may, in research, use such techniques as flame photometry, spectro-photometry, chromatography, or use radio-isotopes.

SCHOOLS, SIXTH FORM AND TERTIARY COLLEGES, COLLEGES OF FURTHER EDUCATION

Technicians help teachers and lecturers. This used to be rather a menial job but conditions and prospects have now improved considerably. The work combines science with dealing with children and young people; it covers preparing, setting out and maintaining demonstration materials and apparatus as well as helping students and pupils in the classroom.

In smaller establishments there may only be one technician; in one day the technician could then help in and prepare for classes in physics, chemistry and biology. In large establishments several technicians work under the direction of a chief technician, and there are opportunities for progress, with training, to a more senior post, and to specialize in either biology, chemistry, or physics.

SCIENCE GROUP OF THE CIVIL SERVICE

Technicians are called Assistant Scientific Officers. They are part of a team led by a scientist engaged in research in any of the scientific disciplines.

Large museums and research councils also employ laboratory technicians.

HOSPITALS

Apart from medical laboratory scientists (see p. 420) there are technician jobs which involve regular day-to-day contact with patients.

Technicians work with a large range of apparatus, used for physiological measurement in anaesthesia, audiometry, cardiology, electromyography, electroencephalography (brain investigation), heart lung machine operations in surgery, intensive care monitoring, radiation protection and isotope and nuclear physics. They work under the supervision of medical staff, but they have considerable individual responsibility. Physiological measurement technicians often work with patients under varying degrees of stress; the work can occasionally be harrowing.

Radiation protection is an important branch of *medical physics*. Technicians' exposure to radiation is kept to a minimum. Regular monitoring using detector systems ensures that any increase in radiation level is noted, its cause investigated and action taken.

The application of electronics (see pp. 168–70) to medicine is another specialist field. Technicians are responsible for design, development and construction of a wide range of electronic apparatus. They also check and re-calibrate electronic measuring and counting equipment and assist with research.

In *audiometry* – measuring hearing loss – they work with children as well as adults. Technicians also fit hearing aids.

ANIMAL TECHNICIANS

They work in all the settings, but particularly in pharmaceutical research. In 'animal units' they are concerned with breeding, husbandry, and housing of laboratory animals and with associated research. Animal technicians must be fond of animals and have an aptitude for handling them but they must not be sentimental about their charges: the animals are well looked after, but the reason for their being in the lab is for experiments to be carried out with or on them – so some are inevitably going to die unpleasantly.

Prospects – technicians generally
Very good. Technicians can usually switch from one setting to another – though their adaptability depends on the degree of initial specialization. On the whole, physiological measurement technicians are the least adaptable. Promotion normally depends on passing examinations. It is possible for technicians to qualify for entry to degree courses; but senior technician jobs do not necessarily require a degree.

There are some possibilities, with experience and qualification and relevant language, to work abroad.

Pay: Medium (see p. xxiii).

Training
Usually on-the-job with day- or block-release for T.E.C. *Science Certificate* (see p. xv). Students take basic sciences and specialist options to fit in with their work – for example in Animal Technology, Medical Physics, Medical Laboratory Practice and Physiological

Measurements; there is a great variety of options. Not all specialist subjects are available at all colleges – it depends largely on local job opportunities. Specialists like *medical physics technicians* or *animal technicians* can also study for their own specialist bodies' examinations, but T.E.C. training is more broadly based and therefore it enables students to switch specializations later on, should they want or have to do so. (Once qualified to T.E.C. Certificate or Higher Certificate standard, they can still take specialist bodies' Final Membership examinations.) Length of training varies mainly according to entry qualifications. With 4, sometimes 3, relevant O-levels, part-time training normally takes two years; with 3 Grade 2 or 3 C.S.E. in relevant subjects it usually takes three years (not all colleges have facilities for lower-entry-level students).

Students with fewer than 3 Grade 3 (sometimes Grade 2) C.S.E. can work for the *City and Guilds Science Laboratory Assistants Certificate* by part-time study while in relevant employment. With experience, they may then be able to go on to T.E.C. Certificate training.

Pre-entry training: There are full-time or sandwich T.E.C. Diploma courses normally lasting two years in all the T.E.C (part-time study) Certificate subjects. Entry requirements for these courses are, in most colleges, 4 relevant O-levels; but there may be full-time 'catching up' opportunities for students who want to become science technicians but are lacking appropriate O-levels.

Higher or Senior Technician training

Students with T.E.C. Certificates containing sufficient units (see p. xv), T.E.C. Diplomas, or at least 1 science A-level and, usually, another science subject studied at A-level and 3 or 4 O-levels, take a T.E.C. Higher Certificate (part-time) or T.E.C. Higher Diploma (full-time or sandwich). Again, there are a great many specializations.

For the next few years, some colleges may still be running Ordinary and Higher National Certificates (part-time) and Diplomas (full-time); these are the old-established qualifications which the T.E.C. awards are replacing. OND/C entry requirements are normally 4 appropriate O-levels.

Personal attributes generally

Manipulative skill; patience; scrupulous attention to detail; a sense of responsibility; willingness to take orders; ability to work both independently and as one of a team.

Position of women

There are about equal numbers of male and female science technicians, but far more men are senior technicians. This is not entirely due to discrimination: women often are unwilling or unable to do the evening study which has to accompany day- or block-release. As general employment conditions deteriorated in the last few years, more men (often graduates) became technicians, and women's relative position, specially in senior jobs, has deteriorated further.

Career-break: As this is a rapidly changing area, only technicians who systematically keep up with developments can return.

Late entry: Not much scope, because training vacancies are likely to go to school-leavers with up-to-date science. However, women can take full-time T.E.C. science courses at any age.

Part-time: Very limited scope – but no reason why this type of work should not be done part-time (especially in schools).

Further information   Institute of Animal Technicians, Peter Gerson, Central Public Health Laboratory, Colindale Avenue, London NW9 5HT
City and Guilds of London Institute, 76 Portland Place, London W1N 4AA
Technician Education Council, 76 Portland Place, London W1N 4AA

Related careers   *Engineering Technician – Medical Laboratory Scientist – Physiotherapy – Optical Work – Orthoptics*

Food Science and Technology

Entry qualifications   All educational levels, see **Training**.

The work   *Food science* is concerned with the chemical and biological nature of food and its behaviour under natural conditions, during processing and during storage. *Food technology* is the application of relevant sciences, including engineering, to the processing, preservation and development of raw materials and manufactured foods. Food scientists and technologists work in quality control and product development departments (see Science, p. 400) of food companies which make anything from fish fingers to fruit cake or canned soup. They also work for flavour makers, public analysts, or in research centres where experiments with new food products using unorthodox materials (such as sea-weed, or plankton) may be carried out. Some research jobs are for food *scientists*; production jobs tend to be held by *technologists*; but there is no clear-cut division between the two and both types of specialists are found in most job areas.

Prospects Generally good: the industry is less affected than many by economic slumps. Its diversity provides opportunities to specialize. The broad-based training allows for flexibility. As in other industries, technologists now often move into top general management (see line management, Management in Industry, p. 259).

Pay: Medium (see p. xxiii).

Training See *Science Technician Training* (p. 415) for below-degree-level training for T.E.C. and City and Guilds Certificates, with specialization in food science and technology at the various levels of entry qualifications from laboratory assistant (City and Guilds qualification) to T.E.C. Higher awards.

For entrants with at least two A-levels including chemistry, and physics and another science normally at least at O-level: degrees in Food Science and/or Technology. Degrees vary in emphasis and content; some are more research-orientated, others include substantial management content. C.N.A.A. degrees normally last 4 years and include industrial experience.

For science and engineering graduates there are post-graduate courses in Food Science, Food Quality Control, Food and Management Science, Food Microbiology, Food Engineering.

Personal attributes A meticulous approach to technical problems plus an interest in people as consumers. For many jobs a real interest in food is desirable, as is the ability to work as part of a team. For *management careers*, ability to organize people and work, to work under pressure and to take decisions.

Position of women There is still some bias against women in production jobs where they are in charge of a lot of men, but they have little difficulty in entering other areas.

Career-break: Provided you stay in touch through professional institutes there should be no problem.

Late start: Fair opportunities for those with fairly recent chemistry O-level.

Part-time: Possible, but not very common.

Further information Institute of Food Science and Technology, 105–111 Euston Road, London NW1 2ED

Forensic Science

Entry quali- *Scientific Officers*: T.E.C. Higher award (see p. xv), or degree in a
fications scientific, engineering or mathematical subject.

Assistant Scientific Officers: At least 4 O-levels, including English
language *and* a science or mathematics subject, or T.E.C. award in
Science.

The work Forensic scientists and their assistants are a kind of scientific detective.
They apply scientific knowledge to the investigation of crime. They
work closely with the police and examine material obtained from the
scene of a crime, using the standard experimental techniques to examine
and identify traces of soil, paint, glass, etc.; identify drugs; determine
the quantity of alcohol in blood samples, etc. They use sophisticated
experimental techniques, including chromatography, ultra-violet and
infra-red spectrophotometry and neutron activation analysis. They are
employed by the Home Office in its central research establishment and
in regional laboratories. Most of the openings are for *chemists* and
biologists, with occasional opportunities for physicists, geologists and
others.

Biologists identify body-fluid stains and determine blood groups.
They also identify hairs, fibres, seeds and fragments of plant and animal
tissues. They use microscopes – including scanning electron microscopes
– and increasingly, molecular biology techniques.

Some forensic scientists specialize in working on documents and inks;
others become experts on firearms or explosives. They spend most of
their time in the laboratory, but may visit the scene of a crime to collect
material, and may appear in court as expert witnesses.

Prospects Good for promotion from one Civil Service grade to another.
Pay: Medium to high (see p. xxiii).

Training Normally on-the-job under the supervision of experienced scientists,
with day-release.

Personal As for scientists, plus willingness to be exposed to some sordid aspects
attributes of crime and to withstand gruelling cross-examinations in the witness
box.

Position Very few women at the moment, but only because very few have applied.
of women See Civil Service (p. xxiii).

Further in- The Civil Service Commission, Alencon Link, Basingstoke, Hants
formation RG21 1JB

Medical Laboratory Scientist

The term 'medical laboratory scientist' may be confusing. Whatever terms are used in individual job descriptions and examinations, until a 'medical laboratory scientist' has at least a T.E.C. Higher award she is not, in the usual meaning of the term, a professional *scientist*, and she will work under the overall supervision of a scientist.

In the National Health Service, the title is now Medical Laboratory Scientific Officer.

Entry quali-
fications
4 O-levels in academic subjects, of which at least 2 must be scientific and at least 1 must indicate an adequate command of English. See **Training** for *A-level* and *graduate* entry.

The work
Medical laboratory scientists and technicians are concerned with laboratory investigations for diagnosis and treatment of disease, and research into its causes and cure. While training, medical laboratory technicians work under the overall direction of scientists who have specialized in the application of their particular discipline to medicine. Work is done in hospitals, universities, blood transfusion centres, public health laboratories, veterinary establishments and pharmaceutical firms. In hospital there may be some contact with patients.

Medical laboratory technicians and scientists specialize in: *clinical chemistry*, the analysis of blood and other biological materials; *medical microbiology*, the isolation and identification of bacteria and viruses from patients with infections or in water and foodstuffs; *haematology* and *serology*, the study of blood; *histopathology* and *cytology*, the study of tissues removed during surgical operations and at post-mortem examinations, and in investigations for the early detection of cancer.

Prospects
Good. Technicians and scientists can move from one type of laboratory to another; some scope in E.E.C. and developing countries.

Pay: Medium to high (see p. xxiii).

Training
As the job covers such a wide range of levels of responsibility, there are training opportunities at various levels of entry qualifications; all train for membership of Institute of Medical Laboratory Sciences which leads to State Registration. This is required for National Health Service (and most other good) jobs:

Either: on-the-job in approved laboratory (I.M.L.S. knows which are and which are not approved) with day- or block-release for T.E.C. Certificate or Diploma (see T.E.C., p. xv) in Sciences with Medical Laboratory Science units;

Entry requirements for courses vary from one college to another: i.e. an applicant with fewer than the 4 O-levels required for student membership of the Institute *may* be accepted at a college course; but she would probably have difficulty finding a training vacancy with day-release. It depends on supply and demand. Length of course depends on entry qualifications: entrant with 4 O-levels including maths and a science would normally take two years; someone with lower qualifications would take longer.

Or: full-time T.E.C. course which could lead to Certificate and take 1 year, or take 2 years full-time and lead to Diploma (same level of study, but more subjects studied). Again, entry qualifications vary, but on the whole 4 O-levels with science and maths are likely to be required.

Or: for entrants with one A-level science: part-time day-release (2 years), or full-time course for T.E.C. Higher award. Length of full-time course depends on length of practical experience in laboratory which is always part of the course. (T.E.C. awards and specially T.E.C. higher awards are still new and arrangements vary very much.)

Or: science graduate entry: one year on-the-job with day-release. For some posts, only graduates are accepted.

Personal attributes   An interest in the medical applications of science; scientific aptitude and technical skills; patience; liking for experimental and routine work.

Position of women   The ratio is about 50:50, proportion of men increasing in senior posts.

Career-break: Opportunities for returners if they have kept up with developments.

Refresher courses: A few 'up-dating' lectures, but would not help women who are out of touch.

Late start: Possibly, for those with up-to-date science and willing to work for very low pay while on day-release. Better opportunities for career-changers from related fields (nurses, for example).

Part-time: Few opportunities.

Further information   Institute of Medical Laboratory Sciences, 12 Queen Anne Street, London W1M 0AU

Related careers   *Medicine – Pharmacy – Pharmacy Technician – Radiographer – Scientist – Technician Engineer*

SECRETARIAL AND CLERICAL WORK

Secretary – Shorthand/Audio Typist – Clerk – Word Processor Operator

1. SECRETARY

Titles have no precise meaning: executive secretary, private secretary, personal assistant are used indiscriminately. Some of the most high-powered secretaries prefer to call themselves merely 'secretary'; some 'personal assistants' just do junior executives' typing and telephoning.

The confusion over titles arose because traditionally there is no promotion ladder and career-structure, and no precise definition of the secretary's work or of the differences between *personal assistant, secretary, shorthand-* or *audio-typist,* and *clerk.* Differences between these jobs are considerable, but in employers' and employees' minds they are blurred, which leads to disappointment and frustration on both sides of the desk. However, with the wider choice of career opportunities for women, fewer able women are now willing to stay in jobs without prospects of advancement. Mainly for that reason, some organizations are now introducing something resembling career-structures. For example, the difference between 'personal assistant' and 'secretary' is now often being taken seriously. A secretary follows her boss's instructions; when she fully understands the department's work, she becomes a 'personal assistant' and in that capacity makes her own decisions. For example, as a sales manager's secretary she would, if a salesman falls ill, ask her boss to whom the sick person's work should be allocated. As personal assistant she would re-allocate the work herself, without asking her boss.

Another development which is changing the secretarial scene is the 'team secretary' (in another office, she might be called an 'administrative assistant'). She 'manages' a group of, say, several junior architects in an architectural partnership, or overseas marketing people in an export department. She organizes her charges' appointments, travel schedules, etc., and keeps track of their various projects and assignments. If the head of the department or partnership wants to know where X is, or how project Y is progressing, the team secretary knows the situation exactly.

Both Personal Assistant and Team Secretary are in fact junior/middle management jobs but they are not necessarily recognized as such (see Management, p. 259 and **Position of women**, p. 431).

In the past, secretarial work was the best way into management for women. While *some* (very few) secretaries – not necessarily graduate secretaries – still succeed by this route, there are much better ways into management (see p. 262). The vast majority of secretaries remain secretaries throughout their working lives. Promotion usually still means becoming secretary to someone higher up in the hierarchy – for example, from secretary to sales manager to secretary to finance director to secretary to managing director to secretary to chairman. In this promotion system, expertise gained in one job tends to be fairly useless in the next, therefore the opportunities for independent work, for becoming P.A. (or *acting* as P.A. at least) or executive, tend to be less in the new job than they were in the previous one. Many secretaries find that the higher up in the hierarchy their boss, the less the boss is likely to delegate. So secretaries who want a career and not a job need to find out far more details about what an advertised job involves than do people who go into structured careers with accepted work-content, qualifications, promotion prospects, etc.

The work   Traditionally a *secretary* usually works for one person or perhaps two. (This is of course the 'office' secretary, not the administrator in charge of an institution, learned society or similar organization.) It is the secretary's task to husband her boss's time and energy so that he or she can concentrate on whatever the job is at that moment.

The secretary acts as buffer between her boss and callers and phone calls, and takes minor decisions on her/his behalf. She must understand her boss's work well enough to know when to act on her own initiative and when to ask for instructions. This is one of the most challenging secretarial skills. Secretarial duties may involve:

(a) Acting as link between individuals and various sections in an organization; this could be departments in a university, company or store, or individuals in a management-team, and may involve writing memos, ringing people up, going to see them.

(b) Collecting information from a variety of printed and personal sources – this involves knowing where to go for whatever the information required, perhaps telephoning trade associations or government departments.

(c) Preparing agendas for meetings and collecting documents supporting the various items, distributing the papers at the right time to the right people; taking minutes at meetings, editing them and writing them up.

(d) Looking through the day's mail and deciding which letters the boss has to deal with personally and which ones she can cope with herself;

summarizing lengthy letters and documents; drafting her own replies to some letters and presenting them to her boss for approval and signature. (e) Making travel arrangements and arranging meetings, at home or abroad, for several busy people: this is a time-consuming task which requires meticulous attention to detail and may involve international trunk calls and lengthy correspondence until finally a time and place suitable to everyone has been agreed upon.

The amount of typing a secretary does varies. In a large office she may only deal with her boss's confidential correspondence, other matters being dealt with by a 'junior secretary' or someone from the typing-pool or word-processing unit. She may be in charge of one or several juniors, or cope single-handed.

Invariably, being a secretary is a self-effacing job. A good secretary rarely gets the kudos she deserves when, thanks to her efficiency, a crisis is avoided, but she is likely to be blamed if things go wrong – say if she forgets to remind her boss of an appointment which she/he too had forgotten and which is written down in the appointments diary.

SPECIALIST SECRETARIES

Though there is no *need* to decide on any specialization before training, there are 3 specializations for which special training is useful:

1. *Medical Secretary*: She works in hospital, for one or several consultants; in consultants' private consulting rooms; or for general practitioners. She requires knowledge of medical terminology and of health and social services organization. In hospital, secretaries have less contact with patients than in consulting rooms and general practice, but they have more companionship. In G.P.s' group practices the work involves organizing/administration.

2. *Farm or Agricultural Secretary*: Farm secretaries deal with the paperwork which modern farming entails. They fill in forms, keep accounts, keep and analyse records, and deal with correspondence, often on their own initiative. Only very big farms employ full-timers; most need part-time help. So farm secretaries either work as freelances, spending a number of days a month on different farms, or they are employed by farm-secretarial agencies and are sent out to different farms. The work is varied, as it involves working on different types of farm; and it requires experience and self-confidence because farmers, unlike other employers, usually know less about the work to be done (accounts, filling in V.A.T. and other forms) than their secretaries. Specialist training is a great advantage.

3. *Bi- or Multilingual Secretaries*: They translate incoming mail; then may compose their own letters in a foreign language from notes dictated in English, but most outgoing mail is written in English. They sometimes

read foreign journals and search for and translate or summarize relevant articles. Occasionally they may act as interpreter. Their scope varies: some secretaries hardly use their languages at all; others are relied upon totally by their mono-lingual bosses. Foreign Office secretaries must be proficient in 1 language but many never use that knowledge even when working in embassies abroad (see Civil Service, p. 126). There are commercial opportunities abroad for truly bi-lingual secretaries with, occasionally, the relevant shorthand. International organizations usually require previous senior secretarial experience. Overall, the greatest demand is for French/English, German/English and French/German/English. There is a small, steady demand for Spanish, for other European languages, and for Russian.

At home, foreign shorthand is rarely required; in order to master it, it is essential to be *absolutely fluent* in the language(s) concerned. For most linguist-secretary jobs a grasp of the relevant country's economic and social set-up is far more important than shorthand and 100% speaking and writing fluency.

2. SHORTHAND- AND AUDIO-TYPISTS AND WORD PROCESSOR OPERATORS

Many so-called secretaries are really typists. Shorthand- and audio-typists and word processor operators normally work for a number of people, often in a typing pool or central word processing unit or 'station', and not for individuals as secretaries do. Their job is far more impersonal, concerned with producing texts efficiently and economically rather than dealing with people and all the various jobs the secretaries cope with. It is work for people who like getting on with the job without having to talk much to their bosses; but it can be a step to secretarial work too.

The demand for *shorthand*-typists is still greater than for *audio*-typists and for word processor operators – but that is likely to change soon. At the moment there are still executives of, say, 45+ who cannot get used to dictating machines and insist on dictating to an individual. Younger executives now all use dictating machines, the use of which cuts the time wasted by shorthand typists while executives think, change their minds, are interrupted by telephones, etc. So the need. for shorthand-typists is rapidly dwindling.

Copy-typists have virtually disappeared. Small offices now usually use photocopying machines; in larger organizations word processors are being introduced.

The term 'word processor' has caught on and is now firmly established. However, most manufacturers would have preferred 'text processors' because the equipment's strength lies in processing texts.

A 'word processor' basically consists of a typewriter-like keyboard connected to a visual display unit (v.d.u.) which looks like a TV screen, and to a 'memory' in which previously 'keyed-in' texts are stored, coded, filed ready for 'retrieval', i.e. for future use either in further printed texts, or for 'call up' on v.d.u. screens. The keyboard is also connected to equipment which prints the text; it may be connected to other v.d.u.s, either in an office next door, or in one, or several, offices hundreds of miles away. One operator could be transmitting a message instantly to other v.d.u.s as well as producing the text in printed form.

Operating word processors is easy and can be learnt in a few weeks, usually on the job. (There is no need to understand how a word processor works any more than there is a need to understand how a television works. It is only necessary to know which knob to turn to achieve which result.) The operator 'keys in' text exactly as she would type it. The text then appears on the screen.

[Word processors may also be linked to other data processing equipment (see Computing, p. 134).]

Briefly, the word processor's main advantages over conventional office equipment are these:

1. It enables the operator to correct typing mistakes easily and quickly;
2. It can produce any number of perfect 'top-copies' instantly;
3. It automatically files, codes, sorts and has ready for future use not only whole printed texts but individual paragraphs or sentences;
4. It can combine individual sections with new texts and/or with lists of addresses, or with other sections of text stored in the 'memory'.

The preparation of original letters, memos, reports is not necessarily very much quicker on a word processor than on an electric typewriter operated by a competent typist. Word processors will not necessarily be replacing typewriters in small professional or commercial offices. The saving in time and effort occurs when (a) texts have to be amended several times, as happens frequently in offices where reports/ memos/letters are drafted by one person and then circulated for approval/amendment by others; (b) where reports are highly complex and, even though composed by one person, are likely to need several drafts before the final version is ready; (c) in offices from which long and complex documents, which vary only *slightly* in content, are sent out in their hundreds. For example legal documents sent to clients often contain several standard paragraphs, as well as one or two original ones; the same applies to estate agents, banks, mail order firms, etc.; (d) in offices where hundreds of standard letters have to be produced, each looking like top copies.

Word processors are used differently in different organizations. There is no agreement yet on which is the best method of using this new technology. In some offices several word processors are combined in one central 'station', all the organizations' work being processed there; in other offices each department might have its own word processor, and possibly several secretaries/typists as well as clerks (see below) use the equipment; in some cases each secretary has her own individual word processor.

3. CLERKS

This may involve some typing or word processing or micro-computing (see Computing, p. 138). Clerks' work varies even more than secretarial work. Some clerks work on their own all day; others are in constant contact with colleagues and/or the public. A clerk in a travel agency may send out brochures to customers or hand them out over the counter; in a mail order firm she may check incoming orders to see whether the right postal orders are enclosed; in a hospital or a bank a junior may do nothing but photocopy. She may work in a post-room, collecting and distributing mail from and to various departments and individuals. In a personnel department, she may work on staff records, entering details about absence, wage increases, etc. In large organizations, whether town hall, store or manufacturing company, there is often a computerized filing system. In a small office a clerk may still do 'old-fashioned' filing, answer the telephone, make the tea and do some typing. The extent to which clerks' work has been affected by the introduction of computerized equipment varies enormously. At the moment, the majority of offices still rely largely on the old-fashioned methods of entering and updating facts and figures, transmitting messages, collecting and distributing information. But, at least in large offices, this is likely to change in the next few years. For example in insurance offices, when updating clients' policies, clerks first have to look for the file then re-type part of the policy and file it again. With computerized equipment however, the clerk 'keys in' the reference code, the policy is 'called up' (appears on) the video display unit, the clerk 'keys in' the necessary amendments and, at the press of a few buttons, the policy is amended as required, printed, *and* stored in the equipment's memory – the electronic file. Any telephone inquiry dealt with by clerks, whether from a supplier in a manufacturing industry or an airline customer, is dealt with now by keying in the question and getting the answer instantly on the v.d.u.

Clerks may also become telephonists or receptionists. The receptionist's job may be rather more complex than it appears – receptionists are expected to have a good knowledge of who does what in the organization so that they can direct callers to the right person or department.

Prospects   *Secretaries*: Good. They can pick and choose the environment they want to work in, whether the City, a public institution or for an individual. Prospects of going up the management ladder are not at all good generally, but there are some possibilities in fashion, in public relations, in travel, employment, and estate agents – in areas where specialist training is not expected. *Very* few secretaries in television manage to jump the abyss between secretarial and creative work. Demand for real secretaries and personal assistants is likely to remain high, despite the introduction of electronic office equipment. Secretaries with administrative ability may in fact have better prospects – they may run word processing units, plan new office systems, or move into sales and customer (advisory) services.

Bi-lingual secretaries: They get jobs easily, but not necessarily with much scope for using their language proficiency. Graduates are often overqualified. O-level or A-level language plus knowing how to use a dictionary is often all that is needed, even when the job was advertised as for a linguist. There are more secretaries who want to work *abroad* than there are jobs available. However, good linguists with about 3 years' secretarial experience can get jobs in E.E.C. countries and elsewhere, mainly in British or multinational companies' offices.

Medical secretaries: Excellent – a secretarial growth area.

Farm secretaries: Good opportunities in most rural areas.

Typists: Word processing equipment is beginning to reduce demand drastically.

Clerks: Electronic equipment is rapidly reducing demand.

    Pay: *Secretaries*: medium to high; *Clerical work*: low to medium; *Word processor operators*: medium (see p. xxiii).

Training   No set pattern. A secretary must still be able to write shorthand, preferably at 90–100 words per minute (and transcribe it adequately), and audio-type at 50 words per minute. She must be able to spell. She must know how to use, and where to find, sources of reference. She needs a good grasp of who does what in the commercial world, in the community, in government. She must be able to draft and summarize letters, reports, etc. – both verbally and in writing.

    Where, and how, she acquires the 'secretarial core skills' is totally immaterial. Certificates and Diplomas awarded by colleges, the Royal Society of Arts, the London Chamber of Commerce and Industry, Pitman's, for example, and specialist ones by the Association of Medical Secretaries, are useful when there are more applicants than vacancies. Qualifications secure a first interview, but they count for far less than impression made at interview.

A 6th-form education, preferably taking A-levels in such subjects as geography, English, economics, plus a short typing course, is far more useful than leaving school at 16 and taking a 2-year secretarial course. O-level English language is essential: a degree is rarely an advantage. Even when an employer specifies 'graduate secretary', an intelligent, well-informed 6th-form leaver is usually acceptable. There are so many graduate secretaries simply because arts graduates cannot think of anything else to do – not because many secretarial jobs are so intellectually demanding that only graduates could fill them. Graduate secretaries do not even have significantly greater chances of getting into management than 6th-form leavers.

There is a tremendous variety of secretarial courses, but there is no pecking order, no 'best buy'. Education and training for secretarial/general office work is sadly unorganized, with several overlapping qualifications. Certain qualifications, such as the Royal Society of Arts', are well known and carry considerable weight, but individual colleges, teaching methods and equipment vary enormously. At this stage in the 'office revolution', when new office equipment and routines are being widely introduced, a course for a good qualification at a college with antiquated equipment, and teachers who know little of present-day office practice, may be less useful than a course in a college which arranges visits to modern offices, and which has teachers who understand 1980s office technology, even if the college only awards its own diploma.

One cannot even always judge the usefulness of secretarial courses by their entry requirements. There are some courses which only accept entrants with at least 2 A-levels (some even insist on a degree) which *may* lead fairly quickly to senior secretarial jobs. But it is quite likely that students who take these courses would have got equally far, equally quickly, if they had merely taken a short sharp typing-only course.

Courses broadly fall into these categories, each with many variations:
(1) Courses for students with 2 A-levels or with degrees or comparable qualifications, lasting between 3 and 9 months; a 3 months' crash course, learning the core skills, should be sufficient.
(2) 6-month to 2-year courses for students with at least 5 O-levels and an undertaking to study for an A-level. Unless 2-year courses include something like medical, farm or linguist secretarial work, or A-level study, 2 years is unnecessarily long.
(3) 1 or 2-year courses for students with 3 to 5 O-levels. They often include O- (or A-) level study. Courses are likely to lead to typing or clerical rather than secretarial jobs.
(4) Courses for students with fewer than 4 O-levels. These are not strictly speaking *secretarial* courses (whatever their title!). They should

last 2 years and include general educational subjects if they are eventually to lead to secretarial work.

(5) 1-year courses in English, shorthand, typing, office routine, lead to *clerks'* and *typists'* jobs. (This applies also to commercial courses at school.)

(6) Business Education Council (B.E.C., see p. xvii) courses, part-time or full-time, 2 or 3 years normally. Broadly, 'General' awards – no specific entry requirements – lead to clerical work; 'National' awards – 4 O-level entry – lead to secretarial work if secretarial options were included.

Many of the courses under (1) to (5) are likely to lead to B.E.C. awards as well as to college diplomas, etc.

There are a few private schools running word processing courses, but the quality and value of such courses vary greatly. Different manufacturers' equipment is operated differently, and any job applicant who can type (for key-boarding) will be taught how to operate word processors, or microcomputers, on the job, or on companies' or manufacturers' own courses.

Specialist Training

Bi- or multi-lingual secretary: Entry requirements from 'O-level pass' or 'A-level standard' in the relevant language to language degree. Most courses last 2 years. Prospective secretary-linguists who intend to take a language degree should look out for degree courses including 'area studies' – which means the course covers the relevant country's history and social and economic institutions, etc. That type of knowledge is also very important for getting jobs abroad with commercial firms and international agencies.

Medical secretary: *Either* – 2-year course for Association of Medical Secretaries' Diploma. Entry requirement 4 or 5 O-levels; *or* general secretarial course with medical shorthand.

Farm secretary: 2-year course. Farm Secretaries' courses at Agricultural Institutes *or* general secretarial course with Farm Accounts.

Clerks and typists: Clerks do not necessarily need any preliminary training.

Personal attributes

Secretaries who hope (probably in vain) to become executives: exceptional organizing ability, self-confidence, determination and ambition, a logical brain, business acumen, willingness to take responsibility *and* willingness to take orders; ability to communicate easily with people at all levels of education and status in the organization; willingness to work long hours.

Personal assistants: the above qualities without the ambition and business acumen; the willingness to take responsibility must be coupled with the willingness to remain in a supportive role; a sympathetic manner, a desire to be of use to others; ability to ignore getting undeserved blame when things go wrong and not getting well-deserved praise; indifference to seeing less able 'executives' have higher status and pay, and more responsibility.

Typists/word-processor operators: wanting to get on with one's work without involvement with people and in the organization's business; accuracy.

Clerks: depends on type of job – some require a liking for quiet backroom work dealing with paperwork; others a liking for dealing with people; most require attention to detail and willingness to do as told.

Position of women

This is still almost 100% women's work, but recently some men have become secretaries. Some word processing units are being organized/ run by young male (as well as female) graduates who come into the organization with computing experience or as management trainees.

Career-break: Should be no problem for *real* secretaries, but in a few years' time when women want to return to work, the office revolution will have changed prospects for typists and clerks – *far* fewer opportunities for unskilled and semi-skilled office work will exist.

Late start: Secretarial work is easy to start late. While there are *some* employers who will not consider anyone over 35, there is a growing number of employers who *prefer* the over-35s.

3-month to 1-year courses geared to mature students are available under T.O.P.S. (see p. xl) (including specialist secretary's courses).

Refresher courses: available under T.O.P.S. (see above).

Part-time: Excellent opportunities for *typists* and *clerks*. Not quite as many for *secretaries*, who are expected to be available whenever the boss wants them. However, even here part-time work is gradually becoming accepted, but part-timers are never likely to have as wide a choice of jobs as full-timers. The fewer the hours they are willing to work, the more restricted the choice of job.

Part-time can be anything from 6 hours a week, to 4 full days; 2 or 3 full, or 3 or 4 half days are the most usual. A flexible number of hours, to suit both secretary and employers and varying week by week, is sometimes possible. A new variation on the part-time theme is 'twinning': 2 women doing one job, either handing over to each other – overlapping perhaps in the middle of the day, or leaving each other detailed notes, anything which minimizes the disadvantage of lack of continuity. There are a few jobs which can be done in term-time only, leaving mothers free during the children's holidays; and occasionally some 1 week (or fortnight) on, 1 week (or fortnight) off jobs.

'*Temping*' is a kind of part-time work. It is particularly suitable for actresses, artists, models, etc., people who have to 'fill in' while waiting for their own kind of work; for mothers who cannot get a term-time-only job, and for secretaries and typists who prefer a frequent change of environment to getting involved with one set of people and one type of work. Temps normally work for agencies who send them to employers on a weekly or daily basis; only those with very good contacts and experience can work as freelances.

Further information   No central organization. Local education authority for lists of local courses.

Related careers   *Accountancy – Broadcasting – Company Secretary – Hospital Administration – Linguist – Management – Personnel Work – Public Relations*

THE WOMEN'S SERVICES
(W.R.A.C., W.R.A.F., W.R.N.S.)

NON-COMMISSIONED RANKS: technical – clerical and communications – catering and stores – medical and dental – miscellaneous trades. COMMISSIONED RANKS: including cadet entrants and permanent and short service commissions – nursing

Non-Commissioned Ranks

The Services are, to a great extent, self-contained communities, and offer many different jobs. The Women's Royal Naval Service, the Women's Royal Army Corps, and the Women's Royal Air Force need secretaries, telephonists, drivers, photographers, people to look after welfare, etc.

Apart from jobs which can be done both in the Services and elsewhere, there are the Service careers, concerned with the defence of the country. Women work on radar, aircraft, and radio maintenance, meteorology, gun sites, and communication systems.

Entry quali-
fications
Minimum age for W.R.N.S., W.R.A.C., and W.R.A.F., 17. The Services often rely on aptitude tests and interviews, and do not demand O-levels for all jobs. There are some opportunities to study for O-levels in the Services.

The work
and training
Junior ranks in the Women's Services lead very much of a community life, both on and off duty. They are rarely alone, they may share bedrooms for 2 to 4 people, but their quarters normally have comfortable sitting-rooms. Discipline and regulations are no longer as rigid as they used to be, and officers, far from being formidable, are usually specially chosen for their pleasant personalities and their ability to get on with and understand other, younger, women. Many officers are themselves in their early 20s. The amount of free time given is generous. Civilian clothes may be worn in off-duty hours, and dances, concerts, films, and games are frequently organized. In all three Services, most women work with men and may share a mess with them. Airwomen and Wrens may live out.

The three Services encourage girls to continue their education. There is no compulsion to do so but promotion normally depends on passing examinations. In the W.R.A.C. and the W.R.A.F. especially, students may be given time off for study in duty hours.

After an initial period of service at home there is a chance but no guarantee of a foreign posting. Individual preferences are taken into consideration as far as possible.

Recruits sign on for a 9-year 'Notice Engagement' (22-year in W.R.A.C.). This means that after completing 18 months' service from age 18 or completion of training, whichever is the later, they can at any time give 18 months' notice to end their engagement. Therefore they can, if they wish, serve for a minimum of 3 years. In all Services release can be obtained on marriage or compassionate grounds. In the W.R.A.C. and W.R.A.F. it is possible in some areas to sign on for what is known as 'local service', which means living at home, and working at local Army and Air Force stations. Married women often do local service.

Every recruit starts with a few weeks' basic training. This is usually followed by specialist training for the chosen category.

In all three Services recruits are given interviews and tests *before* acceptance: they are 'entered' only if there is a vacancy in the category for which they seem suitable.

The type of work does not necessarily vary greatly between the three Services.

The various careers are called 'trades' in the W.R.A.C. and the W.R.A.F., and 'categories' in the W.R.N.S. There are a large number, and to most of the trades and categories there are many branches. Broadly they fall into 5 main groups:

1. Technical, including Transport
2. Clerical and Communications
3. Catering and Stores
4. Medical and Dental
5. Specialists including Provost (military police), Physical Training Instructor, Kennel Maid/Groom, Photographer.

1. TECHNICAL

Acceptance is *either* on the basis of aptitude test; *or* on O-level maths and/or physics, and geography; for W.R.N.S. photographers, O-level maths or C.S.E. Grade 1 Photography is acceptable.

In all Services, servicewomen operate electrical and electronic equipment. They send and receive messages by teleprinter, plot and record positions of ships and aircraft. Women also train as radio and radar mechanics, and in the W.R.A.F. as technicians in the various trades, and repair complicated instruments. In the W.R.N.S. and the W.R.A.F. they work in control-towers of air stations, logging times of incoming and out-going aircraft and recording aircraft movement. In the W.R.A.C. they work on gun positions, spotting and recording shell bursts. Delicate equipment is used to measure the speeds at which shells travel and the work requires great accuracy. Much of it is on the Secret List.

In the W.R.N.S. and in the W.R.A.F. servicewomen work on the maintenance of aircraft. Other technical trades and categories include tracers, draughtsmen, electricians, aircraft and electronic technicians, instrument mechanics, and weapon analysts.

Specialized training is given after acceptance.

A new development: women can work with the Royal Electrical and Mechanical Engineers (R.E.M.E.) on the repair and modification of the Army's telecommunications, radar, control and computing equipment. They are trained to T.E.C. Higher Certificate. R.E.M.E. women belong to the W.R.A.C. for administrative purposes, but share the R.E.M.E. mess.

2. CLERICAL AND COMMUNICATIONS

Acceptance depends on an aptitude test.

Recruits are taught office work to suit the demands of their particular Service. Suitable recruits are given further training, and specialize in accounts, shorthand, coding and decoding morse, teleprinting or switchboard operating. Entrants with secretarial training or experience stand a good chance of early promotion in the W.R.A.C. and W.R.A.F.

3. CATERING AND STORES

Acceptance depends on an aptitude test.

Cooks work in men's, women's and mixed messes. These may range in size from a small officers' mess at an outlying station, to one for hundreds of people.

Duties include meal-planning, ordering, budgeting, some diet-cooking. There is scope both for the untrained keen to learn, and for those with relevant qualifications. Stores work covers food, clothing, furniture and technical items. (See also under Commissioned Ranks, p. 437.)

4. MEDICAL AND DENTAL

Acceptance: *either* on O-levels or A-levels, as required for equivalent jobs in civilian life, *and/or* on suitability tests.

The three Services differ:

(a) QUEEN ALEXANDRA'S ROYAL ARMY NURSING CORPS (Q.A.R.

A.N.C.): Trains girls for State Registration, State Enrolment, dental clerk assistants, dental hygienists, medical clerks and ward stewardesses. It offers 5 training schemes, much the same as those given in civilian hospitals and medical schools.

(i) For girls with minimum 5 O-levels, including English language or history, maths or science, and 1 other subject: 3-year State Registered Nurse. Training is exactly the same as in civilian hospitals (see p. 305) but it takes place in military hospitals at home and/or abroad. State Registered Nurses may be recommended for commissions.

(ii) 2-year State Enrolled Nurse (see p. 308) training is the same as in civilian hospitals, but takes place in military hospitals.

(iii) Dental clerk assistant, dental hygienist. Both categories are trained at the Royal Army Dental Training Centre and then work in Army dental departments at home and overseas.

(iv) Medical clerks are trained in clerical duties with particular emphasis on medical terminology. After training they are employed in Army hospitals at home and overseas.

(v) Ward stewardess (hospital housekeeping service).

No G.C.E. requirements for (iii), (iv) and (v), except dental hygienist, who needs 4 O-levels including English language and biology.

(b) QUEEN ALEXANDRA'S ROYAL NAVAL NURSING SERVICE (Q.A.R. N.N.S.): trains girls for State Registration and State Enrolment. The W.R.N.S. also trains dental hygienists and dental surgery assistants.

(c) PRINCESS MARY'S ROYAL AIR FORCE NURSING SERVICE (P.M.R.A.F.N.S.): takes and trains S.E.N.s at R.A.F. training hospitals. A qualified S.R.N. may apply for a commission in the P.M.R.A.F.N.S. The W.R.A.F. offer training for medical assistant, dispenser, physiotherapist, laboratory technician, hygienist, radiographer, operating theatre technician, electrophysiological technician, dental surgery assistant, and dental hygienist. There are also openings for professionally qualified entrants to most of these trades.

5. OTHER MISCELLANEOUS TRADES AND CATEGORIES IN THE SERVICES

(a) Administration.

(b) Driver: no previous experience necessary.

(c) Hairdresser (W.R.A.C. only): previous experience essential.

(d) Musician (W.R.A.C. only): acceptance based on ability to read music and play an instrument.

(e) Photographer: aptitude rather than previous training required (except W.R.N.S., see p. 439).

(f) P.T.Instructor: all Services train their own P.T. Instructors.

(g) Policewoman: no previous experience necessary.

Prospects   Promotion prospects to N.C.O. vary according to trade or category, but are generally good for girls able to take responsibility. Servicewomen with good educational qualifications and the right personal attributes are encouraged to apply for commissions and have a good chance of acceptance for officer training (see Commissioned Ranks, below).

Fair chance of being posted abroad, except in W.R.N.S.

Pay: Medium (see p. xxiii).

Personal attributes   An equable disposition; a gregarious nature; ability to mix and work well with people of all ages and both sexes and to take discipline without resentment; adaptability to new people and places; a spirit of adventure.

Further information   See end of section, p. 440.

Commissioned Ranks

The work   All officers specialize in a branch of work, such as administration or telecommunications or catering. In most establishments women officers work with their male colleagues as part of a team. They may also be responsible for the discipline and welfare of the servicewomen in their unit, but in any case are expected to take an active interest in the welfare of those (male and female) working under them.

Men and women usually share the officers' mess. Messes are not unlike hotels, with dining-room and lounge, and staff to do the chores. Each officer has her own bedroom. Senior officers also have their own sitting-rooms. During working hours officers wear (individually tailored) uniforms; off duty they wear civilian clothes. Outside duty hours they can normally come and go as they like.

Training   Three ways:

1. By promotion from the ranks.

2. By direct entry into a Permanent Commission (except for W.R.N.S.), for women who intend to spend all their working lives in the Service.

3. By direct entry into a Short Service Commission, which varies from 2 to 8 years. The method of selection is by oral and written tests or exercises, and interview.

Details for the three Services:

1. W.R.A.C.

Entry qualifications   Minimum age 18 years 5 months. Upper age limit varies according to type of commission.

(a) For Permanent Regular Commission – 5 G.C.E.s (1 English language, 1 mathematics or a science subject, and only 1 other may be non-academic) including 2 academic A-levels.

(b) Special Regular and Short Service Commission – O-levels as above, but A-levels not required.

Graduates are eligible for all types of commissions.

Training   Candidates for all types of commissions complete a course at the W.R.A.C. College, Camberley. This is either 8 months or 8 weeks, depending on age and experience. Graduates take the 8-week course.

Instruction is both academic and practical and covers a wide field of general and military subjects. More specialized training may be given after a period of commissioned service.

Women with maths and physics A-levels are now trained by the Royal Electrical and Mechanical Engineers to become chartered engineers (while in the W.R.A.C.), or they can join as engineering graduates. They live in the R.E.M.E. mess.

2. W.R.A.F.

Entry qualifications   Minimum age 18.

(a) Officer entry into Permanent and Short Service (4–6 years) Commissions: a degree, or professional qualification, is required for the engineering, administration (education, catering and physical education specializations), medical and dental branches. Degrees or suitable civilian experience may also confer 'officer entry' status for other branches.

(b) Cadet entry: 5 O-levels, including English language and mathematics, for aircraft and fighter control, photographic interpretation, supply and administration (secretarial specializations) branches.

(c) Officers commissioned from the ranks normally require entry qualifications as in (a) or (b).

Training   1. Officer entrants are commissioned on entry and receive 4 months' training at the Officer Cadet Training Unit. This is followed by professional training for their branch.

2. Cadet entrants enter as officer cadets and receive 4 months' training at the Officer Cadet Training Unit. They are then commissioned and receive professional training for their branch.

3. W.R.N.S.

Entry quali-
fications

Direct Entry into Short Service Commission: Age on entry 20½–26. Degree or comparable qualification in a field relevant to the branch in which the candidate wants to specialize.

Cadet entry: Minimum age on entry 18½. 2 A-levels, 3 O-levels, including English language.

Rating entry: Minimum age 20. 5 O-levels, including English language and mathematics, and officer potential.

All officer training starts with 5 months' service as rating, and is followed by a 13½-week Officer Training Course at the Royal Naval College, Dartmouth. Further training follows, either on a specialist course or on-the-job at a Naval establishment.

The three Services welcome, and commission, State Registered Nurses. In the Army there are also often vacancies for radiographers and physiotherapists.

Prospects

Promotion prospects are good – if only because the marriage rate is high.

In the W.R.N.S. promotion is automatic to second officer and thereafter by selection.

In the W.R.A.C. promotion for efficient officers is automatic up to and including Captain; above that promotion is by selection after examination.

In the W.R.A.F. (as in R.A.F.) promotion up to Flight Lieutenant is by time, thereafter by examination and selection.

Undergraduates are eligible for W.R.A.C. or W.R.A.F. sponsorship during their studies.

The three nursing services all offer direct promotion from the ranks and Direct Entry Short Service Commissions to State Registered Nurses. In Q.A.R.A.N.C. and Q.A.R.N.N.S. commissions are also sometimes offered to non-nursing personnel for employment in the administrative, welfare and personnel management field. Opportunities for overseas postings vary between the Services.

Pay: Medium to high (see p. xxiii).

Personal
attributes

For all officers: initiative; qualities of leadership; organizing ability and/or special skills; the ability to get on with both men and women at all Service levels; an understanding of the problems of young people; a reasonably gregarious personality; spirit of adventure.

Position
of women

The Sex Discrimination Act does not apply to the Services. In the Navy and Army, men's and women's Services are separate entities, with separate promotion structures, so equality of opportunity considerations do not apply. In the R.A.F. there is an integrated career pattern by branch or trade and the principles of the Act are followed where possible.

Career-break: In theory return is possible, but it rarely applies to married women, owing to mobility requirements.

Late start: Varies according to type of work and previous qualifications, but generally upper ages for joining are: W.R.A.C., 33; W.R.N.S., 28; W.R.A.F., 39.

Further information   Ministry of Defence, Lansdowne House, Berkeley Square, London W1X 6AA, or nearest Army Careers Information Office.

For the W.R.N.S. and the W.R.A.F. the recruiting offices are called Careers Information Offices: Addresses are available at post offices, careers offices and local telephone directories.

Related careers   *Nursing – Police*

NOTE: The Services are the only section in this book in which careers for men and women are very different (the Sex Discrimination Act does not cover the Forces). The information given here only applies to women's career opportunities. There is no space to cover *both* sexes' opportunities, and information for men is readily available from the Services and from l.e.a. careers officers.

SHIPBROKING, AIRBROKING, AND FREIGHT FORWARDING

Entry quali-
fications
All educational levels; in practice at least 4 O-levels. Also graduate entry.

Shipbrokers, airbrokers and freight forwarders are concerned with the efficient and economical movement of goods from one part of the world to another. The shipbroker uses only ships, the airbroker only aircraft, the freight forwarder uses any means of transport. The work is a vital part of world trade and at the centre of the country's commercial activities.

1. SHIPBROKERS

They match up empty ships with cargoes and negotiate terms on behalf of their clients. This process is known as 'fixing', and is rather like solving a giant jigsaw puzzle. The shipbroker may use a regular cargo run or charter a ship for a single voyage or a series of voyages, or a part of a ship's freight space. She also acts as agent for shipowners when their ships are in port and deals with customs formalities, loading documentation, arrangements for the crew and any problems that may crop up. Shipbrokers also buy and sell ships for their clients.

Shipbrokers often work long and irregular hours, as they have to be in telephone contact with people all over the world during *their* working hours.

The *Baltic Exchange* in the City of London is the world's only shipping exchange. The 700-odd members comprise shipbrokers, grain traders, and others concerned with shipbroking. They meet 'on the floor of the Exchange' to trade (see also Commodity Broking, p. 464) and exchange mutually useful shipping information.

2. AIRBROKERS

They also match cargoes (and people) and carriers from and to all parts of the world. Air-chartering is done mainly by telephone; air-charterers rarely meet each other or see the aircraft they are chartering or the people whose goods or clients they are carrying. Work can be very hectic, as charters may be arranged only a day or so before take-off. However, most of the work is carefully planned ahead. The variety of aircraft for charter is much smaller than the variety of ships; the variety of cargo carried is growing steadily. The bulk of air-chartering is still concerned with two types of cargo: (1) people – aircraft are chartered 'on time charter' to tour operators or, for example, construction firms which transport personnel to and from the Middle East; and (2) perishable foods. Air broking is still evolving, with airbrokers constantly looking for new business – especially to and from and in the Middle East, Far East and Africa.

3. FREIGHT FORWARDERS

They arrange transport of all types of freight to and from anywhere in the world. They search out the most efficient method or combination of methods of transport in each particular case, evaluating respectively the need for speed, security, refrigeration; the fragility of the goods, etc. Goods may be sent by traditional methods such as rail, or something more modern such as container ship or jumbo jet, or by a combination of several modes of transport. The freight forwarder must be well-acquainted with the advantages and disadvantages of the various methods of transport (which she is likely to learn by experience and from colleagues rather than from the transporters themselves), and with the intricacies of freight handling and storage and the different techniques and arrangements in the various ports and airports all over the world. She must make it her business to find out routes which, though possibly longer in mileage, may be more efficient because turn-round arrangements in some ports and airports are quicker than in others.

She is also responsible for documentation, such as Bills of Lading, import and export licences, and for specialized packing and warehousing.

Some freight forwarders specialize in certain commodities or geographical areas; others in certain methods of transport and/or types of packing or warehousing.

Prospects Depend largely on world trade conditions, but London is one of the world's largest shipping, air chartering and freight forwarding centres and specialized freight forwarding is an expanding industry. There are some opportunities for experienced shipbrokers and for freight forwarders to work *abroad* for a spell.

Pay: medium to high (see p. xxiii).

Training On-the-job. Experience is the most important part of training. While there are specific institutes – the Institute of Shipbrokers, the Institute of Freight Forwarding, the Institute of Export – students now normally first take a Business Education Council (B.E.C.) award (see p. xvii for various levels of award). This is a more broadly based and a more useful qualification if a broker or freight forwarder has or wants to change to another commercial function later in her career. With a B.E.C. National award or Higher National award, students can then take the specific Institutes' final examinations.

A few big charter firms take graduate and occasionally A-level trainees.

There are also relevant Export Management options in some Business Studies degrees and post-graduate management courses.

Then there is a Foundation Course in Overseas Trade for entrants with at least 4 O-levels including English and maths. This course is being phased out, to be replaced by a B.E.C. (see p. xvii) Post-Experience Certificate, for people in relevant employment or with relevant past experience. The Certificate course covers Part 1 of the syllabuses of both the Institutes mentioned above and also of the Institutes of Export and of Marketing, and of the Society of Shipping Executives.

Although foreign languages are not required for any of the examinations, fluency in at least 1 language is a great advantage.

Personal attributes

Interest in commercial geography and world trade; a practical approach; a liking for paperwork, a good telephone manner; *especially for ship- and airbroking*: an entrepreneurial spirit and ability to win people's confidence.

Position of women

On the whole firms are reluctant to appoint women to responsible positions because, they say, shipbrokers and freight forwarders deal with countries in which women are not at all equal, and a woman negotiator might therefore lose the firm some business. However, there is no reason why women should not succeed in this field – practicality and getting on with people easily are important ingredients, and women are supposed to be good at both. In *airbroking*, which is a newer career area where there were no traditions to break down, the few women who have tried have done well.

Career-break: Might not present any problems for experienced ship-brokers/freight forwarders – except that methods of transport change rather rapidly and competition from young people is very keen.

Late start: Possible only for women with related industrial experience.

Part-time: Not at the moment – no reason why it should not be possible.

Further information

Institute of Chartered Shipbrokers, 24 St Mary Axe, London EC3

Institute of Freight Forwarders Ltd, Suffield House, 9 Paradise Road, Richmond, Surrey TW9 1SA
Institute of Export, World Trade Centre, London E1 9AA

Related careers *Management in Industry – Purchasing and Supply – Stock Exchange – Travel Agent*

SOCIAL WORK

Casework – Groupwork – Community work – Social services departments – Hospital social work – Probation work – Residential social work (including children's homes) – Youth work

Entry qualifications

Vary according to age and type of course; see **Training**, but about half of entrants are *graduates*.

The work

Social workers basically help individuals and families who have problems with which they cannot cope without professional help. The precise terms of reference, the most effective way of organizing social work – and what areas of 'helping people' constitute social work – are issues which have been debated for years and will go on being debated and changed.

An important change in organization took place in the early 1970s: the former social work specializations, child care, medical and psychiatric social work, blind and deaf welfare, were integrated into one social work profession. (In England and Wales probation still keeps its separate entity, but not in Scotland.) Social workers are now general social work practitioners, 'generically' trained, i.e. trained to deal with any type of practical, personal or social problem, any age range (any 'client group'). Social work is now 'people-orientated' rather than 'problem-orientated'. For example, in the past a family in which a child had to be committed into the care of the local authority because it was badly neglected and/or disturbed, because the mother was deeply depressed and the father physically disabled, might have had three social work specialists coming to help; now one social worker would try and cope.

The range of work done and settings worked in by individual social workers are therefore much wider than they used to be. Nevertheless, there is still scope for anyone who wants to work mainly with a particular client group – for example, the elderly or children – or who wants to work in a particular setting – in a hospital or day centre, or with foster parents and children. Local authorities' social services departments are organized in geographical 'area teams', and it is the *teams* which must be generic, i.e. able to cope with any situations. Within area teams workers can often specialize in work with a particular client group.

In fact, though specialization has been done away with theoretically, it is creeping back – as any collection of job advertisements in the press shows.

Social work can be frustrating: often problems arise from causes beyond the clients' or the social workers' control, such as bad housing or unemployment. Social workers are increasingly involved with questioning social policies which are often responsible for clients' situations, and with articulating clients' needs. Also, whether problems are caused by personal inadequacy, bad luck, ill health, the housing shortage or a combination of circumstances, there are rarely neat solutions, and social workers must be able to get job satisfaction from *trying* rather than only from *succeeding*: they may support a depressive, an alcoholic, an unstable family in an overcrowded flat or whatever the type of social casualty, for years and yet see the situation deteriorate.

Whatever the client group with whom they work or the setting in which they work, social workers use two 'social work methods': *casework* and *groupwork* (community work is often confused with groupwork, but in present-day social work organization (and jargon) the two mean totally different kinds of work – see below).

Casework

Casework continues to be the main social work method. It involves establishing a relationship of trust and understanding with the client, jointly identifying the client's problem and then 'working through it' to resolve it or to enable the client to live as normally as possible in the circumstances. Social workers always try and work themselves out of a job: however serious a client's problem, the social worker helps her client to remain or become independent and not to rely on the social worker's permanent support.

Clients' problems may be short-term and practical – arranging for a braille course for someone who is going blind; arranging for a child to be taken into care while the mother is seriously ill; or they may be long-term, and possibly requiring daily contact at least over a period, for example supporting a depressive client; or disturbed child in foster-care.

In most area teams, 'intake' or 'assessment' workers see new clients. So new social workers need not fear that they may be confronted with clients with whom they are unable to cope.

Caseworkers may have to work with whole families: for example, to help a client understand what led up to a situation (the first step towards resolving it) – whether it is a child's delinquency, despair due to disability, alcoholism, or whatever – the social worker may have to be involved with several members of a family, also with those who are not aware of, or do not want to be involved with, whatever the problem is. This is known as 'family casework'.

Groupwork

Groupwork is a far newer method of social work; it is used much less than casework, but its use has been increasing in the last few years. It is not as clearly defined as casework. In groupwork a number of clients share their similar problems, for 'therapeutic' reasons. Some people find it easier to discuss personal problems with fellow-sufferers rather than in a one-to-one situation with the social worker; through talking about their experiences and anxieties under the guidance of the social worker, clients help themselves and each other. Groups may be depressed patients, the physically handicapped, disturbed or retarded youths, etc. Not all groupworkers agree with 'labelling' of clients and some now use groupwork to help clients with various kinds of problems.

Groups can also be practical (and then the work may overlap with community work, see below). Young mothers on a new estate may be brought together to avoid their isolation and loneliness developing into serious psychological problems, and/or to encourage them to start a playgroup, etc.

A new form of groupwork is done in 'Intermediate Treatment Centres'. Under recent legislation, children who have been in trouble with the law may be committed into the care of the local authority but go on living with their families. They may have to attend an Intermediate Treatment Centre where they are encouraged to take part in various activities (it can be a bit like a special kind of youth club) and are also given individual casework attention.

Social workers work in a variety of settings:

1. SOCIAL SERVICES DEPARTMENTS

Most work in local authorities' social services departments. Their hours are often irregular – clients have to be visited in the evening or at weekends; someone always has to be on emergency stand-by in case of crises – anything from getting an abandoned baby into a nursery to coping with an evicted family. The social worker plans her own work within the team and has a great deal of scope for decision-making.

Most spend about two-thirds of their time seeing clients; the rest writing up reports, or in discussion with colleagues. This is a very important part, when having to take such vital decisions, for example, as whether to leave a baby with a disturbed mother or whether there is a danger of 'non-accidental injury' (baby-battering).

Possible post-training specializations include adoption and fostering; the elderly and/or handicapped; psychiatric patients discharged from hospital but still needing support; dealing with children whom the Courts have put under Supervision or Care Orders – which means children might be living at home but the social workers are responsible for them. This may involve occasional, or almost daily, contact.

2. HOSPITALS

Many hospitals have a social work department or team of social workers led by a Principal Social Worker. Although hospital social workers are employed by local authority social services departments, they are also members of the hospital team, together with medical colleagues. They assist patients and their families in coping with social and psychological problems which might impede the patient's recovery if left unattended. When working with an orthopaedic surgeon, for example, work may involve organizing help at home for a mother about to be discharged after a hip-replacement; when working with obstetricians, the social worker may help an unmarried mother work out her own and her baby's future – both in practical and psychological terms. Often she may have to help patients and their relatives come to terms with disabling or terminal illness; she may also cope with purely practical matters such as organizing home helps for new mothers; or meals on wheels for geriatric patients. With psychiatric patients, the hospital social worker may herself give 'on-going' support, and she may arrange for continued casework after the patient's discharge.

Hospital social work is relatively more of a 9 to 5 job than any other social work, and it does not usually require as much vital on-the-spot decision-making.

3. CHILD GUIDANCE CLINICS

Much smaller numbers of social workers work in child guidance clinics, where they are part of multi-professional teams with psychiatrists, psychologists and other professionals, helping in the diagnosis and treatment of difficult children. This may involve intensive long-term casework with both children and their parents.

4. EDUCATION WELFARE OFFICERS/ SCHOOL SOCIAL WORKERS

Another small group are education welfare officers or school social workers, acting as link between school and home. They are alerted by teachers when children first show problems such as truancy or learning difficulties. They visit parents and hope to diagnose and deal with the cause of the problem, or refer children and parents for help to other agencies.

5. SOCIAL WORK IN RESIDENTIAL CENTRES

Residential work is really a misnomer: it is the *client* who is residential: by no means all workers in residential establishments have to live in, and to confuse matters even more, 'residential work' may include work in day-centres. Residential homes and day-centres vary in size, purpose, client group. They can be for old people; the physically or mentally handicapped; for various groups of children: nurseries, older children, hostel for adolescents.

Residential child care officers are the most clearly defined group of 'residential' workers. They work in community homes (the comprehensive term for children's homes, including former approved schools, reception centres, remand homes, hostels for adolescents), in residential schools and homes for handicapped children. The title 'housemother' has officially been changed to 'residential social worker' or 'residential child care officer' but 'housemother' is still used.

The majority of children in residential care are 'deprived'; they tend to react with suspicion and hostility to new faces: social workers must be able to understand the underlying causes of the children's behaviour, to know how to help them. The work varies according to the extent of the children's deprivation and disturbance, and social workers can choose the type of home they want to work in. In a 'family'-type home for six or a dozen school-age children, several may be quite happy and in care for a short time while their mother is in hospital; in some homes most children suffer from some emotional disturbance, and duties include observing the children's behaviour, their relationships with and response to other children and adults.

Residential social workers in children's homes also organize such activities as drama, art and sport. Hours are necessarily long, but regular off-duty times are arranged.

Residential social work ('residential care') can mean very different levels and types of work – from housekeeping-plus-sympathy as assistant, to highly skilled diagnostic psychiatric support and rehabilitation. Under new agreements the same qualifications for both residential and fieldworkers (see **Training**) now apply. Residential work also provides excellent pre-training job opportunities.

6. PROBATION WORK

Probation officers are social workers attached to the Court; their function is, broadly, to help older delinquent children, young people and adults who have been in trouble with the law, to lead more satisfactory lives. Their main tasks:

(a) *Social Inquiry Reports*: To help the Court decide the best method of dealing with an offender, the probation officer inquires into the offender's background. This may involve having several exhaustive talks with the offender and possibly his/her family, to find out what circumstances led up to the offence and to enable the offender, possibly for the first time in his life, to think about the whys and hows of his or her life. On the basis of the probation officer's report, the Court may decide not to send the accused to prison, but to use one of the alternatives to prison:

Probation Orders: Offenders who are put on probation become the probation officer's clients. They report to her at regular intervals and discuss with her any problem – job, housing, relationship with family or girlfriend – anything which has any bearing on the client's way of life. While some clients are only too glad to have someone sympathetic to listen and advise, others are very difficult to make contact with and deal with.

Experiments with New Alternatives to Prison: New methods of dealing with offenders are being tried out. Under *Community Service Orders* offenders are required, under supervision, to do work which is of benefit to the community. Work may consist of helping in homes for the disabled; decorating old people's homes; building adventure playgrounds.

Day Training Centres: Offenders (usually aged between 25 and 35) may be ordered to attend such centres. They have work (art, craft, etc.) therapy, and intensive group discussion sessions where they are encouraged to come to grips with themselves, discuss what made them behave as they do, what they themselves can do to change their way of life, etc.

(b) *Prison Welfare and After-Care*: Probation officers may work *in prisons* (then they are called prison welfare officers) or in remand centres. They help prisoners keep alive links with their families (they may visit prisoners' families) and, towards the end of the prison sentence, help them plan their future.

After-Care: Ex-offenders aged under 21 *must*, over 21 need not but may, keep in regular touch with the probation officer.

The challenge of probation work is that it involves working towards change: in individuals – helping them towards a life which is both more satisfying for them, and for the community – and in society (experiments with alternatives to prison constitute such change), which may have treated individuals badly. The probation officer has a dual role: she must win and keep her client's confidence and yet must protect society from potentially harmful citizens; she must at times exert authority and yet not lose her client's trust. Probation officers are attached to Courts in England and Wales, but in Scotland local authority social work departments are responsible for work with adult offenders.

Voluntary organizations such as the N.S.P.C.C. or the Invalid Children's Aid Society and a number of similar organizations also employ trained social workers, and they may offer practical pre-training experience.

Community Work

If casework and groupwork are methods of dealing with individuals with problems, community work can be said to nip problems in the bud. As a 'social work approach' it is still evolving. Different community workers all see their jobs differently; many do not see it as 'social work' at all. The only point on which they all agree is that their job is different from the traditional community worker who ran a settlement (and still does so) in a poor area and whose work overlaps with *Youth and community worker* (see below). Terminology is utterly confused and confusing; terms of reference of, and training for, community work are vague and varied and changing.

Broadly, the new type of community worker tries to improve the quality of life of the community in which she works. She is part information point, part link with the local authority and other organizations which could be of use to the community, but whose services are not necessarily known to the majority of people. In order to make herself known in the community, the community worker makes it her business to meet as many people as possible. Having discovered what issues people are concerned about – or which may lead to problems – she may bring together people with similar concerns: for example, parents of children with educational problems, and help them form a parent–teacher association. She helps people to help themselves by giving advice and information. She also advises people to know what their rights and options are: she may advise old age pensioners to apply for benefits they are entitled to, or shoppers that they can refer their shoddy shoes to the consumer protection people. She may work closely with immigrant communities and community relations officers. Her terms of reference are vague and wide and call for initiative and insight, tact, and understanding.

Community workers initiate social action and help communities peacefully and lawfully to change the local *status quo*. It is a tricky job at times, as their loyalties may be divided between the community which needs better services or amenities, and their employers, the local authority, which is short of cash.

By no means all local authorities employ community workers. Community workers may have had social work training or relevant experience. There is no set pattern. The job requires great judgement and maturity.

Youth Work and Youth-and-Community Work

Job definition is again vague and confusing. The Youth Service comes under the local education authority, not the social services department. Youth workers, youth-and-community workers and community centre wardens can all be different jobs, or one person may combine the activities.

The *youth worker* is the most clearly defined job, and the oldest established. She initiates a wide variety of activities, usually for the 14–20-year-olds. All interests, from dancing to classical music, sailing to dressmaking, drama to sport, have to be catered for. The youth worker's most difficult tasks are to find the right balance of activities; to let members do as much organizing and planning for themselves as possible; never to let the club resemble an evening institute, and yet to bear in mind that the youth service is 'educational' in the widest sense. She must take an interest in all club members, especially in those who have personal problems. She may occasionally do a little unofficial social casework.

Her duties also include management of premises; recruitment and selection of voluntary helpers; dealing with administration; keeping in touch with social workers; attending committees; trying new methods of attracting 'unclubbables', which may mean going into discos and cafés to meet young people who do not come to youth clubs.

Increasingly, youth workers are '*youth-and-community workers*' and try and involve all ages. Youth clubs are attached to or part of a community centre where citizens of all ages meet for recreation, education or entertainment. Activities may include morning mother-and-toddler clubs; adventure playgrounds; painting or pottery classes for adults; reading classes for illiterates; English for immigrants; discussion groups. This type of work overlaps with community work (see above), but it is usually rather more administrative and traditional in aims. The main difference between the work of new-style community worker and the youth-and-community worker probably is that the former spends as much time as possible in the community; the traditional 'community centre warden' type of youth-and-community worker is busy in the centre.

Prospects generally

Though there is a shortage of social workers in many areas, level of recruitment depends on level of public expenditure. On the whole, however, the greatest difficulty is getting pre-training practical experience in social services departments, which is required for admittance to most social work training courses. The best opportunities for such vital experience are in residential social work.

Pay: Medium to high (see p. xxiii).

Training

The pattern of courses is very confusing. To qualify as professional social worker the Certificate of Qualification in Social Work (the C.Q.S.W., awarded by the Central Council for Training in Social Work) is required. Several types of courses lead to this qualification. Which type to take depends mainly on candidates' academic qualifications and on the stage in their lives at which they decide on social work.

Courses within each category also vary in emphasis on particular aspects – groupwork, community work, mental health, hospital, probation, residential, etc. Candidates should look at latest course curricula before choosing a course if they are interested in a particular social work setting or approach.

Course types leading to the C.Q.S.W.
Minimum age 20, although most entrants are older and have had relevant experience (for example, in residential or day centres as unqualified assistant). Courses leading to the C.Q.S.W. are available for non-graduates, graduates and undergraduates at polytechnics, universities and other educational institutions. Courses are usually full-time and half the training is practical work.

Courses for non-graduates normally last 2 years full-time. (In Scotland there is also one course, which lasts 3 years, where students can start at 19 instead of 20.)

Candidates aged 20–25 must normally have at least five O-levels including English or Welsh. In England and Wales colleges normally require 2 A-levels (in Scotland, 2 S.C.E. O grades and 3 'Highers').

Candidates aged 25 and over do not need G.C.E.s but must show evidence of ability to study at an advanced level, such as recent part-time or evening studies in an academic subject.

Courses for graduates last either 1 or 2 years. Graduates with 'relevant' degrees, diplomas and certificates can take 1-year C.Q.S.W. courses. Individual C.Q.S.W. courses decide which pre-professional awards are 'relevant'; they usually require studies to have covered social administration, policy and services and practical work in social service agencies. (C.C.E.T.S.W. is currently reviewing this.)

Graduates with 'non-relevant' degrees take *either* 2-year C.Q.S.W. courses; *or* a course leading to a 'relevant' post-graduate diploma in social administration or social studies followed by a 1-year C.Q.S.W. course.

Degree courses leading *also* to the C.Q.S.W. last 4 years.

Preliminary Training: For 16-year-olds with a few or no G.C.E.s: 2-year courses at further education colleges leading to Preliminary Certificate in Social Care (P.C.S.C.). Students spend about half the time on general education; most work for O- (possibly A-) levels; and half learning about the social services, about people and how the social services help them. Students spend some time in day and residential settings such as playgroups, day-centres, children's homes and homes for the elderly and handicapped.

The P.C.S.C. courses are an *introduction* to, rather than training in, professional social work; they lead to jobs in day and residential settings, but with experience, there is a possibility of becoming professionally qualified by attending a C.Q.S.W. or new Certificate in Social Service (see below) course.

All C.Q.S.W., and many C.S.S. courses include some teaching about *work with the deaf and blind*. Some C.Q.S.W. courses and C.S.S. options emphasize these areas of work. There are also post-qualifying study opportunities for people wishing to specialize in these areas.

Community work: C.Q.S.W. courses include community work, but there are also specific community work courses which do *not* lead to the C.Q.S.W. – in other words they qualify students for community work but not for 'orthodox' social work. Most full- and part-time courses are at post-graduate level, but candidates with relevant experience may be accepted. Courses are held at polytechnics and universities. Length: 1 or 2 years.

Youth and community work: Courses lead to work as youth worker and community centre warden rather than (at least without further experience) the new style community worker (see above). Courses last normally 2 years for non-graduates, 1 year for graduates. Entry requirements for under-25s: 5 O-levels. Some teacher-training and some degree courses include a youth or youth-and-community work option.

Certificate in Social Services (C.S.S.): Training leading to

C.C.E.T.S.W.'s Certificate in Social Service is designed to qualify non-social worker staff in the personal social services, including staff in residential homes and special schools, social work assistant, volunteer and home help organizers, and managers, senior staff and instructors in day services. Most students are employees on in-service training. Minimum age 18. If under 21 entrants need 5 O-levels or relevant experience. The courses, which consist of 3 units, last at least 2 years. All C.S.S. students complete a common unit and choose 1 of 4 standard options, relating to either children and adolescents, adults, the elderly, or communities. Within her standard option each student develops her particular interests in, for example, the under-5s or 'handicaps'. She also takes a special option to develop further one specific aspect of the work.

C.S.S. training does *not* normally lead on to professional social work training.

Personal attributes (all social work)

The desire to help people irrespective of one's own personal likes and dislikes; the ability to communicate with every level of intelligence, cultural or social background or emotional state; perseverance in the face of apparent failure when clients/groups show no sign of improvement or appreciation of efforts made for or on behalf of them; stability; a ready understanding of other people's way of life and point of view; sympathy and tolerance of human failings; the ability to take an interest in other people's problems without becoming emotionally involved; a sense of humour; wide interests unconnected with social work (to keep a sense of proportion); patience and empathy.

Position of women

Women do well up to middle-level jobs, then proportionately far fewer go up the ladder – while there are more women than men in social work, the proportion of women heads of departments is small but increasing.

Career-break: Returners are welcomed. *Refresher* training mainly on in-service basis.

Late entry: Mature entrants are welcome on all types of courses. Over-25s (sometimes over-30s) may be accepted on 2-year C.Q.S.W. courses without the normal G.C.E. qualifications; acceptance depends on course tutors' assessment of candidate's ability to cope with the course.

Courses specially for mature entrants and those with domestic responsibilities:
(1) For candidates aged 30-plus: 2-year C.Q.S.W. courses. A large number of places are reserved for prospective probation officers.

Courses are geared to people with 'experience of life' but not necessarily high educational attainment, though graduates also take these courses. (2) 3-year C.Q.S.W. courses for people with domestic responsibilities. Students work short days, have school holidays – hence the extra year. Flexible G.C.E. requirements. (3) Part-time course at London University Extra Mural Department for holders of relevant degree or diplomas.

Part-time: Not as many opportunities as one would have thought: Local authorities vary in their attitudes: some go to any lengths to enable women with children to work part-time; others take young full-timers rather than more mature and experienced part-timers. However, as the proportion of single women over 50 is decreasing, social work, like other professions with large proportions of women, may well have to make it easier for married women to return to work on their own (i.e. often part-time) terms.

Further in-formation   *C.C.E.T.S.W. Information Services*: Derbyshire House, St Chad's Street, London WC1H 8AD; 9 South St David Street, Edinburgh EH2 2BW; 14 Malone Road, Belfast BT9 5BN; West Wing, St David's House, Wood Street, Cardiff CF1 1ES.

Related careers   *Careers Officer – Nursery Nurse – Nursing – Personnel Officer – Police – Prison Work – Teaching*

SOCIOLOGY

Entry quali- 2, or more often 3, A-levels and 3 O-levels; mathematics or statistics at
fications either level.

The work The sociologist must not be confused with the social worker: the latter
deals with people with problems, whereas the sociologist studies the
conditions under which such problems arise and develop. While social
workers must have some knowledge of sociology, sociologists do *not*,
without further training, have the professional skill needed to deal with
people's problems and do casework (see p. 446). The distinction
between sociology and social work is a very important one.

Sociology is the study of social relationships and social structures. It
is concerned with how society functions, both in matters regulated and
organized by government and in those which depend on custom and
convention. Subjects of study include race relations, the relations
between labour and management, and the origins, function, change,
and development of established social institutions such as the family,
the religious sect, the political party, or the village or urban community.
It also considers such social phenomena as student revolts and the rise
in illegitimacy and delinquency. Sociologists examine how individuals
behave in any given setting – at home, in the neighbourhood, in the
club, in the 'gang'. They examine how individuals in these various
groups, and the groups themselves, 'interact', i.e. behave towards each
other. For example, the same person is a family man at home, a
colleague at his work, a customer in a shop and an old inhabitant in a
village expanding into a new town. In each of these roles he meets
different people and behaves in a different way. The sociologist studies
these 'behaviour patterns'.

Sociologists collect information in a variety of ways, mainly by
observation and interviewing. This may involve joining a youth club,
moving into a new town or an industrial slum, or working in a factory
and becoming a 'participant observer'. It may mean interviewing as an
outsider with the help of systematically prepared questionnaires. Apart
from this field work, there is the collation, analysis, interpretation and
presentation of the information collected. Statistics and computers are
used for this part of sociology. The academic and theoretical aspects of
sociology are what distinguish it above all from social work: it is by no
means entirely or even mainly 'dealing with people'.

Sociology is closely allied to and overlaps with other social sciences such as social psychology (p. 374), economics (p. 161), and social anthropology. In the past anthropologists have concentrated on studying the primitive societies, and sociologists the modern ones, but today the difference between these two disciplines is not as clear-cut.

Prospects

A sociology degree is not a vocational qualification, but mainly a basis for further specific training. The best scope is in social work, personnel management, planning. In industry, sociologists may be employed to research into industrial relations and general job satisfaction and productivity questions. There are some opportunities (without further full-time training) in the police and in market research, but there are more sociology graduates than jobs/trainings for which a sociology degree is useful.

Pay: Depends on job.

Training

Honours degree in sociology or a combination of social science subjects. The choice of the right course is important, and complicated: the wording used to describe courses varies, and the combination of subjects covered and the emphasis given to the different aspects of sociology cannot necessarily be deduced from the title given to a particular course. It is essential to study up-to-date prospectuses, and to consult the *C.R.A.C. Degree Course Guide* before choosing a course. It is not wise to go by the experience of people who read sociology even recently, because of the many changes and innovations in this field.

During their first year, students study the rudiments of the social sciences generally: economics, politics, social institutions, social and/or economic history, psychology, statistics, geography. During the second and third years they concentrate entirely on sociology or choose 2, occasionally 3, subjects from among: sociology, economics, geography, social administration, politics, philosophy, and statistics. There are also a few courses where sociology can be combined with physics and/or mathematics, with engineering, with education, with management studies, with computer studies.

Degree courses are largely theoretical; field work is not normally an integral part of the course. During vacations, or before starting her studies, the student is expected to do some work which brings her into close contact with unfamiliar aspects of life. Such work could be, for example, as a hospital orderly, a factory worker, or a helper in a youth club.

Personal attributes

A deep but detached interest in how people live, think and behave; a scientific approach to contemporary social problems rather than emotional involvement; the ability to get on well with all kinds of people at all levels of intelligence, at least sufficiently well to interview them successfully; above-average intellectual ability; an analytical, logical brain; the ability to discuss and write lucidly, and some mathematical ability.

Position of women Depends entirely on type of job: on the whole women sociology graduates do not encounter special problems. As the degree is a preparation for a wide variety of jobs, it could be a useful preparation for women who intend to return to work after a break and who are not quite sure what they want to do eventually. More women than men take sociology degrees.

Further information British Sociological Association, 10 Portugal Street, London WC2A 2HU

Related careers *Economics – Health Visitor – Market Research – Personnel Management – Planning – Police – Psychology – Social Work – Work Study*

SPEECH THERAPY

Entry quali-
fications
2 A-levels and 5 O-levels. Subjects should normally include English and 2 of the following: biology or zoology; mathematics; a foreign language; English literature; music.
For degree: chemistry *or* general science *and* A-level biology or zoology must be included.
Graduate entry: see **Training**.

The work
A speech therapist treats defects of voice, speech and language. Most patients are children: they may stammer, have an articulation problem or be excessively slow in learning to talk. In hospital clinics, therapists work with children and adults – many of whom have suffered brain damage or disease. Patients who have had their larynx or voice box removed have to be taught an alternative method of sound production.

Every patient needs a different approach – in helping each case the therapist must apply her knowledge of phonetics, psychology, anatomy and physiology, neurology, acoustics, and her common sense.

Most speech therapists work in clinics for children or in hospitals. Some patients are treated in groups, most individually. Most speech therapists work on their own, some as members of a team. In rural areas considerable travelling may be necessary.

A speech therapist meets a great many people – teachers, social workers, doctors, as well as her patients.

Prospects
Good, but jobs are not available everywhere. Some opportunities in Commonwealth and English-speaking developing countries.
Pay: Medium (see p. xxiii).

Training
For (essential) examination set by College of Speech Therapists:
Either: 3 years full-time at Speech Therapy Training Schools; courses may be shortened to 2 years for graduates, depending (a) on degree subject and (b) on individual training schools' policies. Syllabus includes: speech pathology and therapeutics; phonetics; linguistics; anatomy and physiology; psychology; neurology. Students are given an insight into related fields, such as physics of sound; paediatrics; the social services; plastic surgery in relation to speech therapy; audiology; diseases of the ear, nose and throat. During practical work in hospital and in school clinics students first observe then assist with treatments.
Or: Degree courses, at several universities.
Both methods are equal in job-getting terms.

Personal attributes	Understanding of people, whatever their age, temperament, background, and mood of the moment; desire to help, ability to detect personal problems which may have a bearing on the cause and treatment of the defect; tact, unlimited patience. Because so much of the work is with children, and sometimes with emotionally disturbed ones at that, the knack of gaining children's confidence; a pleasant voice – young patients are apt to imitate; a sensitive ear to detect slight sound differences; a calm manner and stable temperament; *for senior posts*, organizing ability.
Position of women	This used to be an all-female job: now the ratio is about 25 women to 1 man.
	Career-break: No problem. *Refresher courses* available.
	Late start: Usually welcome: over-25s may be accepted with lower-than-normal qualifications.
	Part-time: Good job opportunities, but not for head of department jobs.
Further information	College of Speech Therapists, 6 Lechmere Road, London NW2 5BU
Related careers	*Acting – Social Work – Teaching (Speech and Drama, p. 492).*

STAGE MANAGEMENT

Entry quali-fications None specified.

The work The stage manager and her team are responsible to the director, during rehearsals, for the implementation of her/his instructions. This usually includes such things as the recording of actors' moves and other stage directions in the prompt book; collecting props, sound effects, etc. for the director's approval; relaying of the director's requirements to the scenic, costume and lighting departments; ensuring that the actors are in the right place at the right time for rehearsals, costume fittings, etc. During the run of the play the stage manager is in charge of everything on stage and backstage, and is responsible for seeing that each performance keeps to the director's original intention. The stage manager may also conduct understudy rehearsals. She often works all day and is in the theatre until the lights go out. Stage managers are engaged by theatrical managements for one particular production, or for a repertory season, or occasionally on a more permanent basis.

Prospects Fair. There is a shortage of trained and experienced stage managers. Many directors start as stage managers. First jobs are the most difficult to find.

Pay: Low to medium; very occasionally high (see p. xxiii).

Training Full-time stage management courses at drama schools for 1–2 years. Admission to the courses is by interview and only those who are interested in stage management for its own sake or as preparation for work as a producer or director, but not as a stepping-stone to acting, are accepted.

The subjects studied include history of drama and theatrical presentation; literature; the elements of period styles; stage management organization and routine: play study; carpentry; stage lighting; voice; movement; make-up.

Note: Stage management training does *not* lead immediately to work in television and films, but, if supplemented with experience, it may do so. See also Arts Administration course, p. 64.

Personal attributes Organizing ability; natural authority and tact for dealing with temperamental and anxious actors; a practical approach; ability to deal with emergencies from prop-making to mending electrical equipment; calmness during crisis; interest in the literary and technical aspects of theatrical production; the ability to speak well – both lucidly and concisely; visual imagination; a genuine desire to do stage management in preference to acting – frustrated actors do not make good, or happy, stage managers.

Position of women Proportions of men and women have always been fairly equal; women are welcome in the profession and do well in it.

Career-break: Should be no problem if good experience before the break – and if willing to work all evening *and* often during the day.

Late entry: Should be good opportunities – maturity helps in a job which involves organizing others.

Part-time: Sporadic rather than part-time.

Further information Local theatre; drama schools.

Related careers *Acting – Broadcasting – Teaching (Speech and Drama,* p. 492)

STOCK EXCHANGE AND COMMODITY MARKETS

STOCK EXCHANGE: Stock jobbers – stock brokers – investment analysts – administration staff. COMMODITY MARKETS: Commodity brokers – dealers – market clerks – research staff.

**Entry quali-
fications**

Nothing rigidly laid down: but at least mathematics and English O-level normally expected (see **Training**). *Graduate* entry usual for *investment analysts* and *research staff*.

The work

(a)*The Stock Exchange*:

The Stock Exchange is a market at which individuals and institutions with money to invest buy stocks and shares in private companies and Government Securities, and where companies raise money by selling their shares. These 'securities', as they are called, may be in established firms or may be created when a company is formed, or following a merger. There are a few provincial exchanges; nearly all Stock Exchange people work in London.

(b) *The commodity markets*:

London is one of the world's main commodity trading centres, both for 'physical' commodities, that is raw materials, as well as 'futures', which concern the promise (or contract) to buy or sell a certain quantity of a commodity at a future date at a price agreed in advance. That means a producer or purchaser of, for example, sugar, who invests a large sum of money in planting or in buying a crop, will minimize losses – and gains – if the price fluctuates because of changes in supply and demand, between the times of planting and of harvesting the crop. Speculators neither produce nor use the commodity, but hope to make a profit by buying and selling 'contracts' at what they hope is the right time. 'Soft' commodity markets (sugar, cotton, etc.) are housed at the Corn Exchange (except for grains at the Baltic); five metal markets at the Metal Exchange. Physical trading is no longer carried out on the floor, but directly between companies; but futures markets are conducted by an 'open outcry' system, in which dealers sit in a ring at the Exchange calling out their bids and offers.

JOBS IN THE STOCK EXCHANGE

1. *Stock jobbers* are wholesalers of shares, specializing in certain sectors of the market. They buy and sell to stockbrokers and other jobbers 'on the floor' of the Exchange, never directly to the public. Some now have police-type radios while 'on the floor' to communicate with their office.

2. *Stock brokers* are agents who advise their clients on which securities to buy or sell at any given time. They deal with jobbers on behalf of their clients. Most large firms of stockbrokers delegate the actual dealing on the Stock Exchange floor to *authorized clerks*. Brokers spend much time talking to clients and studying information provided by the research department's investment analysts.

3. *Investment analysts* are mainly employed by broking firms to provide the information on which to base advice to clients. They analyse company accounts and economic reports and confer with senior management of companies in order to assess trends and forecast market movements. Most specialize in one section of the market. (Investment analysts also work for merchant banks.)

4. *Administration staff* process the transactions arranged by the brokers and jobbers. Routine work is done by computer; the rest is highly specialized and involves the preparation of documents and calculating and arranging payment of commission and taxes.

JOBS IN THE COMMODITY MARKETS

1. *Dealers*, or market traders, carry out the actual trading in the dealing ring, as described above. Their assistants, called *blue buttons*, sit in the dealing room relaying information and instructions to and from the dealers by phone or two-way radio.

2. *Market clerks* work for the market organizers themselves and chalk up the trading moves on a large blackboard as dealing is in progress. They usually progress to dealing.

3. *Commodity brokers* advise clients on when to buy and sell which goods at what price (like stockbrokers).

4. *Research staff* (like investment analysts) collect and analyse data with which to brief the brokers. They study information on climatic, political, economic conditions, gluts, shortages, price trends and market movements all over the world.

Prospects These are not the most secure of occupations; success depends on the economic climate and on drive and personality. Openings are not plentiful, but, once in a job, promotion prospects for the right type of person are reasonable, regardless of academic achievement. Clerical staff can become authorized clerks, 'blue buttons', dealers, brokers and jobbers. Employees who are considered suitable to become members of the Stock Exchange usually receive assistance towards their membership fee – which is considerable – from their sponsoring firms. Commodity dealers usually progress to posts on the 'physical trading' side of their companies.

Pay: Medium to high (see p. xxiii). Stockbroking firms generally offer lower salaries than jobbers, but give bonuses, as do commodity brokers.

Training

Varies. There are no formal training schemes for the commodity markets – junior staff learn on-the-job. Some stockbroking firms operate training schemes for clerks for the Stock Exchange Certificate. Membership of the Stock Exchange, a precondition of partnership, requires a pass in the 'Stock Exchange Examination', which can be taken in stages over any length of time, and is studied for by correspondence course, day-release (rarely), or private study.

Graduates entering the Stock Exchange or commodity markets are most likely to go into investment analysis or research departments. Useful degrees are statistics, law, economics, modern languages.

Personal attributes

Entrepreneurial and gambling instinct, flair for dealing with figures, extrovert personality, ability to communicate easily on the telephone, personally and in writing; mental agility; quick-wittedness; high powers of concentration; exceptional self-confidence; memory for people and figures.

Position of women

The City is still very much a male preserve; women need great motivation to break down sex-barriers. About 30 out of over 4,000 stockbrokers are women. Women were officially admitted to the Stock Exchange in 1973; but they have only established themselves in research and investment analysis departments.

Career-break: Would present problems, except, possibly, in research.

Late start: Only if professionally qualified in a related field, such as economics, accountancy, banking.

Part-time: Unlikely.

Further in- Public Relations Department, Stock Exchange, London EC2N 1HP
formation London Commodity Exchange Co., Cereal House, 58 Mark Lane,
London EC3R 7NE

Related *Accountancy – Banking – Economics – Insurance*
careers

SURVEYING

Chartered surveyor – surveying technician

Chartered Surveyor

Valuation surveyor – estate agent – auctioneer – quantity surveyor – building surveyor – planning and development surveyor – land agent/agricultural surveyor – land surveyor and hydrographic surveyor – minerals or mining surveyor – general practice surveyor

Entry quali-
fications

For membership of the Royal Institution of Chartered Surveyors and the Institute of Quantity Surveyors: 2 A-levels, 3 O-levels; mathematics and an English subject to be included, at either level.

For membership of the Incorporated Society of Valuers and Auctioneers: 5 O-levels, including an English and a maths subject.

The work

Surveying is an umbrella term for a variety of jobs which are all, to varying degrees and in varying proportion, concerned with, to quote the R.I.C.S., 'the measurement, management, development and valuation' of virtually anything: oceans, rivers, harbours, earth's surface, all land, and anything that is in or on land or water, whether natural or man-made. Many surveying jobs are also concerned with protecting improving the urban and rural environment and the efficient use of resources. The various surveying branches each involve a different mix of technical, commercial, practical, academic ingredients, and different amounts of time spent on dealing with clients, dealing with other professionals, and on office and outdoor work. Each branch, therefore, suits people with different temperaments, interests, aptitudes. For example, the urban estate agent-surveyor has little in common with the hydrographic surveyor charting oceanic depth, or with the planning surveyor doing research into shopping centres.

The professional surveying specializations are grouped into 'Divisions' by the *Royal Institution of Chartered Surveyors*: 'General Practice' which covers valuation, estate agency, auctioneering and urban estate/housing management; quantity surveying; building surveying; planning and development; land agency and agricultural surveying; land and hydrographic surveying; mineral surveying.

The Incorporated Society of Valuers and Auctioneers' qualification covers much the same ground as the R.I.C.S.'s General Practice Division *except* urban estate/housing management. (See also Housing Management, p. 213.)

The main surveying branches:

1. VALUATION SURVEYOR (also called Valuer, or simply Surveyor)

She assesses the value of any type of property at any particular time. It may be in connection with rating, insurance, death duty purposes, as well as for general commercial purposes. There are various valuation methods; the most commonly used one is the 'comparison' method. This is an intricate mixture of basing judgement on ascertainable facts – value of property in the neighbourhood or other similar property; quality, etc., as well as on 'getting the feel'. When assessing the value of residential property, or a row of shops, for example, factors taken into account include possible future development in the area (motorways, one-way traffic schemes, housing estates, parking restrictions); amenities (open spaces; swimming baths; entertainment facilities generally); proximity to schools, shops, transport; noise; as well as type of neighbourhood and informed guesswork as to whether the area is likely to go down/come up; does it have any feeling of community (which might affect quality of school or be of interest to the elderly, etc.).

Valuers also assess contents of houses. Though they are expected to be able to tell a Rembrandt from an amateur's efforts, valuers do not normally assess the value of works of art but call on experts in that field as necessary. If working for a property developer or local authority they may value land. They may inspect, for example, a plot of land which is up for sale, assess its potential in terms of houses, shops, flats, etc., to be built there, and do a rough 'costing' of whatever type of building is being considered.

Apart from working for estate agents, local authorities, property developers and other commercial concerns, valuation surveyors also set up in private professional practice. While work for property developers requires a certain amount of gambling instinct and very pronounced business acumen, local authority valuers' work is more concerned with valuing according to laid-down criteria.

2. ESTATE AGENT

Valuation surveyors (as described above) may be estate agents, but estate agents are not necessarily valuation surveyors. Within surveying, estate agency is probably the most commercially and least technically oriented specialization. There is at the moment no need for estate agents to have particular qualifications (but this may soon change). However, most firms of estate agents have at least one R.I.C.S. or I.S.V.A. qualified partner. Estate agents negotiate the sale, purchase, leasing of property – not only of houses but also of industrial and commercial premises, agricultural and other land. They arrange and advise on mortgages and on implications of Rent Acts, and on relevant law generally. They manage property for clients, which involves drawing up leases, collecting rents, responsibility for maintenance, etc.

House agents' clients may be property managers of vast commercial empires, or first-time house purchasers who need to be guided through the complexities of making the most expensive purchase of their lives. House agents may specialize in one type of property (residential, or commercial or industrial), or they may deal with a mixture of types of properties. 'Negotiators', who deal with clients, often specialize in dealing with one type of client. Traditionally, women often specialize in dealing with house purchasers, helping them to sort out priorities: few can afford their dream house, i.e. what they want exactly where they want it. Negotiators help weigh up advantages of, say, sunny garden or 'good neighbourhood'; solidly built but no garage; not-so-solid but near shop/school/transport/parks, etc.

Estate agents advise vendors on the price to ask, so they have to understand something about valuation, even if they are not professionally qualified valuers. The work involves a lot of client-contact, of getting about and getting to know an area and being aware of changes in type of inhabitants and property.

3. AUCTIONEER

Most estate agents are also auctioneers. (Normally estate agents employ different people as negotiators and as auctioneers, but in small firms everybody might do everything.) Some firms specialize in auctioneering commercial, industrial, residential or agricultural property; others specialize in furniture, machinery, works of art. (The few well-known auction rooms where paintings, etc. are auctioned are staffed by art specialists who have learnt about auctioneering rather than by the estate agent-valuer-auctioneer.) An auctioneer outside London may well auction the contents of a house one day, cattle in the local market-place the next, and a row of shops the day after that. Work varies according to whether done in country town or big city. The actual auctioneering is only part of the work: it also involves assessing value and advising vendors on 'reserve price', and it involves detailed 'lotting up' and cataloguing items to be sold.

While some firms of auctioneers, especially in the country, engage people specially for auctioneering and teach them the necessary skills and techniques, it is advisable to train as valuer (see above) as well.

4. QUANTITY SURVEYOR

Quantity surveyors are also called 'building economists', 'construction cost consultants', 'building accountants'. The quantity surveyor is an essential member of the design team on building projects of any size. She translates architects' or civil engineers' designs into detailed costs – of labour, materials, overheads; and she breaks down all materials and processes to be used into detailed quantities and timing. She evaluates alternative processes and materials and may suggest alternative design technologies and materials to those suggested on the original design. Her thorough and up-to-date knowledge of construction technologies enables her to find ways of getting work carried out in the most speedy, economical and efficient way, without impairing the design. Calculations involved may be very complex – for example future maintenance costs have to be considered when evaluating the use of alternative materials and processes. Calculations are often done with computers.

Quantity surveyors are normally appointed by the designer of the project, i.e. the architect or civil engineer. At a time of soaring costs and constantly changing technologies, the quantity surveyor's status in the design team has risen enormously in the last few years and, although the architect/civil engineer has the last word, the quantity surveyor's suggestions or modifications are taken very seriously indeed. Sometimes a quantity surveyor is appointed the project manager.

The quantity surveyor is responsible for cost control during the whole project. She advises on cost implications of any proposed variations to the design, makes interim valuations of completed work, checks contractors' interim accounts and settles final accounts. She is also involved with financial administration of contracts for supportive services (mechanical and electrical engineering services for example) and may be responsible for overall project management.

The quantity surveyor's work is a combination of straightforward figure work, complex calculations, and negotiating skills. She must be able to deal with colleagues from other disciplines, contractors, clients. She spends more time at her desk doing calculations or writing reports and at negotiations than on the building site, but the time spent on the various ingredients of the job varies from project to project, and according to the type of employer.

About 60% of quantity surveyors are in private professional practice; others work for contractors, consultant engineers, in government departments, local authorities, commercial and industrial firms.

5. BUILDING SURVEYOR

This is the most practical specialization. Building surveyors make structural surveys of and diagnose type of defects of buildings of all types, for prospective purchasers, vendors, owners, building societies. They assess maintenance costs and control maintenance programmes; they prepare plans for conversion and improvements. They draw up plans and specifications, go out to tender, and may supervise contractors' work and check accounts. They advise on building, planning, health and safety regulations, and they may also be involved with restoration or maintenance of ancient monuments and historic buildings. They spend a good deal of time clambering about on buildings to check roofs, lofts, drains, fire escapes and general structural soundness, so their work requires agility.

Some work in private professional practice; the majority are employed by any type of organization which owns, sells, buys, builds, manages property. This includes housing associations, contractors, all types of industrial and commercial firms, local authorities and central government.

6. PLANNING AND DEVELOPMENT SURVEYOR

This used to be part of 'general practice surveying' and became a separate R.I.C.S. Division in 1975. The work overlaps with Town and Country Planning (see p. 356).

Planning surveyors are concerned with the efficient allocation of resources in planning and with planning economics and planning law. The work is largely desk research (including statistics) and communicating with other specialists concerned with planning. A planning surveyor, for example, investigates the economics of a proposed shopping area. That would involve collecting facts and figures from various sources and writing up the findings. She might have to find a suitable site for an industrial plant which has to be somewhere within a given area, must be near an inland waterway, near transport and must not be within an area of scenic value. That would not necessarily involve travelling, but consulting maps and relevant organizations.

The planning surveyor also advises clients on planning implications of proposals to buy and develop a property. This could involve visiting the site, taking photographs, and then appraising the proposal from a civic design point of view.

Planning and development surveyors work for planning consultants, local and central government, as specialists in general practice surveying firms.

Graduates can take a post-graduate (day-release) course in town and country planning and move into planning itself. As planning degree courses are oversubscribed and surveying courses are not, this is a useful route into planning.

7. LAND AGENT/AGRICULTURAL SURVEYOR

Terms are confusing. Traditionally, land agents were (usually resident) managers of farms or other rural properties. There is now a tendency for firms of agricultural surveyors (or land agents) in professional practice to manage farms and estates on a contract basis, i.e. a firm manages a number of farms and/or rural estates, etc., rather than one individual being employed by one farmer, though that may also be the case (see Agriculture, p. 27). Agricultural surveyors do much the same work in rural areas as general practice surveyors do in towns. They may do valuation (including livestock and agricultural plant), estate agency, auctioneering, or they may concentrate on farm management (see Agriculture, p. 27). Increasingly they advise on alternative uses of land, for recreational purposes such as country parks, caravanning and camping sites, country trails, long-distance footpaths, nature reserves. They would then also develop/manage land so used.

Agricultural surveyors may also conduct sales and auctions of country properties, contents of country houses, livestock, agricultural machines, plant, forests and forest products.

Many agricultural surveyors are in private professional practice. According to the size of the practice, other specialist surveyors (valuers, building surveyors) may be employed. Agricultural surveyors sometimes now do farm business management as well, perhaps employing specialists to advise on mechanization, diversification (see alternative land use above) and other ways of improving farm profits.

They also work for A.D.A.S. (see Agriculture, p. 26), local government, the National Trust and other bodies which own/manage land.

Agricultural surveying is an unusual combination of business, technical, environmental and agricultural work, and one of the few professional jobs which include getting about the countryside.

8. LAND SURVEYOR AND HYDROGRAPHIC SURVEYOR

Land surveyors must not be confused with land agents/agricultural surveyors. Land surveyors are surveyors in the strict sense of the word. They use sophisticated technologies (including aerial photography) to measure and plot the precise shape and position of natural and man-made features on land for the purposes of map-making, including large-scale maps which are used for engineering constructions. (Before motorways can be sited, for example, or bridges built, the minutest physical details of the area have to be plotted and mapped.)

Land surveyors do not draw maps; that is done by cartographers (see p. 94). Land surveyors work in private practice, or they work for the government (Ordnance Survey, Ministry of Defence mainly), or for consulting engineers and big contractors. Some work for the Directorate of Overseas Surveys which sends (experienced) surveyors to the developing – and other – countries to survey land, some of which has never been surveyed and mapped before.

Hydrographic surveyors are the smallest and most scientific branch. They survey oceans, waterways, harbours and ports for purposes of producing nautical charts which show the precise shape, size, location of physical features of the sea bed, etc. and hazards, currents, tides, sunken wrecks. The information sent by hydrographic survey ships operating in most parts of the world to the Navy's Hydrographic Department is being continuously revised and is done with highly sophisticated equipment. British Admiralty Charts are used by seafarers all over the world.

Most hydrographic surveyors are also naval officers. This is fairly tough outdoor work.

9. MINERALS OR MINING SURVEYOR

This is the smallest specialization. Mining surveyors are responsible for mine safety and for mapping mineral deposits, and are involved with the potential use, value, properties, management and exploitation of mineral deposits, which means combining technical, scientific, managerial and commercial aspects. They are also responsible for minimizing environmental damage to the countryside where mineral deposits are mined.

In this country mining surveyors are concerned only with coal mining, but overseas minerals surveying covers a variety of other minerals.

Prospects   Vary according to economic conditions, but are reasonable generally; best opportunities are for general practice, quantity, and building surveyors. Some opportunities in E.E.C. countries (for those who speak the relevant language fluently!), especially for quantity surveyors, who are also in demand in Africa and the Middle East.

Pay: Medium to very high (see p. xxiii).

Training   For membership of the Royal Institution of Chartered Surveyors (any surveying specialization) and of the Institute of Quantity Surveying: over 50% now take full-time 3-year (or 4-year sandwich) degrees or diplomas which lead to full or partial exemption from R.I.C.S. Membership examinations; others study while in appropriate employment, which takes 5 to 6 years of part-time study. Day-release is automatically granted only in public sector employment. In the private sector, students usually have to study in their own time by correspondence course and evening classes. However, quantity surveying students are an exception: because the demand here exceeds the supply, they may find it much easier than others to be given day-release.

Choosing a full-time course is complicated. Some courses allow students to choose between several allied specializations during the second year, but for other specializations, such as mineral surveying, the decision has to be made before starting a course. It is essential to study the R.I.C.S.'s up-to-date lists of exempting degrees and diploma courses in each division. Course titles, especially for general practice, vary and are often misleading. For example there are several different titles for courses leading to General Practice Division exemptions; the titles are not necessarily an indication of course emphasis either.

Quantity surveyors may qualify with the Institute of Quantity Surveyors instead of the R.I.C.S.

(Though it is usual to work initially in the specialization in which one qualified, it is quite possible to switch specializations later. In practice some specializations (such as, for example, building and quantity surveying) are more easily interchangeable than, for example, general practice and hydrographic.)

Graduates from any discipline may study for the R.I.C.S. Graduate Entry Scheme examination by part-time study or correspondence course, while in appropriate employment. Study takes about 18 months to 3 years. Though theoretically an arts graduate could qualify as a land and hydrographic surveyor, it is more usual, in practice, for Graduate Entry students to choose something like building or planning and development, and, perhaps, for physics graduates to choose hydrographic surveying.

General practice surveyors (i.e. valuers, estate agents, auctioneers) normally train *either* for the R.I.C.S. General Practice Division, as above, *or* for membership of the *Incorporated Society of Valuers and Auctioneers* (see entry requirements). I.S.V.A. training is *either* by 3-year full-time course (courses only at a few colleges and polytechnics); *or* by day-release; *or* (the most common method) by correspondence course, taking 4 to 6 years, while in appropriate employment.

The I.S.V.A. qualification is now recognized by the Civil Service and local government as equivalent to the R.I.C.S. General Practice Division for employment of valuation surveyors.

However, in estate agency and professional general practice surveying it is considered less prestigious.

Personal attributes

Practical approach to problem-solving; ability to inspire confidence in clients; ability to take complex decisions on own initiative and work as one of a team as well; for some jobs – ability to handle labour; for consultancy, business acumen; liking for being out of doors; for women, indifference to working in what is still largely a male preserve.

Position of women

There is no logical reason whatever why there should be so ludicrously few women surveyors. Only 0·9% of qualified R.I.C.S. members are women, and even of its student members only 4·5% are women. The I.S.V.A. has 3·4% women members.

So far the few women in the profession are doing well, although some have changed employers rather often because promotion was blocked for them. A comparatively high proportion has gone into teaching (and at least one polytechnic has a woman as head of the surveying department).

Only mining and hydrographic surveying should present any problems. Mining surveyors during training must go down the mines and women are not yet allowed to *work* in the mines (which surveying trainees do not actually have to do), and hydrographic surveyors are trained, partly, by the Navy, on naval vessels. No woman has made any effort to overcome the down-the-mines problem, and no Wren has, apparently, yet asked to be trained for hydrographic surveying. These two are, in any case, a tiny minority of surveyors. No other surveying makes demands on physical strength or presents any hazards women, however traditional in outlook, cannot cope with as well as men. (Building surveyors go up scaffolding, but women have no worse heads for heights than men.)

Career-break: Should not be difficult in, for example general practice surveying; possibly more difficult in areas where technologies change rapidly, but here keeping up with developments by reading journals should help. No refresher courses so far.

Late start: Requires very strong motivation. No women seem to have tried yet; no problem getting training, but first job may be difficult for over-30s.

Part-time: Not so far, but no reason why established surveyors should not suggest to their employers that part-time – with flexible hours – should work well.

Further information

Royal Institution of Chartered Surveyors, 12 Great George Street, Parliament Square, London SW1P 3AD;

Institute of Quantity Surveyors, 98 Gloucester Place, London W1H 4AT

Incorporated Society of Valuers and Auctioneers, 3 Cadogan Gate, London SW1X 0AS

Related careers	*Agriculture and Horticulture – Architecture – Cartography – Engineering – Housing Management – Surveying Technician – Town and Country Planning*

Surveying Technician (includes managerial jobs in the building industry)

Entry quali-fications   Theoretically 3 Grade III C.S.E.s, in mathematics, a science and English language, gain entry to a T.E.C. Certificate course (see p. xv). In practice most employers and colleges require slightly higher qualifications; these vary according to supply and demand from Grade II C.S.E.s to 4 O-levels.

The work   It overlaps in at least some of the specializations with supervisory and management jobs in the building industry (see p. 85), where titles vary: the term 'technician' may not be used, even when the qualification required *is* a technician qualification.

Individual technicians' work varies enormously; some are desk-bound draughtsmen, some are out and about using sophisticated procedures and equipment for taking measurements; some have a great deal of 'client contact' etc. Almost invariably they are part of a team.

The majority work under the overall direction of chartered surveyors, architects, civil engineers or planners. Some of their work is indistinguishable from that often done by chartered surveyors: until a few years ago, chartered surveyors qualified almost exclusively by on-the-job plus part-time training, and they had only slightly higher entry qualifications (5 O-levels) than technicians often have now. While chartered surveyors' training is now certainly much more demanding than technicians', many tasks are still the same as they always were and do not require the chartered surveyors' in-depth training. Technician-level qualifications are sufficient for the majority of those 'surveyors' who, while wanting a certain amount of responsibility and professional training, do not aspire to initiate and take charge of complex projects.

Surveying technician specializations:

1. BUILDING SURVEYING TECHNICIAN
(see Building Surveying, p. 472)

Sub-divisions cover construction and assessment of structures; administration of building regulations; preparation of plans; specification for and organization of work to be carried out by contractors; estimates of cost before projects start; dealing with tenders and contracts and checking and passing contractors' accounts; advising lay public on soundness of construction of property they consider buying (while ultimate responsibility for such advice lies with the employing chartered surveyor, the actual surveying on which surveyors' reports to clients are based is often carried out by technicians – which the customer is not necessarily aware of); advice to property owners on maintenance and repair. This may include drawing up schedules for redecoration, advice on eradication of damp, dry rot, etc.

Building surveying technicians work in a great variety of settings – and under a great variety of titles (for example *building manager, building surveyor, building inspector*). They are employed by virtually any type of organization which owns or is responsible for the building and/or maintenance of property, and by firms of consultants. When they work for building contractors, they may also be called *Planning* or *Contracts Manager*, or *Contracts Surveyor*. Their work may be mainly organizational – ensuring that manpower and equipment are used efficiently; this means planning all the operations which are involved in completing a contract to build whatever it is. For example, if a firm of building contractors is engaged simultaneously on converting several houses into flats and building office blocks, the contracts planner or manager has to estimate how long how many workers and which equipment will be required on each job; when the various specialists such as heating engineers, plasterers, electricians, should be where.

While in the past only very large contractors had contract planners, now middle-sized firms often engage such staff (under various titles, and not necessarily *only* engaged on this type of planning).

Another job for building surveying technicians is *site manager*. She is responsible for organization of the sequence and smooth working of operations on site.

Technicians who prefer desk-bound work can become draughtsmen and eventually be in charge of a drawing office, or work for estate agents, where they meet the general public (see p. 469).

Training On the job with day- or block-release for T.E.C. Certificate in Building Studies followed by Higher Certificate; or full-time Diploma in Building

Studies followed either by part-time day-release study for Higher Certificate or by full-time Higher Diploma.

Entrants with 1 appropriate A-level start training for Higher Certificate or Diploma. Each Certificate course normally takes 2 years' part-time study, a Diploma course 2 years' full-time (see p. xv for T.E.C. details).

2. QUANTITY SURVEYING TECHNICIAN

This offers probably the greatest scope. It has three main sub-divisions (with rather quaint traditional titles):

(a) *Taker Off*: She abstracts and measures from architect's, surveyor's or engineer's drawings every item of labour and materials to be used on a project, and lists them in recognized terms. The information is needed to arrive at 'cost plans' and bills of quantity. The job is almost wholly office-based, and usually involves contact with architects, engineers and surveyors as well as cooperation with other technicians.

(b) *Worker Up*: She works out volumes, quantities and areas which have been measured by the taker off, and classifies all items in recognized units. Every item of labour and/or materials used on a project is then recorded on the Bill of Quantities. Other information may be 'banked' for future reference, in computers. Workers up are entirely office-based; they may be responsible for a whole project or section of a project.

(c) *Post-Contract Surveyor and Site Measurer*: She divides her time between office and site. Work includes measuring for purposes of producing periodic valuations of work done by contractors, and discussions with sub-contractors employed on the site. Post-contract surveyors (the word 'surveyor' is used though they are surveying *technicians*) may be physically measuring work on site one day, attending a site meeting with a number of colleagues from different building-work spheres the same afternoon, and negotiating final payment with a sub-contractor the next day. They must have been workers up and takers off before becoming post-contract surveyors. Their job overlaps very much with that of chartered quantity surveyors (see p. 471).

Training   As for building surveying, with different course units.

3. GENERAL PRACTICE TECHNICIAN

This Division covers the work done by chartered general practice and planning surveyors (see p. 468). (At chartered level, a new *Planning and Development division* was set up recently; at technician level, it did not seem necessary to start an additional Division. Most technicians who intend to help chartered planning division surveyors would, probably, take the general practice technician training.)

General practice technicians may specialize in valuation, estate agency, estate management, town planning (see Chartered Surveying, p. 468). Openings are very varied, ranging from suburban estate agency's negotiator (see p. 469) to Inland Revenue or insurance company's valuation technician. This specialization offers scope both to those who are mainly interested in meeting members of the public and to those who want to do mainly drawing office work.

Training As for building surveying, with different course units.

4. LAND SURVEYING TECHNICIAN

These work with chartered land surveyors (see p. 473). There are opportunities for work with sophisticated instruments such as electronic distance-measuring equipment, for photographing and tracking man-made satellites, or in aerial photography.

This is one of the most adventurous of technician specializations, with work for oil companies and air survey companies at home or abroad.

Training T.E.C. Certificate and Higher Certificate in Surveying, Cartography or Planning. Each Certificate normally takes 2 years' part-time study while in relevant employment.

5. MINERAL SURVEYING TECHNICIANS (see Chartered Mineral Surveying)

This is a small Division and involves the preparation of accurate plans in connection with safety, operation and development of mines, and geological formations in connection with mineral deposits. Much of the work is underground.

Training T.E.C. Certificate and Higher Certificate in Mineral Surveying or Mining. Each Certificate normally takes two years' part-time study while in relevant employment.

6. HYDROGRAPHIC SURVEYING TECHNICIAN (see Hydrographic Surveyor, p. 473)

Making and up-dating charts of seas and coastlines, and profiles of sea beds; 'sign posting', on charts, of shipping lanes. This can be arduous outdoor work on surveying ships and requires practical seamanship; only few draughtsmanship, office-based, jobs.

Training   Mainly at Royal Navy Hydrographic School, Plymouth. A few courses at polytechnics; or special option in T.E.C. Land Surveying.

7. AGRICULTURAL SURVEYING TECHNICIAN

This work overlaps with *agriculture* (see p. 23) and *land agency* (see Surveyors, p. 473). Agricultural surveying technicians have only limited scope.

Training   Unlike other technicians who have the choice between full- and part-time training, agricultural surveying technicians all take full-time courses at Agricultural Institute or College (see p. 29).

Prospects   *Surveying technicians* generally are in demand in all spheres, but demand is greatest in quantity, general practice and building surveying. There are, in these specializations, usually about 5 vacancies for every 1 vacancy for chartered surveyors.

It is possible, but only after about 10 years, for surveying technicians to take the Direct Membership Examination of the Royal Institute of Chartered Surveyors and become fully professionally qualified – even without having got any A-levels. Experienced technicians, especially in quantity surveying, have some opportunities in E.E.C. countries, especially if they speak the relevant language fluently.

Personal attributes   Some mathematical ability; interest in finding practical solutions to technical problems; liking for outdoor work; ability to work as one of a team and also to take responsibility, coupled with willingness to work for people more highly qualified than oneself; meticulous accuracy; self-confidence (see **Position of Women**); ability, or willingness to learn, to be in charge of building-site workers.

Pay: Medium to high (see p. xxiii).

Position of women   The proportion of women technicians is minute (though there have been draughtswomen for a long time): well below 1%. However, especially in planning, estate agency (general practice) and quantity surveying opportunities for women are there; but very few women are applying for training or jobs. Only tradition is keeping this area of employment virtually a male preserve.

In some offices women may still be unwelcome, but there are many more where they are welcome. Training courses invariably welcome women students (if only because many of the courses are under-used). (However, women may not be able to train for mineral and hydrographic surveying because of the practical work down the mines and on survey ships. Apparently no girls have *tried* to train.)

Career-break: It is too early to know how returners would fare, but, if they have kept up with developments, there is no reason why experienced technicians should not return to work. It would probably be easier in general practice and quantity surveying than, say, in agricultural surveying.

Late start: So far none seem to have tried, but theoretically there is no reason why women should not start in their twenties or thirties.

Part-time: Not at the moment, except, perhaps, in quantity surveying; but no reason why experienced technicians should not try and make their own part-time arrangements, especially in estate agency work.

Further information	Society of Surveying Technicians, Aldwych House, Aldwych, London WC2B 4EL

Related careers	*Architectural Technician – Architecture – Building Management – Chartered Surveyor – Housing Management*

TAX INSPECTOR

Entry quali-fications Honours or post-graduate degree in any subject.

The work The Inspector of Taxes' main duty is to examine the accounts of business concerns in order to agree the amount of profits for taxation purposes. This brings her into contact with the whole range of Britain's industry and commerce in her own district. There are Inland Revenue Offices in all areas.

She deals with many kinds of people – accountants, lawyers, industrialists, farmers, small shopkeepers – by personal interview as well as by correspondence. She also represents the Crown before an independent tribunal when she and the taxpayer concerned cannot agree on the amount of tax assessment.

Prospects Generally good, but jobs not available everywhere. Promotion prospects good for people willing to move to where there happens to be vacancy.

Pay: Medium to high (see p. xxiii).

Training During the first 3 years of service inspectors take part-time training and residential courses to a professional standard and have to pass examinations which qualify for promotion. Tax Officer (Higher Grade) entrants are given part-time training for 2½ years.

Personal attributes Common sense; judgement; administrative ability; keen intellect; the ability to sum up people and situations; impartiality; equanimity; enjoyment of responsibility.

Position of women Twice as many women as men join as tax officers, but the higher up the ladder, the smaller the proportion of women. This is apparently at least partly due to the fact that (a) far fewer graduate women than men join Inland Revenue, and (b) because women are not often willing to move round the country for promotion. However, it is also likely that women have to have more drive and determination than men to reach the higher grades.

Career-break and *Late start*: See **Civil Service**, p. 130.

Further information	Civil Service Commission, Alencon Link, Basingstoke, Hampshire

Related careers	*Accountancy – Actuary – Banking – Insurance*

TEACHING

Nursery – primary – comprehensive – secondary modern – grammar – technical – special schools – further (and higher) education establishments

SPECIAL SUBJECT TEACHERS: home economics – physical education – speech and drama – art – Froebel – Montessori – music – higher education

Entry quali-
fications

Since 1980: *either* 2 A-levels and 3 O-levels including English language and mathematics for Bachelor of Education degree; *or* any degree or equivalent qualification for post-graduate professional teacher training. (See **Training** for people with certain specialist qualification and mature entrants.)

The work

It is unwise to judge teaching as a career by one's own experience of being taught. There are many different types of school, and the atmosphere and work differ greatly from one school to another – it depends partly on local education authorities' policies; partly on Heads' and teachers' personalities and views on educational theories, and partly on the size and location of school (but differences do not depend as much on type of neighbourhood as people outside teaching often think). New techniques for communicating knowledge and enthusiasm are tried out extensively. Among these are programmed learning; a new approach to the teaching of mathematics and of languages; the linking of different subjects into 'projects'. These ideas give teachers scope for experiment. The emphasis is more and more on encouraging children to learn by experience and discovery. Pupils are encouraged to 'research' into anything from local history to moon-shot history, or indeed into any subject the children themselves or the news, local or national, may suggest. It is for the teacher to 'use' the children's own interest to some purpose in her teaching.

However, fashions in education change from time to time. At present there is a tendency to have a rather more structured curriculum than was fashionable a few years ago. The fact that teaching is now a graduate profession is significant: to be able to use children's curiosity and to guide them effectively through planned courses which the children enjoy, *and* in which they acquire knowledge, requires teachers to be highly proficient, and creative. Teachers need a thorough understanding of conflicting educational theories; of the 'learning process' of children's intellectual, social and emotional development. Another important point is that teachers' scope is much wider than pupils can easily appreciate: the purpose of school is by no means just to get as many children as possible through as many exams as possible, but to make them *want* to learn; it is also to prepare children for work, leisure and adult life generally. The more outside interests teachers have, the better they are likely to be at their job – which is why many teacher training courses much prefer students who have had a job, or travelled extensively, in between school and college.

NURSERY SCHOOLS AND NURSERY CLASSES

(For the 2–5s.) Classrooms look like a cross between workshop and nursery, with toys, paints and handicraft equipment, plants and often pets easily accessible. Children make things, play by themselves or in small, informal groups. Teachers encourage the timid and less able, calm down the boisterous and aggressive, tell stories, organize games or acting to music, and above all answer unending streams of questions. Normally, one teacher is in charge of her class for the whole of the school day. Nursery assistants (see p. 298) help in nursery schools and classes.

PRIMARY SCHOOLS

(For the 5 to 11s.) Infant classes (for the 5–7s) are much like nursery classes: teaching still takes the form largely of play and 'activities'. Formal teaching starts gradually.

Subjects are integrated into 'projects', the emphasis is on keeping alive and stimulating children's natural enthusiasm for learning and for widening their experience; this is considered just as important as teaching facts and figures. A primary school teacher normally teaches the whole range of subjects to her own class but there are some specialist teachers, for example in mathematics and science, in some schools.

Neither nursery nor primary school teachers do much marking of exercise books, but they do a good deal of lesson-preparation.

MIDDLE SCHOOLS

The majority are for 8 to 12s or 9 to 13s; some cover a shorter age-span. As middle schools are fairly new, teachers have scope for working out new approaches to learning, and for using experimental methods.

For the first 2 years, children tend to stay with their class teacher, later they have subject teachers; in some schools subjects are integrated and several subject-specialists work as a team.

SECONDARY EDUCATION

Several types of institution:

6th-form and Tertiary Colleges

For academic and non-academic pupils working for O-levels and A-levels; the atmosphere is more like college than school.

Comprehensive Schools (the vast majority)

They provide courses for pupils of 11 (or following middle schools from 12 to 13) to 18, of all abilities and interests. (In some areas pupils transfer to 6th-form college at 16.) The organization of individual schools varies enormously. In some, for example, pupils work in 'sets', each set comprising all levels of abilities; in others pupils are 'streamed' according to their abilities. Often a mixture of these two systems is used. Some children work for no examination at all; some for Royal Society of Arts examinations in commercial subjects or for City and Guilds exams in vocational subjects; most work for C.S.E., or G.C.E. O-levels and A-levels. (A modification of the secondary-education examination system is under discussion.) The range of subjects taught is extremely wide. It may for example include photography; use of office machinery; woodwork; engineering subjects; technical drawing; dress-making; as well as A-level courses in computer science, astronomy, sociology, and of course orthodox school subjects at all levels. Staff in comprehensive schools represent a wide range of interests and special-izations. In many schools challenging experimental work is being done with older children who are not interested in academic subjects but have to stay on at school till 16, and new ways of rousing the interest of the unacademic are being tried out.

Secondary Modern Schools

Secondary modern schools provide a general education to a minimum school-leaving age. Many pupils do not work for examinations, an increasing number do.

Grammar Schools

They provide academic courses for pupils who intend to go on to higher education.

Technical Schools

There are now very few indeed. They provide courses for pupils of 11 to 16 who want to specialize in vocational subjects. The work previously done in these schools is now usually done in comprehensive schools.

The vast majority of teachers work in State schools, but there is also scope in the various kinds of independent day and boarding schools. (Training requirements are essentially the same.)

SPECIAL SCHOOLS

Special schools, hospital schools and special classes in ordinary schools provide for various categories of handicapped children, including physically handicapped, blind, deaf, maladjusted and educationally subnormal children.

Teachers of deaf and of blind children must acquire an additional qualification, either by in-service training or by a 1-year full-time course of special training. (There is also a 4-year B.Ed. in audiology and education of the deaf, as an alternative to teacher training plus the 1-year special training.) Special training for teachers of educationally subnormal and other handicapped and maladjusted children within the ordinary school system is not yet compulsory, but it is strongly encouraged. Courses last from 1 term to 1 year. On some B.Ed. courses (see **Training**) students can specialize in teaching mentally handicapped children and in work with maladjusted educationally subnormal and severely handicapped children.

Handicapped children are taught in much smaller classes. Work with them is as much forming relationships and gaining their confidence and support as formal teaching. 'Training programmes' in special schools for mentally handicapped children and in subnormality hospital 'schools' are designed to help the children develop self-confidence and the capacity to relate to people around them; to help them move, eat, play and walk as best they can in spite of their handicaps. Mentally handicapped children learn slowly, but they can usually acquire simple skills. Painting, movement to music and creative activities generally play a large part in work with these children.

Prospects   There is a general shortage of mathematics, physical sciences, craft, design and technology teachers. Modern language, music, religious education specialists are in short supply in some areas. But for other subject specialists, and non-specialists, prospects are not good, because of cut-backs in expenditure on education. Teachers who do not want to teach any of the 'shortage subjects' would be wise to choose one of the training methods which lead to a wider choice than just teaching.

Chances of promotion to head of a department and other posts carrying special responsibility allowances are quite good. There are some possibilities of changing from school teaching to college of education teaching, to further education, and to doing research into teaching methods, television teaching and production of schools programmes. Altogether there is a considerable variety of work for teachers away from the classroom.

The National Council for Educational Technology needs teachers to work on the development of computer-based learning techniques both for work in schools and for industrial training. As a result of the Industrial Training Act, training at all levels in industry and commerce, from unskilled clerks and operatives to management, is expanding. Experienced teachers can go into industry as training officers and organizers of training schemes.

There are excellent opportunities for teaching in the underdeveloped countries, where European teachers are greatly needed to help establish or consolidate new education services. There are also exchange and other schemes for teaching work in Europe and in the U.S.A.

Pay: Medium (see p. xxiii).

Training Because of the fall in child·population, a reduction in the number of teachers changing to other professions, and because of the cut-back in public spending, the number of teacher training places has been drastically reduced. At the same time organization of training has changed:

(a) Teaching is becoming an all-graduate profession.

(b) Training is now more flexible: students can postpone the final decision whether to teach or not.

(c) Institutions where teachers train have changed. Until recently there were about 160 colleges of education, solely concerned with teacher training. These colleges have either merged with polytechnics or other institutions of higher or further education; or several colleges of education have merged into one larger institution (Institutes or Colleges of Higher Education) which also award degrees and/or Diplomas in Higher Education; a few colleges of education continue to remain single institutions, solely concerned with teacher training.

At present there are alternative methods of training:

(1) 3-year Ordinary B.Ed. (4 years for honours) degree. Most degrees are awarded by the C.N.A.A.; some by the university with which the institution running the course is associated. Course content varies from one institution to another, but always covers academic and professional studies and practical experience.

(2) Degree in any subject followed by 1 year's professional teacher training. People who want to teach in grammar schools or do A-level work in comprehensives should choose this method – first taking a degree in the subject they particularly want to teach.

(3) Degree with an education option (for example in mathematics, science, music), usually 4-year sandwich courses including 1 year's professional teacher training. There are very few of these courses.

(4) For those who do not wish to commit themselves to teaching at the outset; 2-year full-time or 3-year part-time Dip.H.E. course, at the end of which students can decide whether to take a further 1- or 2-year course for B.Ed. or, possibly, another degree or professional qualification.

The Dip.H.E. is a new qualification available at non-university higher education establishments. Entry requirements are as for a degree (with exceptions for older entrants). The Dip.H.E. is intended to be a qualification worth something in its own right, but its value in the job market cannot yet be assessed. Professional organizations may grant partial exemptions to holders of Dip.H.E.s in relevant subjects, but they do not grant as much exemption as to degree holders.

The Dip.H.E. enables students to postpone final career and subject decisions. A wide variety of courses is offered. In some colleges students specialize in 1 or 2 subjects, but more frequently they choose a number of 'modules', usually within a main area of study: for example, sciences or humanities. They must complete a set of modules to obtain the Dip.H.E.; they can usually go on to study for a further year at the same institution, and get a degree. If the first 2 years contained sufficient relevant modules the student can usually get a B.Ed. (Ordinary) in 3 years (honours in 4); but more years are required if the student changes direction during the Dip.H.E./B.Ed. course. The same applies to other degree subjects: it depends on the relevance of the modules studied during the first 2 years whether a further 1 or 2 years for a degree will be required.

All this applies to the Dip.H.E.-degree sequence *within* the same institution: Dip.H.E. students are also able to transfer to relevant degree courses at universities, but usually they will slot into the second, rarely the third, year of a university or C.N.A.A. degree course.

Before choosing a Dip.H.E. course it is essential to research the variety of courses and to study individual course prospectuses carefully.

Teacher training includes: (a) 'education' subjects which are the professional studies linked with learning how to teach and include the theory and history of education, teaching techniques, psychology, the development of children; and (b) teaching practice, where students work in schools at intervals throughout the course. Generally, students also study 1 or 2 'main' subjects throughout the course and 1 or 2 'subsidiary' subjects for a part of the course (many institutions have introduced unit or modular study arrangements).

Before choosing a particular type of course and institution, it is important to get all the up-to-date information possible: atmosphere, approach to teaching, and breadth of activities vary greatly from one institution to another. Prospective students are advised to study college prospectuses thoroughly.

Personal attributes   A liking for and understanding of children; a desire to help them develop and express their personalities; keen interest in the art and techniques of communicating knowledge by stimulating enthusiasm; patience; a friendly manner; energy and organizing ability; a good speaking voice. There is also scope in teaching for students who are not interested in teaching young children, but who are interested in senior-school work.

TEACHING IN FURTHER EDUCATION ESTABLISHMENTS

Further education colleges cater for a very wide range of students; there is a need for almost every kind of specialist. There are opportunities for graduates, especially in mathematics, science and technology; for members of professional institutions, and for those who have qualifications and experience in anything from catering to business and engineering. Nurses, art college graduates and scientists are also wanted. General or 'liberal' studies are taught to a wide range of students, from apprentices on day-release to full-time degree students. General studies teachers are normally graduates.

Further education teachers need not take special teacher training but they can do so (full- or part-time) at Further Education Teacher Training Centres.

Teachers taking on degree-level work normally have done post-graduate work – exactly like university teachers (see p. 495).

Special Subject Teachers

1. HOME ECONOMICS (HOUSECRAFT OR DOMESTIC SCIENCE TEACHER)

The work   Her function is much wider than merely teaching cookery and dress-making. It covers the principles of hygiene and nutrition; wise budgeting; how to choose well when buying equipment; what to look for when buying a house and points to consider when furnishing it (including aesthetic appreciation and fitness for purpose); the organization of social and welfare services, and elementary economics (how money is earned and spent).

Home Economics teachers have professional studies and teaching practice in the same way as general subject teachers. (See also p. 209, Home Economics.)

Prospects   A home economics training may also lead to jobs outside teaching – in catering, institutional management, home economics.

Pay, Training and *Further information* as for teachers generally.

2. PHYSICAL EDUCATION TEACHER

The work   P.E. teachers teach games, gymnastics and swimming; archery, riding, skiing; and dancing – ballroom and national, but not normally ballet. They also do remedial gymnastics with children who have bad posture, flat feet, etc. They often organize or help to organize camping and other out-of-school activities. In fact P.E. covers a much wider range of activities now than it used to. The aims of P.E. include preparing schoolchildren for intelligent, enjoyable use of leisure, of which adults will have much more in the future than they do now.

Pay, Training and *Further Information* as for teachers generally. (See also Remedial Gymnast, p. 394, and Dancing, p. 143.)

3. TEACHER OF SPEECH AND DRAMA

The work   The functions of the speech and drama teacher are to help children develop their personalities, widen their interests in literature and drama and enable them to use speech more effectively to communicate. She teaches mime and improvisation; movement; verse-speaking, public speaking, and simply holding conversations; playwriting; acting and producing plays. Some of the work with school plays has to be done out of school hours. She also deals with pupils' minor defects in speech, and improves articulation. (For helping children with defective speech, see Speech Therapist, p. 460.)

Prospects   An increasing number of secondary schools employ these specialists; there are also opportunities in special schools for backward children, as county drama advisers and in youth clubs, amateur dramatic societies, etc.

Pay and *Further information* as for Teachers generally.

Training   *Either* specialist B.Ed course in conjunction with (but not, as in the past, entirely *at*) an approved drama school, *or* B.Ed. course at teacher training institution which specializes in speech and drama (possibly as one of several option modules).

The composition of courses varies slightly, and a second subject (usually music or English literature) is always studied. All courses include every aspect of play production, verse-speaking, movement, phonetics, English poetry and prose, theory of education, and actual teaching practice as for other teachers (see p. 490).

There are also degree courses in drama. Studies can be combined with related subjects. Syllabuses vary from one university to another, but usually include all aspects of play-production and construction, history and literature of the theatre, theories of acting and production, actual acting, and other practical theatre work. The emphasis in these courses is not on producing actors, but on narrowing the gap between the actor's approach and the literary approach to the theatre.

4. ART TEACHER

Training

Normal training *either* for B.Ed. at a teacher training institution which specializes in art, *or* a 1-year course of teacher training at art training centres for holders of the degree in Art and Design or of some other advanced qualifications in art.

Prospects

Limited opportunities. There are more candidates for jobs than vacancies.

5. FROEBEL TEACHER

B.Ed. or post-graduate course at Froebel Institute College, Roehampton Institute of Higher Education, London. The Froebel method of teaching does not differ substantially from methods now generally used in infant teaching, which is why there is only one special Froebel course.

6. MONTESSORI TEACHER

Training for the internationally recognized Montessori Diploma is given by the private Maria Montessori Training Organization, 26 Lyndhurst Gardens, Hampstead, London NW3 (very expensive, grants rarely given). The Diploma does not lead to 'qualified teacher status', i.e. only to jobs in private schools and nurseries, not local authority schools and nurseries. It is advisable, therefore, to add a Montessori qualification to a B.Ed. as private school jobs are not available everywhere. There are 3 courses:

(1) 1-year full-time for people over 21 with 7 O-levels, or 5 O-levels and 1 A-level.

(2) 2-year full-time for those with fewer qualifications.

(3) 2-year evening course, suitable for mature students. Entry requirements normally as in (1) but may be flexible.

7. MUSIC TEACHER

See Music, p. 293.

Position of women

In 1976 (latest available figures) 77% of full-time primary school teachers were women, but women held only 43% of primary school headships. 44% of full-time secondary school teachers were women, and women held only 18% of secondary school headships. The proportion of women heads is *declining*. This is only partly due to the fact that more women than men leave the profession and that many women who stay while bringing up a family are too busy to take on the head's extra responsibilities. In the last few years, as more schools became co-educational and small schools amalgamated into comprehensives, more men were appointed to headships than women; and as teachers' pay improved, fewer men left the profession; so the trend for more top jobs for men continues.

Local education authorities (responsible for appointing heads) state categorically that not enough women with the right experience apply for headships. Women who do apply say that they have to have at least as many years (with as much variety) of teaching experience as men to stand equal chance of appointment. Their 'life experience' and experience of bringing up a family (which may have shortened the period spent actually teaching) is, illogically, not taken into consideration.

Late start: Until 1975 mature students were very much encouraged to train for teaching; many were accepted with lower-than-normal entry qualifications. Since the drastic reduction in teaching jobs, the situation has changed. They are not at all barred from training courses, and there are still a few extended part-time courses specially for mature students (usually over 23). However, it is likely that, in competition with school-leavers for training places, young candidates may be given preference: there is at least no policy to discriminate *in favour* of mature students.

As teaching jobs are now not necessarily available when and above all where candidates want them, teaching is no longer the ideal job for mothers: holidays may be long, but so may be the daily journey to the nearest vacant post. Mature students should try and train as specialist teacher in one of the shortage subjects, if that fits in with their interests.

Career-break: Depends on local supply-and-demand and on individual's subjects. In theory, returners have always been very welcome in schools, but new college-leavers are cheaper to employ and may be given preference when jobs are scarce. However, by the time today's students are at the return-to-work stage, the cut-back in teacher-training should have evened out the supply-and-demand situation.

There are 1-year 'retraining courses' for qualified teachers interested in teaching mathematics, craft, design and technology, Business Studies and the physical sciences. Some of these courses also admit people with relevant qualifications or experience who are *not* qualified teachers. For example people with science degrees or H.N.C.s/D.s. There are also some, though limited, opportunities to train as teacher of English as a foreign language. These courses normally qualify candidates for mandatory or T.O.P.S. awards (see p. xl).

Refresher Courses: Both short full-time and in-service courses are available.

Part-time: Depends on area and subject. Very little scope for primary teachers; fair scope for maths, music, crafts, science specialists.

Further information   Booklet from Department of Education and Science, Elizabeth House, York Road, London SE1 7PH

HIGHER EDUCATION TEACHING

A good honours degree plus post-graduate research is the usual qualification. Teaching is almost invariably combined with research.

Notes on the Scottish System

The system is different in several respects. The main differences in educational requirements and methods of training and qualifications for those straight from school are:

Entry qualifications   (For admission to college of education courses): *Either* 4 subjects at the Higher grade; *or* 3 at the Higher grade and 2 at the Ordinary grade. All students must have a pass in English at the Higher grade and a pass in arithmetic or mathematics or statistics.

Candidates educated in England and Wales must have at least 2 subjects at A-level and 4 at O-level. Passes (at either level) must be in approved subjects and must include English language, English literature and mathematics. (Candidates who do not have a pass in mathematics must provide evidence of a reasonable standard in arithmetic or mathematics.)

English in the Scottish Certificate of Education covers both language and literature, and there are no separate passes in these subjects. The English language and English literature passes in the G.C.E. may be offered at either O- or A-levels.

Training   Only teachers who have registered with the General Teaching Council for Scotland may be appointed to permanent posts in education authority and grant-aided schools. To be eligible for registration, it is necessary to hold a Teaching Qualification awarded by a Scottish college of education or an equivalent qualification approved by the Council (e.g. an English teaching qualification). There are 3 types of Scottish Teaching Qualifications:

(a) Teaching Qualification (primary education). Awarded to those who complete either a degree course followed by a 1-year course of professional teacher training or a 3-year course at a Scottish college of education.

(b) Teaching Qualification (secondary education). Awarded to those who hold an honours degree or ordinary degree that includes passes in 2 graduating courses in a subject taught at school, and who have completed a 1-year academic course of training at a college of education, and to persons who have taken a 4-year B.Ed. degree. Teachers of certain subjects, such as homecraft and physical education, normally obtain this qualification after a 3-year course of training at a college of education which specializes in the relevant subjects. In subjects such as art and music the qualification may also be awarded to those who have relevant qualifications of comparable standard, plus a 1-year academic course of professional teacher training.

(c) Teaching Qualification (Further Education). F.E. teachers do not need a professional teaching qualification, but for permanent jobs they must have the *entry* qualifications required for professional F.E. teacher training. In practice this normally means they must have technical or commercial qualifications and experience.

Persons who have successfully completed comparable courses in England and Wales may also be admitted to the Register of teachers.

Holders of Teaching Qualification (primary education) may be appointed to posts in secondary schools in England and Wales, but not to do grammar school or grammar stream work.

NOTE: Honours degree courses in Scotland last 4 years, ordinary degree courses 3 years.

Further information   Advisory Service on Entry to Teaching, 5 Royal Terrace, Edinburgh EH7 5AF

TRADING STANDARDS OFFICER

Entry quali- 2 A-levels, 3 O-levels, including English, a mathematics and a science
fications subject. *Graduate entry*: about 44%.

The work Trading Standards Officers are employed by local authorities to ensure
a fair system of trading between consumers and traders, and between
traders themselves. They are responsible for the enforcement of consumer protection legislation, such as the Trade Descriptions Act, which
makes it illegal to supply goods and services which are wrongly or
misleadingly described. Complaints and investigations may concern, for
example: a holiday brochure which misled travellers into expecting a
luxury hotel on the beach when in fact they bought a holiday in a guest-
house in a back-street; a 'showerproof' coat which does not withstand
the briefest of showers; a 'pre-shrunk' shirt which is two sizes smaller
after the first wash. Officers ascertain facts, which involves getting
expert opinion and/or having articles examined in a testing laboratory,
and get matters put right. If necessary, they take offenders to court.

They also check the accuracy of weighing and measuring equipment
– from the nip used to sell whisky in a pub to the weigh-bridge which
weighs lorry-loads in the docks (the Trading Standards Administration
developed out of the Weights and Measures Department). They use
elaborate electrical equipment to check quantities in, for example,
prepacked goods; they use straightforward methods to check that, for
example, petrol pumps dispense correct amounts.

Britain's entry into the E.E.C. has greatly affected and expanded the
trading standards officer's work, as British quantity and quality control
methods have had to be brought into line with Continental practice.

Officers divide their time between dealing with traders and with
individuals who have complaints and/or queries; inspection, report
writing. The higher up the hierarchy, the less actual checking of
equipment and quantities the trading standards officer does. They meet
a great variety of people and have much scope for decision-taking.

Prospects This is an expanding area but opportunities depend on local authority
spending priorities. It may be necessary to move to get a job or obtain
promotion.

Pay: Medium to occasionally high (see p. xxiii).

Training   3 years on-the-job, with block-release, for the Diploma in Trading
                 Standards. The syllabus covers relevant legislation, structure of trade;
                 trading standards inspection techniques and administration; sampling
                 techniques; quantity and quality control administration.

Position   This has been an all-male preserve till very recently, and even now very
of women   few are women. This is rather illogical as so much of the work is
                 concerned with women shoppers' complaints. It is a hangover from the
                 days when the trading standards officer's predecessors, the weights and
                 measures inspectors, had to do some (though never very much) heavy
                 physical work – for example, weighing sacks of coal. The Trading
                 Standards Administration genuinely wants more women to take up this
                 work; the few qualified women in this career have done very well.

                 Career-break: Too early to say whether return to work will be easy;
                 there should be no difficulty in theory if those in temporary retirement
                 keep up with legislation and other developments.

                 Late start: No women seem to have tried, but no objection from
                 employers.

                 Part-time: Not at the moment – not enough women have asked for it.

Further in- Institute of Trading Standards Administration, Estate House, 319D
formation   London Road, Hadleigh, Benfleet, Essex SS7 2BN

Related   *Environmental Health Officer – Factory Inspector – Home*
careers   *Economics*

TRAVEL AGENT/ TOUR OPERATOR

Clerical work – Counter work – Planning

Entry quali-fications None for work in a travel agency. 4 O-levels including English for the Institute of Travel and Tourism's examination. To get a good job: a 'tourist country' language; good geography; numeracy.

The work There are 2 types of travel company: travel agents who are the retailers, and tour operators who put together and organize package tours. Travel agents sell tour operators' holidays, as well as tickets for rail, air and coach travel.

Travel Agency: the work can be divided into clerical and counter. *Tour Operators* concentrate on planning – with such sub-divisions as British and foreign, summer and winter; business and holiday; party and individual marketing.

1. CLERICAL WORK

Keeping elaborate filing systems with cross-references; every member of staff must be able to find quickly details about block and individual bookings.

Each booking involves filling in forms, sending them out, filing, and checking. There may be several letters full of intricate detail. Itineraries and currency-conversion have to be worked out; timetables checked. Minor clerical errors can have disastrous consequences when affecting clients' holidays. Increasingly, clerks use computerized equipment. See Clerical Work (p. 427).

2. COUNTER WORK

This is just selling. Clients (never called customers) may know what they want and simply buy a ticket for a train journey, or book a world tour, or want some travel literature. But most have no idea of what they want. Their leisure-time tastes must be summed up, and 'channelled' into what the counter-clerk thinks is the holiday they will most enjoy in a price range they can afford.

The counter-clerk usually has not been to the places she suggests – but she should know, from travel literature or from colleagues, as much about them as possible. She must take trouble with each client; her responsibility is far greater than that of most other sales assistants. Most people 'buy' only one holiday a year, and if this one is not a success, they will go to another agency next year.

3. PLANNING

This is done by directors and 'travel technicians' (i.e. experienced clerks). 'Planning trips' last from 2 to 8 weeks twice a year and are exhausting. 2 or 3 resorts and perhaps 12 hotels may be investigated in a day. Local transport, garage facilities, food, amusements, beaches will be checked and local tourist officials consulted. Planning of the tour later involves checking timetables and maps, costing, and conferring with transport and accommodation services suppliers.

Staff work long hours and most Saturday mornings.

Prospects Ample scope for clerical and counter work; slim chance of promotion to manager of section or agency. There is a high proportion of junior to senior staff, and competition for senior posts is very keen indeed. Opening one's own travel agency needs a great deal of experience and capital.

Pay: Low to medium (see p. xxiii).

Training Training for the Institute of Travel and Tourism's examinations (taking these is not compulsory but highly advisable):

Either (and usual): on-the-job with correspondence course or part-time day-release and/or evening classes; *or*: 2-year full-time course for B.E.C. National award with travel/tourism option modules (see B.E.C., p. xvii), followed by Higher National award.

The syllabus includes: geography; law; a European language; travel agency operation; 'tourist value'; transportation and administration systems; tourist regions; economics; major festivals and special events; travel.

Graduate entry: Some Business Studies and some Catering (see p. 108) degrees include tourism or similar options, and there are some post-graduate courses; some also accept B.E.C. Higher National award holders. At graduate and post-graduate level tourism and catering training and work overlap.

Personal attributes Aptitude for figure work; good judgement of people; a friendly manner; accuracy; organizing ability; common sense; a good memory.

Position of women There are few women travel agency managers. In large tour operating companies, women are beginning to do well, though they have to have more paper qualifications (and languages) than the men with whom they compete.

Career-break: Opportunities for returners depend on contacts, on having kept up with changes in the industry, and on economic conditions.

Late start: Training posts are very poorly paid and as there are always more applicants than vacancies, not much chance – except for clerical or counter work – *without* day-release.

Part-time: Only seasonal.

Further information Institute of Travel and Tourism, 53–54 Newman Street, London W1P 4JJ

Related careers *Catering (Hotel Work) – Civil Aviation (Cabin Crew and Groundstaff) – Linguist – Secretarial Work*

NOTE: *Couriers* are normally employed for the season, though some may do secretarial work and/or planning off-season. This is not a career as such but rather a pleasant change for competent secretaries/linguists or simply good organizers.

WORK STUDY AND ORGANIZATION AND METHOD

Entry quali-fications
Nothing specific; anything from a few months' experience as clerk or sales assistant, technician or engineer, or graduate entry.

The work
Work study is part of Management Services, which means techniques designed to help management make the best use of all available resources.

Work study officers are concerned with analysing and improving working methods. Originally *work study* referred to work in production, *organization and method* to office work; but the aims and principles are basically the same, and the two types of specialists now form one profession which is very much involved with the implications of the change from traditional office and shop-floor work to the use of word processors and computerized equipment in manufacturing.

The work has two main aspects:

(1) *Method study*, which is the analysis of how operations – whether workshop or office – are carried out with the aim of devising improvements (both in terms of productivity and work satisfaction).

(2) *Work measurement*, which means using specific techniques to measure the amount of human effort that is contained in any particular job and in the operations contained in a particular job, whether it is work on an assembly line, as supermarket shelf-filler, as shop assistant, as hospital sister or as civil servant. Work measurement plays an important part in settling equal pay matters, where 'work of equal value' has to be defined. Work may also involve designing labour- or time-saving devices and having ideas for such devices.

The success of the work always depends on gaining and keeping people's confidence – employees may have to be reassured that no changes detrimental to them will be introduced; employees may resent being 'measured'; managers may have to be convinced that work which *looks* easy is in fact highly complex.

Work study combines dealing with people and technical, analytical work in an unusual way.

Prospects
Good for people who have had any kind of industrial or commercial 'work situation experience'. This is, says the Institute, very much a 'second career'. (See *Late start* below.)

Pay: Medium to high (see p. xxiii).

Personal attributes

Numeracy; common sense; ability to gain and keep people's confidence and to establish good relationships with people at all educational levels, and of all temperaments; methodical approach; reasonably analytical brain; imagination; average intelligence; ability to organize people as well as their work.

Training

The Institute Certificates and Diplomas are taken mainly by part-time evening or correspondence study (sometimes day-release) over a period of about 3 years. The normal way to learn is as assistant to a work study officer, preferably with some past experience of work (in any capacity) – even if only a few months.

Position of women

The Institute's membership of 21,000 includes 800 women, the majority of whom work in hospitals, local and central government and similar areas concerned mainly with office work; some work in textiles and electronics-manufacturing, where there are many women workers. But women with some kind of past working experience, no matter where, who are willing to do a spell in shop-floor production as assistant work study officer, should have no problem eventually getting good jobs (they may have difficulty getting the *first* job). As the work depends so much on common sense, organizing ability and establishing good relations with people, this is an area in which women who have tried have done well; the trouble is that so very few women know about the job.

Career-break: In theory there should be no problems, but too few have tried to be definite about this.

Late start: Very good opportunities: as mentioned above, this is very much a 'secondary career'; so anyone with any kind of work experience, whether clerical, in retail, catering in hospital or wherever, stands a good chance. There are a number of 3- to 6-month courses under the T.O.P.S. scheme which are sadly under-used by women (see p. xl).

Part-time: Not much scope, but there are occasionally special projects where shift-work has to be studied, and several work study officers may share the working day – this might involve 'unsocial hours'.

Further information

Institute of Management Services, 1 Cecil Court, London Road, Enfield, Middlesex

---

Related careers

Careers Officer – Engineering – Factory Inspector – Management

---

Index

This book uses only the feminine pronoun though the information, unless otherwise stated, applies to both sexes.